How Harvard Rules

How Harvard Rules

Reason in the Service of Empire

edited by

John Trumpbour

South End Press   **Boston, MA**

Manufactured in the United States

Cover design by Lisa Hinds

Typeset and design by the South End Press collective

Library of Congress Cataloging-in-Publication Data

How Harvard rules.

Includes index.

1. Harvard University--History--20th century.
2. Higher education and state--Massachusetts--Cambridge.
3. Industry and education--Massachusetts--Cambridge.
4. Harvard University--Employees--Political activity.
5. Harvard University--Faculty. I. Trumpbour, John.

    LD2153.H69 1989   378.744'4   89-6206

    ISBN 0-89608-284-9

    ISBN 0-89608-283-0 (pbk.)

South End Press, 116 Saint Botolph St., Boston, MA 02115

98 97 96 95 94 93 92 91 90 89 1 2 3 4 5 6 7 8 9

Permissions

"Ideology in Practice: The Mismeasure of Man," reprinted from *The Mismeasure of Man* by Stephen Jay Gould by permission of the author and W.W. Norton and Company, Inc. Copyright © 1981 by Stephen Jay Gould.

"Jackboot Liberals," copyright © 1985 by Alexander Cockburn.

"Living with the Bomb," copyright © 1983 by *The Nation* magazine, The Nation Associates, Inc.

How Harvard Rules is a student institution started in 1969 in the aftermath of the occupation of University Hall. The original edition published numerous documents liberated during the occupation, showing Harvard's cooperation with the CIA and other arms of the national security state.

Table of Contents

V. Education, Ideology, and Social Control

VI. Strategies for Transformation

Preface

On those occasions when Harvard is not accorded fawning praise, it generally can count on deference to its authority from the media and Establishment institutions. Indeed an informal survey of the *New York Times* in the late 1970s indicates that the newspaper made reference to the University three times more than all other schools combined. The consummate Establishmentarian McGeorge Bundy, chastened by the campus rebellions in his midst, reflected on Harvard's customary lack of critical self-examination: "The fame of Harvard covered us...with its radiance, and we all too easily assumed that the honor paid to us because of Harvard was no more than our personal due. The really ruthless critics among us were too few, and the self-critics fewer still."[1]

In recent years, self-styled representatives of the Right, men proudly elitist and anti-student, have unleashed a torrent of books and articles critical of Harvard and its Ivy League counterparts. Patterned after William F. Buckley's early Cold War tract *God and Man at Yale*, new expressions of this genre include John Le Boutellier's *Harvard Hates America* and Benjamin Hart's anti-Dartmouth philippic *Poisoned Ivy*. From a more general perspective, Allan Bloom's *Closing of the American Mind* enunciates many of their views. According to the *New York Times*, as emblazoned on the back cover of the book, it "hits with the approximate force and effect of electroshock therapy." This may well be true.

How Harvard Rules represents a repudiation of the Blooms, the Buckleys, and the Le Boutelliers, who call for an even more hidebound and reactionary academy than exists today. Hardly the den of radicalism they portray, Harvard has a political right-wing that is very right (Pipes, Ulam, Herrnstein, Loury, Banfield, et al.) and a sea of liberals who are not very liberal (the *New Republic* crowd and the Cold Warrior Allison/Kennedy School Axis); beyond this, there are a few mild social democrats (Reich, Galbraith, and Hoffmann)—and, save for the hard sciences and the Law School, a barely visible progressive presence. As Ed Meese recently declared, "The Reagan Administration has the highest percentage of Harvard graduates among its Cabinet and subcabinet appointees of any Administration in American history—substantially exceeding the percentage in the Administration of John F. Kennedy."[2] Michael Dukakis, reviled by George Bush as a Harvard ultra-liberal, is in reality a shallow technocrat who as governor has enacted policies that later led to some of the nation's most grisly black infant mortality statistics: Boston recently ranked worst among the country's largest 27 cities—despite possessing the highest per capita ratio of Harvard antipoverty experts in the nation. (For more details, see footnote six of the book's conclusion.) Meanwhile Dukakis's servility to corporate interests is so pronounced that the co-author of his blueprint for economic revitalization, Harvard Professor Rosabeth Moss Kanter, calls him "CEO" of "Massachusetts, Inc." She means this as a compliment.

Such a description of the governor from Harvard is hardly surprising, for the University's historic role has been to serve corporate power and, more recently, the national security state.

Though this book often focuses on individuals and personalities, the University in its very structure—its governing board, its funding network, its traditions—ensures that it will remain firmly in the service of power and privilege. Founded in the seventeenth century during the checkered reign of Charles I, Harvard no longer pledges allegiance to the British monarchy, but is today ruled by seven oligarchs on a self-perpetuating body called the Harvard Corporation. Insulated from any meaningful form of democratic accountability, the Corporation makes a mockery of the view that were Harvard to replace the worst of the institution's malefactors with a more "enlightened" group of women and men, everything would be all right. Harvard's malady goes beyond that. The institutional matrix at Harvard sees to it that would-be challengers to its misrule are isolated and contained. As a result, Harvard's plunder of local neighborhoods, investment in South Africa, service to the CIA, and training of the U.S. corpocracy continues largely unabated.

This is not to succumb to despair. There will be renewed opportunities for the opponents of Harvard's service to barbarism, and the book's conclusion offers a plan of attack for the student movement and its allies. In the end, however, this book should be regarded first and foremost as a work of demystification.

The book is divided into six sections: 1) Introducing Harvard; 2) Harvard and the State; 3) Harvard, the Corporations, and the Community; 4) Science and Pseudo-Science: Racism and Sexism in the Sciences and Social Sciences at Harvard; 5) Education, Ideology, and Social Control; and 6) Strategies for Transformation. There are three major themes pervading these chapters: the myth of Harvard's independence, the myth of Harvard as a liberal-left institution, and Harvard's contribution to ethnocentrism and the "superiority" of the West. Among the many contributors, there is clearly no "party line"; there are enough views to offend everyone.

One final point: we are in rare agreement with William F. Buckley when he remarked that confronted with the prospect of a government run by Harvard men and women he would much prefer leadership chosen randomly from a Boston telephone book. Through *How Harvard Rules*, we hope to expose the folly of blind obeisance to an elite educational institution long run amok.

Notes

1. *Daedelus,* Summer 1970.

2. *New York Times,* July 15, 1988, p. A31.

Despite his sneers at Harvard in the 1988 Presidential campaign, "Harvard's boutique...a philosophical cult normally associated with extremely liberal causes," Bush, writes journalist David Nyhan, "obviously didn't mean it. His Cabinet is stuffed with Harvardians; his staff likewise." (David Nyhan, "The 20-Year Difference at Harvard," *Boston Globe,* April 9, 1989, p. 75.)

Nyhan adds: "A moderate was picked to head the Kennedy School of Government, which gave Ed Meese a medal for distinguished service. A conservative will head the Law School, where the tenured faculty roster is: two black males, five women, and 52 white males. The university still resists full divestment of companies doing business in South Africa."

Part I
Introducing Harvard

Introducing Harvard
A Social, Philosophical, and Political Profile

John Trumpbour

Russell Baker, the resident wit at the otherwise humorless *New York Times*, summed up the 100th Anniversary Celebration of The Statue of Liberty:

> The plans for the Statue of Liberty business remind me of a song somebody ought to write. Its title would be "America the Blowhard." Patting yourself on the back once in a blue moon is forgivable, but constantly thumping your chest about how wonderful you are soon makes you an embarrassment to friends and neighbors.

Baker's words apply equally well to Harvard University. In a May 25, 1988 *New York Times* editorial a rival university official declares, "For self-congratulation, Harvard remains in a class by itself." That it does is confirmed in the bestselling memoirs of Harvard alumnus and overseer Theodore White, who cannot help but recall his joy when glimpsing "what remains still the most beautiful campus in America, the Harvard Yard. If there is any one place in all of America that mirrors better all American history, I do not know of it."[1]

White's enchantment with the strikingly dull Yard is hardly isolated. Another alumnus explains the allure of Harvard this way,

> My place in the world is still defined by the fact that I went to Harvard... It affected the way I talk, the stripes on my tie, gave me my closest friends and my wife.[2]

It has been remarked that, while Waterloo was won on the playing fields of Eton, the twentieth century battles in the corporate board rooms and the Department of State are settled in the classrooms of Cambridge, Massachusetts.[3]

Harvard's predispositions toward rule are deeply ingrained, for it emerged in the eighteenth and nineteenth centuries as the preferred institution of Boston's self-confident and aristocratic ruling caste. Well into the eighteenth century, Harvard's president kept a list identifying the social rank of each student, a register printed in the college catalog that determined table seating, placement in processions, and speaking privileges in class. By the end of that century, the list was scuttled, as the president could not handle the mounting complaints from student's parents who felt that their family deserved higher ranking. Instead, a whole network of finals clubs developed, Porcellian, A.D., Fly, et al., which persist to this day, imposing elite ranking in a fashion surely as definitive as that of the dons.[4] In his autobiography (1907), Henry Adams, the grandson and great grandson of U.S. presidents, modestly explained his reasons for going to Harvard:

> For generation after generation, Adamses and Brookses and Boylstons and Gorhams had gone to Harvard College, and although none of them, as far as known, had done any good there... custom, social ties, convenience, and, above all, economy kept each generation in the track... All went there because their friends went there, and the College was their ideal of social self-respect.[5]

In the early 1970s, a Harvard senior told author Vivian Gornick, "It's hard to say exactly how it happens. But after four years here you feel as though the world has been created to be led by Harvard men."[6]

There are signs in the street that point to how this happens. The college newspaper, the *Crimson*, in virtually every news story lists the Harvard class of prominent public figures (i.e., "FDR '04," "Weinberger '38," "Rockefeller '36," etc.), reminding students that the most powerful people go to this, the most powerful university in the world. (The fixation on one's graduating class seems a peculiar pomposity of the U.S. bourgeoisie: one cannot imagine an Oxford student newspaper printing "Thatcher '47," "Benn '48," Macmillan '19," "Cockburn '63," etc.) President Bok, ever eager to exalt in its global influence, notes that, much like the British Empire, the sun never sets on Harvard.[7] Then there is the architecture: the imposing Greek columns, the high ceilings and crystal chandeliers, the oaken walls covered with busts and portraits of Anglo-Saxon Harvardians—typically past presidents. Of the Faculty Room on the second floor of University Hall, Gornick reflects:

> If one is not oneself of "good family," it is impossible to escape a sense of outsidedness, and if one should, into the bargain be a woman, one is entirely dislocated... Surely, this room was not made to accommodate or include me in its doings. Here, I was never intended to belong.[8]

Finally, there is the house system modeled after Oxbridge, the exclusive clubs, and the public rituals and revelry. There is the notorious chant of students and alumni when Harvard finds itself routed on the gridiron, "That's all right, that's OK, you'll work for us someday," and, of course, there is graduation. The last is replete with grand processions of famous and not-so-famous alumni and the Overseers dressed in top hats and silken gloves, a formidable panoply surrounded by the shrieking of bagpipes, intermittently halted for addresses in Latin and the football songs of the Harvard Band.[9]

These festivals of the ruling class should not be dismissed lightly, for Harvard makes a considerable investment in their success (as much as $750,000 spent on entertaining an individual alumni class during reunions). It therefore comes as no surprise that on its 350th anniversary in 1986, Harvard put on what is probably the most lavish celebration of a university in history. Indeed what *The New Republic*, referring to the 100th Anniversary of the Statue of Liberty, calls "The Gross-Me-Out Fourth," "the most revolting display of glitz in this country's history,"[10] could well apply to Harvard's celebration, which reproduced many of the excesses of that remarkable Fourth of July. Evidently believing itself worthy of pageantry on a par with the Statue, Harvard hired the same people who put together the Liberty lalapalooza. The opening ceremonies for the University's 350th at times had a strangely populist aroma: Harvard is just another part of Americana.

The Age of Bok

The master of ceremonies was no evangelist of kitsch, no gaudy impresario, but a man of sophisticated styling, Harvard President Derek Curtis Bok. Though he was not one to call off the fireworks, the laser light shows, the 600 foot helium rainbow, and the Harvard licensed 350th chocolates, Bok expressed some unease with his university's excessive gloating, warning that a backlash against Harvard could ensue if people perceived that it won too many accolades, occupied too many of the command posts of society. This was connected to a larger theme: the University is now threatened from without and within by a "harvest of problems our successes have brought us." At stake is the very independence of Harvard. He mordantly intoned that "military and intelligence agencies" try to "engage professors in secret research and to impose restrictions to keep our scientific findings out of enemy hands," and "Businesses search for relationships with our scientists that will help them develop new products." He then added to his litany of threats overzealous social activists and local communities.

Thernstrom said if he believed it was a proposal for feminist indoctrination, he would oppose it. "But this is not the case," he said, "nor is the new chairman [sic] a radical ideologue."[20]

Thernstrom would, therefore, oppose Women's Studies if it were led by any of the premier radical feminists of the twentieth century. His liberal ideological policing would provide ample grounds for the suppression of Simone de Beauvoir, Adrienne Rich, Juliet Mitchell, Christa Wolf, and Virginia Woolf. (Paradoxically to some, Thernstrom recently accused African-American students who charged him with making racist comments in his lectures of exhibiting a dangerous McCarthyism of the left.)

Harvard instead chose as the Women's Studies chairperson Britain's Olwen Hufton, a skilled historian who is, none the less, committed to a safe brand of feminism.[21] Cologne University sociologist Maria Mies comments on the liberal willingness to acquiesce in Women's Studies programs:

> In the U.S.A. departments of women's studies were established in most universities without great opposition. Although this all needed a lot of struggle from the women's movement, there was a certain paternalistic benevolence in granting "the girls" a certain niche in the system. Already at this stage the various patriarchal establishments used their power to co-opt women and to integrate their rebellion into the system.[22]

Now Harvard was a last holdout to this trend, but they gave in when the liberals realized, in Mies's words, that:

> in the field of women's studies a tendency towards academic feminism could be observed. The goal was no longer to transform society and the man-woman relationship, but to get more women into the academic establishment and women's studies and research.[23]

Incidentally, when we asked other feminists to participate in the making of How Harvard Rules, some declined, expressing the fear that contributing to a radical attack on Harvard would jeopardize the upcoming faculty vote on Women's Studies. Their political dilemma illustrates the workings of this ideological intimidation at Harvard: they would moderate their criticism in order not to frighten liberals of Thernstrom's ilk. This is regrettable: a more sustained feminist presence in this work would have been an asset. More recently, Nina McCain of the Boston Globe expressed frustration about the unwillingness of the several Harvard feminists whom she interviewed to speak on-the-record of their criticisms of Harvard and of Radcliffe president Matina Horner.[24]

A final source of the myth of Harvard as a 'liberal-left' institution is its central role in the dissemination of Keynesian economics. A fringe of right-wing alumni at Harvard formed the Veritas Society, which for several decades fought Keynes's "virulent" doctrines by distributing literature to thousands of undergraduates. Their treatment of Keynes as a "pervert" and a Leninist in sheep's clothing helped to associate Harvard economists with subversive "Fifth Columnist" tendencies. Nevertheless, Galbraith is more accurate when he notes in his *Age of Uncertainty* that the capitalist Keynes's "fate was to be regarded as peculiarly dangerous by the class he rescued."[25] Keynes himself stated that he would never join Britain's Labor Party, openly stressing that "the class war will find me on the side of the educated bourgeoisie."[26] The reality is that while liberal Keynesians flourished at the Department of Economics, Harvard regularly bid farewell to radical economists, most notably Paul Sweezy. Lawrence Lifschultz's essay in this book documents the history of these purges. One of the results of these housecleanings is that most of the U.S. Keynesians adopted a sallow, anemic version of the doctrine. Compare the Cambridge University quartet of Maurice Dobb, the great Marxist economic historian, Joan Robinson, a pungent non-Marxist critic of monopoly capitalism, Nicholas Kaldor, author of a robust socialist alternative to Thatchernomics, and Piero Sraffa, friend of Gramsci (and, for what it's worth, Wittgenstein) who later synthesized Keynesian economics and Marxism, with their leading counterparts in the U.S. universities.[27] The Veblenesque John Kenneth Galbraith of Harvard and James Tobin of Yale probably have the most admirable record, though the former's previous belief in the gospel of countervailing power between unions and management became a major ideological prop of the postwar social order and the latter, during his service on Kennedy's Council of Economic Advisors, became an aggressive advocate of military Keynesianism both to pump up the economy and, in his words, "to keep the Western world ahead...in weapons research and development, in armaments in being."[28] The conservative's visceral hostility to Keynes is curious, especially in light of Reagan's embrace of this great false god to accomplish his arms build-up. (Keynes himself in the German edition of his *General Theory* straightforwardly credited the Third Reich with pioneering his techniques in their pre-World War II rearmament program.) After Tobin and Galbraith, leading U.S. Keynesians such as MIT's Paul Samuelson and Lester Thurow, and Harvard's Benjamin Friedman are unabashedly committed to welfare state capital-

Bush, and Thatcher are standing in as defenders of Dante, Shakespeare, and Homer.[32] If we could only be so lucky. In the Persian Gulf of the 1980s, a latter day version of the Crusades unfolded, this time with Reagan the Lionhearted confronting Khomeini.

Now a pervasive assumption in the universities is that people conversant with the highest culture are not inclined towards mass butchery and the maiming of fellow human beings. When Secretary of Defense Robert McNamara was ordering record levels of bombing against the Vietnamese people, an employee of his told Edward Said that "the Secretary is a complex human being: he doesn't fit the picture you may have formed of the cold blooded imperialist murderer. The last time I was in his office I noticed Durrell's *Alexandria Quartet* on his desk."[33] In other words, those who read quality fiction are rich and complex human beings, incapable of the savageries of lesser mortals. This is a peculiar notion, subsequently demolished by the literary critic George Steiner in his commentaries on Nazism. We have since learned of the Nazi officer who in between verses of Rilke would write out orders for the next batch of gas chamber exterminations. The combination of high culture and barbarism among many Nazis, however, has done little to inspire humility in elites soaked in the humanities.

On the other hand, perceptive social critics such as Lewis Lapham suspect that U.S. society does not really

> expect its "best people"…to have read William Shakespeare or Dante. Nor does anyone imagine that the Secretary of State will know much more history than the rudiments of chronology expounded in a sixth-grade synopsis. If it becomes necessary to display the finery of learning, the corporation can hire a speechwriter or send its chairman to the intellectual haberdashers at the Aspen Institute…

…Or to those quick-witted clothiers at the Harvard Business School or the Kennedy School of Government. For these elites, adds Lapham,"Education has become a commodity, like Pepsi-Cola or alligator shoes…"[34]

That being said, even the most hammerheaded and Cro-Magnon of the University's graduates comes away with a certain sense that the system works and that the West is still best. Contrary to Allan Bloom's lugubrious vision of enveloping relativism, this confidence in Western superiority is exhibited even in the most liberal members of the Establishment. Harvard-trained Anthony Lewis of the *New York Times* talks of how U.S. policy in South Africa is at odds with

"Western ideals" and "Western values."[35] One irritated reader responded to Lewis:

> Implicit in this notion is (a) that some such "Western" value system exists; (b) that it is very moral; and (c) that it is morally superior to non-Western value systems.
>
> Can anyone define, for those like me who are perplexed, what exactly these values are? Are they not the same values that produced slavery (in both Europe and the U.S.), inquisitions, conquests of the New World, colonialism, and legal segregation, the brunt of which was borne by the darker peoples? Are they not the same values that produced racists like Hitler, Mussolini, and the Tsar of Russia?[36]

How does Harvard in particular reinforce this presumption of Western cultural and moral preeminence? Some of the blame can be attributed to the content of the curriculum which, despite a core course requirement of Foreign Cultures, is not imaginative in breaking out of the bonds of provincialism. A curious student can certainly find plenty of courses covering non-Western topics. But many scrupulously avoid them, and it is quite possible to get through the Foreign Cultures requirement without taking any courses outside of Western Europe. Meanwhile, several departments have designed curricula that are outright impediments to Third World studies. For instance, the Department of History reports that 80-90 percent of its students major in either European or U.S. studies, but this is encouraged by the full year requirement of a sophomore tutorial which is dramatically slanted towards North Atlantic civilization (only two regions of the world are taught in the four topics, which include Europe 1) before 1700, 2) post-1700; 3) the United States; and 4) historiography, largely confined to European thinkers).

These biases are reflected in the scholarship of Harvard's social scientists. Though probably among the least provincial U.S. intellectuals, the Harvard-trained anthropologist Clifford Geertz, now at Princeton, helped produce a massive study of Morocco without citing a single Arab source.[37] Geertz is regularly accorded the highest praise at Harvard and elsewhere. However, an Arab scholar, notes Edward Said, always has to refer to U.S. and European intellectuals, no matter how trivial, lest s/he be dismissed as parochial and lacking rigor. Despite Harvard's claim to be a world class institution of learning, only a minuscule percentage of the faculty have even rudimentary knowledge of the central literary and philosophical representatives of non-Western civilizations.

It is not surprising, therefore, that the leading figures in the Harvard intelligentsia have such a superficial and patronizing attitude towards other cultures. Henry Kissinger observes that Third World people fail to comprehend "that the real world is external to the observer" because their "cultures... escaped the early impact of Newtonian thinking," causing their "difference of philosophical perspective" which remains "the deepest problem of the contemporary international order."[38] There is ample documentation in this volume's chapter on the national security state of similar profundities uttered by leading Harvard social scientists. Nor have the dominant forces in the humanities at Harvard been free of this subsuming ethnocentrism. A brief examination of perhaps the two most important scholars of the humanities at Harvard in the twentieth century, Irving Babbitt and I.A. Richards, is illuminating in this regard. It is not simply a question of putting more energy into studying foreign cultures: Babbitt, the doyen of the humanities at Harvard in the first three decades of the twentieth century and opponent of Harvard President Eliot's "Rousseauistic" elective system, celebrated the study of Sanskrit and Pali, the latter for understanding "classical" early Buddhism. He even briefly attacked the West for its assumption of cultural superiority in his essay "Buddha and the Occident" (1927). But it becomes clear through a closer reading of his oeuvre that Babbitt's aim is disciplinary, to domesticate the Romantic, "Rousseauistic" excesses of the Asiatic hordes. He writes that "Genuine culture is difficult and disciplinary." Observing that "Greece is perhaps the most humane of countries," Babbitt notes that they "not only formulated the law of measure ('Nothing too much'), but also perceived the avenging nemesis that overtakes every form of insolent excess or violation of this law." He warns that the "masculine" or "virile" spirit of the classical is under threat in both the Eastern and Western world. In Rousseau, identified by Babbitt as the greatest enemy of this ideal, "there is indeed much in his make-up that reminds one less of a man than of a high-strung impressionable woman. Woman, most observers would agree, is...more temperamental than man." With the specter of "temperamental" revolutionaries haunting the interwar world, Babbitt suggests a solution: "Circumstances may arise when we may esteem ourselves fortunate if we get the American equivalent of Mussolini; he may be needed to save us from the American equivalent of a Lenin." For Americans, if we fail to submit to "classical" order, Babbitt advocates il Duce; for the Orient, if they resist classical Buddhist discipline, one can infer that they will require Tojo or, more recently, one of Jeane Kirkpatrick's benign authoritarian dictators.[39]

Babbitt's extreme nostrums of classical discipline would occasion chuckles among some of Harvard's contemporary humanities establishment. Their hero, if any, would be I.A. Richards, a formidable intellectual presence at Harvard during mid-century. This is not the place to develop the major themes of Richards's literary criticism, but he is generally much more committed to cultural pluralism and countering illiberality than most of his Harvard colleagues as shown in his *Mencius on the Mind: Experiments in Multiple Definitions* (1932). Even so, he anticipates the power of cultural imperialism in replacing overt colonial rule. He reflects in *So Much Nearer: Essays Towards a World English* (1969) that two-thirds of the world are currently illiterate, with many coming from cultures in Asia, Africa, and the Middle East that read non-alphabetic script. He asserts that "if there is to be any truly world-wide communication between peoples within a foreseeable future, it will be in some language which is alphabetic. It could be within our lifetime and through English."[40] Richards's context is a period of decolonization, but his program has lineages in Macaulay's famous "Minute of 1835," which demanded that English replace Sanskrit and Arabic in the education of India's peoples. Richards's confidence in English is not presented with the arrogance of Macaulay, who outright denied the value of Sanskrit and Arabic as follows: "...a simple shelf of a good European library [is] worth the whole native literature of India."[41] Richards lacked Macaulay's political clout, as he unsuccessfully pressured Chiang Kai-shek's Nationalist regime in China to require English in its schools. These hopes were not fulfilled in his lifetime, but the new media and the global supermarket are slowly accomplishing the dirty work once carried out by the Macaulays of the British Empire. In the name of greater efficiency and international communication, Richards's grandiose vision provides grounds for overriding Arab, Indian, African, and Chinese cultures in favor of a new information order, the likely terminus of which is a bland North Atlanticized world civilization.

In comparison with the humanists, Harvard scientists have formulated the harshest theories of the inferiority of peoples of non-Western descent. These scientific theories, couched in the "virile" language of "objectivity," probably have had greater impact than those of the humanists, whose findings can more easily be dismissed as "temperamental" and "subjective." Louis Agassiz, among the most influential scientists of the nineteenth century and a forerunner of Harvard's eugenics movement, claimed to be completely dispassionate and objective in his discovery of the racial inferiority of blacks. He considered "the questions growing out of man's physical relations as merely scientific questions," and that he "investigate[d] them without reference to politics or religion."[42] In his recently discovered memoirs, Agassiz destroyed his claim of disinterested inquiry by revealing his fear and revulsion towards blacks, how his first sight of them made him ill, and how he just "knew" they were barely higher than apes. In 1975, Harvard's Bernard Davis, a leading advocate of biological determinism, echoed Agassiz in his assurance that "neither religious nor political fervor can command the laws of nature."[43] Throughout the essays by Beckwith, Hubbard, and Gould, *How Harvard Rules* analyzes and provides a critique of the many Harvard scientists, past and present, who have been in the vanguard of crude theories of genetic and racial determinism.

In the short run, are there any proposals that could contribute to a more humane, less ethnocentric brand of science and social science at Harvard? In terms of the core curriculum, students should be offered a program that directly addresses the epistemology of the human and natural sciences. That is to say, Harvard students need to learn how to identify the ideological biases of the sciences, shrouded as they are in the thick cloak of "objectivity" and "value neutrality." It is through such ideological ruses, as exhibited in Agassiz, that racist and ethnocentric theories gain rapid credibility in the academy and elsewhere. After taking such a class, many students would, of course, continue to embrace reactionary ideology. However, by dismantling science's claims to blind "objectivity," it would in a single stroke remove one of the main pieces of ammunition in the ideological arsenal of the bourgeoisie. Several of the seminal texts of twentieth century philosophy contribute to this unmasking of technology and science as "ideology": Husserl on the crisis of Western science, Bloch on the manner in which capitalism distorts the "innocence" of modern technology, and Kuhn, Feyerabend, and Lakatos on the structure of scientific revolutions. Above all, it is Marcuse who first elaborates how the "political content of technical reason" fits into a mature theory of advanced capitalist society. In his critique of Weber, Marcuse asks that people consider how:

> the very concept of technical reason is perhaps ideological. Not only the application of technology but technology itself is domination (of nature and men)—methodical, scientific, calculated, calculating control. Specific purposes and interests of domination are not foisted upon technology "subsequently" and from

the outside; they enter the very construction of the technical apparatus. Technology is always a historical-social project: in it is projected what a society and its ruling interests intend to do with men and things.[44]

Such a perspective does not require students to embrace a messianic anti-scientism. Rather, in an era of Chernobyl and Three Mile Island, it asks students to abandon passivity when confronted with scientific reason as a legitimation for the prevailing social order. As intellectual historian Mark Poster observes: "The greatest danger today may come not from those who shout 'blood and soil' but from those who scientifically plan for war in the name of freedom. These are the people whose trigger fingers represent the culmination of Western reason."[45]

A second area in which Harvard could overcome some of its insularity is in the teaching of history on a global scale. There is some provision for this in the core, but it is typically executed with the most backward of social science tools, often with pure narrative which amounts to "history as just one damn thing after another." On a somewhat more positive note, two sociologists, Barrington Moore and Theda Skocpol, would have to rank as Harvard's most successful practitioners of a global historical vision. Moore's radical critiques of the capitalist social order during his active tenure at Harvard disturbed many, though his Brahmin background and Weberian pessimism about the prospects for social change may have made him palatable to the powers that be. Skocpol apparently does not have such luck. After staving off a challenge to send her packing from the Department of Sociology, Skocpol has finally been allowed to return, only to be greeted by the likes of Department of Social Studies chairperson David Landes, who harasses her with demands that she "prove" herself "intellectually."[46] (While Skocpol's achievement is internationally recognized, one does not find Landes lecturing the third-rate cast of male faculty in the departments in which he holds tenure about their need to "prove" themselves "intellectually.") There are shortcomings in Moore's and Skocpol's work; Bryan Turner has pointed to lingering aspects of ethnocentrism in this type of grand sociology.[47] By providing tools for grappling with a historical capitalism that operates on a global scale, radical social scientists occasionally marginalize peoples yet to be absorbed by the global economy—or yet to participate in the great revolutions of modernity. While vulnerable to such critiques, Moore and Skocpol have demonstrated how an interdisciplinary social science can contribute to an understanding of the West and beyond.

The chief impediment to this sort of inquiry is the elaborate division of labor in the academic departments, an intellectual inheritance of the industrial revolution. Students and progressive faculty will have to fight for institutions that help overcome the fragmented, departmentalized state of knowledge. Occasionally the area studies programs are more successful in this, but the priorities of the national security mandarins and the foundations undercut such efforts (see my National Security essay). In the academic departments, scholars are hired to be specialists of sixteenth century England, eighteenth century France, twentieth century United States, etc., so they have little incentive to conceive of history on a larger scale. They soon develop a provincialism of time and space.

Progressive intellectuals need to guard against this in their own work. The explosion of new fields of study has greatly enriched recent intellectual life, as exemplified in Afro-American, Third World, and Women's Studies. (For the debate over how Third World studies might fit into a core curriculum, see the essays by Silva and B. Robinson, and the conclusion.) The most successful practitioners in these fields have been those who avoid the compartmentalization that leads to ahistorical and essentialist theories of racism and sexism. More compelling is the work of progressive intellectuals who instead develop approaches which articulate how racism and sexism have been integral parts of larger totalities, how they historically ensure the reproduction of cultural and material life. By abandoning the false boundaries of Western education, the leading figures in Afro-American Studies have produced a formidable body of scholarship, freed from the hollow discourse of liberal historiography. (Compare the work of progressives Manning Marable, Vincent and Rosemary Harding, Cornel West, Henry Louis Gates, Eugene Genovese, Elizabeth Fox-Genovese, Jacqueline Jones, Mechal Sobel, etc. with the crowning achievement of liberal scholarship, *The Peculiar Institution* (1956) by Berkeley's Kenneth Stampp, who writes: "I have assumed that the slaves were merely ordinary human beings, that innately Negroes are, after all, only white men with black skins, nothing more, nothing less."[48]) This critique of compartmentalization should not be construed as a rebuke to feminist intellectuals, who are so often accused of parochialism by self-righteous male colleagues. Women have produced important insights into numerous fields that have been stifled by the limp approaches of the phallocratic academic establishment: i.e., Skocpol on the state and revolution, Natalie Zemon Davis on the Reformation and social change, Victoria Bonnell on the Russian working class, Louise Tilly on demographics, Stephanie Coontz on the American family, Elizabeth Fox-Genovese on capitalist ideology, to name but a handful. Meanwhile, the men, as Perry Anderson points out, rarely reciprocate, save in a few exceptions, scrupulously avoiding sustained research into topics primarily concerning women.[49]

The intellectual gains due to the political agitation of the 1960s are rarely registered by mainstream academicians, who treat the period as an age of barbarism. There are criticisms that can be raised about the focus and tactics of educational reform on the Left. The U.S. New Left was not free of anti-intellectual elements, but neither are other currents in the U.S. political spectrum. Moreover, much New Left critique is not so much anti-intellectual as against intellectuals as a class, who betrayed their calling by putting reason at the service of the state. It is true that in terms of curriculum, the student campaigns against the study of foreign languages in the name of "relevance" may well have been a shortsighted capitulation to a consumerist mentality, at the very least rendering the U.S. New Left less able to engage in the internationalism of their European and Third World counterparts. But even here, there is today a substantial exchange of ideas between the European and U.S. Lefts (see journals such as *Telos, New German Critique, Cultural Critique, Praxis International*, etc.), and between North Americans and the Third World (*NACLA, MERIP Middle East Reports, The Bulletin of Concerned Asia Scholars*, etc.) What is most amusing is that the U.S. Right, with all its wealth and cadre of intellectual mercenaries, repeatedly charges the New Left with anti-intellectualism, when the very student representatives of conservatism in the United States have such an embarrassing record, to say the least. The beer guzzling Neanderthals who put sledgehammers to the shanties at Dartmouth, the self-proclaimed "Aryans" who violently threatened blacks protesting against apartheid at the University of Texas, and the enthusiastic perpetrators of Ku Kluxery at The Citadel are recent examples of reason and intellect at work among self-identified conservative students. The editors of the right-wing *Dartmouth Review*, often a subject for lavish praise by William F. Buckley, are at best the thinking man's answer to Morton Downey, Jr.; at its worst, their discourse raises the specter of white sheets. The Irving Kristols, the Adam Ulams, and the Hilton Kramers who have vigorously attacked the student Left for its alleged opposition to intellect could be taken more seriously if they worked on getting their own house in order. Just as the Left needs to fight against the Stalinists in its ranks, the U.S. Right should work to combat its more racist and authoritarian elements. Contrary to the claims of Norman Podhoretz, the U.S. Right has been quite unimpressive in this regard. The charge that the Left is responsible for the demise of intellectual culture is primarily useful in delegitimizing progressive social movements. As the French sociologist Henri Lefebvre declares, "Counterrevolutionaries would have it that revolutionaries destroy culture and order, whereas it is they who reveal the dissolution of culture and the arbitrariness of order."[50] The forces of counterrevolution preside over such a dissolution of culture in the contemporary United States where 48 percent of its people say they never read a book, 45 percent do not know that the United States and the USSR fought on the same side in World War II, and an Ivy League educated Secretary of State justifies a squalid foreign policy as representing the defense of Western civilization.

In the midst of this cultural and political graveyard, are there any prospects that the university could play a constructive role in the foreseeable future? In the course of the essays by Robinson, Hernandez, and Escalante, it becomes abundantly clear that Harvard, for one, actively harms the interests of many people in its immediate neighborhood. In this instance, there are currently some heartening developments. First, students continue to join with local workers, activists, and politicians who refuse to digest the slick public relations campaign and oratorical bromides of the Bok regime about its concern for the surrounding community. The forging of this alliance has given jitters to an administration previously smug in its composure, now pushed to such oafish measures as locking the gates to the University on May Day 1986, and in November, turning to arrests. The triumph in 1988 of the Harvard Union of Clerical and Technical Workers in its drive for unionization has further shaken faith in Bok's omnipotence. A second related development is the growth of a network of alumni and students concerted in their efforts to fight Harvard, especially its complicity with the rogue regime of South Africa (see essays by West and Hartman and Wolff). In the 1960s, student rebels had to carry out their opposition isolated and resented by large segments of society, including blue collar workers, the so-called respectable middle class, and complacent alumni. There is still a large and vocal flank of conservative alumni to buttress Bok's sagging fortress, but now students can draw on the resources and organizational skills of a substantial base of alumni from the 1960s and beyond who are not inclined to goosestep in line to the cadence of the Harvard Corporation.

But moving beyond Harvard, what are the possibilities for student action on a national scale? The Free South Africa movement has caused substantial buckling among administrators and boards of trustees previously resolute in their opposition to divestment. In spite of this, much U.S. media and academic commentary tends to belittle campus struggles as having little possibility of transforming the wider society. Naturally, student exclusivism or putschism will hardly do as a political strategy. But in the United States where labor unions are numerically weak (16 percent of the workforce), immobilized by a slothful bureaucracy, and debilitated by the absence of a political party of the working class, there are other institutions which must be looked to for political vitality. Workers continue to rebel through wildcat strikes, sabotage, and absenteeism; however, such expressions of alienation have not been articulated into a meaningful political program. In the U.S. context, the churches and the universities are two places which have provided some space for a sustained political intervention. Both have in the past served as apologists for stasis and reaction, but they also permit the modicum of community necessary to organize a sustained political struggle. Students are handicapped by the limited duration of their studies (typically four to five years) and segregation from labor and other social movements, but these can be partly surmounted by 1) maintaining progressive student institutions (see the essay by West), 2) organizing progressive alumni (see Hartman and Wolff), and 3) affiliating the student movement with progressive community organizations. This latter proposal will require some debate and strategic thinking. In a city such as Boston with over two dozen colleges and universities, there is ample reason to engage in concerted actions and united fronts. This is particularly urgent in the case of Boston University where the tyrannical John Silber routinely crushes any voices of dissent with a well-oiled repressive apparatus.

There are several historic examples of national student organizations that have mobilized effectively against state and corporate power. The French student union UNEF spearheaded the opposition to the Algerian War and attracted massive trade union support, a dauntless action in the inhospitable environment of the late 1950s and 1960s. In the South, the Student Nonviolent Coordinating Committee (SNCC) played a pivotal role in smashing Jim Crow and other vestiges of U.S. apartheid. The SDS in Germany (*Sozialisticher Deutscher*

Studentenbund) and the United States (Students for a Democratic Society) sought the democratization of the university, and, despite the later turn of some members to the most desperate varieties of sectarian ideologies, helped bring substantial pressure against U.S. intervention in Southeast Asia. Under repressive conditions in Eastern Europe, students set into motion the revolts of 1956 in Budapest and Warsaw and helped promote the Prague Spring of 1968. Developing societies have watched the toppling of their governments by student rebellions of various ideological colors, including in Bolivia, Venezuela, Indonesia, and South Vietnam. In China, student uprisings have been called the harbingers of governments about to fall.[51] Currently in South Korea, students lead the resistance against the neo-fascist state, and in China their heroism has been met with Communist Party sponsored terror. While there is yet to be a return to the heights of May 1968, the student movement in France helped put a brake on Jacques Chirac's ambitious plans for conservative retrenchment. Much more decentralized than their French counterpart, the U.S. university system provides obstacles to the formation of a national student movement. This will require political organization that is adaptable to a variety of local circumstances.

Though he is to the right of most administrators, John Silber nevertheless speaks for the dominant ethos of the governing boards of the leading U.S. universities when he states that "most institutions ought to be run on an elitist basis."[52] Members of the Harvard Corporation resoundingly endorse this view (see Weismann's essay), rebuffing even the most modest proposals to open their proceedings to public scrutiny. The authoritarian structure of the liberal university remains inviolate. Harvard's meanspiritedness in this regard has thoroughly stifled the enthusiasm and energies of its own community. While the governing board speaks as though democratization is bizarre and alien to the university, they have conveniently forgotten that the very emergence of higher education in the West was rooted in the rise of student-controlled universities. The University of Bologna, one of the two original Western universities, according to historian Alan Cobban, "was, for more than a century, a student dominated institution and the prototype for a large European family of universities either partially or mainly controlled by students."[53] Harvard's relative youth, its founding at the late date of 1636 well after the masters and magistrates of the high Middle Ages and Renaissance had succeeded in snuffing out the powerful medieval student guilds, has left it with a legacy secure in its contempt for advances in rights and self-governance subsequently won at other educational institutions. At the most modest level, there are academic departments at UC-Berkeley and the University of Michigan, in some cases ranked higher than Harvard, which report success with student representation at faculty meetings. Throughout much of Latin America, students and faculty enjoy far greater rights of self-government, often permitting them to vote for senior university officials. Spanning several decades, the Statute of Cordoba (1918) has granted Argentinians and other Latin Americans rights and prerogatives that their North American counterparts can hardly imagine, trimmed and trammeled as they are by corporate and educational elites so quick to deny freedoms while whistling refrains of Yankee Doodle.[54] White liberal feminists are apt to scoff at "primitive" Arab women; yet 38 percent of the faculty at Morocco's leading university are women, who also possess such rights as full maternity leave. Egyptian law schools hired female faculty well before Harvard even opened its doors to women.[55]

Throughout its 350th anniversary, Harvard's representatives fell over themselves in describing the University as "independent," "unconforming," "creative," and "free." Much like the U.S. media, Harvard indulges its critics from the Right, who accuse it of being subversive of established values, a den of heresy; the University's leadership almost loves such taunts. Bok, cheered on by the students, scurries to debate the likes of William Bennett and John Silber. Having heard about this commitment to nonconformity, most outsiders are amused when attending large lectures at Harvard in the humanities and the social sciences. At the end of a lecture, no matter how intellectually empty and uninspiring, Harvard students can usually be counted on to give the professor a big round of applause. At the very least, the applause meters of some professors should be lowered by a reading of *How Harvard Rules*. More importantly, this book might help students gain the understanding to create a movement that is critical and humane.

Notes

1. Theodore White, *In Search of History* (New York: Warner Books, 1981), p. 61.

2. Carl Vigeland, *Great Good Fortune* (Boston: Houghton Mifflin, 1986), p. 236.

3. see Ferdinand Lundberg's foreword to E.H. Lopez, *The Harvard Mystique* (New York: Macmillan, 1979), especially p. xiv for the comparison to Eton and Waterloo.

4. *Ibid.*, pp. 16-17.

5. Henry Adams, "The Education of Henry Adams," excerpted in William Bentinck-Smith, ed., *The Harvard Book* (Cambridge: Harvard University Press, 1982), pp. 251-252.

6. Vivian Gornick, *Essays in Feminism* (New York: Harper and Row, 1978), p. 97.

7. Bok, Commencement Address (June 1987).

8. Gornick.

9. This description is in part adapted from Peter Gomes's enthusiastic account of the commencement exercises in "Our Secular Sacrament" (1979) in Bentinck-Smith, ed., pp. 388-392.

10. *New Republic*, June 23, 1986. The $750,000 figure for an individual class reunion is from Vigeland, *op. cit.*

11. For the listing of the Curtis-Bok clan as the fifteenth richest U.S. family in the 1920s, see F. Lundberg, *America's Sixty Families* (New York: Citadel Press, 1960 [1937]), pp. 26-27. Bok's ideology has other influences. Married into the social democratic Myrdal clan of Sweden, Bok sometimes parrots their progressive rhetoric, while in the end defending institutions and policies that desecrate this family's noble legacy. For example, compare the contempt for the peace movement expressed by the Bok-initiated and approved Living with Nuclear Weapons group with the active support for the European Nuclear Disarmament (END) movement provided by Nobel Peace Prize winner Alva Myrdal. See essay by Kopkind.

12. G. Epps quoted by Seymour Martin Lipset and David Riesman, *Education and Politics at Harvard* (New York: McGraw-Hill, 1975), p. 239.

13. Bundy quoted in booklet, *How Harvard Rules* (1969 edition), p. 35.

14. Quotations assembled by David Bell, "Ghosts of Leftists Past," *New Republic*, August 11-18, 1986, p. 17.

15. E. Schrecker, *No Ivory Tower* (New York: Oxford University Press, 1986), p. 340.

16. Cited by Bell.

17. The campus novels of the British literary critic David Lodge amusingly capture the flavor, as well as the abscence of political engagement, in much

of this nominally left intellectual culture. In his novel *Small World* (1984), he writes of his conference-hopping protagonists: "The same topics, mostly structuralism and poststructuralism, were being debated in identical terms in Paris, Oslo, Ankara, Rome, and New York. And often by the same people." In an interview, Lodge confesses that he came upon this "new cultural phenomenon" after himself attending two conferences in Zurich and Israel in 1979: "All those Joyce scholars converging on Zurich and with one hand explicating these very esoteric texts and with the other looking for the best restaurants and where to go jogging." See Mary Blum, "David Lodge: At Home with the Comic Form," *International Herald Tribune*, May 15, 1989, p. 14. Terry Eagleton, though, has warned of the limits to Lodge's satirical vision. Noting that indeed "structuralism at once mimes the technocratic procedures of late capitalism, and threatens to undermine its protective humanist ideologies," he points out that "if a traditional liberalism thus appears increasingly tarnished and shopsoiled, it remains for liberal bourgeois ideologues such as Lodge...the only available source of social critique and fundamental value. This is so because the political...is part of the problem rather than the solution. Marxism and feminism are yet more instances of theoreticist Eurospeak, to be blandly satirized along with floating signifiers and intertextuality." T. Eagleton, "The Silences of David Lodge," *New Left Review*, 172, November-December 1988, p. 95.

18. Noting that many radical economists have left the academy, one tenured Marxist economist explained to journalist Paul Farhi of the *Washington Post* some of their dilemmas: "You can't get tenure if you don't publish in the mainstream journals. If you have views that don't correspond to the mainstream point of view, you won't get published." Paul Farhi, "Withering Away of Marxism," *International Herald Tribune*, June 8, 1989, pp. 11 and 15.

19. Hilary and Steven Rose, *Ideology of/in the Natural Sciences* (Cambridge: Schenkman, 1980), p. 67.

20. *Harvard Gazette*, November 21, 1986, p. 4.

21. According to the profile of Hufton in *Harvard Magazine* (January/February 1989), p. 63, they happily report that "She eschews radicalism."

22. Maria Mies, *Patriarchy and Accumulation on a World Scale* (London: Zed Press, 1986), p. 15.

23. *Ibid.*

24. McCain, "Matina Horner Moves On," *Boston Globe*, March 6, 1989.

25. J.K. Galbraith, *The Age of Uncertainty* (Boston: Houghton Mifflin, 1977), p. 197.

26. Keynes quoted in R. Skidelsky, ed., *The End of the Keynesian Era* (London: Macmillan, 1977), p. 34.

27. In his previous reflections on the Cambridge University economists and in his eulogy of Nicholas Kaldor, Alex Cockburn has made this point about the pallid quality of U.S. Keynesianism.

28. Tobin quoted by Allen Matsusow, *The Unravelling of America* (New York: Harper and Row, 1984), p. 11.

29. Falk quoted by *Vanity Fair*, April 1985, p. 49.

30. Some of this data cited by Norman Geras, *Karl Marx and Human Nature: The Refutation of a Legend* (London: Verso, 1983), p. 105. Statistics on pesticide poisoning from World Health Organization, cited by *International Herald Tribune*, June 1, 1989, p. 7. After witnessing the massive poisoning of wild life in the Sudan, the agronomist and pesticide expert Arif Jamal noted the proliferation of barrels of pesticide with the label: "Not registered for use in the United States of America." He asked in vain: "How can a country forbid a poison at home and yet manufacture it and sell it to other countries. Where is the morality of this?"

31. Shultz speech cited by Noam Chomsky, *Pirates and Emperors* (New York: Claremont Research, 1986), p. 174.

32. These reflections are in part adapted from a speech by Edward Said, AAUG Convention, Cambridge, MA, 1986.

33. Edward Said, *The World, the Text, and the Critic* (Cambridge: Harvard University Press, 1983), pp. 3-4.

34. Lewis Lapham, *Money and Class in America* (New York: Weidenfeld and Nicolson, 1988), pp. 20-21.

35. See Anthony Lewis's column, *New York Times*, July 24, 1986, p. 25.

36. Anant Sundarum, letter, "What's All this Talk About Western Values?" *New York Times*, August 10, 1986, p. 24.

37. Clifford Geertz, Hildred Geertz, Lawrence Rosen, *Meaning and Order in Moroccan Society* (Cambridge: Cambridge University Press, 1979). For Geertz's lack of any Moroccan sources, see Edward Said, "Orientalism Revisited: An Interview," *MERIP Middle East Report*, 150, January-February 1988, p. 34.

38. Kissinger quoted by Noam Chomsky and Edward Herman, *After the Cataclysm* (Boston: South End Press, 1979), p. 350.

39. This critique of Babbitt and Richards relies heavily on William Spanos, "The Apollonian Investment of Modern Humanist Education," *Cultural Critique*, Fall 1985. See pp. 38 and 47 for quotations of Babbitt. See I. Babbitt, *Rousseau and Romanticism* (New York: AMS Press, 1976 [1919]), *Literature and the American College: Essays in Defense of the Humanities* (New York: Kelley, 1972 [1908]), and *Spanish Character and Other Essays* (New York: AMS Press, 1983 [1940]).

40. *Ibid.*, p. 67.

41. *Ibid.* For a discussion of Macaulay, see also Said, introduction to *World, the Text, and the Critic*; cf. John Clive, *Macaulay: The Shaping of the Historian* (New York: Vintage, 1974), esp. pp. 231-232, chapters 12 and 13.

42. Agassiz cited in Leon Kamin, Richard C. Lewontin, and Steven Rose, *Not in Our Genes* (New York: Pantheon, 1984), pp. 27-28.

43. *Ibid.*

44. Herbert Marcuse, *Negations* (Boston: Beacon Press, 1969), pp. 223-224.

45. M. Poster, "The Modern versus the Postmodern: The Franco-German Debate in Social Theory," in J. Trumpbour, ed., *The Dividing Rhine: Politics and Society in Contemporary France and Germany* (Oxford: Berg Publishers, 1989), p. 74.

46. For the Landes-Skocpol dispute, see Michael Nolan, "Return of Sociologist Precipitates New Conflict," *Harvard Crimson*, October 8, 1986, pp. 1, 6.

47. B. Turner, *Marx and the End of Orientalism* (London: Allen and Unwin, 1978).

48. Kenneth Stampp's famous formulation is briefly discussed by Manning Marable, *How Capitalism Underdeveloped Black America* (Boston: South End Press, 1983), p. 220.

49. P. Anderson speech, New School for Social Research, transcript partly reproduced in "Agenda for Radical History," *Radical History Review*, 36, 1986, pp. 32-37.

50. Henri Lefebvre, *The Explosion: Marxism and the French Upheaval* (New York: Monthly Review Press, 1969), p. 143. The right-wing calls student radicals anti-intellectual when the *Dartmouth Review* regularly delivers such wisdom as Jeffrey Hart's observation that "I support SDI even if it doesn't work—at least it would keep money out of the hands of the poor." (quoted by *Spy*, July 1989), or "We don't owe the Indians anything. We fought them. They lost. That's that." Theodore Crown, *Dartmouth Review*, February 8, 1989. It is also interesting to note that William Kristol and Carnes Lord, both proud political disciples of Leo Strauss, the philosopher who inspired Allan Bloom, are today top staffers for that philosopher-king, Vice President J. Danforth Quayle. David Fields in a letter to the *New York Times Magazine* (July 30, 1989) remarks: "[I]t is not a little ironic that the Straussians, with their elitist convictions, puffery about intellectual rigor and hand-wringing about the loss of virtue (in the classical sense, please) in modern society, have found an opening through Dan Quayle."

51. See comments of Orville Schell, "Nightline," May 5, 1989.

52. John Silber quoted by *Boston Globe Sunday Magazine*, December 14, 1986, p. 34.

53. Alan B. Cobban, *The Medieval Universities: Their Development and Organization* (London: Methuen, 1975), p. 170.

54. For a work that points to The Statute of Cordoba as a great victory for students, see Robin Blackburn and Alexander Cockburn, eds., *Student Power* (Middlesex: Penguin, 1969).

55. Statistics from lecture by Berkeley anthropologist Laura Nader at Harvard University, February 25, 1988.

How Harvard is Ruled
Administration and Governance
at the Corporate University

Robert Weissman

University administrators in the United States learned many lessons from the campus unrest of the late 1960s and early 1970s, but the importance of teaching democratic values by example was not among them. In fact, university administrators have made a virtue of their institutions' lack of democratic governing structures. This was exemplified in a *New Republic* article entitled "Highest Education: Our universities are the world's best," by Henry Rosovsky, past dean of the Faculty of Arts and Sciences and currently a member of Harvard's governing board. Rosovsky wrote, "Governance is another area in which American universities are unusual...We have a system of governance that permits non-consensual and unpopular decisions to be made when necessary. We have learned that not everything is improved by making it more democratic."[1]

At Harvard University, President Bok's vision of administering a modern university is grounded in this anti-democratic philosophy. Bok's vision has consisted of the adoption of a new, corporate style of governance to replace traditional, old-boy models. As Bok has put it into practice at Harvard, this newer model has offered corporate ideals and sophisticated tactics in place of the traditional patriarchal (meaning, in this case, reliance on notions of family, family ties, and beneficent rulers in a setting where male dominance of the governing structure remains almost absolute) and patronizing values, including overtly repressive methods of dealing with dissenters, which characterized the administration of Bok's predecessor. The new management style has not totally replaced the old; vestiges of the past still remain, particularly in the realm of ideology.

The Origins of Corporate Harvard

Bok took the reins of Harvard in 1971, inheriting them from Nathan Pusey, who had been appointed president in 1953. Bok's corporate management system stands in stark contrast to that of Pusey, who embodied the old system, both in his values and management style.

The replacement of Pusey's model of governance with Bok's was not merely a matter of collective personal preference on the part of the six men who selected Bok to succeed Pusey. Two intertwined factors—the growth of student protest and the University's greater integration into society—worked to make Pusey's philosophy woefully inefficient and ineffective, eventually plunging the University into crisis and necessitating the switch to the more modern, corporate management of Derek Bok. On the one hand, beginning with the civil rights movement and blossoming as part of the anti-war movement, student protest at Harvard became the major challenge facing University administrators. On the other hand, broad changes in the political economy significantly altered universities' role in society and affected administrators' duties. Spurred by the rapid growth of industry and the military-industrial complex during the post-World War II and Vietnam War-induced economic booms, major research universities such as Harvard saw their budgets mushroom with federally-supported grants, took on non-traditional functions, and expanded greatly. As David Noble and Nancy Pfund explain, "In the 1940s the universities' primary ties were transferred from private industry to the Federal Government as they became centers of contract research for military and other governmental agencies. This phase reached its full flowering in the policy think-tank multiversity of the 1960s."[2] Developments at Harvard, such as the growth of federally-financed science research, the founding of the Center for International Affairs (C.F.I.A.), and the physical expansion of the University (under Pusey the square footage of University property doubled)[3] helped transform the University into what Clark Kerr called a "multiversity."

Pusey's attitude and model of government were especially unsuited to deal with student protest, where the crisis was particularly acute. Pusey is most remembered for his decision to call in police to end the student takeover of University Hall in 1969, a bust that ended with hundreds of students injured. This decision was indicative not only of Pusey's strategy for dealing with protesters, but of his attitudes as well. For Pusey, the conflict with radical students represented an assault by outsiders on the hallowed halls of Harvard; it fell to him to defend the University from what he called "alien" forces. In stark contrast to the flexible strategy Bok would successfully employ later, compromise was impossible for Pusey; he argued that "if we had compromised, it would have been with something essentially evil." "Pusey's ideal was so outmoded," the *Harvard Crimson* later commented, "few others could recognize it."[4] After the incident, in the fall of 1969, the Harvard Corporation (Harvard's primary governing board; see below) lost confidence in Pusey to such an extent that it took power from Pusey, enmeshed itself in the day-to-day management of the University, and gave full responsibility for handling student protest to Archibald Cox, then a professor at the Harvard Law School.

Pusey's method of administration was as antiquated as his ideal of Harvard and prevented him from adequately coping with the bloated University. Five months before Bok took office, a special University Committee On Governance "recommended augmenting the staff of the President to include six Vice Presidents" so as to "alleviate the...'overburdened' condition of the Administration."[5] Even Pusey realized changes were needed, recommending an expansion of the administration. "I had one vice-president," he later recalled. "But by the time I left the University had grown so vast that no successor could or should go on that way."[6]

Bok's Response I: The Corporate Model of Governance

To extricate the University from the crisis ushered in by its massive expansion and the subsequent rise of a radical student movement, Bok introduced a new, modern form of management to Harvard. While maintaining ultimate control of administrative decisions, he has implemented a new, decentralized structure of administration. Components of this new structure include a division of labor between Bok and his right-hand man, Daniel Steiner, in which Bok focuses on academic issues and Steiner handles management questions, and the insertion of a new tier of five vice presidents to manage different aspects of the University. Mimicking the corporate governance structure was the means by which "Bok rationalized the administration," Steiner has explained. "He moved us to a larger more sophisticated central administration, one that's staffed to deal with any problem."[7]

Old Boy Harvard Goes Corporate

The oldest and most significant of the University's traditional structures is the President and Fellows of Harvard College, commonly known as the Harvard Corporation. Established in 1650, the Corporation is the oldest corporation in the United States. A self-perpetuating body consisting of seven members, the Corporation appointed its first member who is not a white male (a white corporate attorney named Judith Richards Hope) in February 1989. The President and Fellows technically own all of Harvard and have final say in every decision at the University.[8] In practice, the Corporation delegates most of its authority; most significantly, it has little role in academic decisions. This delegation of power takes place at the Corporation's discretion, however.

The Corporation meets one day every other week. Fellows therefore make a substantial time commitment to the University when accepting an appointment. Membership carries tremendous prestige; but those who accept appointment do so to influence Harvard's policies, and, in large part, out of a sense of social obligation (see Trumpbour's essay on Harvard's corporate relations).

The Corporation's meetings are secret, and minutes of the meetings are not disclosed. The members focus on financial and budgetary issues, and long-term planning for the University.

The exact issues and the level of detail that the Corporation addresses are not known by anyone other than the ruling body's members themselves and perhaps several other high-ranking University officials. What is clear is that while Bok has been president the Corporation has given more decision-making power to the president and his appointees. This change is due both to the University's growing complexity and to the Corporation's confidence in Bok's abilities. The Fellows' delegation of authority probably carries over to general policy issues; as president, Bok controls the key University decisions but consults with the Corporation about them. An ex-member of the Corporation supported this view:

> He defines the Corporation's most important functions as: to act as a confidential sounding board for the President on educational and other policy matters; to exercise a collective judgment on business type questions; to detect or identify issues; to warn; to reinforce the President where help is needed.[9]

This advisory role is similar to that played by corporate boards of directors. As the Fellows have ceded power to the president, they have gradually been transformed from one of the active governing bodies at the University and filled the position of Corporate Harvard's hands-on board of directors.

Harvard has another governing body, the Board of Overseers, which is elected by the alumni. While the Board is supposed to oversee the activities of the Corporation, it mostly serves as a rubber stamp for the Corporation's decisions. One function of the Board of Overseers which is relevant to this discussion is its role in legitimizing the Corporation. The Corporation probably could not exist without the Overseers. The extensive power wielded by the Corporation is essential to its effectiveness. Yet the closeness and privacy of the Corporation virtually requires the existence of a senior body which is selected in a more representative way and which more nearly reflects the public nature of the University's charter.[10]

That is, because one governing body—the token Overseers —is relatively diverse, the fact that the other—the powerful Corporation—is secretive and homogenous is less politically noteworthy and offensive.

The Structure of the Schools

Another traditional structure that has been given a new twist under Bok is the University's decentralized system of graduate schools. Each school has traditionally been autonomous, making independent tenure decisions, establishing their own standards of appropriate conduct, raising their own funds, running their own admissions procedure. This decentralization provides a convenient excuse for inaction by the central administration, enabling it to avoid forcing changes at any particular school. In the aftermath of revelations in 1985 and 1986 that Professors Samuel Huntington and Nadav Safran, both of the Faculty of Arts and Sciences, were consulting for the CIA in apparent violation of University rules, Bok explained in an open letter to the University his position on the issue and to what standards he thought faculty members should adhere. He did not, however, force the implementation of these rule changes, nor did he even campaign to have his suggestions adopted. The University's "decentralization" also functions as a rationalization for a lack of accountability on the part of Harvard's highest administrators. Because he is "ultimately responsible, but not directly" for undergraduates, Bok has rejected undergraduate requests that he address College students' concerns in a formal, institutionalized manner, through publishing a paper on the "State of the Students" and attending a forum to address students' reactions.[11]

There are, however, strict limits on the amount of autonomy faculties have, and to that extent, the decentralization at Harvard is analogous to that of a corporation among its divisions. When a division malfunctions, the central administration steps in and takes over.

It is usually unnecessary for the central administration at Harvard to take over, because the various faculties, sharing the values and ideals of the administration, do not usually "malfunction." When problems arise, faculties or departments are usually able to handle them on their own. For example, left-wing professors were totally purged from the economics department without any help from either the University administration or from the Faculty of Arts and Sciences' administrators (see Lawrence Lifschultz's essay). Occasionally, however, problems do get out of control, and it becomes necessary for central authority and power to assert itself.

The current struggle at the Law School over the tenuring of radicals constitutes the most obvious case where Bok has ignored the University's decentralization and taken control. The Critical Legal Studies (CLS) movement, a loosely coordinated "school" which examines the foundations of law and challenges the notion of neutrality in the legal system, has a stronghold at Harvard; many of its leaders— Duncan Kennedy, Morton Horwitz, Roberto Unger—are tenured members of the Harvard Law School faculty. In combination with liberal elements of the faculty, CLS adherents successfully supported the tenure bids of a number of leftist professors during the early 1980s, despite the ardent opposition of conservative faculty members. Fearful of the growing strength of progressives, Bok stepped into the fray in 1985, stating that he would intervene in cases where tenure votes were alleged to be politically motivated. Bok used this justification to review the case of David Trubeck, who had been awarded tenure by the Law School faculty; after reevaluation, Bok set a historic precedent in 1987 by withdrawing the tenure offer.[12]

Students and Structure

For all the admiration Harvard's rulers may express for the corporate mentality, Harvard is not a corporation; consequently while its structure can imitate corporations' to a great degree, it cannot mirror them. Derek Bok has different goals and different constraints than Lee Iacocca. Even where Harvard's rulers are unable to copy corporate structures, however, they approach their problems with a corporate perspective.

As employers promote "team concepts" to divide workers, so the Harvard administration utilizes and manipulates ideals of community and various structures to prevent the conditions that lead to the development of protest. The central thrust of this pre-emptive strategy of diffusing protest is to prevent students from forming into a cohesive social group. Dividing students from one another is therefore the most important technique used to control students.

The division of students is aided by the lack of interaction between students at the nine faculties at Harvard, either informally or formally, through a unitary student senate. For the most part, then, the administration need only turn its attention to the College. For the same reasons that Bok writes "it is the undergraduates who provide most of the energy, excitement, and exuberance responsible for the plays, the football games, the student newspapers, the musical events, and all the other activities that give so much texture and vitality to campus life,"[13] undergraduates also are the main participants in campus protests. Undergraduates achieve this distinction first by virtue of their numerical predominance; students at Harvard College make up approximately 40 percent of those enrolled full-time at the University. In addition, graduate students are increasingly mired in professionalism and careerism. In contrast, undergraduates, not all of whom have shed their idealism, have time to devote to meeting, conspiring, and protesting.

The primary method by which undergraduates are divided is through the housing system. Almost all undergraduates live on campus, with all upper-class students living in a dorm or "House" with which they will stay affiliated for three years. Each House has a dining hall, and most of an undergraduate's social interaction takes place within his or her House. The House system had its genesis and development long before Derek Bok became president of Harvard, but its function is nevertheless to divide students. (Ironically, the House system, begun under President A. Lawrence Lowell in 1930, was initially developed to overcome the lack of community at Harvard. The system was an attempt to create small, autonomous communities to combat the atomizing effects of a large institution.) Students are encouraged to identify with their House and to seek community within their House. Bok has actively promoted the Houses, investing tremendous resources in renovating them; one friend even jokes that Bok may be remembered in Harvard histories as "a great builder."[14]

Structures, both organizational and physical, that might bring students together, such as a student center, are actively discouraged. Thus recent rumblings from the student government about the need for a student center, timid though they were, were of concern to the administration. Addressing the student government of the College, Bok stated that in the fifteen years of his tenure the University had invested $70 million in facilities for housing, education, athletics, and drama. In view of these expenditures, the real limits on resources facing the University, and other competing projects requiring money, he did not feel an investment in a student center could be justified.[15] This response was perceived as quite convincing by almost everyone in the audience, and, taken on its own terms, it was.

From a more removed perspective, however, it demonstrated another aspect of corporate rule: ahistorical and noncontextual analysis. Because given Bok's response, the logical question was "If you spent $70 million on College students' facilities, why didn't you spend any on a student center?" The answer to this question is clear: a student center has the potential to bring students together, to overcome the divisions engendered by the House system, to enable students to develop a common consciousness of their role in the University, and to be politicized. Deprived of this common consciousness, students suffer from atomization and its twin, disempowerment, and are incapable of posing a threat to the administration.

Bok's promotion of the House dormitory system thus turns the system's original purpose on its head. What was developed to create community for students is now used to prevent students from realizing their broader campus community.

Given this set of circumstances, it came as a surprise to student activists when it was revealed in October 1988 that the University was considering constructing a student center. Suddenly, the Dean of the College, who two years earlier stated, "Except for student support, I haven't heard any widespread support for the proposal [for a student center],"[16] was proclaiming that "It's an interesting thing to speculate and dream about—and I think we're at that stage."[17]

Activists' surprise quickly gave way to dismay, both over the process by which the student center had been planned and the specifics of the plan. The administration's infatuation with secrecy— if students can't be told about a student center in the works, what can they be told about?—was almost comical. Unfortunately, the administration's secrecy and unwillingness to allow student participation in the planning of the center, or even to consult students on the prospective idea, had concrete, negative effects. The administration's tentative plans call for the building of a student center and a new dining hall for first year students in Memorial Hall, which presently contains not only two lecture halls, but most of the campus's office space for undergraduate organizations as well. The administration has also proposed changing the building in which first year students currently eat (and which also contains meeting rooms) into faculty office space. Thus, it appears that the effect of the university's proposal, as it now stands, will be a net decline in student office and meeting space—hardly the hopes students might harbor for a student center and hardly a threat to Bok's emphasis on the House dormitory system as a means to divide students.

Bok's Response II: Management Style and Strategies (a focus on discipline)

Accompanying Bok's corporate administrative apparatus has been an enlightened management philosophy and strategy to replace former President Pusey's "outmoded ideal." Bok's administration doesn't react in rage to student protests and enact repressive measures to counter them. Instead, seeking to avoid confrontation, the administration utilizes sophisticated tactics, makes limited compromises, and co-opts moderates, a strategy well illustrated by recent developments in the discipline system at the Faculty of Arts and Sciences.

Since Vietnam-era protests, the disciplinary system at Harvard has been bifurcated, with one system used for political offenses and one used for all other types. Until the fall of 1987, the tribunal which had been charged with trying students guilty of political offenses was the Committee On Rights and Responsibilities (CRR), a body which evolved out of the political crisis at Harvard in the late 1960s.

(In theory, the CRR's mandate went far beyond dealing with political offenses. The document on which the CRR was based, the Resolution on Rights and Responsibilities, listed theft, among other things, as an unacceptable interference with the "essential processes of the University." Theory and practice diverged widely, however; the CRR never dealt with non-political cases.)

Since its inception, the CRR met with student opposition. Students pointed to numerous flaws with the committee, most pointedly its separating out political offenses for special treatment, and its total lack of due process, including closed hearings, a lack of established procedures, and the acceptance of hearsay evidence. Though the committee was supposed to be made up of both faculty and students, students refused to serve on the committee they labeled a political tribunal and a kangaroo court; almost all defendants refused to appear before it as well.

From its creation until 1972, the committee dealt with 368 complaints, issuing punishments that ranged from warnings to dismissals. The harshest penalties went to the most visible activists, making political leadership a hazardous vocation. By 1971, picketing students were wearing bags over their heads. One student leader, who had not yet been informed that she was on probation, neglected to wear her bag, and was suspended.

When student protest died down, the CRR became dormant. Except for a brief revival in 1975, it was effectively non-existent from 1972 to 1985. Student protest over the CRR in the form of the boycott continued, however, and no students served on the CRR. By the early 1980s, the administration no longer even bothered to ask students to serve on the committee.

In the wake of anti-apartheid protest in 1985, the faculty and administration decided to reconvene the CRR. When students declined to serve on the body, the CRR met anyway. In 1986 students reaffirmed the boycott specifically as a repudiation of the perceived unjust nature of the CRR. The student government issued a detailed and far-reaching proposal to abolish both the CRR and the College's other disciplinary body, and to revamp the entire disciplinary process. As a result of this renewed student refusal to participate in the operation of the CRR, the faculty decided to review and revise it.

Initially, there was confusion among the faculty about what actually should be reformed. They wanted to stop student protest, but they did not perceive anything wrong with the CRR. While students pointed out that the discipline system was not characterized by due process and fair procedures, the faculty responded on their own terms. Invoking the old, patriarchal model of governance, one of the most liberal faculty members, Professor Diana Eck, explained that established rules were unnecessary in the University because "A university doesn't pass laws, just like a family doesn't."[18]

But the more sophisticated administration was operating under a different paradigm. With the most militant protests long passed, it no longer found harshly repressive structures necessary. The administration took control of what was supposed to be a faculty review committee (the committee's membership shrunk and the composition was changed to favor administrators) and developed a proposal that granted limited rights to students.

Administrators did not meet students' most radical demands, to treat political offenses according to the same rules as other violations and to have faculty judged by the same system as students. They did, however, lend a minimal air of fairness to the system by establishing clear procedures for the new committee which guaranteed students the right to an open hearing, to challenge evidence, to use a faculty advisor, and to be sentenced according to an established set of penalties. Granting these rights to students will not substantially alter the administration's ability to discipline students, so the administration had no reason to continue to deny them. The implementation of these new procedures has, however, conferred legitimacy on the system, as was exemplified by the termination of the student boycott in December 1987.

Ultimately, this legitimacy will allow administrators greater control over students, even as they act to limit the arbitrariness of the old system. The administration was unable to mete out harsh punishments to activists in 1985, 1986, and 1987 because the discipline system lacked community support; such restrictions are no longer evident.

The reforms in the disciplinary system worked to diffuse protest by turning a subject that had the potential to galvanize students into a non-issue. The seventeen-year boycott of the CRR demonstrated students' deeply felt opposition to the system, and the continued use of the body could have sparked protests that involved liberal students as well as radicals.

Thus, the administration chose to initiate a compromise solution to an issue that deeply divided students from administrators and faculty. The compromise was engineered and carried out by the administration, but it nevertheless was a compromise, offering meaningful concessions to students. These tactics are indicative of the Bok administration's broader strategy of ameliorating and minimizing potential protest by anticipating problems before they fully develop, and, where possible, by co-opting moderates.

The Challenge to Progressives

The challenges, obstacles, and difficulties posed by Bok's corporate model of governance are immense. The extra tier of administration added by Bok accentuates the degree of hierarchy at the University, makes it difficult to locate responsibility at any one individual, and removes the University's leaders further from students, and, in fact, any one they don't want to deal with. "The more sophisticated central administration" to which Steiner referred is distant from all and unknown to most students. The highest administrative official an undergraduate is likely to have contact with is the Dean of Students, who coordinates and oversees student organizations. Those at the top of the governing structure bask in the anonymity they are guaranteed by the buffer of administrators that protects them from critical individuals or organizations. Corporation members even brag about their anonymity; one recently retired member described the Corporation as a "marvel—it's so anonymous—the only voice is that of the president."[19] The combined effect of the University's rulers' increasing hierarchy and anonymity is to mystify the dynamics of power at Harvard and to decrease administrative accountability.

This situation is of great import for students. The manner in which the University is run not only affects students' education, but educates them as well. It teaches them that those who hold power are not, and should not be, held accountable, an important lesson both to those who will become the country's leaders and to those who will be funnelled to the middle-class. It teaches students to be passive, compliant, and accepting if they are ruled; it teaches them to be secretive, removed, and to concentrate power if they are rulers. While the anti-democratic nature of the University is obvious, the contempt with which democratic values are treated exacerbates the situation. While progressive students have angrily accused the Corporation of being similar to the Kremlin and the College of Cardinals, important members of the University cheerfully agree the analogy is correct; Samuel Huntington has, for example, labeled the Corporation "our Politburo."[20]

Students develop their politics while they are in school, and if those who run their university are contemptuous of democracy, students can only conclude, either consciously or unconsciously, that democratic values are irrelevant or counter-productive in other parts of society as well. If efficiency and democracy are opposite values, why should economic institutions be democratized? For that matter, why should political institutions be democratic? Progressive students must reverse the equation: "If our political institutions are democratic, why not the educational one, where we live and study?" But the task of progressives is not easy. Despite the pretensions of decentralization, power at Harvard is highly concentrated. There are no institutional counterweights to the power held by the president, his top aide, and the Corporation; nor are there established channels through which students can influence their rulers. The University, moreover, is structured to prevent organized insurgencies; and the administration utilizes sophisticated tactics, is flexible, and adept at diffusing student movements. Thus the challenge for progressive activists in the years ahead is daunting. While the cyclical divestment movement has attained some meaningful, if partial, victories, it has merely provided glimpses of the type of movement needed to seriously challenge Harvard's corporate structure and the direction in which it allows Harvard's rulers to guide the University. Mounting such a challenge will require a broad-based, self-conscious student movement with a large core of activists. It will need to maintain a sustained effort, work outside the system and in coalition with other University constituencies, and create alternative institutions to pressure the few who hold power at Harvard.

Notes

1. Henry Rosovsky, "Highest Education: Our universities are the world's best," *New Republic*, July 13 and 20, 1987, p. 14.

2. David Noble and Nancy Pfund, "Business Goes Back to College," *The Nation*, September 20, 1980, pp. 233 and 246.

3. William McKibben, "A Gentleman Reflects," *Harvard Crimson*, commencement issue, 1981, p. 74.

4. McKibben, p. 74.

5. *Harvard Crimson*, "Committee Report Says New Structure Needed for President's Office," (no byline), April 2, 1971, p. 1.

6. Quoted in McKibben, p. 74.

7. Quoted in E. J. Kahn III, " Bok to the Future," *Boston Magazine*, September 1986, p. 141.

8. "All the property of every department of the University stands in the name of the President and Fellows. Every faculty is subject to their authority. All the degrees are voted by the Corporation, and in the first instance, all appointments are made by them or their designees. All general changes in the requirements and procedures anywhere in the University are carried out under the authority of the Corporation...It is the Corporation as a whole which is solely empowered to receive gifts on behalf of the University. Moreover, the Corporation can invest the University's funds in purchase of real and personal property and, as is the case with any true corporation, it is the Corporation as a whole who can sue and be sued" (The Committee on the Structure and Function of the Board of Overseers [The Gilbert Committee], "Report Concerning Harvard's Governmental Structure," December 1978, p. 3).

9. Office of the Secretary of Harvard University, "Harvard University: The Governing Boards," February 1985, p. 4.

10. Gilbert Committee, p. 13.

11. Derek Bok, Address to the Harvard-Radcliffe Undergraduate Council, May 4, 1987.

12. Bok's denial of tenure to Trubeck has not in the least diminished the faculty conflict at the Law School. In May of 1987, conservative faculty members succeeded in garnering enough votes to block the tenure attempt of feminist CLS adherent Clare Dalton (a two-thirds vote is required to approve a tenure decision). Intense pressure from progressive (including liberal) faculty members of the Law School, combined with national interest, forced Bok to reevaluate the case. See Raskin's essay below for the outcome of this episode.

13. Derek Bok, *Higher Learning*, (Cambridge, Massachusetts: Harvard University Press, 1986), p. 36.

14. Kahn, p. 140. The friend is Henry Rosovsky, with whose social and historical analysis of the University this essay begins.

15. Bok, Address to the Harvard-Radcliffe Undergraduate Council.

16. *Harvard Crimson*, Jeffrey Nordhaus, "Student Center's Chances Are 'Unlikely' Says Dean," February 24, 1987, p. 1.

17. L. Fred Jewett, quoted in Martha A. Bridegam, "Harvard Considers New Student Center," *Harvard Crimson*, October 6, 1988, p. 1.

18. Quoted in Michael Nolan, "Faculty Group to Review Disciplinary Plan," *Harvard Crimson*, October 26, 1986, p. 6.

19. Andrew Heiskell, quoted in Carl Vigeland, *Great Good Fortune: How Harvard Makes Its Money*, (Boston: Houghlin Mifflin, 1986), p. 202.

20. Samuel Huntington, Introduction to a Speech by Corazon Aquino, Harvard University, September 20, 1986.

Part II
Harvard
and the State

Harvard, the Cold War, and the National Security State

John Trumpbour

"The sort of activities that goes on in the classrooms and laboratories of Cambridge is contributing vastly to the immense national efforts we are making and shall have to make to live up to our nation's acquired responsibilities in the world and to compete effectively in this life-and-death struggle in which it seems that we are to be engaged for a long time with our alien rival, the USSR." So observed Harvard President Nathan Pusey (1953-71) in the early wake of the Cuban Revolution in 1959.[1] Lest there be doubts about Harvard's continued commitment to the American Imperium in the waning Age of Eisenhower, Pusey assured his Cambridge audience that the University would never rest. In waging the Cold War, America should not forget, said Pusey, that: "Harvard is no stranger to such struggles, albeit this is the most serious one we have ever faced. Our university has done its part—and more—in every conflict in our nation's history."[2]

As is manifest in Pusey's portly prose, Harvard initially took great pride in promoting the early Cold War. Harvard men, though sometimes subordinate to Yalies and Princetonians in the Truman and Eisenhower administrations, helped plan and execute most of the major military, paramilitary, and covert interventions of the postwar period—two large land wars in Korea and Vietnam, and the global counter-revolutionary struggle in Greece (1948), Iran (1953), Guatemala (1954), Indonesia (1958 and 1965), Lebanon (1958), Laos (1960), Cuba (1961), the Congo (1964), British Guyana (1964), Dominican Republic (1965), Chile (1973), and, more recently, Angola (1974-76 and 1986-present), Nicaragua (1980-present), Grenada (1983), and Libya (1986). Colin Campbell of the *New York Times* put it mildly, then, when in an essay of June 1986 he reflects that "a kind of international interventionism came to be a leading idea in Harvard's conception of foreign affairs."[3] The Spanish-American War is usually regarded as the salad days of the Harvard interventionist spirit. Historian Samuel Eliot Morison notes that so many Harvard men launched the United States into the war, William Randolph Hearst, Henry Cabot Lodge, and Theodore Roosevelt, among others, that the University could adopt for its own Empress Eugénie's saying about the Franco-Prussian War: "C'est ma guerre, C'est ma petite guerre à moi."[4]

The Federal Government, the Foundations, and the Rise of Area Studies

There were new features in Harvard's postwar interventionist crusade, however. Pusey's predecessor, President James Conant, in 1948 welcomed what he called Harvard's "new, more intimate association" with the federal government. "Indeed," marvelled Conant, "many professors here and elsewhere find themselves perplexed as to how to divide their time between calls from the government and their responsibilities as scholars and teachers."[5] The postwar transformation of Harvard took on several dimensions: 1) Federally-sponsored University research enjoyed a massive increase; these funds were virtually nonexistent before 1940, ballooning to 33 percent of total University expenditures in 1965, and levelling at around 20 percent today. Much of this federal expenditure remains in the hard sciences. Nevertheless, Harvard openly acknowledged that much of this funding was of military origin. As Conant modestly put it in 1946: "At the moment not inconsiderable amounts of government money are being spent in the universities to support research, thanks to the vision of certain leaders of the Navy and Army."[6] 2) At the same time, a network of corporate philanthropies aggressively sought to transform the study of foreign policy. Prior to World War II, the number of centers of international studies could be counted on both hands. By 1968, there were 191, 95 of which were concentrated at twelve universities. The Rockefeller and Carnegie Foundations played the dominant role in this initial transformation, spending immense sums in conjunction with smaller foundations ($34 million between 1945 and 1948) on what came to be known as area studies. After 1950, the Ford Foundation contributed more substantial lucre, funding all or the majority part of 83 centers. As a report from the U.S. Office of Education explained: "It must be noted that the significance of the money granted is out of all proportion to the amounts involved since most universities would have no center program had they not been subsidized. Our individual inventories indicate clearly the lack of enthusiasm as well as of cash on the part of most college administrators for such programs."[7] Out of this marriage of corporate interests with the welfare-warfare state came a rising class of academicians, "the new mandarins," who put reason, sometimes of a specialized, technocratic variety, at the service of the national security apparatus.

Theodore Draper comments on their invasion of Washington after World War II:

> A new breed of politicized intellectuals appeared—the foreign affairs intellectuals. What had been a fairly small field became a minor industry with branches in international politics, international economics, international arms proliferation and control, foreign aid, area specialization, and the like... If anything more were needed to invigorate the war-time and post-war boom in the procreation, care and feeding of politicized intellectuals, the Truman Doctrine of 1947 and the Marshall Plan of 1948 came just in time. They enabled large numbers of American intellectuals to fan out all over the world at government expense, scattering their largesse and advice far and wide.[8]

By the time of the Kennedy administration, JFK's close aide Ted Sorensen could boast that "professors, ex-professors, and would-be professors were all over Washington—in the White House, in the bureaucracy, in Congress and Congressional staffs, in almost all levels of government."[9]

The university, with its reputation as the American institution most resistant to outside pressure, a bulwark against the self-serving priorities of corporate and government elites, proved to be most pliable. Thought to be traditional, conservative, inclined to shun hasty experimentation with new programs, the university, on the contrary, built up with dispatch area studies programs in the Soviet, Asian, and later, African, Middle East, and Latin American fields. Aggressively overriding disciplinary boundaries, bringing linguists, economists, sociologists, historians, and political scientists together under one roof, the area studies programs were typically better funded than the traditional academic departments and became the sites of new buildings, libraries, and journals, sometimes to the consternation of intellectuals on the left or in disciplines largely cut off from the foundation booty. For managers of the national security state, the area studies programs could be relied on as extension schools for the State Department, while providing analysis judged useful for containing upheaval in hot spots throughout the globe.

Former Harvard Dean and National Security Advisor Mc-George Bundy openly declared that the tradition of area studies grew out of the requirements of the intelligence community. Bundy states that "the area study programs developed in American universities in the years after the war were manned, directed, or stimulated by graduates of the OSS." Another former JFK-LBJ advisor Roger Hilsman elaborates: "When OSS, America's wartime secret intelligence service, was set up in 1941, one of the basic ideas behind it was the novel and almost impish thought that scholars could in some respects take the place of spies."[10]

Specializing primarily in what eminent linguist Noam Chomsky calls "the dismal field" of international studies, this academic class possessed great confidence in its ability to rule the planet, an attitude nurtured by the heady triumph of World War II and by faith in the ability of knowledge to impose order on a seemingly chaotic world. As David Halberstam said of McGeorge Bundy, "There was no doubt in his mind about his ability to handle not just...his job but the world."[11] When the idealist conviction of this class in the power of knowledge to transform the world failed to yield results, they were all too willing to succumb to the appeals of brute repression and direct intervention. Intellectuals often feel hopelessly mired in passivity, so they can be quick to surrender to the seductions of power. As Halberstam continues about former Secretary of Defense Robert McNamara: "Sometimes...he seemed so idealistic as to be innocent. He never talked about power and he did not seem to covet it. Yet the truth was quite different. He loved power and sought it intensely."[12] More adept than the generals and even the politicians at masking their abdication of responsibility when the ensuing destruction and carnage was set into motion, the intellectuals scurried under the cover of idealistic internationalism, and later under the twin banners of "value neutrality" and "objectivity" to justify their policy choices. Rather than call attention to the choice involved, the bogus appeal to science put their recommendations in the realm of necessity. The whole baroque façade came to be constructed out of intellectual materials of a most flimsy sort, neologisms, euphemisms, and a rhetoric of elusion designed to insulate them from debate—all too familiar in the Vietnam debacle when "pacification" was used to describe the destruction of villages, "forced urbanization" stood as the equivalent term for obliterating the countryside, and currently "stability" remains the code word for U.S. global hegemony.

As will be seen later, many of these Orwellian terms were of Harvard vintage. One of the more revolutionary aspects of the Reagan foreign policy team may well have been its initial willingness to dispense with this obfuscating discourse, in spite of Alexander

Haig's masterful butchery of the language. Whereas McNamara and Bundy in the Kennedy and Johnson administrations and Laird and Rumsfeld in the Nixon and Ford administrations might refer to scenarios for limited nuclear war with such dazzling antiseptic formulations as "our menu of options," Haig instead blithely told Congress of the need for a "nuclear warning shot," while Weinberger also in 1981 spoke robustly about "our nuclear war fighting capability."[13] When Europe and later the United States erupted in waves of protests (over 800,000 marchers in New York alone in June 1982) the Reagan team learned the folly of directly confronting the public with the reality of U.S. foreign policy. They retreated to the euphemistic excesses of the mandarins: MX missiles became "peacekeepers," contras were reincarnated as "the moral equivalent of our Founding Fathers," and, for those still fearful of a trigger happy administration, the Strategic Defense Initiative (SDI) signalled the end of reliance on mutual assured destruction (MAD) and nuclear utilization strategies (NUTS). Their language in foreign affairs became cloaked in the idiom of Wilsonian internationalism, a divorce of rhetoric from reality so great that Alan Wolfe terms it the triumph of "crackpot moralism." Previous administrations had threatened to use nuclear weapons on at least nineteen occasions; the Reagan people no longer deluded themselves about the costs of glibly telling the truth.[14]

Intellectuals, as Chomsky once put it, are "experts in legitimation." When necessary, they have supplied a euphemistic cover for U.S. foreign policy designs, but they have not been free of hysterical excess either. The intellectuals may think that theirs is a sheltered and monkish vocation, promoting greater restraint against abuses of power than the politicians, the generals, and the wider U.S. public. History, however, does not confirm their flattering self-appraisal. During World War I, Mencken remarked that the professors:

> constituted themselves, not a restraining influence upon the mob run wild, but the loudest spokesmen of its worst imbecilities. They fed it with bogus history, bogus philosophy, bogus idealism, bogus heroics... I accumulated, in those great days, for the instruction and horror of posterity, a very large collection of academic arguments, expositions, and pronunciamentos... Its contents range from solemn hymns of hate...official donkeyisms...down to childish harangues.[15]

After World War II, the intellectuals—again contrary to their self-image as voices of responsibility and restraint—took the lead in promoting the onslaught of Cold War delirium. In his presidential address to the American Historical Association in 1949, Harvard-trained Conyers Read, a renowned historian of Tudor England, told his admiring audience:

> We must clearly assume a militant attitude if we are to survive... Discipline is the essential prerequisite of every effective army whether it march under the Stars and Stripes or under the Hammer and Sickle... Total war, whether it be hot or cold, enlists everyone and calls upon everyone to assume his part. The historian is no freer from this obligation than the physicist. This sounds like the advocacy of one form of social control as against another. In short, it is.[16]

Stanford historian Thomas Bailey, author of two of the century's biggest selling textbooks on U.S. history, in 1948 reassured intellectuals otherwise squeamish about the anti-democratic ethos of the foreign policy elite:

> Because the masses are notoriously short-sighted and generally cannot see danger until it is at their throats, our statesmen are forced to deceive them into an awareness of their own long-run interests.[17]

In 1981, the director of Harvard's Center for International Affairs, Samuel P. Huntington, gave such a view resounding applause, writing that "you may have to sell [intervention or other military action] in such a way as to create the misimpression that it is the Soviet Union that you are fighting. That is what the United States has done ever since the Truman Doctrine."[18]

In the postwar construction of U.S. foreign policy, the intellectuals' greatest genius has been their knack for placing local conflicts and nationalisms in Third World countries into a grand strategic design, exhibited in Bundy and Rostow's repeated demonstrations of how Vietnam's "fall" would adversely affect U.S. "vital interests," Kissinger's proclamation that the Allende government's socialist experiment in Chile had dire geopolitical consequences, and Brzezinski's bluster that Ethiopia's conquest of the remote Ogaden province against Somalia represented a U.S. foreign policy setback monumental enough to scuttle SALT II. Reflecting on the intellectual's special role in these episodes, historian David Kaiser suggests that their pursuit of these grandiose themes has been more unrelenting than that of the politicians:

> Few experienced politicians would have urged Presidents Lyndon B. Johnson and Richard M. Nixon to persevere in Indochina as long as Mr. Rostow and Mr. Kissinger did, or regarded the fate of the Ogaden as critical to American foreign policy.[19]

Among the foreign policy mandarins, Harvard has produced the U.S. political culture's most determined peddlers of crisis and architects of grand design. But before discussing the Harvard component of the mandarin caste, it will be necessary to consider the question: who makes U.S. foreign policy?

The Foreign Policy Establishment: Harvard, the CFR, and the Making of the Empire

The dominant institution of the foreign policy elite is the New York based organization, the Council on Foreign Relations (CFR). On the rare occasions that it is discussed, the media openly acknowledges the preeminence of the CFR: *Newsweek* calls its leadership the "foreign policy establishment of the U.S.," the *New York Times* suggests that it "has made substantial contributions to the basic concepts of American foreign policy," and Marvin and Bernard Kalb term the Council "an extremely influential private group that is sometimes called the real State Department." Richard Barnet has observed that membership in the CFR is "a rite of passage for an aspiring national security manager." Thus, Henry Kissinger could tell Hamilton Fish Armstrong, one of the CFR's leaders, "You invented me."[20] Founded in 1921 to combat the evils of isolationism, the CFR has membership heavily weighted towards the most internationalist wing of the capitalist Establishment: the banks (eight members each from Chase Manhattan and J.P. Morgan and Co., seven members each from First National City and Chemical Bank), the oil companies (seven members from Mobil, six from Exxon), corporate law firms (eight members from Sullivan and Cromwell), and, in particular, the Rockefeller group of financial interests.[21] Muckraking journalist Ferdinand Lundberg reflects on the serious interest these wealthy people take in foreign policy:

> Members of the CFR have a closer and more specific connection with foreign relations. For it is, largely, their properties, branches, and affiliations abroad that are guarded by the State Department and the army, navy, and air force.
>
> Were the sea lanes not fully guarded by the ships of the navy and its submarines and strategic airfields, there might be an interruption in the flow of oil and other materials to the United States. Then many citizens might find themselves without heat and electricity, without gasoline, perhaps without coffee, tea, spices, and Scotch whiskey. There would ensue a terrible public flap,

with irate questions raised about what the government was
doing about the horrible situation.

But propertied members of the CFR would be raising such
questions much sooner than the cold, lightless, and Scotchless
resident. For it is their ships and properties that the navy and the
State Department is specifically concerned about. Interference
with these properties instantly puts the State Department into
action.[22]

The Early Years

Harvard men played a central role in the founding and expansion of the CFR. Several black tie affairs at the Harvard Club of New
York provided the initial setting for the formation of the CFR. Two
important figures were Professor of History Archibald Cary Coolidge, the first editor of *Foreign Affairs*, and Edwin F. Gay, an economic
historian and the first dean of the Harvard Business School. Previously Coolidge belonged to a group formed by Colonel Edward
House and President Woodrow Wilson, the Inquiry, an organization
called "the first attempt to use teams of scholars to plan long-term
foreign policy." He considered Theodore Roosevelt, William Howard Taft, Charles Evans Hughes, Henry Cabot Lodge, and Herbert
Hoover to be among his circle of friends, and liked to brag to his
students that the State Department doorman knew him by name.
"Through aggressive recruiting," according to historian Robert Mc-
Caughey, Coolidge saw to it that Harvard "was well represented in
the early attempt at academic foreign policymaking." Over a third of
the key contributors to the Inquiry, for instance, were affiliated with
Harvard as alumni or staff. Considered a flag waver, a member of
"the drum and trumpet" school of historiography, Coolidge was also
the most influential figure in the expansion of international studies
at Harvard in the interwar period. Edwin Gay, the sole "scholar"
among the leading officers of the CFR, pushed for Coolidge as the
first editor of *Foreign Affairs*. Gay himself edited the *New York Evening
Post* for Inquiry member Thomas W. Lamont of J.P. Morgan and Co.
Back in 1898, Gay articulated a vision that would later appeal to the
CFR's founding fathers: "When I think of the British Empire as our
inheritance I think simply of the natural right of succession. That
ultimate succession is inevitable."[23]

In the late 1920s, Isaiah Bowman, then vice-president of the CFR
and subsequently president of Johns Hopkins, established the objectives of the CFR's expansionist policy. He defined U.S. interests as

global and equivalent to Britain's, subsuming "a region whose extent is beyond the Arctic Circle in Alaska, southward to Samoa, and East and West from China to the Philippines to Liberia and Tangier." In justifying this remarkable dream, Bowman added that "if our territorial holdings are not so widely distributed as those of Great Britain, our total economic power and commercial relations are no less extensive."[24] Between 1940 and 1945, anticipating the United States as the heir to global hegemony, Bowman and other CFR members including Allen Dulles, John Foster Dulles, Hamilton Fish Armstrong, Harvard Professor of Economics Alvin Hansen, and Professors of History William Langer and Crane Brinton participated in the CFR's War and Peace Studies Project, the self-stated goal of which was "to elaborate concrete proposals designed to safeguard American interests in the settlement which will be undertaken when hostilities cease." The militant U.S. interventionism espoused by the CFR came to be cloaked in the language of idealistic internationalism. Among themselves, they admitted the need for some deception in order to sell their ambitious aims to domestic opinion and the wider world. Conceding in 1941 that the "formulation of war aims for propaganda purposes is very different from formulation of one defining the true national interest," the War and Peace Studies group noted that "the interests of other peoples should be stressed, not only those of Europe, but also of Asia, Africa, and Latin America. This would have a better propaganda effect." In a letter to Hamilton Fish Armstrong in 1942, however, Bowman was quite open about U.S. postwar aims: "The measure of our victory will be the measure of our domination after victory." The CFR group developed the concept of The Grand Area, an expanded zone of free trade for U.S. capitalism that would be integrated by a combination of 1) financial institutions and programs (later the IMF, World Bank, Marshall Plan, etc.) and 2) military policing and alliances. The latter was at first demonstrably understated, but the predominance of either financial institutions or policing arrangements in the postwar world led to fissures among the foreign policy Establishment.[25]

Michael Klare calls it the division between traders and Prussians in the foreign policy elite, the split between those who demand more carrot and those who demand more stick in order to secure the interests of the U.S. Empire. A dramatic example of this split came in the Carter administration in which Zbigniew Brzezinski represented the Prussians and Cyrus Vance, ultimately the loser in the ensuing power struggle, spoke for the traders.

Prussians, Traders, and Trilateralists

In the 1970s, the U.S. foreign policy Establishment found itself in growing disarray. Components of the crisis included U.S. economic decline *vis à vis* Japan and Western Europe, the USSR's attainment of relative parity in the arms race, and the eruption of revolutions throughout the Third World (Ethiopia in 1974; Cambodia, Vietnam, Laos, Guinea-Bissau, Mozambique, and Angola in 1975; Iran, Grenada, and Nicaragua in 1979). To address the first problem, conflict among the core countries of the capitalist world, David Rockefeller, a CFR director since 1949 and later its chair, formed the Trilateral Commission. A veritable *Capitalist Internationale*, the Commission brought together leading politicians, industrialists, bankers, and academicians from the United States, Western Europe, and Japan (each region provided about 60 representatives). Besides addressing the crisis of advanced capitalism, the Trilateralists placed a stronger accent on North-South issues than the CFR, which historically fixed more of its gaze on East-West conflict. The Carter administration had an overwhelmingly Trilateralist cast, as at least 25 of the Commission's 65 U.S. members, including Carter and Mondale themselves, filled its highest ranks. This hardly represented a displacement of the CFR, as 84 percent of the Carter Trilateralists belonged to both bodies. Nevertheless, among the Commission's notables, the majority "traders" (Cyrus Vance, Warren Christopher, Andrew Young, Paul Warnke) soon became overwhelmed by the Prussians (Brzezinski, Huntington) and their shock troops outside the administration, now including Kissinger who urged military build-up and the scuttling of SALT II. David Rockefeller himself, apparently miffed at Carter's "human rights" policy which he later ludicrously blamed for the fall of the Shah of Iran and the deteriorating position of other U.S.-backed tyrants, now toed a more Prussian line.[26]

The Committee on the Present Danger

In the midst of this internecine struggle, a new elite organization with a chillingly Cold War cast came into increasing prominence, the Committee on the Present Danger (CPD). Founded in 1976 by Eugene Rostow and Harvardians Paul Nitze and Richard Pipes, the CPD became for the Reagan administration what the Trilateral Commission had been for the Carter era. Out of a preliminary survey of 90

Reagan advisors, cabinet and sub-cabinet appointments, 32 belonged to the CPD including Reagan himself, 31 to the CFR, and only 12 to the Trilateral Commission. Warning that the United States had developed a dread disease diagnosed as "the Vietnam syndrome," CPD ideologue Norman Podhoretz decried what he called the "sickly inhibitions against the use of military force," a pronouncement strangely in the idiom of the Third Reich's Goebbels.[27] While Podhoretz and his sidekick Irving Kristol dared urge the right-wing political forces in West Germany to be more nationalistic as one solution to NATO's alleged impotence, the CPD articulated several themes: 1) the need for a massive arms build-up, 2) the end of détente, and 3) escalation of U.S. intervention for the rollback of Communism. While the CPD had some bases of support in the Ivy League, it built up and sustained a powerful flank of right-wing institutions outside the traditional Establishment: The Heritage Foundation, CSIS at Georgetown, and the Hoover Institute at Stanford, to name a few. Still, there were several influential figures at Harvard giving the enterprise legitimacy. Besides the leadership of Pipes and Nitze, other Harvard cheerleaders for rollback in the CPD include Professor of Education Nathan Glazer and Professor of History Oscar Handlin.[28]

One of the most dramatic aspects of the CPD's history is the revealing prominence of Harvard in whipping up Cold War hysteria. The CPD founded in 1976 was patterned after the enormously successful and influential Committee on the Present Danger established in late 1950 by Paul Nitze and Harvard's President James Conant. Conant's central role in the building of the military-industrial complex and the making of the early Cold War remains to be told in this account. Conant served as chair of the President's Office of Scientific Research and Development after World War II. This important body engineered the linking of university laboratories with the production of weaponry, one of the hallmarks of Cold War science. Conant called this the "beginning of a revolution." He, of course, was well placed to achieve this marriage of the national security state with the university. During World War I, while a professor in the chemistry department, he helped to develop poison gas for U.S. troops to use, as well as the masks to protect them. During World War II, Conant served on the eight member Interim Committee, responsible for advising Truman and Secretary of War Stimson on how the atomic bomb should be dropped on Japan. The Interim Committee had judged unanimously that a target which "would clearly show its [the

Bomb's] devastating strength" was ideal; however, it was Conant who remained insistent on the need to maximize civilian casualties. He clamored for the United States to nuke a population center, one ideally with "a war plant employing a large number of workers closely surrounded by workers' houses."[29] Though understandably regarded as Conant the Barbarian throughout much of the world, he received a thunderous reception at Harvard on his return during the 1946 commencement exercises. As the *Boston Globe* reports:

> The alumni head introduced the President of Harvard by the name all Americans have come to know and respect for his value in an epoch of national emergency: "Conant of Harvard."[30]

Conant's next triumph was the destruction of efforts to control nuclear weapons in the immediate World War II aftermath. A furious debate erupted over the control of the atomic bomb between 1) those who wanted to place it under international control and 2) those seeking U.S. development and a push for nuclear superiority. The proponents of international control were led largely by the scientists who worked on the Manhattan Project. Arguing that the Soviets would develop the Bomb in a few years, they thought it foolhardy to begin a race for nuclear superiority. Conant used the weight of his authority to help crush their movement. J. Robert Oppenheimer, a charter member of the CPD, apparently accepted Conant's views on the Bomb, because he urged passage of the May-Johnson bill to ensure U.S. military control of the weapon. As he said in his congressional testimony:

> I think no men in positions of responsibility, who were scientists, took more responsibility...than Dr. Bush and Dr. Conant. I think if they liked the philosophy of this bill and urged this bill, it is a very strong argument. I know that many scientists do not agree with me on this, but I am nevertheless convinced myself.[31]

The May-Johnson bill was stopped by opponents of "military control" of the Bomb, but was followed by Truman's backing for the McMahon bill, which gave power to a civilian-run Atomic Energy Commission (AEC). U.S. control of the Bomb emerged victorious, though under the thumb of the national security bureaucracy rather than the military. While this might be seen as a minor setback for Conant, Truman offered him the chair of the Atomic Energy Commission, a position he declined, preferring to retain the presidency of Harvard until 1953. He still served on the AEC's General Advisory Committee from 1947 to 1952; during part of that time he reigned as chair of the CPD. Conant's role in scuttling arms control is a lesson in the rewriting of history; he and Nitze are often uncritically praised for promoting a massive conventional arms buildup to forestall the resort to nuclear war.[32]

As leader of the Committee on the Present Danger, Conant rallied elites behind NSC-68, the National Security Council document authored by Nitze that judged the Soviet Union to be "inescapably militant" and "the inheritor of Russian imperialism." "Animated by a new fanatic faith," NSC-68 stated, the USSR "seeks to impose its absolute authority over the rest of the world."[33] Paul Hammond, who interviewed participants in the NSC-68 process, concluded that Nitze purposely exaggerated "the military threat" of the USSR in order to justify a U.S. arms buildup.[34] State Department heavyweights George Kennan and Harvardian Charles ("Chip") Bohlen, fathers of containment who both objected to NSC-68's lurid propositions, found themselves in what Jerry Sanders calls "diplomatic Siberia": Kennan temporarily sent to Latin America and Bohlen transferred to the U.S. Embassy in Paris.

At a spring 1950 meeting of the State Department, foreign policy advisor and leading investment banker Robert Lovett urged that "We must have a much vaster propaganda machine to tell our story at home and abroad." This is where the president of Harvard fit in. NSC-68 called for a tripling, a quadrupling of U.S. Defense spending; the garrisoning of U.S. troops in Europe; and "offensive forces to attack the enemy and keep him off balance," although the report went on: "emphasis should be given to the essentially defensive character" in order "to minimize, so far as possible, unfavorable domestic and foreign reactions." Fearful of a disastrous economic depression due to a dollar gap between Europe and the United States (too many U.S. dollars, not enough European imports), NSC-68 sought some way of continuing Marshall Plan aid, set to expire at the end of 1951.[35]

In the face of serious public dissent from this enterprise, Conant's CPD drove into the nation's mind the sense of impending crisis during a series of radio addresses. In a nationwide radio broadcast shortly after Truman's State of the Union address, Conant declared that "the United States is in danger. The danger is clearly of a military nature...we must take immediate steps to meet the national danger."[36]

The CPD had much success. Opposed by isolationists and fiscal conservatives, it managed to overcome divisions within the U.S. elite by ensuring the triumph of the permanent war economy, already given a major boost by the Korean War. With bases of support in the midwestern and west-coast states, the CPD's opponents had an agenda with a certain popular appeal. The so-called isolationist Right, Taft, Hoover, et. al., were by no means anti-interventionist, but they gave priority to Asia over Europe, the latter region regarded as effete and decadent, the center of Eastern Establishment economic and cultural investment.[37] The isolationist Right saw Asia as the new frontier, the choice *Lebensraum* for U.S. capital and cultural domination; they howled that the Eastern Establishment sold out in China to the victorious Communists.[38] The CPD's stress on rearmament and the garrisoning of troops in Europe in the midst of the Korean War struck them as further betrayal. Much of the isolationist Right also regarded the massive increase in defense spending from $13.5 billion to $48.2 billion in FY1951 as irresponsible profligacy, a budget larded with wasteful transfers of resources to Europe. From a different vantage point, Kennan himself judged $13 billion in 1950 to be more than adequate for U.S. defense needs, but the NSC-68 crowd had him sent to the salt mines of Latin America for raising such objections. Fortified by arguments from Keynesian economics, the CPD, Nitze, Acheson, and McCloy promoted the idea that a bloated garrison state was a healthful tonic for U.S. business. The CPD itself cozied up to General Eisenhower as the successor to Truman. Contributing heavily to the destruction of Taft's Republican nomination bid, they were amply rewarded for their services by Eisenhower, who gave Conant a high-level administration appointment. Assured of the victory of the permanent war economy, they put the CPD to rest in 1953. It would remain dormant until its Second Coming on the eve of the Age of Reagan.

The Relationship of the CFR, Trilateral Commission and the CPD to the Universities

The elite policy bodies such as the CFR, the Trilateral Commission, and the CPD provide three major functions for the ruling class by fostering 1) ideological consensus, 2) elite recruitment, and 3) cohesion among Establishment institutions.

"Consensus"

Though somewhat precarious in the wake of the Vietnam debacle, "The bipartisan consensus...had been nurtured on Wall Street and in the Park Avenue mansion of the Council on Foreign Relations," observe Walter Isaacson and Evan Thomas of *Time*. Henry

Kissinger defends the predominance of a relatively small clique in the construction of U.S. foreign policy: "You need an establishment. Society needs it. You can't have all these constant assaults on national policy so that every time you change presidents you end up changing direction."[39] In terms of the ability to rule, the CFR helps the capitalist class make the transition from what Marx called a class-in-itself to a class-for-itself, from a passive class largely devoid of consciousness to one that actively shapes its own destiny.

"Elite recruitment"

These bodies help to separate the "ins" from the "outs" among policymakers, academicians, and aspiring national security managers. Those without a CFR pedigree are frequently out of the running for top positions in national security management. While serving as personnel chief to Secretary of War Henry Stimson during World War II, John McCloy put it this way: "Whenever we needed a man we thumbed through the roll of Council members and put through a call to New York."[40] Among members of the academic elite and the ruling class itself, it also provides an opportunity to decide who among themselves are more fit for leadership in the command posts of the State. There is occasionally resentment from CFR members over those who make it to the highest echelons of power. As one member said of Kissinger: "Kissinger owed his career to the Council but he never set foot here the whole time he was in office. He is, as you know, extremely arrogant."[41] Still, Kissinger returned as a CFR director after leaving the White House.

Cohesion between elite institutions

Finally, as far as the universities are concerned, the CFR, the CPD, and the Trilateral Commission typically formulate the long-range goals of U.S. foreign policy. The universities, through their international studies programs, tend to work within these larger contours to provide short-range solutions, as well as more detailed research on specific nations and trouble spots abroad. They also pump out many of the middle-level technicians needed for managing the Empire. There are certainly no fixed agendas, but there are ways in which these bodies have influential muscle.

The universities have numerous links with the CFR. For instance, twelve out of 30 of Harvard's Board of Overseers belonged to the CFR in 1973; in 1986, six out of 30 were members.[42] A survey of the directors of the CFR from 1922-1972 indicates that at least 24 percent were officers, overseers, or staff members at Harvard. The latter figures do not even include the sizable Harvard alumni at the CFR.[43]

Another important way in which the goals of the foreign policy Establishment are attained in the universities is through its interlocks with the leading foundations. Earlier it was noted how the vast network of area studies programs came to be constructed after World War II. In the case of Harvard, its Russian Research Center (1947) was financed by the Carnegie Corporation ($750,000 under the first five-year plan), through the intervention of John Gardner, an OSS member and later Secretary of Health, Education, and Welfare (HEW), and Devereux Josephs, a powerful lawyer and alumnus of Groton and Harvard.[44] The tab for the other leading center of Soviet studies at Columbia was picked up by the Rockefeller Foundation. A 1971 survey identified fourteen out of nineteen directors of the Rockefeller Foundation and ten out of seventeen of the Carnegie Corporation's directors as belonging to the CFR. Of course, the Ford Foundation, which finances the majority of area studies programs at elite universities, was run from 1966 to 1977 by CFR member and former Harvard Dean (1953-1961) McGeorge Bundy. Bundy in 1957 had played a central role in the establishment of the Center for International Affairs (C.F.I.A.) at Harvard. Those involved in the creation of the C.F.I.A. included Henry Kissinger; Don Price, a Ford Foundation vice president and later Kennedy School of Government dean; James Perkins, a Carnegie Corporation leader, president of Cornell, and a director of Chase Manhattan; Dean Rusk, similar to John Foster Dulles, president of the Rockefeller Foundation and later secretary of state; and Robert Bowie, the C.F.I.A.'s first director and later an advisor to CIA Director Stansfield Turner. Documents liberated during the student occupation of the C.F.I.A. in 1971 revealed it to be a hotbed of CIA activity, a reputation which continues into the present. Illuminating cases of the interplay between Harvard, the CIA, and the CFR emerged in some of the purloined documents. One of the files uncovered at the C.F.I.A. included the confidential minutes of a June 9, 1968 CFR meeting concerning the CIA. Harvard C.F.I.A. associate William Harris later related to the media that the minutes had luckily been purged of the material most damaging to national security. Nevertheless, in the CFR minutes, the engineer of the Bay of Pigs fiasco Richard Bissell, Yalie and Groton graduate and brother-in-law of former Columbia University Russian Research Institute Director Philip Moseley, confessed that the CIA:

will have to make use of private institutions on an expanding scale, though those relations which have been "blown" cannot be resurrected.[45]

The "blown" relations which Bissell mentioned concerned the revelations that the CIA had funded trade unions, the intellectual journal *Encounter*, the Congress for Cultural Freedom, and the National Student Agency, among others. He continued: "We need to operate under deeper cover, with increased attention to the use of 'cut-outs' [i.e., intermediaries]. CIA's interface with the rest of the world needs to be better protected." Bissell's proposal seems to be in violation of a law accepted in 1967 by the U.S. president stating that: "No federal agency shall provide any covert financial assistance or support, direct or indirect, to any of the nation's educational or private voluntary organizations."[46]

The Saga of the CIA at Harvard Continues

In the two decades since this presidential directive, how have Harvard and the CIA behaved concerning covert funding of University research and intellectual activities? Stansfield Turner, director of the CIA under Jimmy Carter, complains that Derek Bok should lift some of the more onerous restrictions on CIA research at Harvard, while Caspar Weinberger at the 350th anniversary celebration demands that the faculty be unleashed on classified projects. But there are many indicators that Richard Bissell's proposals for University-CIA relations have held some sway at Harvard, notwithstanding Bok's pious appeals to the independence of his institution.

It should be remarked that, despite the revelations and rebellions of the 1960s, the radical view that CIA research must be kept off campus lost out virtually everywhere. The liberal view that CIA research should be permitted so long as it is "open" carried the day. In the liberal interpretation, covert research destroys the spirit of the university because it violates John Stuart Mill's notion of the free marketplace of ideas. The militarization of research and the university's subservience to the priorities of the national security state met with approval if they could be done in the open. This is currently the status quo in principle, regardless of Bok's occasional rhetorical flourishes about Harvard's "need to persuade the public...that...we are *not* instruments of national security," which he proclaimed in a September, 1986 speech. The latter statement is mocked by Bok's own handpicked choice as the Dean of the Kennedy

School of Government, Graham Allison, who throughout his reign openly ran extension courses for the Pentagon's national security elite (for example: his "Program for Senior Executives in National and International Security" still brings droves of CIA agents, admirals, generals, and NSA staffers to Harvard annually, with nary a complaint from self-styled liberals). It is further belied by a recent study of 20 major universities, which indicates that from 1982-1986 Harvard had the greatest percentage leap in defense sponsorship of research (up 156 percent), exceeded only by Ivy League counterpart Brown.[47]

But in practice, Harvard routinely violates even the most permissive guidelines against "covert" research. The cases of Nadav Safran and Samuel Huntington, both Harvard C.F.I.A. people and professors at the Department of Government, are instructive in this regard. In 1985 and 1986 respectively, the *Crimson* and the *Boston Globe* exposed Huntington and Safran's connections to the CIA. After much Bok-esque teeth gnashing about threats to the University's independence, the Dean of the Faculty Michael Spence and his predecessor Henry Rosovsky confessed that it was mere administrative error which led to a failure to tell the public about Safran's and Huntington's "open" research activities for the CIA. (While the administration denied he committed improprieties in the CIA's financing of his book on Saudi Arabia, Safran, however, was mildly faulted for not reporting to the proper University authorities the CIA's bankrolling of a Harvard conference on Islamic fundamentalism. Some cynical observers thought that Harvard might have expected a larger cut of Safran's CIA largess.)[48]

An important question about the Bok regime (1971-present) is whether his lieutenants in the Harvard administration actively protect professors working covertly or semi-covertly on CIA projects. In 1967, in the face of the directive from President Johnson against secret research, Dean Franklin Ford, a former OSS person himself, scribbled a note suggesting that "a confidential file on such relationships" be set up for CIA operatives on the faculty.[49] One can only speculate if Ford's successors Rosovsky and Spence follow this practice, but the circumstantial evidence in the Safran and Huntington affairs makes their claims of "misplacing" the paperwork highly dubious. Prior to the crisis, the administration apparently raised no objections to Safran's contract, which both permits the CIA to censor his writing and forbids him from revealing the government source of funds. His book, *Saudi Arabia: The Ceaseless Quest for Security*, salutes the Rand Corporation and the Rockefeller Foundation for funding his research, but leaves no mention of CIA sponsorship to the tune of $107,430. It was also revealed in January 1986 that Harvard University Press, which previously denied knowledge of the book's CIA funding, had been informed in 1984.

Paradoxically to many observers, Dean Spence's own investigation into the CIA affair reserves its severest attacks for the critics of Safran. Denouncing the three Middle East scholars on the Center for Middle Eastern Studies' (CMES) six-member Executive Committee who called for Safran's resignation, Spence ordered the disbanding of the body. Spence believes *they* should have waited for the completion of *his* investigation. Much to the chagrin of these critics, he provides no reproach of the members of the Executive Committee who throughout the crisis applauded Safran's work, an economic historian of Western Europe David Landes and former Undersecretary of the Navy Bob "Battleship" Murray. Long close to the sweaty armpits of power, Murray, it may be recalled, was an architect of policies later leading to the rehabilitation of such nuclear capable ships as the U.S.S. *New Jersey*, a battle wagon now notorious for the shelling of defenseless Lebanese civilians with its sixteen-inch guns. Murray and Landes continued their campaign on behalf of Safran, in spite of a crushing 193-8 vote condemning Safran's actions by the Middle Eastern Studies Association (MESA) at their conference of November 24, 1985 in New Orleans.[50]

Meanwhile, Professor Richard Frye, described by *Time* as one of the "center's defrocked committeemen," called Spence's report "a whitewash."[51] Doubting that "the Middle East center will ever recover from this," Frye essentially argues that the University has blamed the victims of Safran's unscrupulous behavior. Another critic asserts that Safran behaved like an "Egyptian pharaoh," accountable to no one. In his defense, Safran responds that prior to his meteoric rise to power in 1983, the Center "was moribund;" he told public television station WGBH that if the Center was previously nothing, it was thanks to his building it up that there was at least "something to destroy."[52]

Lest the Safran affair be seen as an accidental misstep by a wayward scholar, it should be recalled how actively the CIA has cultivated what journalist Jeff McConnell calls its "Charles River Connection." In 1950, the CIA relied on MIT and Harvard intellectuals in the establishment of Project TROY, a covert effort seeking to beam U.S. propaganda into Eastern Europe. Out of this project emerged the Center for International Studies (CENIS), a joint MIT-

Harvard think tank, based at MIT apparently because it had fewer formal restrictions against classified research. According to the Senate Select Committee on Intelligence (1976), the CIA "assisted in the establishment in 1951 and the funding" of CENIS "to research world-wide political, economic, and social change." Meanwhile, in the summer of 1950, the ubiquitous Richard Bissell became their first choice as director, but he declined in favor of his Yale friend Max Millikan, who later performed consulting work with MIT economic historian Walt Rostow on covert psychological warfare. During these years, there was plenty of social lubrication among aspiring national security managers, area studies directors, and foundation leaders: CFR members Rostow and Millikan joined the same upper-class club, the Cosmos Club, as other prominent figures in our story—Kissinger, Price, Moseley, Gardner, and Perkins.[53]

Also in the early 1950s, William Langer, probably Harvard's most distinguished historian and head of the OSS's research division during World War II, was called back to Washington. Confronting the tarnished image of intelligence services at the outset of the Korean War, CIA Director Walter Bedell Smith called on Langer to improve its research division. According to John Ranelagh, a historian sympathetic to the CIA: "The achievement of Langer and Smith in reorganizing the CIA's analytical and estimating procedures was one of the most important in the Agency's history." Harry Truman remarked that Smith and Langer made certain that the CIA became "an efficient and permanent arm of the Government's national security structure." Langer returned to Harvard as the Director of its Russian Research Center from 1954 to 1959.[54]

Despite lacking a more formal tie to the CIA, as with MIT's CENIS, Harvard still provided many openings for CIA operatives. Jeff McConnell in the *Boston Globe* ticks off a few:

> With top level White House approval, the CIA set up annual summer seminars at Harvard for foreign leaders and scholars. A consulting relationship was created with the head of Harvard's Center for International Studies, Robert Bowie. Durwood Lockard, Kermit Roosevelt's deputy to the Agency's Near East Division, resigned in 1957 to become assistant head of the Center for Middle Eastern Studies...Several officials and faculty members of the Harvard Business School founded and helped to administer front organizations for the CIA.[55]

All was going smoothly into the 1960s when mass protests and a barrage of exposés (in *Ramparts* and David Wise's *The Invisible Government*) forced a re-examination of university ties with the Agency, as MIT severed its formal connection with CENIS. Several professors scurried for cover, cutting their ties with the CIA; a handful became outspoken critics, particularly those who, without their prior consent, had been working on research financed through covert CIA conduits. More recently, Harvard's Stanley Hoffmann, a representative of the liberal wing of the foreign policy Establishment (CFR), proved to be one of the more eloquent opponents of Safran's shenanigans.

Nevertheless, the CIA and the Pentagon have had success in restoring some links, though the cover of Huntington and Safran has been "blown." Graham Allison, recently a consultant to former Secretary of Defense Caspar Weinberger and on occasion a part of Massachusetts Governor Michael Dukakis's foreign policy menagerie, has provided a most hospitable environment for the training of national security managers. The Harvard Business School maintains an important structure of connections for those seeking to become management experts for the Pentagon, especially in procurement, as a study sponsored by Ralph Nader's Center for the Study of Responsive Law reports on The Harvard Business School's (HBS) earlier background in this field:

> The Harvard Business School became a gathering place for defense management officials and private management activities carried on at Cambridge. Business School faculty members developed a curriculum on defense management, and promising defense officials were continually being sent there to study. The Business School in turn enrolled Ph.D. candidates whose defense-related theses provided further content for the curriculum. The brightest candidates were offered jobs in Livingston-related enterprises [Pentagon consultants] and soon made their own way as defense experts.[56]

But today it is both MIT and Harvard which the Pentagon and the CIA complain about when it comes to restrictions on classified research. They have instead turned to the last leg of their Charles River triad, Tufts University, which former CIA director Bill Casey saluted for being in the center of the war against terrorism. Safely bunkered off the streets of Medford, Tufts faculty contribute to the fastest growth industry in academia, the sub-discipline of terrorology. Professor Uri Ra'anan and his colleagues at the Fletcher School of Law and Diplomacy publish some of the most lurid tracts since the high water mark of the Cold War in the 1950s, including the phantasmagorical anti-terrorist philippic entitled *Hydra of Carnage* (1985).[57] Perhaps a boon for Tufts, the Huntington and Safran revelations came at a bad time for the CIA, just when its entrenchment at Harvard began to resume progress. The CIA was originally built out of the elan of World War II, its recruits coming from a social base of largely prep school and Ivy League elites. Those from this social base have become less pliable, many preferring the fast track life of Park Avenue yuppiedom and, in a smaller number of cases, outright rebellion against the seductions of Wall Street and the national security state. There are still plenty of mandarins of Huntington's ilk willing to do legwork for the Empire, but the Agency's position is now more exposed and precarious.

In the wake of unfolding opposition to the Sam Huntingtons and the Graham Allisons, one can expect a renewed mobilization of pseudo-liberal argument on behalf of training more Pentagon and CIA personnel in the coming years at the Kennedy School and the C.F.I.A. In 1988, Bok applauded a new $1.2 million study of intelligence by Professors Ernest May and Richard Neustadt "openly" sponsored by the CIA, as well as the Kennedy School of Government's hiring for its faculty CIA Africa expert William Kline.[58] In this call for expanded programs, Harvard will supposedly humanize and mellow the most savage elements of the national security leadership, particularly those shabby upstarts from the armed forces. Such oratorical bromides have a certain appeal to the Boks and the Cold War liberals. But, if postwar history is any indication, it has been the civilians, the Harvard people at the top of the foreign policy Establishment, who brought on NSC-68 and the permanent war economy, Guatemala and political support for bloodthirsty despots, and Vietnam and the rest of the global interventionist crusade. It will do little good to blame the military personnel for the misdeeds of Harvard's national security elite. This is sheer cant. The university will never attain a critical and independent understanding of its role in society while it remains shackled to the priorities of the national security state.

Harvard's National Security Mandarins

Fifteen years ago, Yale students issued a booklet entitled "Go to School, Learn to Rule." This section will briefly explore the most recent batch of Harvard faculty and graduates who have taken this educational mission to heart.

The most successful of these figures is, of course, Kissinger. "Power," he declares, "is the great aphrodisiac." Historian John

Lukacs, a conservative, has recently speculated on the sources of Kissinger's success. While at Harvard, writes Lukacs:

> Kissinger became a protege of Nelson Rockefeller—another giant of independent thinking—and the two of them came up with the nuclear shelter and "the missile gap." Of course, we know there was no gap between '57 and '61. But that didn't hurt Kissinger's reputation at all. He was an "expert" in a democracy which likes to take the word of experts. In this respect he didn't differ from sociologists, economists or those sex therapists whose contribution to marital unhappiness is yet to be measured.[59]

But why Kissinger? His immediate classmates at Harvard included several eminent figures with visions of shaping U.S. foreign policy: Huntington, Brzezinski, and Hoffmann. In their intense competition "over who would go the farthest," political scientist Alan Wolfe speculates on why Kissinger ultimately won:

> It cannot be because he is the most ambitious: Brzezinski can match him on that score. Nor is it because he is the most reactionary; on cold war issues, Huntington is farthest to the right. Nor, finally, is it because Kissinger is the smartest; Hoffmann not only has a more analytical mind, he is a genuine intellectual. Kissinger succeeded more than the others because only he recognized how far America had traveled down the road to empire and, as a result, how only the most ruthless and completely cynical Realpolitik would suffice to govern it.[60]

Turning Washington into "a place of extreme tension and nail-biting paranoia," writes Wolfe, Kissinger tapped phones and withheld information from even the secretaries of state and defense in his belief that the Empire could "go about its business without nasty interference from interest groups, the press, and prickly politicians."[61]

Who will be the likely successor to Kissinger in the foreign policy elite? Anyone with a lingering nostalgia for this foul man[62]— and there are many at Harvard—will likely give the foreign policy nod to Huntington, among Harvard's aspirants to the national security throne. It is indeed the Democrat Huntington whose post-Vietnam intellectual preoccupations have come the closest to mimicking those of Kissinger. While Weinberger and Carlucci of Harvard recently tasted power, they were not explicitly trained to be national security mandarins. Huntington's own concerns have neatly dovetailed with Kissinger's. Kissinger's aversions to nasty interference from Congress, the press, and the general public have been enunciated in several post-White House writings. In a series of essays for *Time* magazine, Kissinger wrote of ways to insulate NATO from the interference of European public opinion, which had become jittery about the U.S. arms buildup and scenarios for limited nuclear war. He championed Margaret Thatcher's management of news during the Falklands crisis, arguing that U.S. national security managers had much to learn from her example, since it was the U.S. media which lost the Vietnam War. In the midst of the Palestinian uprising, Kissinger offered this advice to the Israeli government:

> Israel should bar the media...and put down the insurrection as quickly as possible—overwhelmingly, brutally, and rapidly...The first step should be to throw out the television á la South Africa.[63]

Huntington provides a similarly systematic and relentless version of Kissinger's anti-populism. In his chapter on the United States in the Trilateral Commission's book, *The Crisis of Democracy*, Huntington mourns the decline of authority, while decrying the public's willingness to challenge "the legitimacy of hierarchy, coercion, discipline, secrecy, and deception—all of which are, in some measure, inescapable attributes of the process of government." Huntington finds it unsettling that "people no longer felt the obligation to obey those whom they had previously considered superior to themselves in age, rank, status, expertise, character, or talents."[64]

Huntington called for a strengthening of the presidency and the Establishment:

> To the extent that the U.S. was governed by anyone during the decades after World War II, it was governed by the President acting with the support of key individuals and groups in the executive office, the federal bureaucracy, Congress, and the more important businesses, banks, law firms, foundations, and media, which constitute the private sector's "establishment."[65]

The problem, as Huntington diagnosed it, is that the U.S. suffers from a "democratic distemper." This "excess of democracy" has been caused by "previously passive or unorganized groups in the population...blacks, Indians, Chicanos, white ethnic groups, students, and women," who have "now embarked on concerted efforts to establish their claims to opportunities, positions, rewards, and privileges, which they had not considered themselves entitled to before." These "minorities" and the "special interests," who just happen to be the majority of the people, do not realize, in Huntington's words, that "The effective operation of a democratic political system usually requires some measure of apathy and noninvolvement on the part of some individuals and groups."[66]

For the national security manager, Huntington raises the specter that in a time of international crisis, public opposition could put constraints on the president's menu of options—or more precisely, the ability to brandish nuclear weapons, which is threatened by mass public protest. Nixon admitted in his memoirs that his increasing desire to use nuclear weapons in Vietnam had to be scuttled because of the realization that the ensuing mass protests would make the United States ungovernable. While Huntington is not always this direct, it is clear that he gives the problem of military escalation much consideration in his fears of "ungovernability."

Brzezinski's concerns are not that far removed from Huntington's nor, for that matter, Kissinger's. During the 1970s, Brzezinski was said to be more preoccupied with the Trilateralist North-South slant than Kissinger, who put more energy into the traditional CFR East-West agenda. Recently their positions have been somewhat reversed: Kissinger ran a Reagan-appointed commission on Central America while Brzezinski wrote *Game Plan* (1986), a tract on dealing with the Soviets. After completing his Ph.D. and holding a junior faculty post at Harvard, Brzezinski, who is based at Columbia and Georgetown's CSIS, retained ties much more tenuous with Harvard than the other two.

Both Brzezinski and Huntington have forged an ideology conducive to the rule of the new mandarins. Huntington declares that "higher education is the most important value-producing system in society," though he warns ominously that in the 1960s "students who lacked expertise...came to participate in the decisionmaking process on many important issues."[67] In the post-industrial age, Brzezinski adds that "power will be based increasingly on the control of skill" and that "Knowledge [will become] a tool of power." Brzezinski talks of the coming of "the post-national age" in which transnational elites "composed of international businessmen, scholars, professional men, and public officials" can build what his fellow Trilateralist and Harvard Ph.D. Richard Cooper elsewhere calls an "international system that is pluralistic enough to permit cultivation of the values of trilateral countries in all those countries that choose to cultivate them."[68] The euphemistic term "cultivation" is a thin mask for imperialism, as Brzezinski is quick to acknowledge in his *Between Two Ages: America's Role in the Technetronic Era*:

> To be sure, the fact that in the aftermath of World War II a number of nations were directly dependent on the United States in matters of security, politics, and economics created a system

that in many respects including that of scale, superficially resembled the British, Roman, and Chinese empires of the past... The empire was at most an informal system marked by the pretense of equality and non-interference... [Today] it works through the interpenetration of economic institutions, the sympathetic harmony of political leaders and parties, the shared concepts of sophisticated intellectuals, the mating of bureaucratic interests...[69]

Both Brzezinski and Huntington understand the role of intellectuals in maintaining empire as a way of life. But the favorite activity of Harvard's foreign policy mandarins is what has come to be known in the profession as crisis management.[70] Much ink and pulp are expended on the intellectual study of a problem that would seem nerve racking to most, but the Harvard experts handle it with characteristic aplomb. They consider the finest hour for their profession to be the Cuban Missile Crisis, which in separate books by Graham Allison and Professor of Government Richard Neustadt and Professor of History Ernest May is held up as a model for future national security managers to follow. "The best and the brightest" had seriously contemplated a thermonuclear showdown with the Soviets should they balk at removing weapons near the U.S. coast, despite the presence of U.S. nuclear weapons on the Soviet borderlands since the 1950s. Allison himself observes that

Had war come, it could have meant the death of 100 million Americans, more than 100 million Russians as well as millions of Europeans. Beside it, the natural calamities and inhumanities of earlier history would have faded into insignificance. Given the odds on disaster—which President Kennedy estimated at 'between one out of three and even'—our escape seems awesome.[71]

Noam Chomsky reflects that "surely this must be one of the low points of human history."[72] Instead, Professor Thomas Schelling of the Kennedy School at the 1987 reunion of JFK's foreign policy team retorts, "I firmly believe the Cuban Missile Crisis was the best thing to happen to us since the Second World War... I'm willing to take a one-shot risk to reduce the risks [of nuclear war] over the long-run."[73] Schelling's "one-shot risk"—at worst converting the planet into thermonuclear soup, at best diplomatic humiliation of Khrushchev for an action even McNamara openly concedes had no effect on the strategic balance—later led the Soviets (then behind 12 to 1 in nuclear arms) to pursue a massive arms buildup of thousands of nuclear weapons. "You Americans will never be able to do this to us again," warned Soviet negotiator V.V. Kuznetsov.[74] And yet, Graham Allison finds this to be a splendid moment, what he calls "one of the finest examples of diplomatic prudence, and perhaps the finest hour of John F. Kennedy's presidency."[75] Contrary to Allison's syrupy account, recently declassified documents show the Harvard managers at work on the Cuban Missile Crisis to have been bumblers, hardly the crack team of national security managers adroitly maneuvering the United States out of danger as presented in the political science folklore. Now it may be that these transcripts show Kennedy's belief of a 1 in 3 or even chance of war to be an overestimate, but whatever conciliatory gestures the President contemplated came largely against the advice of his Harvard advisors, who mostly urged hard-fisted humiliation of Khrushchev (no *public* face-saving deal on obsolete Turkish missiles, let alone Robert Kennedy's eventual private gambit.) Though these transcripts have been "sanitized" of the most damaging revelations, they provide a new perspective on the Kennedy foreign policy team. Robert Kennedy, portrayed by court historian Arthur Schlesinger as a dove throughout, at one point longed for an invasion of Cuba. Here is a sample of their follies:

- McNamara (excerpts from Oct. 16, 1962): "I would submit the proposition that any air strike must be directed not solely against the missile sites...there would be associated with it potential casualties of Cubans, not of U.S. citizens, but potential casualties of Cubans in, at least in the hundreds, more likely in the low thousands, say two or three thousand."

Or, to take another sample:

- McGeorge Bundy: "I would think one thing that I would still cling to is that he's [Khrushchev] not likely to give Fidel Castro nuclear weapons. I don't believe that has happened or is likely to happen."
- JFK: "Why does he put these in though?"
- Bundy: "Soviet controlled nuclear warheads..."
- JFK: "That's right, but what is the advantage of that? It's just as if we suddenly began to put a number of MRBM's [medium range ballistic missiles] in Turkey. Now that'd be goddam dangerous, I would think."
- Bundy?: "Well, we *did*, Mr. President."
- Johnson: "We *did* it. We..."
- JFK: "Yeah, but that was five years ago."

Another example:

- RFK: "...one other thing is whether, uh, we should also think of, uh, uh, whether there is some *other* way we can get involved in this through, uh, Guantanamo Bay, or something, er, or whether there's some ship that, you know, sink the *Maine* again or something."[76]

To be fair to the Kennedys and their courtiers, Nixon's Harvard people on occasion outdid them in such antics. Kissinger, fulfilling Goethe's axiom that there is nothing more terrifying than ignorance in action, once burst into Bob Haldeman's office and cried out, "This could mean war, Bob," war evidently made imminent—not because of nuclear missiles—but because of the presence of soccer fields in Cuba. "Cubans play baseball. Russians play soccer," he proclaimed, unaware that Cuba had previously fielded teams for World Cup competition. Not to be outdone by this act, Kissinger on other occasions proudly declared his contempt for blacks, constantly complaining about their smell and stupidity. These incidents are amply documented in Seymour Hersh's devastating biography.[77]

The remarkable thing about the Harvard foreign policy Establishment is that by and large none of them lost good repute, none of them had to pay the price for the failure of their foreign policy in Vietnam and elsewhere. There are many Harvard faculty who will grumble about Kissinger, but less on principle and more out of spite for his enormous success. In many circles, Kissinger remains literally the life of the party, recently receiving an enormous birthday bash well in excess of five figures thrown by Harvard's Center for European Studies Associate Director, Guido Goldman. He serves as an advisor to the University's richly endowed McCloy Scholars program, a Harvard version of the Rhodes Scholarship for Germans. Kissinger later joined Graham Allison as one of the special guests at a New York party for the Harvardian McCloy. Concerning Harvard's eagerness to honor McCloy, it may be recalled that he distinguished himself during World War II by helping to engineer the internment of Japanese-Americans, by urging the president not to bomb the tracks for the trains carrying Jews to the death camps at Auschwitz and elsewhere, and finally by absolving some of the most pro-Nazi German industrialists of their grisly war crimes in his service as U.S. High Commissioner for Germany (the predecessor of James Conant in that post). Other Harvard national security people besides Kissinger have been rewarded handsomely in their post-Vietnam service: first Bundy at Ford, then McNamara at the World Bank, where he presided over what has been called his second Vietnam, the development debacle in Marcos's Philippines. Huntington's "forced urbanization" concept legitimized a level of bombing unparalleled in human history (14 million tons of explosives dropped on tiny Vietnam, compared to 2.5 million tons used by the United States in all of World War II. One out of 30 people in all of Indochina ended up dead; nearly three million of those killed were Vietnamese);[78] yet he received a top level appointment at NSA by Carter and is currently received with fawning admiration by goggle-eyed graduates and undergraduates at Harvard's Department of Government. Despite his message to Europeans that the Eastern foreign policy Establishment is in decline and his reputed lack of skill in bureaucratic in-fighting, he could someday be slated for power in a future regime, whether Republican or Democrat.

The tragedy of U.S. diplomacy is that these few who have done so much to shape the world's destiny are rarely held accountable. Such a condition fosters what Richard Barnet terms the "myth of mass guilt which denies the connection between power and responsibility and proclaims the American people as a whole are all equally responsible" for a foreign policy of manifest peril to global survival.[79]

The Cold War Intellectual Establishment: Soviet Studies

From its very outset, the discipline of Soviet studies in the United States found itself imprisoned by the imperatives of combating Bolshevism. Prior to the Bolshevik triumph, most of the nation's Slavic experts studied under the intellectual power broker, Archibald Cary Coolidge, who urged Harvard to put more resources into the study of "the unhealthy countries." Harvard medieval historian Charles Homer Haskins, apparently not anticipating the later rise of Langer, Bundy, and Kissinger, noted that Coolidge's death in 1928 "has snapped a link between us and the world of big affairs."[80] In any event, the U.S. State Department began the training of the first Soviet specialists by appointing Harvard graduate and instructor Robert F. Kelley the chief of the Department's Eastern European Affairs division from 1924 to 1938. During the early months of his career, Kelley earned his spurs, testifying before the Senate on the dire threat of Bolshevik propaganda in the United States, thus receiving the salute of his State Department superiors as "a man of rare and exceptional ability."[81]

In these early years, without programs in the United States, Kelley made sure that Soviet experts received their training by either attending Paris or Berlin—the former the place of study by later U.S. ambassador to the USSR Charles Bohlen, the latter the training ground for George Kennan. Kennan's own warm praise of German culture and disdain for Russian civilization became reflected in his early writings and first memoirs, indeed in some sense reproducing the old nineteenth century division between Teutons and Slavs, the former seen as dynamic and civilized, the latter unchanging and barbaric.[82]

Just as Edward Said in his *Orientalism* noted the common belief of the passivity and immutability of the Orient, short of Western penetration, a similar construction has been used in formulating the demonology of the USSR. Harvard has perhaps been the most aggressive in producing experts who deny the possibilities for change in the USSR. At the time of Stalin's death, the corps of Soviet experts at Harvard were surveyed on whether change might ensue in Soviet society. All rigidly denied the possibility of de-Stalinization, with the signal exception of Barrington Moore, who, as it turns out, eventually gave up contributing to this intellectually barren field.[83]

Throughout the postwar world, the national security elite has warned of bomber gaps, missile gaps, windows of vulnerability, and a whole torrent of Soviet threats and lurking hobgoblins. Have the dominant forces in the Soviet studies establishment provided some sobriety and sane analysis in the face of these miscalculations and hoaxes? On the contrary, they have egged on the theorists of the worst-case scenario, often with reckless abandon.

A dramatic example of this is exhibited in the long-running story in the U.S. media (1982-84) claiming that the Soviet leadership and the KGB through the Bulgarians plotted to assassinate Pope John Paul II. Of the five most important figures in disseminating this claim—Michael Ledeen, Claire Sterling, Richard Pipes (Harvard Department of History), Marvin Kalb (NBC news and now Harvard faculty and administration, JFK School), and Paul Henze (Georgetown, CSIS), the latter three hold graduate degrees in Russian studies from Harvard. Kalb did a one hour documentary fanning the flames; Pipes and Henze provided most of the expert testimony for the newspapers and talk show circuit.[84]

When their elaborate tale was exposed as a fraud, after extensive investigation and court testimony in Italy, none of these figures came forward to apologize for their reckless disregard of elementary facts. Kalb was indeed rewarded for his deeds by Graham Allison, who named this mediacrat director of the JFK School's new mass media center. (While working in Robinson Hall, I recall Kalb's frequent phone calls to Harvard's Department of History when this

Bulgarian plot was in the process of being hatched.) Reflective of his great concern for human rights, Kalb, with his brother Bernard, wrote a 600-page study of Kissinger without even mentioning the destabilization of Chile, a Nixon-Kissinger triumph which has produced fifteen years of grisly torture and repression.

The propensity for the Russian studies establishment to feed the permanent Soviet threat thesis is compounded by the stark reality that many Kremlinologists outright hate the nation that is their object of study. In 1946-47, Harvard's Lauriston Ward and Carleton Coon offered a pioneering survey course, in Coon's words, on "the historic cultures of key peoples in what is now the Soviet Union," featuring "the Mongols of the days of Genghis Khan...the heathen Finnish tribes of the Volga Basin...and such 'primitive' groups as the Chukchi, the Tungus, and the Lapps."[85] Unlike the pioneers of Asian studies, Fairbank and Reischauer, who have a certain affection for the Chinese and Japanese respectively and are repulsed by "Yellow Peril" appeals, the dominant forces in Soviet studies operate in a field that rewards those with an extraordinary contempt for the Russians. This is probably most dramatically exacerbated in Harvard's program, founded at the infancy of the Cold War through a concerted Pentagon-Foundation drive to reorient the production of academic knowledge. Indeed Langer, who ran Harvard's Russian Research Center in the aftermath of McCarthyism, repelled charges that Soviet studies at Harvard could be, in his words, "fronts for Communist propaganda and activity" by pointing to the long list of military personnel in its programs and the bountiful supply of military contracts supporting its research enterprise.[86]

At its most lurid moments, such Cold War activism brought the marriage of liberal idealism and reactionary realpolitik, a political blend that Alexander Cockburn has elsewhere dubbed jackboot liberalism. At the urging of then Russian Research Center director Clyde Kluckhohn and "liberal" sociologist Talcott Parsons, Harvard Professor Edward Mason, a member of the Russian Research Center's Executive Committee and the State Department's policy planning staff, eagerly used his pull with George Kennan to permit suspected Nazi collaborators entry into the United States in the hopes that they would deliver valuable information on the USSR. Kluckhohn and Parsons even pushed for a Harvard faculty appointment for language expert Nicholas Poppe, an employee of the notorious SS thinktank, the Wannsee Institute, the site of the announcement of "the final solution to the Jewish question." Fortunately, University officials denied him the appointment, though he eventually landed a post at the University of Washington.[87]

In denying Parsons's role in this squalid affair, Harvard sociologist James Davis has declared, "Talcott Parsons did not go around with jack boots and a riding crop. He was a gentle scholar of the old school."[88] That Parsons's own notions of campus sartorial grace, his marked preference for pin stripes and Harris Tweed, precluded him from sporting "jack boots and a riding crop" hardly absolves him and his compatriots from Jonathan Wiener's charge of having "contributed to some of the most anti-democratic and anti-intellectual trends in postwar American political life." Parsons's later difficulty with fanatical McCarthyites has only further encouraged liberals to deny that he ever sought to enlist the Russian Research Center in the service of barbarism.

Soviet Studies Today: the Age of Pipes and Ulam

Soviet studies at Harvard is today towered over by two emigré intellectuals from Poland, Adam Ulam and Richard Pipes. Their backgrounds from Poland make their revulsion towards the Soviet Union axiomatic, according to most observers. Nevertheless, it is worth recalling that one of the greatest historians of the Soviet Union, Isaac Deutscher, also came from a Polish Jewish social milieu. But unlike Pipes and Ulam, Deutscher produced critiques that punctured Cold War pieties, while retaining a commitment to a Marxism from its outset resolutely anti-Stalinist. Arriving in England after Stalin had successfully liquidated many of his comrades in the Polish Communist Party, Deutscher was shunned by the dominant Cold War Sovietologists at Oxford, the Sorbonne, and Harvard, not so much as receiving a permanent appointment at even less illustrious universities. When Deutscher visited Harvard's Adams House in 1950, he was not allowed to speak publicly, according to the terms of his visa. Harvard's administration did nothing to protest against this McCarthyite infringement of his freedom of speech.[89]

Meanwhile, Pipes and Ulam's careers flourished. Adopting the right script in the Cold War has its intellectual costs, however. In the case of Pipes, his scholarship is colored by a marked intolerance and chauvinism. Astonishingly this has elicited little commentary from most of his critics. In his portrayal of the Russians, Pipes unwittingly ascribes to them the features of Shylock, in a bizarre replication of imagery from Europe's anti-Semitic literary traditions. (At other times, he subscribes to the standard Slav-Teuton polarities referred to earlier.) Pipes begins his *Soviet Strategy in Europe* with the following observation, so redolent of Shylock:

> Travelers who had visited Russia between the seventeenth and the nineteenth centuries liked to stress the unusually low business ethics of the native population. What struck them was not only that Russian merchants, shopkeepers, peddlers, and ordinary *muzhiks* engaged in the most impudent cheating, but that once they were found out they showed no remorse.[90]

Lest this be thought of as simply a faithful reporting of the scribblings of travelers to Russia, Pipes uses it to assert a much more ambitious ideological doctrine: "The idea of human equality, the noblest achievement of 'bourgeois' culture, is also the source of great political weakness because it denies a priori any meaningful distinctions among human beings, whether genetic, ethnic, racial, or other, and therefore blinds them to a great deal of human motivation." Instead of exploring the genetic, ethnic, and racial sources of Russian "cheating," "the commercial-liberal mind," says Pipes, mistakenly prefers to attribute this to "uneven economic opportunity and the resulting cultural lag."[91]

Ulam is generally more nuanced than Pipes when it comes to contemporary Soviet society, although there are occasional exceptions. Pipes finds the great Russian nationalism of Solzhenitsyn to be distasteful, especially for his outbursts of anti-Semitism, a noxious feature of his writing about which Ulam is inclined to be apologetic. Ulam absolves Solzhenitsyn by noting the novelist's deep-seated hatred of all foreigners, as well as his faithfulness to the canons of literary realism which dictate the need to portray anti-Semitism in the character make-up of his protagonists. This defense on Ulam's part is peculiar because he flatly rejects other positions of Solzhenitsyn's, such as his critique of the modern West's overly legalistic morality. Even if one were to grant Ulam's points on Solzhenitsyn's xenophobia and artistic license in the novels, there is the reality of vol. III of *The Gulag Archipelago*, which in contrast to the muted tone of vol. I, warmly embraces those Soviet people who during World War II collaborated with the Nazis. It is hard not to have ethical revulsion for a writer who terms the Soviet fighters of German occupationists "foolish calves" (*telyata*).[92]

There are other propositions of Ulam's that are seriously flawed. In odd years, he teaches what is sometimes the University's only survey course on radical thought, perhaps the saddest testimony to the poverty of Left intellectual culture at Harvard. Ulam's crude lampoons of Marx are typically laced with apologetics for capitalism. He writes in *The Unfinished Revolution* that Marx could not foresee "that the capitalist would grow more humane, that he would slacken in his ceaseless pursuit of accumulation and expansion."[93] Even conceding the great transformations in industrial capitalism since the nineteenth century, those living through the "second Gilded Age" of the 1980s may have doubts about the finding that T. Boone Pickens, Ivan Boesky, Lee Iacocca, Leona Helmsley, and the Queens-born casino operator Donald Trump have somehow slackened in their ceaseless pursuit of accumulation and expansion.

Ulam's specialty is international relations, and this is where his pronouncements are treated as most authoritative. He finds that the hallmark of Western foreign policy is its fundamental generosity, especially towards the Third World: "Problems of an international society undergoing an economic and ideological revolution seem to defy...the generosity—granted its qualifications and errors—that has characterized the policy of the leading democratic powers of the West."[94] This generosity of the democratic West includes U.S. support for numerous colonial wars (Portuguese, French, British), butchery in South America, Central America, Africa, Indonesia, and Southeast Asia where until recently the CIA funneled military aid to Pol Pot's murderous Khmer Rouge.[95] In the formation of foreign aid programs, U.S. public officials such as Truman's Assistant Secretary of State for Latin American Affairs admitted quite openly: "The State Department is not disposed to favor large loans of public funds to countries not welcoming our private capital."[96] In December 1947, George Kennan, one of the architects of the Marshall Plan, said how it should be implemented: "It doesn't work if you just send the stuff over and relax. It has to be played politically, when it gets over. It has to be dangled, sometimes withdrawn, sometimes extended. It has to be a skillful operation." As John Saville remarks, "As a statement of American magnanimity in the world after 1945, it will not be bettered."[97]

Whereas Ulam's intellectual corpus is probably more influential in the universities, Richard Pipes has as of late made a bigger impact politically. Tracing the roots of his political ascendancy is not always easy. His first step towards national prominence came in 1972 with his participation in Eugene Rostow's hawkish Coalition for a Democratic Majority (CDM) Foreign Policy Task Force, whose members later formed the nucleus of the Committee on the Present Danger: Pipes, Podhoretz, Kirkpatrick, Decter, Kampelman, and Roche. Adhering to Pipes's world view, Rostow wrote then Secretary of State Kissinger: "We deny that relaxation of tensions between the two countries had in fact occurred." And later: "Soviet policy never changes."[98]

The first triumph of the CDM came in the 1972 general election when it urged a scorched earth policy on fellow Democrats, who were expected to vote for the Nixon White House against the challenge of George McGovern. It was Henry "Scoop" Jackson's political allies who found Pipes's writings most alluring. Still unreconciled to Kissinger's détente policies, they then formed the Committee on the Present Danger. Pipes's first coup for the CPD was his chairmanship of the government's notorious Team B, whose report on Soviet military strength claimed that the CIA had been soft on the Russians. Appointed by the Ford administration, specifically by then CIA Director George Bush, Team B was formed in response to critics such as General Daniel Graham who had charged that "there are more liberals per square foot in the CIA than any other part of the government." Pipes argued why his Team B would be closed to other views on the Soviets: "There is no point in another, what you might call, optimistic view. In general there has been a disposition in Washington to underestimate the Soviet drive." The CIA regulars displaced by these Team B outsiders were naturally disgruntled. Herbert "Pete" Scoville, formerly the CIA's deputy director, snapped that Team B was "dedicated to proving that the Russians are twenty feet tall." The Team B report became heavy ammunition in the arsenals of those wanting to claim that the Soviets were achieving military superiority.[99]

Meanwhile, Pipes spent the years of the Carter administration arguing for the attainment of U.S. nuclear superiority. In an op-ed piece for the *New York Times*, he explained his rejection of the view that both sides have enough nuclear weapons:

> More subtle and more pernicious is the argument, backed by the prestige of Henry A. Kissinger, that nuclear superiority is meaningless. This view was essential to Mr. Kissinger's détente policy, but it rests on flawed thinking. Underpinning it is the widely held notion that since there exists a certain quantitative level in the accumulation of nuclear weapons that, once attained, is sufficient to destroy mankind, superiority is irrelevant: There is no over-trumping total destruction.[100]

Pipes then gave his alternative vision:

Unfortunately, in nuclear competition, numbers are not all. The contest between the superpowers is increasingly turning into a qualitative race whose outcome most certainly can yield meaningful superiority.[101]

There was a happy ending in this for Pipes. Kissinger, the previous villain of his piece, later recanted, confessing to the *London Economist*, writes Pipes, "that he erred in adhering to the MAD doctrine: nuclear supremacy did, indeed, matter very much."[102]

Later in 1977, Pipes wrote his famous analysis in *Commentary* asserting that the Soviets do not view nuclear war fundamentally differently from conventional war. Entitled "Why the Soviet Union Thinks It Could Fight and Win a Nuclear War," his article noted that the Soviets lost 20 million people in World War II, and could, through civil defense plans, absorb similar casualties in nuclear war. "Clearly a country that since 1914 has lost, as a result of two world wars, a civil war, famine, and various 'purges,' perhaps up to sixty million citizens, must define 'unacceptable damage' differently from the United States," he reflects.[103]

Pipes then became a Reagan advisor. He argued for the decisive importance of Team B and the CPD in laying the groundwork for the right-wing offensive:

> By the time President Reagan took office, the views of Team B and CPD were unmistakenly in the ascendent... Several commentators, seeking to define President Reagan's views on foreign and defense policies, found their source in Team B... The officials whom Reagan...chose for high posts in the first weeks of his Administration belonged to the Committee on the Present Danger, an organization that saw eye-to-eye with Team B. President Reagan's distaste for arms control as a political tool, his insistence on building up first offensive nuclear forces and then anti-nuclear defenses, all rested on the premise that the USSR held a different view of the ability of nuclear weapons from the U.S., regarding them as guarantors not of peace but of victory.[104]

But when will the Soviets attempt to launch this victorious nuclear strike? The *Washington Post* in April 1982 reported that "Pipes says he is more worried about his children driving safely, and not getting sick, than nuclear war." The article continues: "He has never thought of building a bomb shelter," though he admits that the likelihood of nuclear war is 40 percent. Since Pipes is so committed to the efficiency of bomb shelters for the Soviets, journalist Robert Scheer wonders if "it is possible that Pipes and others on the CPD don't really believe their own alarmist rhetoric about the Soviet nuclear threat and the 'window of vulnerability.'"[105] Five years ago, columnists Evans and Novak reported that Pipes felt the urgent need to re-educate President Reagan about the predatory nature of the Russian people. This was necessitated by the Gipper's recent bedtime reading including such books as Robert Massie's biography of Peter the Great; his attitude toward Russia was softening after learning about the many invasions and massive loss of life the nation had suffered. Pipes apparently worked to nip that in the proverbial bud, a move helping to delay progress in U.S.-Soviet relations until Reagan's Contragate debacle.

Sadly, people in power defer to the wisdom of Richard Pipes on the great issues of our time. This is puzzling because even Jack Ruina, MIT professor and former senior consultant to the White House's Office of Science and Technology, concedes: "Pipes knows little about technology and about nuclear weapons. I know him personally. I like him. But I think on the subject of the Soviets, he is clearly obsessed with what he views as their aggressive intentions."[106]

Despite a temporary thaw in the Age of Gorbachev, the Harvard experts have for too long contributed to what Stephen Cohen calls "the greatest failure of American democracy": "the absence of a real national debate on U.S. policy towards the Soviet Union."[107] Richard Pipes is symptomatic of a problem that promises not to go away.

Middle Eastern Studies: Double Standards Serving Single-minded Interests

Middle Eastern studies languished for centuries as an adjunct of language studies, Harvard itself providing its first academic chair in Semitics in 1640 and Arabic in 1660. In 1842, the field of Orientalism became institutionalized with the founding of the American Oriental Society (AOS), an organization with a large Harvard representation. The opening AOS journal argued for a community of interest between scholars and missionaries:

> While experience has shown, that the Gospel is the only effective instrumentality for awakening the lethargic heathen mind, and giving it a healthful excitement and direction, it has also shown, that the best use of this instrumentality involves more or less attention, on the part of the missionaries, to nearly all departments of knowledge contemplated by the AOS.[108]

The expansion of multinational oil corporations and U.S. involvement in the Middle East military theater during World War II brought a dramatic turn in the fortunes of Middle Eastern studies. Oil companies began with complaints that the American university's failure to pump out scholars and personnel with a broader knowledge of the Middle East hindered their expansion in the region. In a November 1950 memorandum, Harvard Deans Fox and Ward and Professor Richard Frye discussed "the Arabian Oil Company's...great difficulty in locating young men for positions in the Middle East." The company made "funds available to the University of Michigan to establish a department of Middle Eastern studies," while seeking out "additional sources of training" (meaning Harvard).[109]

It would not be until the Spring of 1954 that the Harvard Center got off the ground, temporarily chaired by the peripatetic Langer. In its 1962-63 Annual Report, the CMES reported that:

> the strongest feature of the financing of the Center over the nine academic years of its existence has been the consistent support of the corporations with operations in the Middle East...American Independent Oil Company...Gulf Oil...Socony Mobil Oil Company...SOCAL, SOHIO, Texaco, Inc., Westinghouse...[110]

Langer himself was soon replaced as director in 1957 by the doyen of Middle East studies in the Anglo-Saxon world, Sir Hamilton Alexander Roskeeb Gibb, a Scotsman previously distinguished as the Laudian Professor of Arabic at Oxford. Then Dean McGeorge Bundy bragged of landing Gibb, and pandered to his every need, even in the face of much faculty hostility railroading a professorship without any departmental affiliation to Gibb's right-hand man and chief fundraiser, oil consultant A.J. Meyer. Meyer, with his multifarious connections to oil executives and Arab sheiks, had a limo waiting for him in virtually every Middle East petrocapital and was treated with greater regal splendor than most U.S. ambassadors and other dignitaries.[111]

While Gibb lent an air of old-world academic respectability to the enterprise, several key figures had close ties with the CIA (Associate Director Durwood Lockard, Nadav Safran), the State Department (William Polk), and British intelligence (George Eden Kirk), as well as to the oil companies (Meyer). Among the members of the Center's Board of Overseers included superspy Kermit Roosevelt, the mastermind of the coup that installed the Shah of Iran into power in 1953. Two tensions developed in the unfolding of the Center's history. First, there were the conservative Arabist sentiments of the oil men and Gibb's protégés versus the growing Zionist sympathies of Washington and the wider Harvard faculty, especially after the 1967 war. Pro-Arab Orientalists, however, prevented this controversy from breaking into the open by confining their energies largely to studies of classical literature, the arts, and architecture. Supported by the administration and the larger intellectual community, Zionists were freer to publish admiring tracts of the putative achievements of modern Israel. Still, when Harkabi, the Israeli general touted as an expert on pacifying the Palestinian resistance, arrived at Harvard, he received a C.F.I.A. affiliation, but no sponsorship from the Center for Middle Eastern Studies (CMES). Zionist power at the Center slowly mounted in the 1970s and 1980s, culminating in the naming of Nadav Safran as Director in 1983. Zionist elements indeed in 1982 blocked a professorship to the distinguished Palestinian intellectual Walid Khalidi, who was penalized primarily for his concern with the fate of contemporary Palestine.[112] A second tension emerged between Gibb's progeny, well steeped in the culture and literature of the region, and a younger coterie of thinkers, enthralled with Safran, who instead prefer bland Parsonsian theory, social science surveys of "attitudes," and concern with the strategic balance of power, the latter scholarship thinly veiled commentary for the national security cognoscenti. Harvard Dean and former Secretary of Labor John Dunlop apparently referred to this division when he would tell academicians in Middle East studies that "We need you Widener Library types," referring to those cob-webbed scholars with Gibb's preoccupations. One cynical Arabist at CMES interprets this to mean that the monkish Widener Library men and women give the operation academic respectability, supplying a cover for the national security hacks who can then continue to flood the field with their "pseudo-expertise."[113]

The CIA's penetration of Harvard's Center for Middle Eastern Studies has previously been discussed. Despite his close links with the Agency, Nadav Safran, the departing CMES director, has many defenders who argue that his scholarship is free from ideological bias. Edward Banfield, the pro-Nixon Professor of Government famous for his intriguing thesis that the unemployed are responsible for their unemployment, wrote a letter to the *Boston Globe* claiming that Safran's "work would be honest if it were funded by the devil." Martin Peretz, the publisher of the most influential organ of U.S. liberalism, *The New Republic*, told Harvard Hillel that Safran "is a remarkably honest, dispassionate scholar."[114]

Safran's scholarship is typically found to be "remarkably honest" by the more dogmatic adherents to U.S.-based Zionism, but this honesty does not extend to the Palestinian peoples currently struggling under Israeli occupation. In his most celebrated work to date, *Israel: The Embattled Ally*, Safran nonchalantly observes that Israel "has no masses of land-hungry peasants confronting a few big land-owners." This is surely misleading. The "land-hungry" Arabs do not confront big landlords, but rather the Jewish National Fund which controls the National Land Authority that administers 92 percent of the land within the Green Line (the pre-1967 boundaries). Having had their land expropriated, the Palestinians, concedes Safran, "still suffered the agonies of identity and alienation," but they overall "made up a generally free, prosperous, healthy, educated community."[115] This observation flies in the face of evidence from several studies of Arabs in Israel, even from the commentary available in the Israeli press. The forced proletarianization, the direction of development funds and land privileges away from Palestinian peasants, the harassment and censorship of Arab schools and universities, and the horrible squalor and terror in the West Bank have all contributed to the deterioration of life for these people. Meanwhile, a survey put out by General Har Even of the Van Leer Institute in Jerusalem and published in *Ma'ariv* in 1980 showed that 36 percent of Israeli Jews consider Arabs to be "dirty"; 42 percent, "primitives"; and 33 percent, incapable of "valuing human life."[116] All commentators agree that such bigotry has only worsened in the intervening years. Knesset member Shulamit Aloni comments on the savagery of the police and security forces in the West Bank, a situation which raises "painful associations to those who had lived in Fascist Europe." In 1980, she noted that:

> When a Jew is murdered in the West Bank, a whole town is put under curfew (not all citizens, only the Arabs), and investigations and inquiries are held. But when Jews hit Arab citizens no inquiry file is opened and if they investigate at all, then the investigation is done in such a way and with such speed that the guilty man will never be found. Those who maltreated youths in Hebron two years ago, stripped them naked and let large dogs attack them, were not brought to court. One of the boys died since...[117]

These are aspects of Israeli reality not conveyed at that time by the "remarkably honest, dispassionate" Safran. But compared to the scholarship and journalism of some of his most ardent Harvard supporters, Professor David Landes and lecturer Martin Peretz most notably, Safran and his apologetics read like pungent social criticism. (Safran has the decency to admit that in 1948 the Israelis forcibly expelled at least half of the Palestinians.) Landes, a former director of the Center for Middle Eastern Studies in the mid-1960s, intervened in the *Christian Science Monitor* back in 1977 with the bogus claim that most of the Palestinians were latecomers to the region, people who were drawn there by the economic vitality of Jewish settlements from the late nineteenth century until after World War II. Landes writes that "no one will ever know the extent of illegal [Arab] immigration to Palestine during the [British] Mandate years," but in 1947-48 when "some 500,000 or 600,000 Arabs fled the country (not 900,000), it was primarily these newly located Arabs who left."[118]

Landes, of course, anticipates most of the major themes of Joan Peters's fraudulent work *From Time Immemorial* (NY: Harper & Row, 1984), or rather what Alex Cockburn calls "From Lies Immemorial." She indeed cites his work with glee in promoting the thesis that most Palestinians did not arrive until after Zionist colonization. "To read Peters and her supporters," comments the literary critic Edward Said, "is, for Palestinians, to experience an extended act of ethnocide carried out by pseudo-scholarship."[119]

The theses of Landes and Peters have often been objects of ridicule in Israel itself, but in the United States almost all of the initial reviews of *From Time Immemorial* were gushing with praise, one of the most ecstatic published in *Commentary* by CMES and KSG affiliate Daniel Pipes, whose venomous attitudes towards the Arab people mirrors his father's views towards the Russians.[120] *Commentary* initially balked at publishing a response to Pipes and Peters by Princeton's Norman Finkelstein, an expert on Zionism and the man most responsible for exposing the book's fabricated documentation. As Finkelstein says of *From Time Immemorial*, "[It] is among the most spectacular frauds ever published on the Arab-Israeli conflict," noting that "in a field littered with crass propaganda, forgeries, and fakes, this is no mean distinction."[121]

Landes himself was confronted with serious problems with his demographic evidence. For instance, the overtly pro-Zionist Arieh Avneri in his *Claim of Dispossession: Jewish Land-Settlement and the Arabs, 1878-1948*, argues that at most 100,000 Arabs, both legal and illegal, came to the region during this period. (Oxford's Albert Hourani notes that one of the few pieces of evidence for illegal immigration comes from a Syrian official who in 1934 said that 30,000 Syrians had entered Palestine, but the British Mandate representative responded that this figure was "grossly exaggerated.") Moreover, linguistic studies of the region have turned up little or no evidence of an influx of Arabs from different regions. Landes is forced to rely on a worn out observation by Mark Twain that the region was desolate. He seems ignorant of statistics indicating that the nineteenth century population density of Palestine well exceeded that of the United States (until as late as 1950). Finally, claims by Landes of the economic vitality of Zionist colonization are vitiated by several pertinent realities which he ignores: the widespread Jewish boycott of non-Jewish labor, British economic activity including the building of the oil pipeline and refinery at Haifa, the British Mandate government's public works construction such as the port of Haifa, and, finally, the economic growth in neighboring regions lacking a Zionist presence. When confronted with such evidence in a letter, Landes, according to Professor William Cleveland, made a vague reference to Arabs fleeing conscription under Mohammed Ali and then followed with "uncomplimentary remarks about the character of the challenge and an announcement that the correspondence on the subject was closed."[122]

This is particularly curious in Landes's case because he is often admired for painstaking scholarship and openness to dialogue in his main area of expertise, the economic history of Western Europe. But he may well be a practitioner of what William Burton calls "double standard history"; that is to say, scholarship which "involves the use of rigorous standards of evidence and appropriate goals of objectivity and the exhaustion of pertinent sources of research and publication of analyses of events in the United States and the West, and the abandonment of those same standards when the subject of analysis is a Third World country, relations between the Third World and the West, or a so-called minority within the West."[123]

Another example of Landes's "double standard" scholarship is his recent history of Haiti for The New Republic (March 10, 1986). In it, he hails the "benevolent occupation" of Haiti by the United States from 1915-34. Landes calls the "American presence" the "only period of tranquility" in Haitian history, despite an estimated 13,000 deaths in the rebellion against U.S. occupation in 1919-20 (which he conveniently neglects to mention). The U.S. Marines hired southerners to police Haiti on the theory that they were "better equipped to deal with Negroes," according to historian Roger Guillard in Les Blancs Debarquent.[124]

But Landes is by no means the worst of the Harvard faculty on this score. Martin Peretz can be counted on to plunge into the foulest depths of distortion when it comes to Third World peoples. Discussing a character in a recent play, he remarks:

A crazed Arab to be sure, but crazed in the distinctive ways of his culture. He is intoxicated by language, cannot discern between fantasy and reality, abhors compromise, always blames others for his predicament, and in the end lances the painful boils of his frustrations in a pointless, though momentarily gratifying, act of bloodlust.[125]

There, of course, is nary an objection about this from Peretz's Harvard colleagues, many of whom line up at his trough to publish articles in *The New Republic*, what George Will admires as "the nation's most important political journal."[126]

Some of the most atrocious swill pumped from Peretz's stall came in the aftermath of the bloody conflict in South Yemen in February 1986. Peretz reflects again on the Arab: "Nonviolence is so foreign to the political culture of the Arabs generally and of the Palestinians particularly. It is a failure of the collective imagination for which no one is to blame." Contrary to Peretz, the remarkable reality is Palestinian patience in the face of Israeli occupation. According to statistics published in *Ha'aretz* in July 1982, Palestinians were responsible for 282 Israeli deaths between 1967 and 1982. Meanwhile, in Lebanon during the summer of 1982 alone, the Israeli army killed over 19,000 people according to conservative estimates, and many thousands of them were Palestinians. Between 1967 and 1982, in the Israeli occupation of the West Bank, 200,000 Palestinians found themselves expelled, thousands had their homes blown up, and over half the land in the West Bank and the Gaza Strip was expropriated. Israeli bombing of refugee camps throughout the 1970s resulted in several thousand deaths.[127]

Nietzsche once reflected that "Power makes stupid." In a recent interview, even Elie Wiesel, noted for his abstinence from criticizing Israel, admits that Israel is not a home to thinkers and poets, but to warriors and generals.

Martin Peretz has labored hard to discredit or ignore the voices of Jews who are critical of this belligerent, rejectionist Zionism: Maxime Rodinson in France, George Steiner in England, Israel Shahak in Israel, and Noam Chomsky in the United States, to name but a few. His favorite target for abuse is Chomsky; but more damaging has been the almost complete suppression of meaningful debate on the Middle East in American intellectual culture. The euphoria over Peters's work from Peretz, Bellow, Wiesel, Tuchman, Dawidowicz, and Theodore White is symptomatic of the shallow level of discourse; the book received scorn and ridicule in Western European, as well as Israeli circles. Despite the broad impact of *From*

Time Immemorial, receiving over 200 favorable book reviews according to Peters's count, no one prominent in the Harvard intellectual establishment stepped forward to repudiate the work. Although Harvard was not in the forefront of this recent crusade, the stampede to destroy Marxist David Abraham of Princeton for errors in his history of Weimar Germany is an illuminating comparison. Abraham encountered a campaign of savage denunciation and threats of never receiving another academic appointment for blunders surely sloppy, but relatively minor when set in relief against Peters's grand fabrication. Though some people have repudiated her work, with even Daniel Pipes now conceding its shoddy errors, Peters's name is still in good standing among some of the American intellectual mainstream; Abraham is treated as a leper in the groves of academe. While Abraham offered to correct his mistakes and was refused by his publisher, which rushed it out of print,[128] the unrepentant Peters has released her book in paperback unchanged and full of plaudits from *The New Republic* and *Commentary* crowd.

Perhaps most alarming is that the Peters ethos seems to pervade even those organizations whose very mission is to defend the cultural integrity of stateless peoples. The Harvard founded and dominated human rights organization Cultural Survival, "concerned with the fate of tribal peoples and ethnic minorities around the world," has avoided addressing the plight of the Palestinians, despite the organization's extensive coverage of the Kurds and refugees from Guatemala, Ethiopia, Afghanistan, and elsewhere. Its president, Harvard anthropologist David Maybury-Lewis, has steadfastly refused response to letters inquiring into the reasons for this silence.[129] At the Harvard Law School in 1982, its dean cancelled his welcoming address to a conference on the plight of indigenous peoples when he heard that a Palestinian representative had been invited. Objecting to the speaker's brief work as a researcher for the PLO's mission to the UN, people identifying themselves as Jewish law students at Harvard called in death threats, and security workers had to bring in dogs to search for explosives. Police confiscated several knives and meat cleavers.[130] While the Harvard administration has denounced students for obstructing the free speech of Caspar Weinberger, the contras, and representatives of the regime in South Africa, they never seem to comment on the issue of actual death threats against Palestinians who have sought to speak at the University.

The reasons for this administration timidity is a subject for speculation, though Bok himself is so enthralled with the Israeli leadership that he has called Labor Party leader Shimon Peres a "most illustrious statesman."[131] A primary way in which Peretz, and for that matter Safran, insulate themselves from criticism and debate is to accuse their opponents of anti-Semitism. Safran complains that he was a victim of "the Jewish factor,"[132] his ethnic background driving people to expose him as a CIA operative (even though it was primarily Jewish journalists on the *Harvard Crimson* who heroically brought the story to the public's attention). Meanwhile, a June 9, 1986 lead editorial of *The New Republic* remarks that "It may be that here and there is an anti-Zionist who is not an anti-Semite...it will be hard to find an anti-Semite who is not also an anti-Zionist." The truth is that nothing could be easier. Most of the Nazis were ardent supporters of Zionism because they thought it would be a quick way to purify bloodlines. Mussolini counseled Italian Zionists in 1934: "You must create a Jewish State. I am myself a Zionist."[133] Today, the crypto-fascist leader of the National Front in France Jean-Marie Le Pen laces his speeches with praise and support for Israel, the better to keep the French ethnically pure.

The complex relationship between fascism and Zionism has been untangled elsewhere.[134] It is worth remarking, however, that the Jewish people, having undergone some of the greatest persecution and suffering in the history of our time, are now done a disservice by key members of the Harvard intellectual establishment, who try to impose on this diverse and multifaceted people a rigid, pro-Israeli orthodoxy. The *New Republic,* dominated by a certain Harvard set, is part of the problem, with its aversion to reviewing books critical of Israel, its constant barrage of slurs against Said, and its repeated failure to publish letters by Chomsky, despite Peretz's claim that the right to reply to direct attacks is "axiomatic" in his forum. The few positive gestures towards the Arab world are predicated on their helping "us" to secure "our" interests in the region: the cynical and manipulative manner in which Safran and his closest allies, such as the former Associate Director of the CMES Laurie Mylroie, have embraced representatives of the most repressive Arab regimes, in particular the bloodthirsty government of Iraq's Saddam Hussein, hardly inspires confidence in their willingness to bring reconciliation to the Middle East.[135] Today the courage of the intifadah has at last opened a space for debate on the Palestinian question. There is little doubt, however, that the few Harvard intellectuals less than enthusiastic about Israeli behavior—Hoffmann, Kelman, Wald, Hubbard, and junior faculty such as Lockman—will continue to be confronted by the sleepwalk-ing complacency of a faculty majority.

The Asian Studies Establishment

Having emerged out of missionary work of the nineteenth and early twentieth century, Asian studies began to mature as an aca-demic enterprise in the postwar period. Dean Rusk, then president of the Rockefeller Foundation, told a Congressional committee in 1952 that through service to military intelligence during World War II he himself came to recognize that "it was of the greatest importance for us to encourage concentrated attention on what was then called the weird languages, such languages as Indonesian, Burmese, some of the Indian dialects, some of the languages of Indochina... So we [the Rockefeller Foundation] have attached considerable importance to these area studies."[136] In 1956, Harvard opened its own East Asian Research Center (EARC), funded by the Carnegie and Ford Founda-tions in response "to the rise of a powerful and unfriendly Chinese State," according to the *Official Register of Harvard University* (vol. LXI, No. 16). Further funding came in subsequent years from the Depart-ment of Defense, the U.S. Arms Control and Disarmament Agency, and the U.S. Air Force. Nevertheless, the profession came out of the McCarthy era heavily traumatized by the phantasmagorical ques-tion, "Who Lost China?"

The response of most scholars of Asia was either withdrawal from work on problems confronting contemporary Asia or else ser-vile catering to the needs of Washington (Berkeley's Robert Scalapino, MIT's Lucian Pye are prototypes of the latter). At Harvard, the CIA's Charles Neuhauser ran the EARC's Red Guard Translation project, while the CIA's Sidney Bearman spent 1968 as a visiting fellow there. When a pro-Chinese Communist student sought to return to complete his dissertation, the center blocked his readmis-sion on the grounds that his project might serve as "propaganda."[137] Of the eight major national petitions *against* the Vietnam War (circa 1965-67), signed by thousands of faculty and graduate students, almost all of the area studies establishment declined participation (0 of 36 members of the University of Chicago's Committee on South Asia Studies, 1 of 39 of Michigan's program on Far Eastern Studies, 0 of 25 of Stanford's Hoover Institute, and 0 of 9 of Harvard's executive committee of the Committee for International Affairs). Through this abdication, it is thus no surprise that for expertise on the realities of the U.S. invasion of Vietnam, the public had to turn to professors of biology at Harvard, professors of linguistics at MIT, and journalists largely from the alternative media.[138]

Before the rise of these dissenters, the Asian studies establishment and the elite journalists could barely muster a peep of protest, the latter the most active in orchestrating sonorous praise for a hard-boiled policy in Southeast Asia. Harvard itself produced perhaps the three most influential U.S. journalists of the twentieth century, Walter Lippmann, Joseph Alsop, and Theodore White. Of this trio of pundits, White, student and confidant of John King Fairbank and a member of the visiting committee overseeing the University's program in East Asian Civilization, was typically lionized as a journalistic expert on Asia, having undergone training in Asian studies at Harvard and completed extended stints in China during World War II. In Cockburn's words, White "approached unfolding history with an ecstatic sentimentality that ignored process and caressed the powerful in a way that, as Lenin once remarked of an opponent, would be touching in a child but was repugnant in a person of mature years." When LBJ launched war on Vietnam through the Gulf of Tonkin ruse, White chirped enthusiastically: "The deft response of American planes to the jabbing of North Vietnam's torpedo boats had been carried out with the nicest balance between boldness and precision." Defining himself as a Sinophile, White's last writings focused on the fortieth anniversary of the end of World War II, epistles designed to revive old atavistic hatreds of Japan (see his *New York Times Magazine* cover piece proudly entitled "The Danger from Japan").[139]

Alsop also had absurd pretensions of Asia expertise. A member of Harvard's Porcellian Club and a student of classical Chinese, Alsop thought that the United States could have prevented the triumph of Maoism in China by helping to install in power the Harvard-educated millionaire T.V. Soong. When the Vietnam War commenced, Alsop, a great advocate of escalating bombing, was so cozy with military elites that Everett Martin, the bureau chief of *Newsweek* in Saigon, noted that he had open use of a military jet and that he "doesn't get briefed by Colonels, he briefs them."[140]

Lippmann is often regarded as being outside the Cold War consensus, especially because he attacked Alsop in 1946 for writing essays of such unmatched silliness as "Why Not Be Russia Obsessed" for *The New Republic* (October 14, 1946). But Lippmann's forays into Asia show the limits of acceptable dissent in the postwar United

States. In 1950, he saluted the dispatching of the Seventh Fleet to Formosa, and by 1952 was declaring that it would be a "catastrophe of enormous proportions...if Southeast Asia were to fall into the communist orbit." Though he later discovered that the war was not such a brilliant master stroke, in its early years he mimicked White and Alsop, calling the opening bombing of North Vietnam a "test of American will" and later that retaliatory air strikes were called for because they place the United States in "a better bargaining position for a negotiation." He reassured Eric Sevareid's listeners on CBS that war hawks are "not found in the interior and at the top of the White House," and in the course of that year gave his seal of approval to the U.S.-supported coup in the Dominican Republic. It would take the rise of a younger generation of radical journalists and academicians before power confronted any meaningful challenge—these newcomers at least free from Alsop's and White's delusions of Asia expertise.[141]

So what about the reigning scholars of Asia at Harvard itself? Among the most important intellectual figures in Harvard's postwar history include a historian of China, John K. Fairbank, and a scholar of Japan, Edwin O. Reischauer. Both made substantial contributions to their discipline and have produced memoirs chronicling their achievements.

A victim of McCarthyite hysteria, Fairbank retreated to intellectual work, in many ways reorienting U.S. understanding of China. While under oath before McCarthy's Congressional partisans, he, nevertheless, left little doubt about his ideological sympathies, declaring himself a "loyal American" and a capitalist: "I am engaged in one form of American free enterprise. My university is a private American corporation..." Reischauer on the surface possesses a congeniality that endears him to the Japanese people, a sensibility that caused Clyde Haberman, a reviewer of his memoirs for the *New York Times*, to question whether his loyalty to them came before the people of the United States.[142]

This is not the place to develop a systematic critique of these men. But the limitations of their scholarship and politics are worth noting because of the prevalence of their views in the Asian studies discipline. First, in many circles, Reischauer and especially Fairbank are treated as politically progressive because they spoke out against the U.S. crusade in Indochina. However, both of them considered the intervention to be based largely on policy blunders, Fairbank stressing the "factor of ignorance" at the root of "our Vietnam tragedy."

Reischauer concurs, using the language of "cost-benefit" analysis: "The real lesson of the Vietnam War is the tremendous cost of attempting to control the destiny of a Southeast Asia country against the cross-currents of nationalism."[143]

By treating the war as a "tragic error," a grand "mistake," they blind themselves to the patterns of U.S. foreign policy. As Philip Rahv put it in the *New York Review of Books* in 1967:

> So it would seem that our repeated interventions, covert and overt, in Latin America and elsewhere, our brutal assault on the Vietnamese people, not to mention our benign inattentiveness to the abolition of democracy in Greece by a few crummy colonels wholly dependent on American arms and loans, are all mere accidents or mistakes perhaps.[144]

Fairbank attributes our "error" to misperceptions about the relationship between Communism and nationalism. But many of the foreign policy planning documents from the 1950s onward indicate that national security managers privately were quite aware of the nationalist appeal of the Viet Minh and shaped their imperial policies accordingly. While national security discourse is permeated with rant about monolithic Communism, Fairbank takes this too much at face value, neglecting the U.S. propensity to crush non-Communist nationalists as well (Mossadeq in Iran, Arbenz in Guatemala, Bosch in the Dominican Republic, etc.).

Secondly, there is a tendency to provide scholarship that is instrumentalist in its aim, which in their version meant that understanding should serve U.S. interests. Reischauer is more guilty than Fairbank on this score. At a State Department conference in October 1949, he stressed that Asia's peoples "are asking for an ideology. We have in many ways failed to give it to them. There is a crying need for people to have our ideology. We aren't in the habit of giving it."[145] Reischauer's concern with promoting "our ideology" took many shapes: 1) He called for a crusade against Marxism; he saw the "loss" of China less as treason, in contrast to the McCarthyite view, but rather as an intellectual defeat: "While we strengthened the arms of the Chinese and attempted to fill their bellies the Communists won their minds..." With the United States in the midst of undermining the Geneva Accords, Reischauer wrote about "the particularly absurd mismanagement of our cause that we appear to many Asians to be relying primarily on force and the Communists on arguments..." In scholarship, Reischauer promoted "modernization theory" as an antidote to Marxism.[146]

2) He promoted the "battle of ideas" in Asia's schools and universities, stressing the centrality of intellectuals in furthering U.S. interests:

> If we exploit the special prestige position of the scholar [in the Far East]…it would seem to me that propaganda work, information aimed primarily at them would be the most effective kind of information work. It might be advisable to try to put American professors in every university to the extent that the universities can absorb them. I am sure that there are many places in the Far East where they would like to have good American professors if we can get right in. To what extent have we been bringing future intellectual leaders of that area to this country for extensive training?[147]

3) He emphasized the importance of putting U.S. ideology in Asian idioms. In a 1955 manifesto entitled *Wanted: An Asia Policy*, Reischauer cleverly suggested that U.S. policymakers work at "consciously underplaying America in our intellectual dealings with Asia." A concrete case is his willingness to dispense with the Western vocabulary of capitalism to facilitate its triumph in Asia. He writes:

> Take for example the term 'free enterprise.' For us this implies freedom from the stultifying restrictions of the bureaucratic superstate. It suggests a healthy and desirable freedom for all men on their own initiative to work for the common good…But both 'free enterprise' and 'individualism' suggest entirely different concepts to most Asians. These terms raise before their eyes the picture of the ruthless monopolist, the economic gouger, the foreign or native exploiter of the economic ills of colonial Asia…The Asian may assume that they are symbols of the disregard of all social conscience. Obviously terms such as these cannot be used safely in Asia, and the ideas behind them must be translated into some other idiom.[148]

Reischauer had the opportunity to put some of these ideas into practice as U.S. Ambassador to Japan under the Kennedy administration. In postwar practice, the U.S. struggle for global hegemony is waged on three levels—military, economic, and ideological. Whereas most of the national security managers, Huntington, et al., give priority to the first two levels, Reischauer was fixated on the last, the ideological.

As for Fairbank, during the late 1960s and early 1970s when dissident scholars called for the Association of Asian Studies (AAS) to investigate the growth of ties between experts on Asia and the military, he responded by equating their efforts at restoring academic integrity to the McCarran witchhunt at the defunct Institute for

Pacific Relations (IPR). Despite many disclaimers to the contrary, Asian Studies at Harvard became reason in the service of Empire.

Sociology and the Cold War

As an intellectual response to the crisis of modernity, sociology arose in the nineteenth century, initially a strange blend of scientism and admiration for the most retrograde features of medieval civilization. Its founder, the Frenchman Auguste Comte (1798-1857) himself proclaimed, "Long live the retrograde school, the immortal group under the leadership of Maistre," a reference to a social *couche* of fanatical papists, race-mystics, and monarchists who are considered the forerunners of twentieth century currents of clerico-fascism and anti-Semitism. Comte's own aim was to revive medieval hierarchy in a revamped scientific guise, forming a new academic priesthood able to interpret society on behalf of conservative social reconstruction.[149]

Comte's vision of sociology met resistance in the United States, where its early practitioners came to be influenced by Protestant meliorist currents. Still one of its dominant figures, Edward A. Ross of the University of Wisconsin, called on the sociologist to take the lead in "social engineering," which by "turn[ing] over the defense of society to professionals" could avert the consequences of class war. The vision of the sociologist as a servant of entrenched power remained seductive, probably regaining its first great impetus in 1927 when the Western Electric Company at its Chicago plant hired a team of Harvard cultural anthropologists and psychologists, including the Harvard Business School's Elton Mayo, to figure out how workers acting collectively initiated slowdowns in production. (See the discussion of scientific management in my essay on science.) In the United States, the Depression temporarily cut short sociology's own expansion through this avenue; but by World War II the Pentagon came to recognize a need for teams of sociologists who were contracted to help officers manage and control millions of fresh recruits. By 1968, I.L. Horowitz in his survey of sociology concluded on the sources of the profession's explosive postwar expansion:

> Given the complex nature of social science activities and their increasing costs...the government becomes the most widespread buyer. Government policymakers get the first yield also because they claim a maximum need. Private pressure groups representing corporate interests are the next highest buyer of social science services...The sources of funds for research tend to be concentrated in the upper class.[150]

This may seem at variance with the image of Harvard sociology, as its leading figure Talcott Parsons is commonly regarded as a contemplative theorist rather than an engaged activist. But during the interwar period, Parsons came under the spell of the physiologist Lawrence Henderson, the founder of Harvard's elite academic circle, The Society of Fellows. Henderson made a blunt distinction between "sickness" and "equilibrium" in the social system, believing that the medical doctor, rather than the passive biologist, should serve as the model for the sociologist. Like their predecessor Ross, he and Parsons foresaw sociology as the ideology for the expanding professional classes. At the level of social control, Parsons especially admired the work of cultural anthropologist Clyde Kluckhohn, OSS figure and an early director of Harvard's Russian Research Center, especially for his analysis showing how to maintain effective administrative control of the Navajo Indians.[151]

In the ensuing postwar epoch, U.S. sociology came to be dominated by the Harvard triumvirate of Talcott Parsons, Seymour Martin Lipset, and Daniel Bell. Bell had previously been based at Columbia, while Lipset eventually left Harvard for Stanford, where today he plies intellectual wares at the conservative Hoover Institute on War, Revolution, and Peace.

Through most of his life, Parsons stood as North America's preeminent sociologist. What Weber is for Germany; Durkheim, for France; Pareto, for Italy, Parsons became for the United States. Today radical sociologists regard Parsons as a spokesperson for stasis and conservatism, but his thought needs to be set into context. He represented a rebellion against the sociological tradition of Herbert Spencer, the nineteenth-century Social Darwinist once warmly embraced by the U.S. bourgeoisie. Commager notes that Spencer "dominated the thought of the average American—especially the middle-class American—during the half-century after Appomatox," selling close to 400,000 books and receiving a lavish banquet in his honor by scientists, writers, politicians, and tycoons at New York's Delmonico Hotel.[152]

In the liveliest prose ever mustered in his checkered intellectual career, Parsons began his seminal work, the two volume *Structure of Social Action* (1937): "Spencer is dead. But who killed him and how?"[153] Through a critique of English utilitarianism, under which he lumped Hobbes, Locke, Smith, and Spencer, Parsons decided that its "theory of action" was inherently flawed, unable to explain how the conflicting interests of individual actors led to social cohesion, rather than dissolving society into a war of all against all. Parsons's solution was to stress the power of norms and values. His theory, therefore, was idealist (some would say idealistic): people are driven not so much by self-interest, whether based on instinct or reason, but rather by the need to adhere to social norms. The Italian Pareto provided some of the central concepts of Parsons's sociology: the distinction between logical and non-logical actions, and the role of force and fraud in maintaining social equilibrium. During the 1930s and early 1940s, Harvard was overrun by a rage for the Italian's ideas, so much so that historians talk of "The Harvard 'Pareto Circle.'" Charles Curtis, Bernard DeVoto, Crane Brinton, George Homans, Lawrence Henderson, Joseph Schumpeter, and Elton Mayo were among the Harvard faculty who came under Pareto's spell. Sociologist George Homans explained his enthusiasm for Pareto: "As a Republican Bostonian who had not rejected his comparatively wealthy family, I felt that I was under personal attack, above all from the Marxists. I was ready to believe Pareto because he provided me with a defense." The historian Crane Brinton was disturbed by "the favorite smear phrase for Pareto...'Karl Marx of the bourgeoisie.'" "The liberals," according to Lawrence Henderson, hated Pareto, identifying him "with their favorite word of abuse—'fascist.'" Brinton elaborated why Pareto's "social system of equilibrium" was useful to society: "The concept of equilibrium helps us to understand, and sometimes to use and control, specific machines, chemicals, and even medicines. It may someday help us to understand, and within limits to mold, men in society."[154]

What has all this to do with the Cold War? During World War II, Parsons's fight against fascism led him to more practical political concerns. He turned to an aggressive defense of "the rationalized liberal culture of the Western world." Enunciating a view that carried into peacetime, Parsons called for "strengthening attachment to the basic institutional patterns and cultural traditions of the society," as well as "deliberately and systematically counteracting the very important existing deviant tendencies." He soon put an accent on developing common norms and values.[155]

Lipset took up some of Parsons's challenges. Deeply committed to Cold War liberalism, he became involved in the CIA and Ford Foundation-financed Congress for Cultural Freedom, which, Christopher Lasch observes, argued that "the conventional political distinctions had become irrelevant in the face of the need for a united front against Bolshevism."[156] Among the most prolific social scientists of the twentieth century, Lipset called for studies "locating the sources of U.S. resistance to extremes of right and left during the Depression." Preoccupied during the 1950s with the phenomenon of McCarthyism, he argued that social scientists should put most of their energy into explaining its decline, rather than searching for the basis of its support. Too many political sociologists, he thought, gave no consideration to the "erection of a social theory to explain why some societies are healthy and relatively invulnerable to such threats."[157] On the eve of the most widespread eruption of protests in the history of the modern university, Lipset declared with aplomb that "a brief comparative look at the situation of the university and educated youth in the emerging and industrially developed societies suggests that student activism cannot take on major proportions in the latter."[158] His dismissal of the political potential of students was mild compared to his disparagement of the working and lower classes, whose inherent intolerance and "authoritarianism" is due to a lack of aptitude for democracy: "Acceptance of the norms of democracy requires a high level of sophistication." Though there are notable exceptions in his oeuvre, Lipset became preoccupied with how to prevent social movements, rather than exploring the sources of their vitality. In terms of providing positive political models, he held that political sociology in clarifying "the operation of Western democracy in the mid-twentieth century" could "contribute to the political battle in Asia and Africa." His vision was not confined to the Third World. The United States as "the most advanced society technologically," with "the most developed set of political and class relationships...has presented the image of the European future."[159]

The implications of this advanced technology for society itself became the staple of Daniel Bell. Bell has helped provide many of the central concepts in the discourse of modernity, most recently on the legitimation crisis of late capitalism. In the 1950s, he developed what historian Ellen Schrecker calls "perhaps the most influential contemporary interpretation of McCarthyism," the view that it was a populist phenomenon generated by the "status anxieties" of downwardly mobile WASPs and upwardly mobile ethnics. Working with Parsonsian sociologists (including Parsons himself) and liberal historians such as Hofstadter, Bell downplayed both the politics of McCarthy and the role of elites in fomenting anti-Communism, instead stressing it as a reaction to the dislocations of modernity. Many of his school's theses were rudely cast aside in 1967 with the publication of Michael Rogin's *The Intellectuals and McCarthy*, which showed that the roots of McCarthyism were less grounded in popular rebellion than in the jockeying for power among elites in the Republican Party. Unlike his predecessors, Rogin took the time to study who in fact voted for McCarthy. In the meantime, revisionist historiography showed how the Cold War liberalism of the Truman administration and the foreign policy elite gave impetus to McCarthyism.[160]

Bell's place in modern intellectual history was assured in 1960 by his proclamation of "the end of ideology" in the United States and the prediction of its demise in the West. In the face of the twin catastrophes of Stalinism and fascism, the hopes of modernity had effectively been liquidated, while the triumphs of the corporate order and the Keynesian welfare state elevated those whose claim to power is based on disinterested knowledge and technique.[161] Bell hails this development, for "ideology makes it unnecessary for people to confront individual issues on their individual merits." He believes that ideology appeals to the pre-rational, that it emerged largely as a response to the disintegration of the religious world view of traditional society.[162]

Bell became the oracle of post-industrial society, noting the increasing prominence of "the scientists, the mathematicians, the economists, and the engineers of the new computer technology." His heady optimism about its prospects was hardly tempered by the concession that "it has been war rather than peace that has been largely responsible for the acceptance of planning and technocratic modes in government."[163] As Bell was writing these words, he lost little faith in his humane, non-ideological technicians, who at that very moment were beginning to escalate the war in Vietnam. "McNamara, his systems analysts, and their computers are not only contributing to the practical effectiveness of U.S. action," marvelled Max Ways of *Fortune*, "but raising the moral level of policy by a more conscious and selective attention to the definition of its aims."[164] For Bell, the Cold War in some ways remained an obstacle to the full-fledged decline of ideology and the reign of the technocrats, but this was the fault of the Soviets. U.S. behavior is totally reactive, according to his narrative of Cold War history:

> When the Russians began stirring up the Greek guerrilla EAM in what had been tacitly acknowledged at Teheran as a British sphere of influence, the Communists began their cry against Anglo-American imperialism. Following the rejection of the Marshall Plan and the Communist coup in Czechoslovakia in February 1948, the Cold War was on in earnest.[165]

This is as unimaginative and vapid a Cold War history as they come, but in the absence of revisionist historians at Harvard it goes unchallenged. From outside the halcyon gates of Harvard Yard, there were many storms which his "end of ideology" thesis would have to weather. It was the cockcrow of 1968, Paris, Prague, and Berkeley, denying the power of the technocrats and the party functionaries, that lifted the spell of impotence, showing that ideology did indeed matter. Still it would be foolish to deny that Bell's thesis has staying power. Reformulated and repackaged mostly by thinkers who would be anathema to him, the claim of an "end to ideology" has been adopted in the 1970s and 1980s by disillusioned Marxists such as Italy's Lucio Colletti and swept into prominence by the tidal wave of poststructuralisms imported from what has surprisingly become a contemporary center of intellectual reaction, Paris. But whereas Bell, Lipset, and company were seduced to the end of ideology by the siren song of postwar prosperity and Keynesian economic management, the poststructuralists are drawn to it by the dual breakdown of welfare state capitalism and sixties-style political unrest. Expelling the sober liberalism of Bell from their theory, the poststructuralists wedded "the end of ideology" to the philosophical vision of Nietzsche. The Apollonian Bell became smothered in the frenzy of Dionysus.[166]

An obvious shortcoming in Bell's thesis is its marked irrelevance to people living in most of the world, its silence concerning the political and anti-colonial struggles throughout the Third World. This became the terrain of Rostow, Parsons, and Lipset, who promulgated what reigned for two decades as social science orthodoxy: modernization theory. For them, Bell's de-ideologized political order in the West was mimicked by benign modernization in the Third World, with unrest and rebellion treated as the pre-rational yammerings of a rapidly declining traditional society. Implicit in their model was the view that rapid economic growth would transform the political and ideological structures of the Third World. Lipset's declaration that the United States provided the political ideal for the rest of the world endeared the modernization theorists to the administrators of foreign aid programs. For example, from 1961 to 1963, Kennedy's Agency for International Development (AID) escalated development funds to an average of $4 billion per year, over a third higher than in the five previous fiscal years. Buoyed by modernization theory, AID stressed "developmental" over national security assistance. But with the eruption of six military coups in Latin America in 1962 and 1963, the Kennedy mandarins began the shift away from economic assistance and towards security concerns. The U.S. Army-funded Project Camelot, though eventually cancelled by the State Department because of a combination of domestic and foreign outrage, became the new prototype for social science. It sought to combine the latest social science with the formulation of strategies for effective counterinsurgency in developing countries.[167]

The high prophet of this new social science and the gravedigger of classical modernization theory was none other than Samuel P. Huntington. Whereas modernization theory assumed that economics determines politics, Huntington boldly asserted the priority of politics. His frontal assault came from three directions:

1) He opposed the myth that the U.S. model is exportable. North American political systems, according to his *Political Order in Changing Societies*, are likely "to reproduce in Latin America" a government "simply too weak, too diffuse, too dispersed to mobilize the political power necessary to bring about fundamental change." Noting that Moscow and Beijing have learned this lesson, he argues that "the primary need" of developing nations is "the accumulation and concentration of power." The weakness of the U.S. model is reflected in its archaic institutions and its susceptibility to a "democratic distemper." He elaborates that "democracy...can very easily become a threat to itself in the United States. Political authority is never strong here, and it is particularly weak during a period of intense commitment to democratic and egalitarian ideals."[168]

2) He offered as an antidote what he blandly called "institutionalization." Huntington accents the need to build new and stronger political institutions, but these should be tailored to the needs of the specific country in question. He sees room for optimism insofar as the United States "supported and attempted to promote the development of the most varied types of political systems around the globe," among them Iran's "essentially authoritarian monarchy," "one-party systems in Tunisia and Bolivia, a military led dominant party system in Korea, monarchical-bureaucratic regimes in Thailand and Nepal, and also, of course, a variety of competitive democratic systems..." The effectiveness of political regimes, rather than their convergence with the U.S. model, was seen as the new lode star for the policymaker.[169]

3) He argued that political scientists must engage in political engineering, rather than consign their craft to a theoretical science. MIT's Lucian Pye was himself disturbed that the "disinterest" so

prominent in the "scientific enterprise" of Parsons places too much trust in "the ultimate utility of pure science," thus restraining one from intervening actively in the "pressing public policy issues of the moment."[170]

Huntington's political science became so shackled to the immediate needs of the national security state that many liberals found the distinction between the state and the academy obliterated. Compared with the practice of Huntington and Pye's minions, the sociology of Bell, Lipset, and Parsons in retrospect acquired a certain nobility. Bell's more recent cultural pessimism about the prospects for capitalism is indicative of this autonomy. As for the successors to Parsons, Lipset, and Bell, liberal sociology at Harvard appears to be in a sustained period of disarray.

Latin America

Save for the vitality of Harvard's literary studies (Carlos Fuentes, et al.), Latin America shares with African studies a relative latecomer status at Harvard and is still treated as a field of peripheral studies. It is instructive to note that at the Department of History, for instance, three professors, one assistant professor, and ten to fifteen teaching fellows specialize in Great Britain (population 55 million); one professor and two teaching fellows cover the entire region of Latin America (population 500 million); no professors, one associate professor, and one teaching fellow cover the entire continent of Africa (population 600 million).

Not all Harvardians wanted it this way. Back in the 1840s, Alexander Everett, Harvard valedictorian, elite Bostonian, and brother of the president of Harvard, proposed setting up U.S. institutes of Spanish studies, which he expected to encompass Latin America. Among Everett's motivations was his fear of Cuba, which on a different occasion he described as:

> a moral and political volcano—teeming, under an outside of forced tranquility, with a fiery ocean of insurrection and massacre—ready at any moment to spread by explosion, its boiling lava over everything in its neighborhood—separated from our Southern states by a channel that may be traversed in a few hours...[171]

But for many with an imperial mindset, Latin America for the next century could be ignored. There was a brief spurt in the opening of Latin American studies centers in the interwar period, but interest in the postwar period began to wane. When Harold Macmillan, British Prime Minister from the later 1950s to early 1960s, was asked by Raymond Carr how often Latin America came up in Tory Cabinet meetings, he declared with exaggerated aplomb, "We once had a few discussions on Argentinian beef."[172] Even Kissinger, oblivious to the strength of the revolutionary forces in Nicaragua, has barely a reference to Central America in over 2,000 pages of memoirs.

But in reality it was Cuba and Castro that represented a breach in this patrician indifference. Replacing the geological metaphors of Everett with biological ones, Cuba for a new breed of experts became treated as a disease spreading its socialist bacilli throughout the Caribbean and the continent's southern cone. Carr continues on the early 1960s:

> Latin America became what the Near East is today, with Castro as a secular ayatollah preaching a continental revolution. Academic interest followed political concern. Professors would supply policymakers with the basic materials on which to base a counter-revolutionary strategy...The Ford Foundation pumped money into Latin America studies in U.S. universities; the Parry Committee, set up by the British government, published a report that was to lead to the setting up of Latin America centers in the United Kingdom. A generation of scholars were provided with the tools to set to work.[173]

The trouble with all this is that as the 1960s progressed, fewer and fewer Latin America scholars desired to be recruited for this counter-revolutionary social science crusade. True, at Harvard, non-specialists such as Huntington and psychologists including McClelland churned out studies devoured in Washington. McClelland's *The Achieving Society* in particular argued that Latin America could not develop economically because its peoples lacked an achievement ethic; in other words, they have a "bad attitude"—forget inconvenient arguments about imperialism and a reactionary social structure. But overall the unwillingness of scholars of Latin America to support such nostrums caused the hero of Contragate, Michael Ledeen, in a speech at Harvard in late 1987 to denounce Latin American studies as "a real junk area" in academia. Coming from the mouth of Ledeen, notorious for slovenly crafted scholarship, it is one of the highest compliments ever paid to the field.

Latin America happens to be one of the few regions of the world in which Harvard has a specialist who dissents from government policy, historian John Womack. In U.S. universities, the abundance of progressive intellectuals in the Latin American field can be attributed to the integrity of its professional organization, the Latin American Studies Association (LASA), which has resisted putting reason at the service of the national security state. For speaking out against the contras and the death squad democracies of the region, Womack is, of course, vilified by conservative columnists such as William F. Buckley, Jr., contributors to *The Harvard Salient* who argue that his commitment to Marxism warrants his removal from the faculty, and Accuracy in Academia sympathizers who warn that his classes will be monitored by that right-wing body. In response to the last threat, Richard Fagen, the leading Latin Americanist at Stanford and akin to Womack as a radical critic of Reaganismo, arrives at lectures in a t-shirt emblazoned with the words, "Minister of Propaganda."

Thanks to LASA's vigilance, the Latin America field is not littered with the intellectual hacks and apologists for Washington so dominant in other area studies. But the right can also take solace in the presence at Harvard of several prominent contra defenders. Huntington and Peretz are both drum majorettes for PRODEMCA, an organization that takes out full-page advertisements in the *New York Times*, the *Washington Post*, and elsewhere on behalf of Washington's war in Nicaragua. In lieu of a prominent Latin Americanist, the chief "expert" on Central America for Peretz's *New Republic* is Washington-based Robert Solin Leiken, a Harvardian and ex-Maoist who previously taught at MIT and Harvard. In 1987, Leiken nailed down an appointment to Harvard's C.F.I.A. In the 25th Anniversary Report of the Harvard Class of '61, he notes his own opposition to the Vietnam War and claims a continued commitment to progressive values as the basis for his hatred of the Sandinistas: his "support for popular self-determination and national independence." Leiken's supposed commitment to progressive "principles" wore thin by the end of his Harvard Anniversary Report, as he could not contain himself when it came to the subject of women. He moans that his time-consuming work as a waterboy for policymakers focussed on Central America has made it difficult for him to indulge in relationships with his female students. "'The sleek expensive girls I teach,/Younger and pinker every year,/Bloom gradually out of reach...'" he laments, citing verse that no doubt is illustrative of his professed dedication to self-determination for all peoples.[174]

But anyone who wanted a debate on Central America policy at Harvard in Spring 1986 had their hopes dashed when the Kennedy School of Government caved in to the demands of Assistant Secretary of State for Latin American Affairs Elliott Abrams, who asked that

Robert White, Carter's Ambassador to El Salvador, be disinvited to the Forum. Graham Allison's apparatchiks promptly complied with this diktat and only then did Abrams agree to speak. Though considered a milksop of a liberal in other circles, White instead became touted at Harvard as a representative of dangerously crypto-Bolshevik left views and unfit for the forum with Abrams. The moderator, Harvard professor of government Harvey Mansfield, introduced by the Orwellian title of "John Olin Foundation Distinguished Lecturer in Philosophy and Free Institutions," explained to the *Harvard Crimson* the reasons for revoking White's invitation: "White is a representative of the far left. [The forum was intended] as a debate between liberals and conservatives and [we did not want to] allow the liberal point of view to be drowned out by the far left."[175]

The poverty of U.S. political discourse is exhibited when the likes of Morton Kondracke of *The New Republic*, who routinely refers to the Somocista-infested contras as Nicaragua's "democratic resistance," and the *Washington Post*'s Richard Cohen, a supporter of stores which have policies that refuse entry to black males, are called on to represent liberalism in debates with conservatives. It is no wonder, as Gore Vidal remarks, that "we Americans [have] become a people almost evenly divided between conservatives and reactionaries."[176] The Central America debate at Harvard dramatically demonstrates the processes of political closure at work.

The Ramboization of Harvard

In February 1986, The Hasty Pudding Theatricals, one of the more renowned student organizations at Harvard, gave its coveted Man of the Year Award to none other than Sylvester "Rambo" Stallone. Amidst much media attention, this action also brought expression of outrage within the Harvard community. A slaughterer of senior citizens in the epic movie *Death Race 2000* and an exterminator of Third World peoples in *Rambo*, Stallone surely does not merit one of the University's most prestigious honors. So said his Harvard critics.

Rejecting the logic of Stallone's enemies, I hold the opposite position. Stallone in many ways is an exemplar *par excellence* of the dominant values of the Harvard establishment. What is remarkable is that he was not so honored years earlier.

After all, most of the major architects of the Vietnam War were Harvard men, who behind a façade of technocratic and peaceful rhetoric revelled in the Rambo values of machismo. When his car was surrounded by Harvard students opposed to the war in 1967, Secretary of Defense McNamara stood on the hood and with Stallonesque élan screamed, "I was tougher than you are then [in World War II] and I'm tougher than you now!"[177] More recently, the driving forces behind Reagan's Rambo-style foreign policy carry the Crimson banner with pride: Cap Weinberger, Elliott Abrams, Richard Pipes, Don Regan, et al.

There are other obvious similarities between Stallone and the Harvard establishment. It will be recalled how the Harvard men gladly sent off blacks, Hispanics, and working-class whites to die in Vietnam, while their pampered children enjoyed the luxury of a "safe" upper-class education. One might wonder: where was Rambo while the United States was losing the war in Vietnam? Stallone, according to Jack Newfield, "ducked the draft during the Vietnam War (although he looks physically fit to me.)"[178] It seems Stallone went to an elite private school in Switzerland and then continued to avoid action by studying acting at the University of Miami. It is probably unfair to single out Stallone for his support of a macho foreign policy, while himself avoiding the draft. After all, there are many young Harvard graduates in the Reagan-Bush administrations who did likewise: most notably Elliott Abrams. At the time, Abrams wailed that he had a bad back and could not serve. In a recent interview on Vietnam, he now says: "We had business being there. And if it would have required a few thousand troops stationed there for years in order to prevent this extraordinarily damaging American defeat, then I think most Americans would have been willing to do it." Despite a sizable contingent of latter-day neoconservatives and Cold War liberals, the class of 1970 at Harvard, according to a survey, sent only two out of its 1,200 graduating males to Vietnam.[179] David Stockman sat out the war at the Divinity School. The Harvard Right is not alone in this; most of the leading Reaganites of draft age did likewise: Richard Perle, George Will, Paul Trible, Pat Buchanan, Newt Gingrich, Paul Weyrich, etc. It is remarkable, however, that this Rambo coalition, known to some as the "war wimps," became the dominant voice of U.S. foreign policy for much of the 1980s. U.S. elites have become quite loose in risking the lives of the less privileged, for goals which "the best and the brightest" are ultimately not willing to fight for themselves. As Norman Birnbaum puts it: "A willingness to fight to the last poor black, Hispanic, or impoverished white (or professional officer) is the one warlike trait that unites our political elite."[180]

Harvard, of course, has a great history of cuddling up to the high priests of militarism and war-mongering. Hasty Pudding's celebration of Stallone was portrayed by critics as an isolated case, outside the bounds of Harvard's ordinarily humane traditions. Yet, at the 1986 commencement, there was no moral outrage expressed when Paul Nitze, an engineer of the national security state and a subverter of arms control, was given an honorary doctorate amidst profuse praise from Derek Bok for his contributions to peace. The Kennedy School of Government and Graham Allison caught some flak for awarding Ed Meese a medal for Distinguished Public Service, but again most critics treated this behavior as distinctly at odds with Harvard's past. This is to forget that Harvard in the postwar period has offered honorary doctorates to the most truculent of the military men ranging from Douglas MacArthur to George Patton. (MacArthur apparently did not accept; Patton came to Harvard Yard in a blaze of glory.) Upon receiving his honorary doctorate, Admiral Chester Nimitz was introduced as the "Bold innovator in the years of mounting power, the conquering Admiral of the Pacific Basin,"[181] assuredly the language used by people whose natural idiom is Empire as a way of life. Some would excuse this as an expression of euphoria after triumph in World War II, but there are truly few signs of departure from this in the recent past. The decision in the late 1960s to present the Shah of Iran with an honorary degree is perhaps the most pathetic reminder of Harvard's age-long commitment to upholding social justice and human decency.

Conclusion

> The Program was outstanding. I cannot think of a more effective way to gain a better perspective on so many aspects of national security... I am certain this framework will serve me well for the rest of my career.
>
> **—Division Chief, CIA**
> **on his studies at the Kennedy School of Government, 1988**

Harvard University has proudly stood as a pillar in the construction and maintenance of the Cold War consensus. This essay has identified two features in the University's ongoing contribution to what W.A. Williams aptly called "Empire as a Way of Life." One is the marked contempt for democracy exhibited by most of Harvard's national security mandarins, graphically underscored by Kissinger's formulation that he and his cohorts are free to do with the world as they please because, "A scientific revolution has, for all practical purposes, removed technical limits from the exercise of power in foreign policy."[182] Second is the very limited range of views entertained by this intellectual elite. At the height of the war, McGeorge Bundy correctly noted that "on the main stage...the argument on Vietnam turns on tactics, not fundamentals," though, he conceded, "there are wild men in the wings." Harvard represents this stage center, and its intellectual establishment has been unwilling to challenge what Bundy calls the "fundamentals" of U.S. foreign policy.[183]

Now that Gorbachev has called off the Cold War, the Harvard intellectual component of the anti-Soviet industry should, in journalist Joe Conason's words, "start looking for honest work."[184] More than likely, however, those of us brusquely dismissed as "the wild men in the wings" will have to continue the resistance to their orthodoxies in the perilous years ahead.

Notes

1. Nathan Pusey, *Harvard and Cambridge* (pamphlet, 1959). Pusey's text was delivered in May 1959 at the Commander Hotel in Cambridge.

2. *Ibid.*

3. Colin Campbell, "The Harvard Factor," *New York Times Magazine*, July 20, 1986, p. 45.

4. Morison quoted in *ibid.*

5. Conant quoted in Mike Hirschorn, "What do you give a University that has Everything?" *New England Monthly*, June 1986, pp. 41-47.

6. Conant quoted in *Financial Report to Board of Overseers of Harvard College 1983-84* (Cambridge: Harvard University, 1985), p. 49.

7. Statistics and quotation from David Horowitz, "Sinews of Empire," *Ramparts*, October 1969. Much of the analysis which follows is indebted to this essay.

8. Theodore Draper, "Intellectuals in Power," *Encounter*, 49, 1977, p. 51.

9. Sorensen quoted in *ibid.*, p. 53.

10. Bundy quoted by Robin Winks, *Cloak and Gown: Scholars in the Secret War, 1939-61* (New York: Morrow, 1987), p. 115. For Hilsman, see R. Hilsman, *Strategic Intelligence and National Decisions* (Glencoe: Free Press, 1956.)

11. David Halberstam, *The Best and the Brightest* (Hammondsworth: Penguin, 1986 [1972]), p. 80.

12. *Ibid.*, p. 267.

13. Alexander Cockburn and James Ridgeway, "The Freeze Movement versus Reagan," *New Left Review*, 137, January-February 1983, pp. 7-10.

14. For a listing of the episodes in which nuclear weapons were brandished by U.S. policymakers, see Michio Kaku and Daniel Axelrod, *To Win a Nuclear War* (Boston: South End Press, 1987); and Fred Halliday, *The Making of the Second Cold War* (London: Verso, 1986), p. 50.

15. Mencken from *Prejudices: Second Series* (1920) quoted by Russell Jacoby, *The Last Intellectuals* (New York: Basic Books, 1987).

16. Read quoted by Noam Chomsky, *The Culture of Terrorism* (Boston: South End Press, 1988), pp. 2-3.

17. Bailey in *ibid.*, p. 2.

18. Huntington in *ibid.*

19. Kaiser, "The Right—And Wrong—National Security Advisors," *New York Times*, July 20, 1987, op. ed.

20. These quotations and sources have been compiled by Lawrence Shoup and William Minter, *Imperial Brain Trust* (New York: Monthly Review Press, 1977), pp. 4-5.

21. *Ibid.*, pp. 97-98.

22. Lundberg, *The Rockefeller Syndrome* (New York: Zebra/Lyle Stuart, 1976), pp. 289-290.

23. Shoup and Minter, pp. 13-19. For the quotations and account of Coolidge, see Robert McCaughey, "Four Academic Ambassadors," *Perspectives in American History*, 1979, pp. 574-583. See also Herbert Heaton, *A Scholar in Action: Edwin F. Gay* (Cambridge: Harvard University Press, 1952).

24. Shoup and Minter, p. 22.

25. *Ibid.*, chapter 4; pp. 162-163 for Bowman and War and Peace studies group quotations. See also Noam Chomsky, "The U.S.: From Greece to El Salvador," in Chomsky, Gittings, and Steele, eds., *Superpowers in Collision* (Hammondsworth: Penguin, 1984), pp. 24-58.

26. Halliday, chapter 1 and p. 92. For lists of Trilateralists and cogent analysis of its major doctrines, see Holly Sklar, ed., *Trilateralism* (Boston: South End Press, 1980).

27. Podhoretz quoted and Goebbels analogy from Noam Chomsky in *Granta*, 15, 1985, p. 129. Norman Birnbaum at the Spring 1985 *Salmagundi* conference spoke about Kristol and Podhoretz's homilies to the German right-wing.

28. It should be remarked that the neoconservative Glazer has been much more open-minded on the Middle East question than most of his liberal colleagues at Harvard.

29. Conant quoted by Jerry Sanders, *Peddlers of Crisis* (Boston: South End Press, 1983), p. 73. This is the definitive history of the Committee on the Present Danger. James Hershberg is currently completing what promises to be the most authoritative account of Conant's own role in the development of U.S. foreign policy.

30. *Boston Globe*, June 7, 1946, p. 11.

31. Sanders, pp. 73-76.

32. *Ibid.*, and chapter 3.

33. Text of NSC-68 in John Lewis Gaddis and Thomas H. Etzold, *Containment: Documents on American Policy and Strategy* (New York: Columbia University Press, 1978), pp. 385-442.

34. Paul Y. Hammond, "NSC-68: Prologue to Rearmament," in Schilling, Hammond, and Snyder, *Strategy, Politics, and Defense Budgets* (New York: Columbia University Press, 1962), pp. 267-378.

35. Sanders, pp. 44-53. Lovett quoted on p. 51.

36. To respond to the danger, Conant had previously criticized the Selective Service Act of 1948 as being inadequate for U.S. defense needs. According to Sanders, he wanted a system of universal military service and training, "whereby every eighteen year old would be enrolled in a program of training through a national militia system for ten years." He continued his crusade for universal military service throughout the 1950s, but modified his militia plan by endorsing direct enrollment in the armed forces. *Ibid.*, pp. 63 and 90.

37. Their hero was MacArthur, the aspiring shogun who at his most apocalyptic extreme during World War II declared that "Europe is a dying system. It is worn out and run down, and will become an economic and industrial hegemony of Soviet Russia... The lands touching the Pacific with their billions of inhabitants will determine the course of history for the next ten thousand years." MacArthur quoted in D. Horowitz, *The Free World Colossus* (New York: Hill and Wang, 1971), p. 102. See also Sanders, chapter 2.

38. The term *Lebensraum* is Sanders's.

39. Isaacson and Thomas, "When Wall St. Ruled the World," *Manhattan, Inc.,* September 1986, p. 162.

40. Shoup and Minter, p. 59.

41. Mark and Leonard Silk, *The American Establishment* (New York: Basic Books, 1980), p. 208.

42. Statistics derived from: Shoup and Minter, pp. 76-77 and *CFR Annual Report 1985-86* (New York: CFR, 1986).

43. Shoup and Minter.

44. See Horowitz.

45. John Marks and Victor Marchetti, *The CIA and the Cult of Intelligence* (New York: Dell, 1975), p. 69.

46. *Ibid.*

47. See J. Feldman, "Economic Conversion: An Alternative to Military Dependency in the University," unpublished manuscript, for the National Commission for Economic Conversion and Disarmament, Washington, D.C. Also see his *Universities in the Business of Repression: The Academic-Military-Industrial Complex and Central America* (Boston: South End Press, 1989).

48. Richard Higgins, "Harvard Probing Scholar's CIA aid," *Boston Globe,* October 11, 1985, p. 1. See also Colin Campbell, "Harvard Widens Inquiry in CIA Aid to Professor," *New York Times,* October 20, 1985, and later "A dillar, a dollar, an Embattled Scholar," *Newsweek,* January 13, 1986, p. 75.

49. Ford note published in *How Harvard Rules* (1969 edition).

50. Kristin Goss, "Scholars' Association Condemns Safran," *Harvard Crimson,* November 25, 1985, p. 1.

51. "Unhappy Times in Cambridge," *Time,* January 13, 1986, p. 62.

52. J. Trumpbour, "The Fall of Safran," *MERIP Middle East Report,* 138, January-February 1986, p. 38. Considering that Safran had received substantial help from staff and graduate students on his projects, the University's leniency also appeared to be at odds with a policy announced in 1977 amidst great fanfare that Harvard forbids faculty from making "unwitting use of any person for the CIA or other intelligence agencies..." *New York Times,* May 22, 1977, p. 40. To this day, Safran is entrusted by Harvard with the selection of the next generation of Middle Eastern scholars as a board member of the prestigious Kukin Fellowships for area studies.

53. Horowitz, *loc. cit.*, and Jeff McConnell, "The CIA's Charles River Connection," *Boston Globe*, October 13, 1985, p. A24.

54. John Ranelagh, *The Agency* (New York: Simon and Schuster, 1986), p. 192.

55. McConnell.

56. Daniel Guttman and Barry Willner, *The Shadow Government* (New York: Pantheon, 1976), p. 178.

57. One of Reagan's key Middle East advisors, Geoffrey Kemp, came from Tuft's Fletcher menagerie, as did the Israeli spy Pollard, a proud student of Ra'anan's.

58. Louis Wolf, "CIA Officers as Role Models," *Covert Action Information Bulletin*, Summer 1988, p. 68. For a profile of Neustadt and his utter contempt for democracy, see "The Neustadt Dossier," *New Left Review*, 51, September-October 1968, especially the introduction by Andrew Kopkind. A State Department official in the 1960s declared that under JFK, "Dick Neustadt was a senior pro-consul of the Empire." Neustadt himself is a much more modest chap, once telling an interviewer: "I'm a second-generation bureaucrat."

59. John Lukacs, "The Intellectual in Power: A Discussion," *Salmagundi*, 71, Spring-Summer 1986, p. 263. For Kissinger's view of power as an aphrodisiac, see *Time*, April 24, 1989, p. 31.

60. Alan Wolfe, "Henry's Nemesis," *The Nation*, July 23-30, 1983, p. 86.

61. *Ibid.*

62. The notion of nostalgia for the foul Kissinger is a theme of Alexander Cockburn in his "Beat the Devil" column for *The Nation*.

63. "Kissinger Urged Ban on TV Reports," *New York Times*, March 5, 1988, p. 5.

64. Michael J. Crozier, S. P. Huntington, and J. Watanuki, *The Crisis of Democracy* (New York: New York University Press, 1975), pp. 75 and 114.

65. *Ibid.*, p. 92.

66. *Ibid.*, pp. 61-62, 113-114. The term "democratic distemper" is introduced on page 102. He cites Harvard historian David Donald, on the consequences of the Jacksonian revolution in politics, as the architect of the term "excess of democracy."

67. *Ibid.*, pp. 75, 185. The remark on "higher education..." is co-authored in the study's appendix.

68. Zbigniew Brzezinski, *Between Two Ages: America's Role in the Technetronic Era* (New York: Viking Press, 1970), p. 18, and Cooper, Kaiser, and Masataka Kosaka, *Towards a Renovated International System*, Trilateral Commission: Triangle Paper 14, 1977, p. 19.

69. Brzezinski, pp. 32-33.

70. Beyond the vicarious pleasure received from pondering the United States perched upon the precipice of nuclear war, these theorists may be drawn to crisis management by some of its anti-democratic tendencies: leaders make

decisions of global magnitude free of interference from Congress, let alone wider publics. Crisis management theorists contributed to the dominance of "short war theory" in U.S. strategic thinking, the doctrine that any outbreak of global war would quickly go nuclear and, hence, that all battle planning should be contained within 90 day scenarios. United States Army Colonel Harry G. Summers observes, "This was deliberate. Short war theorists argued that in modern war there would be no time to follow constitutional procedures and involve Congress (and thereby the people) in the decision-making process." He adds that it was the army, and not the civilians, who raised objections to the short war theory, in particular Brigadier General John Vessey who was probably denied promotion for asking in the mid-1970s, what will happen on the 91st day? "As it then stood," concludes Summers, "on the 91st day, we'd either lose the war or be forced to resort to nuclear war, for our mobilization procedures were virtually non-existent." Harry G. Summers, "The Weapons of Bankruptcy," *The Guardian* (UK), July 10, 1989, p. 3.

71. Graham Allison, *The Essence of Decision* (Boston: Little, Brown, 1971), p. 1. See also E. May and R. Neustadt, *Thinking in Time* (New York: Free Press, 1985.) This critique relies heavily upon Noam Chomsky, *Turning the Tide* (Boston: South End Press, 1985), p. 172, and Stephen Shalom, "The Cuban Missile Crisis," *Zeta*, June 1988, p. 79.

72. Chomsky.

73. Thomas Schelling quoted in J. Anthony Lukas, "Class Reunion: Kennedy's Men Relive the Cuban Missile Crisis," *New York Times Magazine*, August 30, 1987.

74. Kuznetsov quoted by Shalom.

75. Allison, p. 39.

76. "Documentation: White House Tapes and Minutes of Cuban Missile Crisis," *International Security*, Summer 1985, pp. 164-203. See also Mark Trachtenberg's analysis in this same issue. For a commentary on the cited excerpt, see Alexander Cockburn, "Beat the Devil," *The Nation*, September 21, 1985, p. 230.

77. Seymour Hersh, *The Price of Power: Kissinger and the Nixon White House* (New York: Summit, 1983), especially pp. 110-111 and 250.

78. Statistics from Robert Muller, National President of the Vietnam Veterans of America, cited by David Dellinger, *Vietnam Revisited* (Boston: South End Press, 1986), p. 169.

79. Richard Barnet, *The Roots of War* (Baltimore: Penguin, 1973), p. 8.

80. McCaughey, pp. 575, 583.

81. State Department superior praising Kelley was Evan Young, cited by Frederick Propos, "Creating a Hard Line Toward Russia: The Training of State Department Soviet Experts," *Diplomatic History*, Summer 1984, pp. 209-226.

82. For reflections on the early Kennan's Germanophilism, see Ronald Steel, *Imperialists and Other Heroes* (New York: Random House, 1971). For Teuton-Slav polarity, see Caesar Voute, "Whose Europe," in Dan Smith and E.P. Thompson, eds., *Prospectus for a Habitable Planet* (Hammondworth: Penguin, 1987), pp. 149-171.

83. Stephen Cohen, "America's Russia: Can the Soviet Union Change?" *Socialism and Democracy*, 3, Fall/Winter 1986. In the following decade, Huntington and Brzezinski would introduce the concept of "oligarchical petrification" to characterize this inability to change. See discussion of this by Moshe Lewin, *The Gorbachev Phenomenon* (Berkeley: University of California Press, 1988). Given the basis of assumptions, academic Kremlinology failed utterly to anticipate the rise of *perestroika*. Compare the early '80s writings of Pipes and Ulam with, for instance, Daniel Singer's prescient analysis, *The Road to Gdansk: Poland and the USSR* (New York: Monthly Review Press, 1981). Singer, a journalist and intellectual close to Deutscher, quite predictably found himself ignored in the universities. It should be said that Ulam's record was marginally better than Pipes's, the former at least willing to entertain the future possibility of Finlandization in Central Europe.

84. Edward Herman and Frank Brodhead, *The Rise and Fall of the Bulgarian Connection* (New York: Sheridan Square Publishers, 1986) documents this episode in intellectual irresponsibility. See also Gilles Perrault, "La grotesque fable de la filière bulgare," in Claude Julien, Jacques Decornoy, et al., eds., *La Communication: victime des marchands*, manière de voir 3 (Paris: Le Monde Diplomatique, November 1988), pp. 25-27.

85. Unpublished letter from Carleton Coon to Benjamin Wright, December 1, 1947.

86. Robert McCaughey, *International Studies and Academic Enterprise: A Chapter in the Enclosure of American Learning* (New York: Columbia University Press, 1984), p. 164.

87. Jonathan Wiener, "Talcott Parsons' Role: Bringing Nazi Sympathizers to the U.S.," *The Nation*, March 6, 1989, pp. 289, 306-309. According to Christopher Simpson, *Blowback* (New York: Weidenfeld and Nicolson, 1988), p. 117, Gustav Hilger, a senior figure in the Nazi Foreign Office, was given research positions at Harvard's Russian Research Center as a "cover" for his CIA activities.

88. *Harvard Crimson*, February 22, 1989, p. 1.

89. Tamara Deutscher recounts this episode in Tamara Deutscher, ed., *Isaac Deutscher: Marxism, Wars, and Revolutions* (London: Verso, 1984), p. xxv. It should be acknowledged that Deutscher's oeuvre has provoked divisions among progressive historians: his caution towards working-class insurgencies in the East and his faith in the emergence of reformist currents within the Communist Party hierarchy, his skepticism towards Bukharin and his case for the inevitability of Stalinism, and his estimate that Stalin's atrocities numbered in the single digit millions rather than 20 million as recently asserted by Medvedev. On the last issue, the historian Sheila Fitzpatrick

(interviewed by A. Cockburn, "Beat the Devil," *The Nation*, March 6, 1989), as well as several demographic historians of the USSR, have recently concluded that Deutscher's figures are probably closer to the mark than Medvedev's, though the jury may still be out. See Barbara Anderson and Brian Silver, "Demographic Analysis and Population Catastrophes in the Soviet Union," *Slavic Review*, 1985, as well as Fainsod and Hough's *How the Soviet Union is Governed* (1979). Currently Broué's monumental biography, *Trotsky* (Paris: Fayard, 1988), has aggressively attacked Deutscher for factual and chronological errors in his Trotsky trilogy. But for all those anxious to dethrone Deutscher from his status as the greatest biographer of the Bolsheviks, his untimely death in 1967 may be enough to explain why the historical profession has still failed to produce a compelling biography of Lenin.

90. Richard Pipes, *Soviet Strategy in Europe* (New York: Crane, Ruzzak, and Co., 1976); pp. 3-42 of this text reprinted in Hoffmann and Fleuron, eds., *The Conduct of Soviet Foreign Policy* (New York: Aldine, 1980), pp. 353-354.

91. *Ibid.*

92. For Ulam's views on Solzhenitsyn and anti-Semitism, see Richard Grenier, "Solzhenitsyn and Anti-Semitism: A New Debate," *New York Times*, November 13, 1985, III, p. 21. For a discussion of Solzhenitsyn's *Gulag Archipelago* and its treatment of Nazi collaboration, see Roy Medvedev, "Solzhenitsyn: Truth and Politics," in Roy Medvedev, ed., *Samizdat Register 2* (New York: Norton, 1981), pp. 295-323.

93. A. Ulam, *The Unfinished Revolution* (New York: Random House, 1960), p. 97. See critique by Chomsky in "Objectivity and Liberal Scholarship," in Noam Chomsky, *American Power and the New Mandarins* (New York: Vintage, 1969), p. 29.

94. *Ibid.*, pp. 4-5. See also Chomsky, p. 32.

95. Many of these examples of generosity are culled from Alexander Cockburn's response to Aryeh Neier and Istvan Deak, *The Nation*, June 23, 1984, p. 754.

96. Truman's Assistant Secretary quoted in Chomsky, *American Power and the New Mandarins*, p. 129.

97. Kennan quoted in John Saville, "Ernest Bevin and the Cold War," *Socialist Register 1984* (London: Merlin Press, 1984), p. 93.

98. Sanders, p. 150.

99. *Ibid.*, pp. 198-199.

100. R. Pipes, "Strategic Superiority," *New York Times*, February 6, 1977, sect. 4, p. 15. Discussed by Robert Scheer, *With Enough Shovels* (New York: Vintage, 1983), p. 55.

101. *Ibid.*

102. Richard Pipes, "Team B: The Reality Behind the Myth," *Commentary*, October 1986, p. 35.

103. Scheer, p. 64.

104. Pipes, "Team B...," p. 40.

105. Scheer, pp. 64-65.

106. *Ibid.*, p. 55.

107. Stephen Cohen, *Sovieticus* (New York: Norton Books, 1986), p. 166.

108. AOS quoted in "Middle East Studies Network in the U.S.," MERIP Middle East Reports, 38, June 1975, p. 3. This essay provided much useful information and an updated version is desperately needed. See also McCaughey, *International Studies and Academic Enterprise.*

109. CMES unpublished documents.

110. *CMES Annual Report 1962-63* (Cambridge: Harvard Foundation for Advanced Study and Research, January 1963), p. 21.

111. It was often said that in his fundraising forays Meyer loved to upbraid skinflint oil executives with such lines as, "$25,000? C'mon John, you guys piss that away in two seconds up there."

112. For the origins of the Khalidi controversy, often presented as a defense of the University's autonomy from Arab wealth, see Fern Reiss, "Donation for New Arab Studies Chair Criticized by Some Faculty Members," *Harvard Crimson*, May 21, 1982, p. 1.

113. Perhaps this is too much of a reading of Dunlop's casual remark, but the recent appointment of Princeton historian Roy Mottahedeh, "a Widener library type," to replace Safran is designed in part to regain the Center's good name. An important intellectual, whose *From the Mantle of the Prophet* could well be to the Iranian Revolution what Edmund Wilson's *To the Finland Station* was for the Bolshevik Revolution, Mottahedeh still considers himself an innocent medievalist, above the fray of politics, and, hence, ultimately less able to check the aspiring national security mandarins. Though they will receive no active encouragement from Mottahedeh, Safran's followers today remain well ensconced at the Center. Quotation of Dunlop from Simha Flapan, interview. Comparison of Mottahedeh to Wilson explicitly made by Val Moghadan, "Socialism or Anti-Imperialism: The Left and Revolution in Iran," *New Left Review*, November-December 1987, p. 15n. While appreciative of Mottahedeh's scholarly contributions, she also provides a critique of the sexist subtext of his work.

Mottahedeh's deep commitment to traditional scholarship and lack of enthusiasm for the frequently worthless ephemera of the national security scholars has probably not endeared him to some of Bok's apparatchiks. They seem to prefer the high profile pretensions of the Kennedy School where heads of state are whisked in and out, and where regions are treated as objects of policy and not subject to the painstaking, richly textured study of the best traditional scholarship. One former member of CMES's Executive Committee has voiced the fear that Harvard will continue to build up programs and initiatives on the Middle East at the more politically pliable Kennedy School and in turn allow the already CIA-damaged CMES to stagnate. Such a scenario could render Mottahedeh's effort at reviving serious scholarship most precarious.

A possible prototype of a new Kennedy School initiative on the region is the Institute for Social and Economic Policy in the Middle East, founded in 1983 at Brandeis and relocated to Harvard in late 1988. Chaired by former HEW Secretary Joseph Califano and directed by Professor Leonard Hausman, the Institute, armed with a one million dollar grant from John Cardinal O'Connor's New York-based Near East Welfare Association, seeks to foster economic, educational, and development cooperation in the Middle East. It is too early to tell how the Institute will evolve, though some judge its Vice Chair Alexander Haig, credited with giving Israel the "green light" permitting the bombardment and destruction of Beirut, Lebanon in 1982 [see N. Chomsky, *The Fateful Triangle* (Boston: South End Press, 1983), p. 215], to be an inauspicious choice for leadership. In Hausman's defense, he has had a measure of success in bringing together Arabs, Christians, and Jews from the region, and in an interview with myself stresses that he would like to have such serious scholars as Mottahedeh and Walid Khalidi on his academic advisory board. Moreover, even a reputed critic of Hausman interviewed for this book regards his aims as modest and up-front, and denounced my suggestion that Harvard and the Kennedy School might have a more ambitious long-term agenda as reckless "conspiracy theory."

114. Peretz speech, Harvard Hillel, 1985-86 term, response to author's question. Banfield letter, *Boston Sunday Globe*, December 15, 1985, p. A6.

115. Safran, *Israel: The Embattled Ally* (Cambridge: Harvard University Press, 1978). The critique that follows relies heavily upon Noam Chomsky, "Armageddon is well located," in *Towards a New Cold War* (New York: Pantheon, 1982), chapter 12.

116. Cited by Chomsky, p. 286.

117. *Ibid.*, p. 279.

118. David Landes, "Palestinians—Another View," *Christian Science Monitor*, January 11, 1977, p. 14. See critique by William Cleveland, "The Palestinians and the Dimensions of Historical Legitimacy," in Glenn Perry, ed., *Palestine: Continuing Dispossession* (Belmont, MA: AAUG Press, 1986).

119. Edward Said, "Conspiracy of Praise," in Edward Said and Christopher Hitchens, *Blaming the Victims* (London: Verso, 1987), p. 30.

120. Pipes was originally recruited to Harvard's Center for Middle Eastern Studies by Safran. He is today stationed at the University of Pennsylvania.

121. Norman Finkelstein, "Disinformation and the Palestine Question," in *ibid.*, p. 34.

122. Cleveland, pp. 108-109.

123. *Ibid.*, p. 108.

124. See response to Landes by Paul Farmer, letter, *The New Republic*, April 7, 1986, p. 2.

125. Martin Peretz in *The New Republic*, May 7, 1984; see critique by Christopher Hitchens, "Minority Report," *The Nation*, May 5, 1984.

126. Will quoted in *The New Republic* promotional leaflet.

127. Alexander Cockburn, *Corruptions of Empire* (London: Verso, 1987), pp. 407-408.

128. Abraham eventually found a new publisher for his corrected study of Weimar Germany. But when a distinguished European scholar, Volker Berghahn, praised the new version in the *New York Times Book Review*, he was denounced by Abraham's U.S. enemies, especially Yale University's Henry Turner.

129. "International Human Rights Organizations and the Palestine Question," *MERIP Middle East Report*, January-February 1988, pp. 15-16 and 20n.

130. Paul Findley, *They Dare to Speak Out* (Westport: Lawrence Hill, 1985), p. 183.

131. This was Bok's way of introducing Peres before the latter's speech at Harvard's Kennedy School of Government.

132. Safran declared this in an interview with the Boston-based *Jewish Advocate*, January 16, 1986.

133. Mussolini quoted by Michael Ledeen, "Italian Jews and Fascism," *Judaism*, Summer 1969, p. 292.

134. Hannah Arendt, *Eichmann in Jerusalem* (Hammondsworth: Penguin, 1977 [1963]), especially chapter 4. For more detailed case studies, see the polemical account of Lenni Brenner, *Zionism in the Age of the Dictators* (Westport: Lawrence Hill, 1983).

135. Mylroie and Safran warmly received Iraqi Ambassador Nizar Hamdoon to CMES in 1986, while Mylroie wrote letters and editorials calling for U.S. support of Iraq, despite the stark reality that Iraq illegally started the Iran-Iraq war and subsequently resorted to chemical warfare, including later against its own Kurdish minority. Baghdad Radio in 1982 announced to Iranians that there was a "certain kind of insecticide for every kind of insect." *MERIP Middle East Report*, November-December 1988, p. 3. While the West is in the midst of congratulating itself for its support of human rights in China, Simon Leys observes in *Le Monde* (July 14, 1989, p. 2) that "in the past year, the Iraqi government has undertaken the annihilation of villages of its Kurdish minority by means of gas and chemical weapons—yet, the reaction of Washington was to double the export credits granted to Iraq."

136. Rusk quoted by D. Horowitz, "The China Scholars and U.S. Intelligence," *Ramparts*, February 1972, p. 33.

137. Lopez, *The Harvard Mystique* (New York: Macmillan, 1979), pp. 134-135.

138. McCaughey, *International Studies and Academic Enterprise*, pp. 232-234.

139. Cockburn, *Corruptions of Empire*, pp. 417-418.

140. Merle Miller, "Washington, the World, and Joseph Alsop," *Harper's*, June 1968, p. 43.

141. For Lippmann critique and quotations see Cockburn's review of Ronald Steel's biography in *Corruptions of Empire*, pp. 193-198.

142. Clyde Haberman, review of Reischauer's *My Life Between Japan and America*, New York Times, August 20, 1986, III, p. 21. For testimony of Fairbank, see Horowitz, "The China Scholars...," p. 34. For a sympathetic view of Fairbank, see Paul Evans's richly documented *John K. Fairbank and the American Understanding of China* (Oxford: Blackwell, 1988). Even so, he shows how slow Fairbank was to challenge the war effort. He also indicates that Reischauer leaned harder to the political right than Fairbank, the Japan expert once accusing his Sinologist colleague of using a "Communist yardstick" during the collaboration on their textbook on East Asian civilization.

143. Fairbank and Reischauer quoted by Chomsky, *After the Cataclysm*, p. 311.

144. Rahv quoted by Chomsky, *Towards a New Cold War*, p. 86.

145. What follows relies on the citations of Reischauer's writing and the critique provided by John Dower in his introduction to *Origins of the Modern Japanese State: Selected Writings of E.H. Norman* (New York: Pantheon, 1975), p. 44.

146. *Ibid.*, p. 46.

147. *Ibid.*, p. 49.

148. *Ibid.*, p. 48.

149. Comte quoted and discussed by Martin Nicolaus, "The Professional Organization of Sociology," in Robin Blackburn, *Ideology in Social Science* (Glasgow: Fontana, 1972), p. 47.

150. Horowitz quoted in *ibid.*, p. 51. For quotation of Ross, see B. Ehrenreich, *Fear of Falling* (New York: Pantheon, 1989), pp. 134-135.

151. This critique is deeply indebted to William Buxton, *Talcott Parsons and the Capitalist Nation-State: Political Sociology as a Strategic Profession* (Toronto: University of Toronto Press, 1985). For the point about Kluckhohn, see Buxton's unpublished manuscript delivered at the Center for European Studies, Harvard University, 1987-88 term.

152. Commager quoted by Göran Therborn, *Science, Class, and Society* (London: Verso, 1980), pp. 15-16. For the sycophantic reactions of U.S. intellectuals to Spencer at the Delmonico banquet, see Richard Hofstadter, *Social Darwinism in American Thought* (Boston: Beacon Press, 1955), pp. 48-49. Parsons's break with Spencer's tradition is explored by Therborn.

153. Talcott Parsons, *The Structure of Social Action* (New York: Free Press, 1968 [1937]), p. 3.

154. Barbara S. Heye, "The Harvard Pareto Circle," *Darwin to Einstein: Historical Studies on Science and Belief* (London: Longmann, 1980,) pp. 134-135.

155. T. Parsons, "Propaganda and Social Control," (1942) in *Essays in Sociological Theory* (New York: Free Press, 1964), cited by Buxton, pp. 96-97.

156. Christopher Lasch, *The Agony of the American Left* (New York: Knopf, 1969), p. 64.

157. S.M. Lipset, "Political Sociology," (1959), reprinted in R.K. Merton, et al., *Sociology in the United States of America* (New York: Basic Books, 1965), pp. 98-100. This critique of Lipset relies on Buxton, chapter 11. Lipset quoted on pp. 230-231.

158. Seymour Martin Lipset quoted by Jürgen Habermas, *Toward a Rational Society* (Boston: Beacon Press, 1970) p. 14.

159. Lipset from *Political Man*, cited by Buxton, p. 234. See also critique by Ehrenreich, pp. 110-111. Anticipating the obvious objection that the working class has found itself at the forefront of numerous progressive and democratic struggles in the nineteenth and twentieth centuries, Lipset writes that the unsophisticated masses were simply following their more cultured leaders, who tended to be better soaked in middle class values. "The fact that the movement's ideology is democratic does not mean its supporters actually understand the implications," he concluded. S.M. Lipset, "Working-Class Authoritarianism," in *Political Man* (Baltimore: Johns Hopkins, [1959] 1981, pp. 114 and 123.

160. For an analysis of Bell and Rogin, see Ellen Schrecker, *No Ivory Tower* (New York: Oxford University Press, 1986), pp. 344-345.

161. In summarizing the thought of Jean-François Lyotard, the intellectual historian Peter Dews is the source of the graphic expression concerning the twentieth century's liquidation of the hopes of modernity.

162. Daniel Bell, *The End of Ideology* (Glencoe: Free Press, 1960), see his epilogue. See also Peter Dews's critique in his introduction to *Habermas: Autonomy and Solidarity* (London: Verso, 1986). The term "end of ideology" may originally have been used by Raymond Aron.

163. Daniel Bell, "Notes on the Post-Industrial Society: Part I," *The Public Interest*, 6, 1967, pp. 24-35. See critique by Chomsky, "Objectivity and Liberal Scholarship," in *American Power and the New Mandarins*, pp. 23-158.

164. Ways quoted by Andrew Kopkind, *America: The Mixed Curse* (Hammondsworth: Penguin, 1969), pp. 234-235.

165. Bell quoted by Chomsky, *American Power and the New Mandarins*, pp. 31-32.

166. Dews.

167. Buxton, pp. 239-240, 265. Contrary to my claim, Anthony Lewis in his column for the *New York Times* (January 29, 1989) argues that Bell's "end of ideology" thesis today applies well to the Third World. For critiques of this emerging view, see A. Cockburn, "Beat the Devil," *The Nation*, April 17, 1989, and S. Shalom, "Triumphant Capitalism?," *Zeta Magazine*, April 1989. As Cockburn remarks, "...when it comes to the matter of whether capitalism is 'winning,' trust the evidence of your senses. Look at the miserable shacks in the *compamentos* on the edges of Santiago. Or the *favela* Rocinha, sprawling up the hillside not 200 yards from the high-rise residential fortresses of Rio de Janeiro's middle class. Or the bodies bundled in niches on New York's

streets and lodged amid the bushes under the Los Angeles freeways. This is victory?"

168. S. Huntington, *Political Order in Changing Societies* (New Haven: Yale University Press, 1968), pp. 136-138. Also S. Huntington, "The Democratic Distemper," in N. Glazer and I. Kristol, eds. *The American Commonwealth—1976* (New York: Basic Books, 1976), p. 37. Both cited and discussed by Buxton, pp. 242-243.

169. S. Huntington, *Military Intervention: Political Involvement and the Un-lessons of Vietnam* (Chicago: Adlai Stevenson Institute of International Affairs, 1968), pp. 24-25. See also Buxton, p. 243.

170. L. Pye, "Description, Analysis, and Sensitivity to Change," in A. Ranney, *Political Science and Public Policy* (Chicago: Markham, 1966), p. 260. See also Buxton, p. 251.

171. Everett quoted by R. Paquette, "The Everett-Del Monte Connection," *Diplomatic History*, Winter 1987, p. 20.

172. Macmillan quoted by Carr, "The Invention of Latin America," *New York Review of Books*, March 3, 1988, p. 29.

173. *Ibid.*

174. Robert S. Leiken, *25th Anniversary Report: Harvard Class of 1961* (1986), pp. 979-980.

175. Alexander Cockburn, "Ashes and Diamonds," *LA Weekly*, May 23, 1986.

176. Gore Vidal, interview, "Surrealism and Patriotism," *New Left Review*, 149, January-February 1985, p. 100.

177. Barnet, p. 115.

178. Jack Newfield, "War Wimps: The Sequel," *Village Voice*, July 23, 1985, pp. 15-17.

179. John Gregory Dunne, "The War That Won't Go Away," *New York Review of Books*, September 26, 1986.

180. Norman Birnbaum, editorial, *The Nation*, January 10, 1987, p. 10.

181. *Boston Globe*, June 7, 1946.

182. Kissinger quoted by Lewis Lapham, *Money and Class in America*, (New York: Weidenfeld and Nicolson, 1988), p. 121.

183. Bundy quoted by Chomsky, "The Responsibility of Intellectuals," in Theodore Roszak, ed., *The Dissenting Academy* (New York: Vintage, 1968), p. 267.

184. Conason quoted in Jamin Raskin, "The People's Mort," *Zeta*, February 1989, p. 69. Now that Gorbachev has called off the Cold War, the *Wall Street Journal* has suggested that the United States should concentrate on issues of development and restoring order in the Third World. Anti-terrorism may provide the cover for many of these interventions, instead of anti-communism. Meanwhile, Gorbachev will likely decline providing support to national liberation movements, giving the U.S. proponents of "restoring order"

and "fighting terrorism" a freer hand. As Kremlinologist Dmitri Simes of the Carnegie Endowment gleefully expressed it in the last *New York Times* think piece of 1988 on the Cold War: "[the] apparent decline in the Soviet threat...makes military power more useful as a United States foreign policy instrument...against those who contemplate challenging important American interests." These are the sort of problems that will preoccupy the national security thinkers during the Cold War thaw. Commenting on the *Wall Street Journal's* editorials, Andrew Edna Duffy summarizes the new view: It is time "to shift attention from the second, communist world to the third world and the threat it constitutes." See A.E. Duffy, "'World's Elsewhere': Reading Third World Novels," *Harvard Graduate Society Newsletter*, Winter 1989, p. 1.

Still there are those at Harvard who call for a renewal of traditional forms of Cold War vigilance. Richard Pipes in "The Russians Are Still Coming," *New York Times*, October 9, 1989, p. A17, declares that Gorbachev's new thinking, "projected with all the propaganda means at its disposal" and with "the desired effect of blurring the perception of the Soviet Union as a hostile power," has allowed the USSR and "its clients in Cambodia, Angola, Nicaragua and Afghanistan" to grow "stronger at the expense of U.S. allies."

Living with the Bomb
The World According to Bok

Andrew Kopkind

In 1983 Mobilization for Survival sponsored a referendum to make Cambridge a nuclear-free zone. Harvard history professor Ernest May led a massive half-million dollar campaign against the proposal, funded by the weapons industry, including Cambridge's Draper Labs. Harvard and MIT presidents both attacked the proposal on the grounds of academic freedom. The largest spending per vote cast in an U.S. election up to that point had its desired effect. The ballot question was defeated.

In the Bok era, Harvard University does see itself as having a special mission in addressing the nuclear arms race. The University's "Living with Nuclear Weapons" project arose explicitly in response to the massive upsurge of protest against nuclear weapons in the early 1980s. Not all were enthralled with this venture. The Living with Nuclear Weapons project, suggests Norman Birnbaum, is the intellectual equivalent of a nineteenth century university announcing a "Living with Slavery" project in the aftermath of the Dred Scott decision. The leaders of the Harvard enterprise, Joseph Nye, Albert Carnesale, and Graham Allison, are particularly close to Massachusetts Governor Michael Dukakis, so the latter's unwillingness to renounce first use and other scenarios for nuclear war may owe something to their counsel. Nye's own magnum opus, *Nuclear Ethics*, is seen as the most "liberal" among the outpouring of books from this group, but in it he expresses thinly veiled contempt for people in the peace movement. This is hardly surprising for the Living with Nuclear Weapons group claims to be above politics, neither hawks nor doves but owls. Owls, they proclaim, are wiser than the others. What they fail to mention is that owls are also among the most predatory of birds, manifestly lethal to numerous living things. In this essay, previously published in *The Nation* (June 4, 1983, © 1983 *The Nation* magazine, The Nation Associates, Inc.), Andrew Kopkind explains the genesis of the Living with Nuclear Weapons project and why their wisdom spells peril.

When Harvard University encounters nuclear weaponry, they do so as equals. The United States's premier intellectual enterprise—and pre-eminent political concern—both command the center of national attention; there they compete for money, media, and moral influence. No wonder, then, that Harvard's historic treatment of the nuclear issue, *Living with Nuclear Weapons*,[1] is written with the kind of respect, reasonableness—even grudging affection—that one rival is expected to show for another. It's a pity that the bomb is in no position to return the favor.

In his commencement address in 1982, president Derek Bok announced that Harvard would join the nuclear debate. Bok was inspired by the columnist James Reston, the middlebrow muse of *The New York Times* who pointed out that the controversy surrounding nuclear weapons was being influenced more by political demonstration than by public education. Anti-nuclear activists staged a massive rally for a nuclear freeze in New York City. Throughout the spring, New England towns within a stone's throw of Harvard Yard had been passing anti-nuclear resolutions. An uncommon political excitement now energized college campuses that had snoozed through the 1970s. "So far," Reston wrote, "the demonstrators have outnumbered the educators" in mobilizing the public response to fear of nuclear war.

The Bok Initiative, as it came to be called around Cambridge, offered a Harvard education of sorts as a substitute for the burgeoning political movement. That education came in three parts. In the first two, Bok proposed courses and meetings for the University community and outreach programs on nuclear matters for reporters. The principal momentum of the initiative, however, would be provided by a book, the projectile of choice in any academic arsenal.

Bok wanted *Living with Nuclear Weapons* to be "an objective account of the basic facts about nuclear arms control." Although no single book could express all the views on the subject represented throughout the University, Bok said the study would express Harvard's "institutional responsibility to educate the public as a whole." Accordingly, five of the institution's most responsible figures were enlisted to produce the study. All are members of one or both of Harvard's foreign policy institutes, the Center for Science and International Affairs (CSIA) and the Center for International Affairs (C.F.I.A.—the "F" is given capital status for obvious reasons). They were:

Paul Doty, a chemist by profession. Doty had worked on the Manhattan Project as a young man, and much later had served in the Kennedy and Johnson administrations. He then raised a bundle from McGeorge Bundy's Ford Foundation and set up the CSIA, which he now runs out of the John F. Kennedy School of Government (a semiautonomous Harvard property) "pretty much as his own shop," as another study group member remarked. Bundy and Doty share an interest in arms control at the highest diplomatic level, and Doty has a reputation as a private go-between for U.S. government interests in Soviet-American dealings.

Samuel Huntington, director of the C.F.I.A., an outfit more integrated than Doty's into Harvard's Arts and Sciences structure. The two centers vie for privileges and prerequisites in the Cambridge constellation. Huntington earned the sobriquet "Mad Dog" for his part in setting up the pacification program in South Vietnam during the late period of war, and he continues to represent the Cold War faction in the foreign policy establishment. He also served on Jimmy Carter's National Security Council.

Albert Carnesale, academic dean of the Kennedy School. He was a SALT negotiator under President Nixon and headed a delegation to the international nuclear fuel recycling talks under President Carter.

Stanley Hoffmann, chairman of Harvard's Center for European Studies. He is associated with the C.F.I.A., although he habitually plays dove to Huntington's hawk (or, as it is sometimes said, pussycat to the mad dog). Unlike the other five, Hoffmann has never been in government, and yet he seems perennially poised for power in the next liberal Democratic administration.

Joseph Nye, Jr., who has feet in both foreign policy centers, enabling him to swing between the two academic power blocs. He was in Carter's State Department and is frequently considered likely for a high office in a future administration.

The careers and institutional affiliations of the members of the study group are significant especially insofar as they shape the book's overall approach. *Living with Nuclear Weapons* is not, after all, an academic treatise untouched by the heated political atmosphere in which it was conceived. Despite Bok's insistence that it serve as a neutral "fact sheet" for the general public, the book performs a political act, an act informed by the interests, the constituencies, the histories, and the aspirations of its authors, as well as those of its sponsoring University.

Bok hoped the study would be ready for commencement in 1983 so that he would be able to announce that it took exactly the year to deliver on his promise. The study group worked through the fall term of 1982, aided by the usual complement of graduate student writers and researchers, and had a draft ready just after the New Year. There was a great deal of wrangling and lobbying in round-the-clock sessions. "On the 30th and 31st of December, we had an eighteen-hour meeting," Hoffmann told me. "Some colleagues were piqued at not being included in the group," he continued. "Nuclear expertise at this university is not limited to these five experts."

The draft was sent to more than a dozen outsiders for comments. Some made minor suggestions: others, like Thomas Schelling, a strategic studies specialist, who submitted a forty-page essay, were more generous with their views. "Outsiders helped us erode one chapter with which I particularly disagreed," Hoffmann reported; given his history of disagreement with Huntington, it's not hard to imagine who was most responsible for the offending segment. At the end, the professors elevated Scott Sagan, a graduate student under Hoffmann and Huntington, to a co-authorship credit for his work on the book.

What finally emerged was a dense and somewhat uneven document which appears to have been "negotiated," as several critics have noted, rather than written. Its organizing principle, if one can be discerned, is the creation of a center in the nuclear debate between the extremes of radical disarmament and frenzied militarization. "It will be criticized by people to the right and the left," Nye told me with a certain satisfaction. "There are not many Edward Tellers or Jonathan Schells among us."

Bok hoped that the book would be factual rather than prescriptive, but when the authors got down to work they realized that analysis logically entails recommendation. For example, the "facts" of U.S. strategic requirements in nuclear delivery systems inevitably lead to a discussion about the need for the B-1 bomber. The group is against that weapon. But the facts lead the authors to favor deployment of new missiles in Europe and development of the Stealth bomber.

Indeed, the facts demand that the authors oppose a full nuclear freeze, disregard George Kennan's proposal to cut the missile stock by 50 percent, and reserve opinion on a "no first use" policy. On the other hand, the facts compel them to argue for moderation in arms-spending increases, for continued arms control negotiations and against abrogation of the Anti-Ballistic Missile Treaty. About the MX, they concede that there is "merit in the arguments on both sides."

Hoffmann finds these recommendations "wishy-washy," the "lowest common denominator" of the various opinions in the group. But the political gravity of the book is centered in the analytical section, which is less factual and much more prescriptive than the authors acknowledge.

"We didn't talk about the shape of the political debate," Nye recalled. "We talked about the issues." In fact, the shape of the debate seems to have been determined without discussion. The book postulates a Hobbesian world of all against all, where only a "balancing act" can avert mutually assured destruction. Deterrence is an unassailable corollary of that postulate. Since the authors live in the bosom of U.S. policy, they see Soviet wolves at every door.

U.S. interests around the world are not questioned in the book, whether those interests involve Middle Eastern oil, Central American tribute, or Far Eastern markets. That U.S. nuclear strategy may be marshaled to advance imperial interests rather than to deter Soviet aggression is a notion that never pops into view. Kennedy's management of the Cuban Missile Crisis is invoked reverentially to exemplify the persistence of the Soviet military threat and the need for forceful deterrence. No mention is made here of Kennedy's hostile and aggressive policy toward the Cuban revolution, or of his crusade to open the Third World to U.S. influence and control.

The unarticulated political function of *Living with Nuclear Weapons* is directly connected to the unexamined political assessment of the global condition that the study offers. A status-quo description must deliver a status-quo prescription: deterrence rather than disarmament. Jonathan Schell argued in *The Fate of the Earth* that it is necessary to "reinvent politics" in order to avert the nuclear holocaust. The Harvard professors have their hearts and minds set on the politics that exist in what they see as the "real world." Schell's suggestion would reinvent them out of jobs, identities, and positions of power.

The freeze and disarmament movements are small attempts to begin the reinvention process, and academic and diplomatic experts—joined in the Harvard study group—are anxious about the process. Harvard is hip-deep in the intellectual apparatus of the national security state. Its two international affairs centers constitute an informal brain trust for strategic policymaking. The competition between them only increases pressure for their representatives to find the exact center of the debate; it also encourages them to define the debate in their own terms so that their University can have it. If an institution can *want*, Harvard wants to own the debate over nuclear weapons.

Bok's book is a major effort to assert proprietary rights on the nuclear issue. Its argument is aimed at the most worrisome scenario: the emergence of a popular anti-nuclear movement. The cold warriors of the Carter and Reagan administrations destroyed the old center of the debate, and in the new disruptive conditions that movement started to flourish. In a way, *Living with Nuclear Weapons* packages old ideas in new, academic colors. It's odd, but understandable, how Harvard manages in every generation to give the best and the brightest a bad name.

Notes

1. By The Harvard Nuclear Study Group: Albert Carnesale, Paul Doty, Stanley Hoffmann, Samuel P. Huntington, Joseph S. Nye, Jr., Scott D. Sagan, with a foreword by Derek Bok (Harvard University Press and Bantam Books).

Jackboot Liberals

Alexander Cockburn

Now that we are in the Age of Bush, it bears reminding that some of the most crackpot reaction of this epoch has been spawned not just by hangers-on from the Heritage Foundation or Reverend Falwell's Liberty College brigade, but by key members of Harvard's liberal and not-so-liberal academic establishment. Written in the early days of Reagan's second term, Alexander Cockburn's parting shot is an antidote to those who naively associate Harvard with iconoclasm and progressive ideas. Ironically, his essay suggests that Harvard liberals Coles and Riesman inadvertently hatched George Bush's 1988 presidential campaign strategy, a strategy that was based primarily on ritual invocation of the Pledge of Allegiance and unflagging denunciation of the ACLU. (Copyright © Alexander Cockburn 1985)

Now that four more conservative years have been officially inaugurated by Ronald Reagan, we may as well remember that much of the damage associated with the rightward swerve of the *Zeitgeist* is not being inflicted by Birchers or kooks from the Moral Majority but by upstanding members of the supposedly respectable intellectual community. Anyone who doubts this should look at the "Thanksgiving Statement" issued by 27 academics toward the end of 1984, urging schools to instill good character in students and warning that "schools in general are not doing enough to counter the symptoms of serious decline in youth character."

This statement is reminiscent of the muscle-and-blood national authoritarianism preached by Thomas Arnold and by subsequent, more explicitly fascist educators. "Character," said the report, "is often revealed in the concern and affection we display toward other members of our group or country. These traits are fostered through the learning of what Sidney Hook called 'the history of our free society, its martyrology, and its national traditions.' Such learning encourages students to be patriotic, to be loyal to our society, and to care about the welfare of their fellow Americans." The report recommended frequent and high-quality ceremonial activities, stressing "contribution."

An article by Charles Claffey in the *Boston Globe* (November 25, 1984) quoted local notables enthusing about this horrible document. Nathan Glazer—one of the report's signatories and a professor at the Harvard School of Education—attributed part of the problems of young people, in Claffey's evocation of his views, to "an over permissiveness arising from the fear of being considered intolerant." David Riesman, professor emeritus of social sciences at Harvard, said that he was heartened by the report and that "critical concerns of character and quality" had to be addressed. "The problem is how—in our delirium of due process and the ACLU—to carry this out."

These barbaric views were capably matched by another "liberal," Dr. Robert Coles, child shrink on the Harvard Medical School staff and recently self-appointed flagellator of "elitist" freezeniks, on behalf of his blue-collar buddies on the faculty. Coles told Claffey he liked the report. In reference to a seventeen-year-old girl's refusal to salute the flag at a school in the Boston area, Coles added: "There's something wrong when you can't salute the flag in a school classroom without creating a constitutional issue. Things like reciting a school prayer and saluting the flag are part of belonging to a society...we are creating a state of anarchy when what kids need are control and discipline."

By an illuminating coincidence, the *Times Literary Supplement* (November 30, 1984) contained a review by Gordon Craig of Christa Kamenetsky's *Children's Literature in Hitler's Germany*. Craig cited the Nazis' plan to emphasize "the duties of the individual to the state and the imperatives of racial awareness and upon character-building and physical training." The proto-Nazi critics of modernist Weimar thought the educational system was "sadly deficient in recognizing its responsibility for promoting a sense of national identification and loyalty among students." Nazi educational theorist Ernst Krieck argued, apropos folklore, that, in Craig's words, "the comparative dimension...must give way to an emphasis upon the specifically German folk community, and folklore and saga must be made to serve as a kind of political science for contemporary Germans." Sidney Hook could not have put it better. There's no Nazi like a liberal in search of the nation's soul.

Part III
Harvard,
the Corporations,
and the Community

The Business-University Revisited
Industry and Empire in Crimson Cambridge

John Trumpbour

The modern university is in the throes of a profound but cryptic crisis. Championed as a haven for open inquiry and scholarship free from the demands of special interests, it finds this self-proclaimed ideal counterpoised by the need for financial and political support from those same interests. Under exemplary circumstances, independent administrators protect educational institutions from untoward influences while simultaneously soliciting private and public support. In the worst case scenario, the god of Mammon suffocates the gods of Spirit and Intellect, with the university becoming a handmaiden to Industry and Empire.

Harvard University is undergoing perhaps the most dramatic of these crises. Outwardly cloaked in the garb of liberal-humane reason, its leadership warns all to steer clear who seek to submit the university to the needs of private and public power. Presidents Bok, and his predecessors such as Pusey, thunder against ideologues of both the Left and Right, the Bolshevik and Birchite birds of prey who would sacrifice the carefully nurtured independence and universality of the institution for narrow political aims.[1] Of all Harvard's conductors, Bok is the most adept at orchestrating this theme, a man with a pianissimo touch when it comes to the University and its discontents.

Yet squatting awkwardly over this effusive ideological discharge from Harvard's administration is the more tangible reality of corporate power pervading the University's structure of governance and institutions. One telling signpost of corporate power is the conspicuous presence of plutocracy on the Harvard Board of Overseers, including the two most powerful representatives of U.S. capitalism in the twentieth century, J. Pierpont Morgan and David Rockefeller, who each served for twelve years on that body. Openly stating that he dropped $5 million into Harvard's coffers in 1986 alone, Rockefeller regards himself as above suspicion, but Morgan's cozy relationship with then president Eliot raised the ire of numerous social critics.[2] Aesthete John Jay Chapman snarled that:

> Eliot goes about in a cab with Pierpont, hangs laurel wreaths on his nose, and gives him his papal kiss. Now...what has Eliot got to say to the young man entering business or politics who is about to be corrupted by Morgan and his class?[3]

The great U.S. social critic Thorstein Veblen was equally scathing in his contempt for Harvard's mode of governance:

> Plato's classic scheme of folly, which would have the philosophers take over the management, has been turned on its head; the men of affairs have taken over the direction of the pursuit of knowledge.[4]

Corporate Muscle and Harvard

As has been explained in the introductory essays of this volume, Harvard is governed by a seven-member corporation, whose decisions are monitored by the 30-member Board of Overseers. In actual practice, the latter body has given its rubber-stamps of approval with such monotonous regularity that the last cited effort to overturn Corporation policy came in 1948 when several Overseers sought to block a tenured professorship to John Kenneth Galbraith.

Why do corporate elites seem so eager to serve on the Harvard Corporation, even though it entails labor unpaid and of a variety more arduous than directorships on ordinary business enterprises? Recently retired Corporation member Andrew Heiskell of Time, Inc. reflects, "I suppose there's a certain pride in being on the Corporation, and I guess most of us are in the position to return some of the goodies we have gotten from the system."[5]

Besides Heiskell's testimony, there are other "objective" indicators of the business presence on the Harvard governing boards. In 1969, the Corporation's members held one corporate chair, three presidencies, and 24 directorships.[6] In 1988, its members possessed five corporate chairs and 34 directorships (though three and fifteen respectively belonged to one man, Robert Stone, who ranks among the greatest of what Richard Rovere refers to as the "interlocking overlappers" of the corporate world).[7] In 1969, the larger Board of Overseers had twelve corporate chairs, five presidencies, and 84 directorships. According to incomplete data (primarily obtained from the University's election brochures), the 1985-86 board had at least seven corporate chairs and 53 directorships. (Several members did not list all of their directorships; this underreporting is confirmed by cross-referencing *Who's Who in America*.) Half of the 30 overseers come from business, manufacturing, consulting, and corporate law backgrounds. Twenty percent are in education (five administrators, one professor). Ten percent come from government service. The remaining 20 percent are lawyers, judges, doctors, and officials in philanthropy/community service. As is the case with the Corporation, finance capital and high-tech are represented in large numbers. Heavy industry is weak, perhaps confirming the view of some social scientists that finance capital is the dominant bloc in the U.S. ruling class.

Whatever the composition of these business elites, the news that Harvard is governed by corporate power is for many people a less than startling revelation, to be greeted with a politely stifled yawn. After all, Harvard graduates wield tremendous muscle in the corporate world, and it seems axiomatic that they would flex it in the running of their university. According to recent figures of Standard and Poor's, Harvard supplies by far the greatest number of top corporate executives in the United States: 5,165. Coming in a distant second is NYU at 2,522, with Yale placing third at 1,941. In its 1985 news release of these findings, Standard and Poor's offered some gratuitous advice: "If you are striving to reach one of the top spots in the corporate hierarchy, a degree from Harvard can be a valuable asset. Just ask the alumni who occupy thousands of executive offices in companies across the nation."[8]

There are a few qualifications to this Harvard clout in the corporate world. Of these 5,165 executives, only a quarter received their undergraduate degrees at Harvard. The majority are products of its graduate and professional schools. Yale College, with 1,542 top executives, has an edge over Harvard College, which supplies only 1,296 undergraduates.[9] According to *Forbes Magazine's* list of the 400 wealthiest U.S. citizens, Yale College also led with 22 contenders, Harvard College following with 17.[10] The Yale thirst for pecuniary aggrandizement apparently remains unslaked, as 400 out of its class of 1,250 seniors in 1985 applied for positions at the investment banking firm of First Boston. (What is the appeal of this outfit? *The New Republic* explains: "The First Boston group that worked on the Texaco-Getty deal—only a handful of bankers—earned a collective $125,000 an hour."[11])

It is, therefore, the professional schools that help Harvard to outflank all other universities in the business world. Harvard MBAs overwhelm Yale MBAs by ten to one in the corporate command posts. Harvard Law School dominates the corporate law scene, as exhibited by data from the most prestigious New York and Washington law firms.

Law Firm	# of Members/ # of Harvard graduates	percent
New York City		
Sullivan and Cromwell	90/40	44
Davis, Polk, and Wardell	83/29	35
Cravath, Swaine, and Moore	64/20	31
Milbank, Tweed, et al.	99/26	26
Dewey, Ballantine, et al.	91/21	24
Washington, D.C.		
Covington and Burling	94/42	45

Source: *Martindale-Hubble Law Directory* (1988)[12]

Each of these firms had made a considerable impact on the national economy. One partner in Covington and Burling explains to Joseph Goulden in *The Superlawyers*: "We've done things for, I'd say, 20 percent of the companies on *Fortune*'s list of the 500 top corporations."[13] Not to be forgotten among Harvard Law School graduates is one of the most powerful global economic movers and shakers of the 1970s and 1980s, recently deposed Saudi oil minister Sheik Ahmed Zaki Yahmani, class of 1966.

Perhaps the strongest influence of Harvard on the corporations is felt in the field of investment banking. According to sociologist E. Digby Baltzell, "investment bankers came to stand at the apex of upper-class authority and social prestige in America." He adds: "Between the Civil War and the First World War, they orchestrated the financial growth of America into the most powerful industrial nation in the world."[14]

Harvard's connections with these financiers were so intimate that muckrakers such as Upton Sinclair referred to it as the University of Lee Higginson, after the prominent Boston investment banking firm later shipwrecked in the Great Depression.[15] When confronted with the narrow, inbred quality of this business elite, Henry Lee Higginson rebuked critics, "Should not we consider all the great advantages that come from interlocking directorates?"[16] In particular,

J.P. Morgan and Co. became known as one of the "Harvard firms" because of its overwhelming preference for its graduates.

What accounts for the dominance of Harvard alumni in today's corporate world? Former Secretary of Defense Caspar Weinberger today attributes the success of Harvard alumni to "their own merits" and not on connections. "Whatever success Harvard graduates have is due to their own talents, honed by their experience at Harvard," he says. But when asked if he had to choose between two job candidates of equal talent, he shot back that without hesitation, he'd hire the Harvard graduate: "The one who obtained the Harvard degree would have a persuasive element" in his or her favor because "people from Harvard are apt to be quite good at their chosen work."[17] A representative from Peat, Marwick, Mitchell, a management consulting firm, was similarly blunt in a November 1986 interview with the *Harvard Crimson*: "We hire a lot of Harvard people and are very disposed to Harvard students."[18] Weinberger and the corporate representative insist that talent, and not connections, explain the success of Harvard people. But many outsiders find what is smugly regarded as meritocracy to be a convenient rationalization for entitlement to power, status, security, and personal gain. Referring to Nelson Aldrich's writings on the upper classes, Kate Wenner of the *Village Voice* writes: "the old elitism of upper class New England at Harvard is on the wane. But it's being replaced by something more efficient, more intractable, more manageable, and also a lot harder to fight."[19]

That valuable observation does not tell the whole story: the old elitism is far from extinguished. David Aloian, former head of the Harvard Alumni Association, stressed that Harvard has the most developed network of clubs in the nation: "If you graduated Harvard and went out to San Francisco to work for Wells Fargo, if you were my son, I'd want you to join the Harvard Club there, where you would meet some of the higher officers of Wells Fargo."[20] Ivan Boesky, the rapacious arbitrageur who recently resigned from the Visiting Committee overseeing the Harvard School of Public Health after the exposure of his illegal insider trading activity, made business contacts and cut deals at the Harvard Club of New York. Even so, the Harvard Club lacks the clout of the more exclusive social clubs for the upper class. Back in the 1950s, C. Wright Mills observed that going to:

> Harvard or Yale or Princeton is not enough. It is the really exclusive prep school that counts, for that determines which of the "two Harvards" one attends. The clubs and cliques of college

are usually comprised of carry-overs of association and name made in the lower levels at the proper schools; one's friends at Harvard are friends made at prep school. That is why in the upper social classes, it does not mean much merely to have a degree from an Ivy League college. That is assumed: the point is not Harvard, but which Harvard? By Harvard one means Porcellian, Fly, or A.D....It is the prestige of a properly certified secondary education followed by a proper club in the proper Ivy League college that is the standard admission ticket to the world of urban clubs and parties in any major city of the nation[21]

It is in such intimate social circles, passing *le sel et le poivre* to fellow rich and powerful, that these young men imbibe the proper values and affectations, acquiring the self-confidence and nerve required to run society. Slowly they are molded into what Mills calls "The Ones Who Decide." One thing they do decide early on is who's in and who's out. For Franklin Delano Roosevelt, his greatest disappointment in life was the refusal of the Porcellian Club to give him membership. Clearly traumatized by this rejection, leaving him with an "inferiority complex" according to his wife Eleanor, he instead joined the Fly Club.[22] In recent decades, there have been transformations in the prep and finals club social scene at Harvard. The renowned racism and anti-Semitism of the "Gold Coast" culture on Mt. Auburn Street is no longer flaunted so openly, though many clubs remain unabashed about their sexism. The Fly Club puts on what they call "Bimbo Bashes," late night parties populated by women sporting the latest in designer label elegance. Off the record, however, some Fly Club members are more candid about their racism. A Fly man in 1988 told a black *Boston Globe* reporter: "You are forced to mix with different races, creeds, and sexes in everything you do at Harvard. It's nice to have a place where you can get away from it all."[23]

Ten percent of Harvard undergraduates belong to finals clubs. Today a sufficiently motivated commoner, possessed with the proper charm and social graces, might gain access to clubs that were absolutely off limits during the years when Mills wrote. In some, however, the atmosphere remains stultifying. Small enclaves exist in which phoney British accents and prep social conventions abound, although most bastions of elitism have become subtler and more accepting of those thought to be less well-bred. One turbid Anglophile at Harvard who recently complained that an acquaintance was dating "a woman on financial aid" encountered scorn and ridicule from other privileged students.[24] Though these colleagues may ultimately think likewise, old wealth in the U.S. upper class learns never to brandish economic superiority so openly. Such inhibitions make it easy for people to delude themselves with the Weinberger doctrine, that Harvard people receive society's highest rewards solely because they are the most talented.

The old elitism is more eager to embrace talent, albeit largely on the former's terms; but there are social costs from the shotgun marriage of the two. As people comfort themselves that all can join the club, there is a corresponding loss of an adversarial culture, a critical consciousness at odds with a social order which, among other realities, is well on its way to becoming the most inegalitarian in the recent history of the advanced industrial world. (A sample artifact: the richest 0.5 percent in the United States own 35 percent of the nation's wealth, according to 1986 Congressional figures, up from the figures of the previous two decades when the same group owned a mere 25 percent.) The old elitism, undiluted by meritocracy, was baleful; but the new ideology of Harvard as the font of superior talent contributes to a higher arrogance. There may be something to Marx's reflection that "The more a ruling class is able to assimilate the most prominent men of the dominated classes the more stable and dangerous is its rule."[25] The men and women whose claim to power is based on technique and knowledge are supremely confident that their rule will be more democratic and benevolent than that of the older order dominated by those of wealth and aristocratic privilege. But their predecessors, observes Noam Chomsky, did not feel "diminished by honesty as to the limitations of [their] knowledge, lack of work to do, or demonstrable mistakes."[26] They were more capable of retreat, unlike those whose overwhelming faith in knowledge's ability to conquer all is falsified and frustrated by a corresponding lack of humility in the face of error. Robert McNamara and his "Whiz Kids" driving the U.S. auto industry and later the U.S. war machine into disaster are representative of this new style of rule. McNamara did all this, doubtless with maximal efficiency: streamlined management, the latest accounting techniques, and generous use of the best computers. Even when their education lacks such technical dexterity, students are inculcated with reverence and awe towards this expertise. The political benevolence and scientific omniscience of these knowledges remains sacrosanct in U.S. elite universities.

The Brave New Curriculum

Those critics who identify the power of the corporations in the modern university's finances and governing structure glide along gracefully, proving their case with ease. It is when they are forced to confront the actual content of much of the university's curricula that they suddenly find themselves skating in theoretical mud. Such venerable courses listed in Harvard's annual *Register* as Alice Jardine's "Introduction to Semiotics," Jan Ziolkowski's "Medieval Beast Literature," and Richard Hunt's "Nazi Culture" hardly evoke images of monopoly capital overrunning the defenseless fortresses of the Ivory Tower.

Universities are caught between two ideals, their contemporary commitment to what Habermas calls neohumanism and technically exploitable knowledge.[27] Historically, Harvard has been more devoted to neohumanism than its neighbor MIT, which is the premier center for technically exploitable knowledge. The interlocking of the corporate world with the universities has much more direct expression in the engineering schools, whose mission, according to Henry Towne, is to see to it that the "dollar is the final term in every engineering equation," or, in the vision of Charles F. Scott of Westinghouse and Yale, that students learn "to work first for the success of the corporation" and "to subordinate their own ideas and beliefs to the wishes and desires of their superiors," in order to "really be efficient." During World Wars I and II, these ideals spread into neohumanist citadels such as Harvard, especially in the growth of industry-education-government cooperation. The extension of this vision from the engineering schools to the liberal arts universities was in part coordinated by the American Council on Education, self-described as "the General Staff organization of education." The ACE's director, Charles R. Mann, identified its central challenge in 1927 as trying to "decide how education can be organized to meet industrial specifications." One of its crowning achievements was the formation of the Educational Testing Service (ETS), which today dominates the setting of standards for U.S. higher education (the SATs, LSATs, GREs, etc.)[28]

In the end, however, Harvard's neohumanism produced some resistance to the proponents of technically exploitable knowledge. It is sometimes said that the Harvard Graduate School of Business was placed on the opposite bank of the Charles River in order to prevent the contamination of undergraduates. Novelist John Marquand wrote that elite George Apley always turned his head away when driving past the Charles so that he would not see this "most damnable example of materialism...the new School of Business Administration."[29] The Brahmin and Anglophile Apley did not seem aware that the Harvard Business School (HBS) also had a more "noble" mission. In Theodore White's glowing account, HBS was "sprung out of the Spanish-American War, when a few public-spirited alumni decided that the United States, for its new empire, needed a colonial school of administration to match Britain's imperial and colonial civil service."[30]

Harvard's neohumanist unease with the business yardstick is partly confirmed in the flourishing of its literary and aesthetic subculture: Conrad Aiken, John Ashbery, e.e. cummings, John Dos Passos, T.S. Eliot, Archibald MacLeish, Norman Mailer, Adrienne Rich, Wallace Stevens, John Updike, among others. From Eliot's flirtation with clerico-fascism to the youthful socialism of Dos Passos, some of Harvard's literary undergrowth adopted values bracingly negative in its assessment of industrial capitalism.

Why, if it is sometimes unreliable, does the U.S. ruling class prefer neohumanism as the leading educational ideal in its universities? Harvard College's own mission is first and foremost to educate the ruling class, whereas MIT trains the managers and technicians who serve this ruling class. Neohumanism is better suited for the former task, while MIT's emphasis on technically exploitable knowledge attains the latter purpose. Harvard provides an education more compatible with a patrician ruling ethos. As once explained by Perry Anderson in reference to British ruling elites and their education in aristocratic values: "a specific training or aptitude would be a derogation of the impalpable essence of nobility, a finite qualification of the infinite." He elaborates that:

> The aristocrat is defined not by acts which denote skills but by gestures which reveal quintessences...The rulers of England were also—uniquely—neither professional politicians nor bureaucrats nor militarists. They were at different times all of these, and so finally and magnificently none of them.[31]

Whereas the British venerate what they call "the graceful amateur," the U.S. upper or equestrian class prefers to speak of "the well-rounded man." The British aristocracy is, of course, much more extreme in upholding this ideal than their U.S. counterparts. As Thomas Gaisford, Regius Professor of Greek and Dean of Christ Church, Oxford, defended the traditional curriculum of classics in the early nineteenth century: "It enables us to look down with contempt on those who have not shared its advantages."[32] However, Harvard's Anglophilia, its constant bowing and curtsying to the British, is not merely the effete snobbery of the Eastern Establishment. (NBC's Tom Brokaw, for one, seemed miffed at Harvard's celebration of the British at the 350th Anniversary: the fawning over Prince Charles, the high profile address of the Vice-Chancellor of Cambridge University, the constant references to Anglo-American history and the special relationship, the later visit of the Archbishop of Canterbury, etc. ad nauseam.) Harvard's adoration of the British and things Oxbridge also serves the needs of a U.S. ruling class which in its most extravagant visions of grandeur places a premium on a patrician and imperial style of rule. This Anglicized humanism is on the wane, threatened by the postwar expansion of Harvard's professional schools, the ascent of the new mandarins (see my essay on Harvard and the state), and the peculiar innovations of the Bok regime.

Lewis Lapham adds that today:

> Nobody wants to say...that we live in a society that cares as much about the humanities as it cares about the color of the rain in Tashkent. The study of the liberal arts is one of those appearances that must be kept up, like the belief in the rule of law and the devout observances offered to the doctrines of free enterprise and equal opportunity.[33]

In the face of these assaults, neohumanism still prevails as the preeminent legitimation for Harvard's educational mission. There are more compelling reasons why the captains of finance and industry who help run the university retain this orientation. The literary critic Terry Eagleton points out that "capitalism's reverential hat-tipping to the arts is obvious hypocrisy, except when it can hang them on its walls as a sound investment." But he also notes that:

> Capitalist states have continued to direct funds into higher education departments, and though such departments are usually the first in line for savage cutting when capitalism enters on one of its periodic crises, it is doubtful that it is only hypocrisy, a fear of appearing in its true philistine colors, which compels this grudging support. The truth is that liberal humanism is at once largely ineffectual, and the best ideology of the "human" that present bourgeois society can muster. The "unique individual" is indeed important when it comes to defending the business entepreneur's right to make profit while throwing men and women out of work; the individual must at all costs have the "right to choose," provided this means the right to buy one's

child an expensive private education while other children are deprived of their school meals... The "sensuous textures of lived experience" can be roughly translated as reacting from the gut—judging according to habit, prejudice, and "common sense," rather than according to some inconvenient "aridly theoretical" set of debatable ideas. There is, after all, room for the humanities yet, much as those who guarantee our freedom and democracy despise them.[34]

In the 1980s, there has been a noticeable revival in the liberal arts, with rapid increases in enrollment in the humanities at many universities. Some of the leading impetus comes from the corporations, who talk of a rapidly changing world that calls for workers with broader, more general skills. The Northwestern Endicott Report, a leading survey of corporate hiring policies, identified a 20 percent leap in interest in liberal arts majors from 1984 to 1985. A 1984 study conducted by AT&T argued that its most successful managers come from humanities/social science backgrounds. According to Shirley Strum Kenny, the president of Queens College and the organizer of a twelve-member board of business executives, "Corporate leaders have been complaining that they want a broader education from their employees."[35] Harvard Business School students are taking more courses in foreign languages, reportedly after being passed over for jobs at such international firms as Chase Manhattan, which often prefers graduates of Georgetown's School of Foreign Service. The recent upsurge in corporate clamor for liberal arts belies the neohumanist claim that their disciplines automatically inoculate the university against insalubrious business priorities.

The Knowledge Factory Revisited

The vitality of the liberal arts is usually enough to soothe critics who are otherwise edgy about Harvard's cozy relations with the corporate elite. Unbeknownst to the humanist Polyannas, who regard their own existence as the last great barrier standing between the Coca-Colonization of the wider nation and the predatory materialism of the elites, Harvard has not hesitated at all in taking steps that place knowledge directly at the service of specific corporations. Instead of serving as a watch dog, Bok has become a lap dog of corporate interests. In reaction to the Harvard administration's proposals to "go commercial" in its biology labs back in 1980, Cambridge City Council member Alfred Vellucci bluntly told the *Boston Globe* that

Harvard "should change *Veritas* [the school's motto] to a dollar sign and change their color crimson to green."[36]

Aside from occasional misty-eyed oratory expressing his concerns for academic freedom, Bok prefers wooden generalities to direct action, thereby failing to fumigate the fouler smelling corporate arrangements now proliferating within the University. To adapt the words of Senator Hugh Scott, Harvard gives the progressives the rhetoric, the business executives get the action. The business-dominated governing board, seeing that Bok delivers the goods, expands his power, which he then uses to promote further corporate incursions. There are two related areas that have been nurtured in the Bok Era in which Harvard's business interest conflicts with the community interest or, more narrowly, the traditional vision of the university as independent of special interests: consulting and biotechnology.

Consulting

A less-than-systematic study conducted by physicist Charles Schwartz in 1975 suggested that nearly half of the Harvard faculty received outside incomes exceeding a third of their regular salaries, most of this largess coming from consulting.[37] How lucrative this activity can be is most dramatically illustrated in the case of Harvard Professor of Economics Otto Eckstein, who sold his consulting firm for $100 million. In late 1986, the Carnegie Endowment's study of higher education sourly concluded that excessive devotion to consultant work has proven deleterious to the quality of teaching at U.S. research universities.[38] This finding is at odds with Bok, who in 1981 proclaimed that consulting aids teaching and research.[39]

To be fair to Bok, he does warn professors not to exceed limits of 52 days of outside consulting per year, while in response to critics he installed additional restrictions on corporate ties in 1983. Certainly there will always be difficulties in judging how to make university expertise available to the wider society. Under capitalist enterprise, however, there are major incentives to abandon one's public responsibilities. As Professor Keith Yamamoto, a microbiologist at the University of California at San Francisco, advises his colleagues involved in consulting: "If you want to go into business, fine—then leave the university. We essentially lose the people who are involved in the companies, anyway... Their attention and energy get drained off."[40]

Harvard currently encourages the draining of professors' attentions and energies from teaching and towards industry. Proposing to cut its professors' salaries in half, Harvard's School of Public Health wants them to raise their remaining income from industry research grants.[41] Should this proposal go through, public health professors will have little choice but to serve the research needs of corporations. An egregious example is Harvard Law Professor Arnold Zack, who recently wrote a report for the State Department on ways to promote "business trade unionism and not ideological trade unionism" among South Africa's blacks. Zack also intervened as a "fact finder" in the Hormel strike in Austin, Minnesota in which he attempted "to convince strikers to accept the company's key proposals."[42] In the regimen under consideration for the Public Health School, the grovelling servility of their Law School counterpart Zack would become less a choice and more a necessity for its professoriate.

Biotechnology

Transformations in the biological sciences have made it a new frontier—in the hopes of some entrepreneurs, a license to print money. Previously biologists were treated as the most "impractical" of scientists, preferring to study the sex life of sea otters over the immediate applied science needs of industry and government. Their colleagues in such subdisciplines as nuclear physics, physical chemistry, and electrical engineering had long ago sold out for a ride on the lucrative grant gravy train driven by major industrial and governmental concerns. Academic biologists largely remained holdovers from an earlier scientific epoch. In the 1970s, pressures mounted from the industrial powers that be, imploring U.S. universities to "go commercial" in biology.[43]

At first, resistance came from many quarters. Duke University turned down a series of well-paying offers to house a biotechnology institute. When MIT agreed to the founding of the Whitehead Institute, the president of the University of Chicago, Hannah Gray, warned that these intimate industry ties "could compromise the traditional process of making faculty appointments within a university." Gray explains that she is "fundamentally very conservative about involvement of universities and corporations," and that "one ought to bend over backwards not to allow things to happen which, however well protected or well intentioned they may appear to be, nonetheless could lead away from some of the essential things universities have to guarantee."[44]

Despite such opposition, industry did not have to wait long for the birth of a new generation of university-industry relations. Its midwife would be an entrepreneur in humanist clothing, Derek Bok. Bok's initiatives on behalf of the new university-industrial complex helped to break down the resistance of other institutions. As Martin Kenney writes, "Harvard's example of signing these large contracts quickly spread to other universities on the East Coast."[45] Harvard took the lead on several fronts. As early as 1974, Monsanto signed a twelve-year contract paying Harvard Medical School (HMS) $23.5 million for the right to secure an exclusive worldwide license in the event of the discovery of a substance to fight tumors. The grant applied to the labs of HMS professors M. Judah Folkman and Bert Vallee. *Science* magazine termed the HMS-Monsanto deal "an agreement that is unprecedented in the annals of academic business affairs."[46]

Bok's enthusiasm for greater university-industry cooperation came to fuller fruition in 1981-82 when Harvard-affiliated Mass General Hospital (MGH) agreed to a ten-year, $70 million contract with Germany's Hoechst Corporation to fund the building of a genetics department by Harvard professor Howard Goodman. The provisions of the Hoechst agreements include "the right [of this corporation] to have four of its scientists in the department at any one time," to read "all manuscripts...thirty days before submission to a journal," and to have "access to the postdoctoral and graduate researches in Goodman's laboratory and in the hospital in general."[47] This agreement elicited greater anger than the Monsanto deal largely because it benefitted foreign capitalists. Referring to the large infusions of federal funds into Harvard's medical-industrial complex, then-Representative Albert Gore fumed when questioning an MGH representative, "Isn't it a little unfair to the U.S. taxpayers after this twenty-year investment that's ongoing at the rate of $25 to $26 million a year, to give the cream of the results to a foreign company that gets exclusive rights?"[48] Harvard Medical School soon let others come to its trough; a month after the Hoechst contract, DuPont funded a $6 million program in genetics in exhange for exclusive licensing rights.

By the advanced date of 1989, Harvard's Mass General Hospital has entered into 40-50 major contracts with individual corporations. According to its director J. Robert Buchanan, the largest is an $85 million agreement with Japan's Shiseido Corporation to establish a

100-member staff Cutaneous Biology Research Center dedicated to researching the production of anti-wrinkle creams, suntanning lotions, and baldness cures. In a pronouncement blandly reminiscent of the president of Hair Club for Men, Dr. John Parrish of Harvard declared that Shiseido and Harvard are good partners because each shares the goal of providing "symptom-free normal skin of pleasing appearance."[49]

With Harvard ready to sell the expertise of professors and graduate students to outside corporations, many of its scientists began scrambling to form their own biotechnology firms. Already Harvard's large contracts had been "very important to the large corporations because of their [previous] inability to convince top researchers to join their companies," according to Kenney.[50] Now researchers felt they had little choice; they either had to serve a large corporation or form their own. Some scholars who initially chafed at this commercialization have become extraordinarily wealthy because of it. Biochemist Mark Ptashne, for one, invested at least $1.4 million in Ivan Boesky's firm. Ptashne made his multimillion dollar fortune through involvement in Genentech, Inc., a company whose shares leaped from $35 to $88 in a single day of trading.[51]

How has this commercialization transformed science research priorities at Harvard? Bok's earlier reassurances of the uninterrupted march of academic freedom ring increasingly hollow as one witnesses the demonstrable effects of his policies. Competition for prestige and recognition has often been brisk in university labs, but the corporate presence poisons this atmosphere in some new and unsettling ways. In many respects, business and science operate under different rules. Standard procedure among scientists is to wait to announce scientific results in well-researched, heavily-documented presentations for academic journals, or before conferences where data and procedure can be challenged by one's peers. While sometimes unable to prevent lab frauds, this procedure helps to protect against charlatanry and false claims of "breakthroughs"; it establishes recognized standards in scientific achievement. Business, on the contrary, puts such a premium on grabbing headlines "as soon as you can get away with it," note Nancy Pfund and Joel Gurin, due to the risk of "losing valuable publicity" that "the result has not been good for either science or the public."[52]

The most prominent episode exhibiting the new corporate rules in action occurred in January 1980, when Harvard biologist Walter Gilbert called a press conference to declare his company, Biogen, the first to produce interferon. This led to an exciting sequence of events: a leap in stock prices for Schering-Plough, an owner of Biogen, and interferon's appearance on the cover of *Time* as the cancer-curing wonder drug. Thus, the day of reckoning came as a shock to many. Later that year, both the American Association for Cancer Research and the American Society of Clinical Oncology debunked the claims for interferon, while Genentech, Inc. showed that it could produce the substance "by a process thousands of times more efficient than Biogen's." However, it turned out that Genentech had obtained the cells to make interferon from the lab of a UCLA biologist David Golde, who thought he was sharing them in the spirit of free inquiry and scientific exchange. He exploded angrily when he found out that his experiments were being used less for public benefit and more for commercial gain. UCLA charged Hoffmann-LaRoche, which worked with Genentech on interferon, with "unauthorized use" of Golde's materials.[53]

Perhaps more treacherous than their need to grab quick headlines and publicity is the corporate inclination towards selective secretiveness. At the Fourth International AIDS conference in Stockholm in June 1988, the Harvard-dominated Cambridge BioScience corporation came under fierce criticism for what the *Boston Globe* calls "an attempted cover-up" of data showing that its AIDS test, Recombigen, came in last among four products by "missing about 15 percent of contaminated blood samples." Dr. Myra Jennings of the University of California at Davis reflects on the contrast between ordinary university researchers and the Harvard corporate scientists at Cambridge BioScience. "All of us in academics are sort of idealistic in that you present whatever you find," she suggests. "I realize that companies don't play that way. They can do some experiments, but they don't necessarily have to present [everything] they find—only the best of what they find."[54]

In this episode, a few Harvard scientists seemed all too ready to permit a greater risk of AIDS contamination in the nation's blood supply, so that they could make fast profits. But such incidents are hardly isolated. On October 19, 1988, the *Boston Globe* again revealed that Dr. Scheffer C.G. Tseng at Harvard-affiliated Massachusetts Eye and Ear Infirmary secretly experimented on patients against FDA regulations and ultimately suppressed test results on his Vitamin A ointment which he claimed cured eye diseases. The thirty-five-year-old Tseng personally made over a million dollars with his fraudulent wonder drug but long escaped detection, presumably because his immediate supervisor, Harvard associate professor Kenneth Kenyon, owned a large chunk of stock in Tseng's small company, Spectra Pharmaceutical Services, Inc. Again the *Globe* concluded that "the practice of publishing favorable results and withholding unfavorable ones could grow increasingly common as more university researchers cross the line between pure science and business."[55]

The new business ethos in the biolabs has also destroyed much of the cooperative spirit within academic departments. Nobel prizewinning biochemist Paul Berg of Stanford talks about the new locks on drawers and hiding of experimental data among colleagues: "Let's say you have one department with three people, each a member of a different company. What does that do to communication within the department?" he asks. "It's war." He tells the story of a top British scientist who could not send his gene splicing research to colleagues because it was up for a patent. Berg explains:"If you put an inducement in patents, you will very definitely get people to clam up."[56]

Berg's prediction in 1980 has amply been confirmed by more recent surveys of scientists. A study of 1,200 faculty members at 40 major universities conducted by Harvard's Center for Health Policy and Management reported the following, according to a summary in the *Boston Globe*:

> Faculty members financially backed by biotechnology firms were four times as likely as colleagues without such support to report that work yielded trade secrets.

The *Globe* points out:

> Trade secrets are results that may become concealed by industrial sponsors, and thus are in contrast to the academic tradition of free and open exchange of research results.

The survey also found that faculty with biotech industry sponsorship were:

> Four times as likely as their colleagues without such support to report that commercial applications had affected their choice of research topics...And five times more likely to report that their research was the property of their industrial sponsor.[57]

Why do university administrators and intellectuals tolerate such levels of uncooperative and secretive behavior in the research labs? Harvard has apparently found the arguments of laissez-faire ideologues to be seductive—that the university must replicate capitalist industry in its structure of incentives and rewards in order for science to progress. The Belgian Marxist economist Ernest Mandel scoffs at such reasoning:

> Throughout history, indeed, most key discoveries and inventions have been made wholly outside any commercial nexus. Profit did not exist when fire was first conserved. Agriculture and metallurgy were not brought into being by the market. Printing was not invented for gain. Most of the great medical advances—from Jenner to Pasteur and Koch to Fleming—were not induced by hope of financial recompense. The electrical motor was born in a university laboratory, not a business workshop. Even the computer, let alone the spacecraft, was designed for public (albeit military) purposes, not for enriching shareholders. There is not the smallest reason to assume that a withering away of market relations and monetary rewards would lead to the disappearance of technological innovation.[58]

Cesar Milstein, who took the Nobel Prize for Medicine in 1984, recently denounced those who wanted him to patent a discovery expected to produce a billion dollar market in the 1990s: "A patent would have meant keeping everything secret while we thought about applications—an outrageous insult to science. Patents are an intellectual swindle."[59]

U.S. universities, state and private, have been built up over decades with the support and labor of a wider public, a social investment made by generations of taxpayers as well as teachers, staff, and alumni. It is a public trust, not to be made the exclusive preserve of a few private corporations, who by slapping down round sums of money gain sole rights to information that justly belongs to all people.[60]

The United States is currently presiding over a decline in pure science, an ideal sacrificed to short sighted private gain. With Harvard helping to shape the new face of corporate power in the U.S. university, a machinery of pelf and privilege has triumphed, winning for business a cheap but major victory over the rest of us.

Whither the Business School?

Confronted by this mounting corporate power, Harvard professors in the arts and sciences are apt to respond that the problem is worse elsewhere in the University. Hardly reassuring to all but the morally invertebrate, the rebuttal carries some truth. Having sketched corporate influence at Harvard, particularly in the natural sciences, this essay will conclude by turning to the Harvard Business

School (HBS), the Harvard institution most pivotal in the maintenance of capitalist enterprise. Today, the Business School leadership is under assault via the dual legitimation crisis of North American capitalism: the apparent erosion of ethics and the decline in U.S. economic preeminence.

Regarded as the West Point of U.S. capitalism, the Harvard Business School (HBS) produces the field marshals—and the field manuals—that guide finance and industry. Though its leaders have been known to express bitterness that its program is now rated academically inferior to Stanford's, HBS takes solace insofar as its graduates still make the most money; in their logic, "He who has the most toys in the end wins." HBS faculty hold directorships on 27 separate companies belonging to the Fortune 500; the nearest business school rival holds a mere seven.[61]

All seemed to be going well until the conjuncture of 1986-1988 in which the U.S. social order found itself convulsed by scandal, ranging from Boesky and insider trading to Contragate to the bawdy exposures of Jim and Tammy Bakker and Jimmy Swaggart.

John Shad, former chairman of the Security and Exchange Commission, vice president of EF Hutton, and graduate of HBS, may have been speaking for the U.S. ruling class when he declared in the *Boston Globe*: "I've been very disturbed by the great number of leading business and law school graduates becoming felons." Shad promptly contributed $20 million to HBS so that it could set up professorships in ethics, now a vast academic cottage industry. Following the cue of the ethicists, Shad attributes the moral laxness of the age to "a change in moral attitude in America" due to "a mobile population, an increased divorce rate, the Vietnam War, the drug culture, and a permissive generation."[62]

These are all convenient targets, but Shad's formulation downplays the centrality of greed in the very ethos of capitalism. As Boesky said to a group of business students in 1985, "Greed is all right by the way."[63] But for those who suggest that business ethics is an oxymoron, Shad in a July 27, 1987 op. ed. piece for the *New York Times* reassures otherwise: "In sum, ethics pays; it's smart (i.e., good business) to be ethical."

Shad and the business school ethicists who repeat this dictum over and over seem unaware that mere expediency is perhaps the shallowest foundation for an ethical system. As John Goldberg remarks:

Reducing ethics to a strategy for achieving profit has the crippling effect of devaluating morality...Suppose crime did pay (even a bumbler who gets himself caught like Ivan Boesky hasn't exactly suffered). Would Mr. Shad then preach a doctrine of crime for the bottom line. Presumably not, but this is what his "ethical system" calls for.[64]

While the capitalist social order has always depended on a large measure of flim-flam and chicanery, there are compelling historical reasons why the Norths and the Boeskys proliferate at this time. The long-term decline in the U.S. economy and world position has brought, in the words of James Petras, "the rise of a new class of ideological desperadoes—from the interstices of politics, academia, the military, and the underworld—to crucial decision-making positions in the international bureaucracy."

Petras elaborates:

> The ascent of this quasi-underworld to power is cause and consequence of the decline of empire. As the industrialist is replaced by the speculator (Rockefellers by Boeskys), so the statesperson is replaced by the military adventurer, the upwardly mobile broker between the State Department and the political gangsters...
>
> The ascent of speculator capital and the decline of productive capital in the economy is based on the same adventurer, illegal, clandestine, insider strategy and activities so characteristic of the lumpen-intellectuals who occupy the netherworld between the White House and the Central American air strips of the narco-contras. The marriage of speculators and lumpen-intellectuals is not coincidental. There are not a few links that bind the two in terms of social background and ambitions, political amoralism, and fanaticism.[65]

Petras's reference to the decline of industrial capital in favor of fictitious paper capital, the replacement of entrepreneurs who must produce a real product with securities-shuffling speculators, is ratified in the business schools, which all too typically shun manufacturing. As *Fortune* reports, HBS

> saw over half its graduating MBAs go into investment banking or management consulting...Another 15 percent of the class headed into venture capital, real estate, commercial banking, investment management, or other financial services. Less than 25 percent of the 1987 MBAs took jobs with manufacturing companies, and most of these were staff, not line, positions.[66]

Now a common response in elite circles to the crisis of U.S. capitalism is the demand that more of "the best and the brightest" from Harvard enter manufacturing. This sober panacea may be fraught with unanticipated dangers. Halberstam's case study of the Ford Motor Company in *The Reckoning* is a chilling tale of what happens when a manufacturing corporation turned cravenly to Harvard MBAs for leadership. When it was all over, these managers nearly left the company "belly up." Speaking of Ford executive Ed Lundy, Halberstam remarks that "he specialized in collecting the brightest young men from the nation's business school campuses." Soon HBS graduates had so infested the company that Charley Beacham complained to Lee Iacocca: "It's a fraternity, Lee, a closed Greek fraternity, and there's no place for people like you or me in it." To designate Ford's most outstanding employees, Lundy used a system of placing strips of green tape under the names of prized personnel on company charts. Iacocca and his friends, eventually squeezed out of Ford, grumbled that too much green tape went to undeserving HBS graduates. When Iacocca's men left for Chrysler, they would often refer to a young executive as a "green tape guy," to which Halberstam adds laconically: "It was not a compliment. It was their shorthand for a man seriously overrated." Iacocca would chide the Harvard MBAs, in his view incapable of contributing anything to sales and production:

> Ed, the great thing about being in finance is, you don't have to worry about ten-day reports, you don't have to worry about sales, you don't have to worry about design, you don't have to worry about manufacturing breakdowns—just what is it you guys do for a living?[67]

While the flaw in Iacocca, notes Halberstam, "was his inability to admit his and the system's culpability," his "constant need to blame someone else,"[68] Ford president Philip Caldwell, a stalwart HBS alumnus, admitted that the massive presence of prima donna MBAs, and not Iacocca, may have brought the company to the brink:

> I think the problem with the Ford Motor Company is that we are growing too many sunflowers, flowers with big heads who rise too high seeking the sun at the expense of all else.[69]

It would be a mistake, however, to regard the Harvard elite as genuinely independent. Lundy's successor, Will Caldwell (no relation to Phil) explained to the just-fired Ford economist Bill Niskanen that he might try to learn how the "successful" ones make it to the top of the company and portrayed Harvard MBAs as a chorus of yes-men:

> The people who do well wait until they hear their superiors express their views. Then they add something in support of those views.[70]

Upper-class iconoclast Lewis Lapham points out:

> The corpocracy does not like to be reminded that an accomplished CEO bears comparison to a butler or gamekeeper—a dull but stouthearted and boyish fellow who can be counted on to look after the porcelain or the grouse: reliable enough to act as the custodian of a large and valuable property, but not clever enough to steal anything important.[71]

Ford's Japanese competitors expressed a certain disdain for their U.S. counterparts. In their view, U.S. executives remained vastly overpaid (two to five times higher than the Japanese) and ultimately unconcerned with production, rarely talking with workers on the assembly line and ignorant of craft issues. When former assistant Secretary of State for Far Eastern Affairs Richard Holbrook asked the Japanese what they thought of U.S. Steel's multibillion dollar acquisition of Marathon Oil, one Japanese manager responded, "We do not understand why a company that is supposed to make steel spends so much time to buy an oil company."[72]

Ironically, in recent years, the Japanese have expressed a desire to send a greater number of students to HBS. While certain "Johnny Walker Japanese" have always been enthralled with U.S. lifestyles, pin-striped suits, and Rolex watches, the Japanese now see HBS training as an opportunity for their country to land the most prominent role in the theater of international finance. Nevertheless, there are those who see HBS training in a somewhat different light; the school is today perceived even by *Fortune* as a force exacerbating the U.S. economic slide. For the most optimistic corporate critics of HBS, the Japanese eagerness to attend HBS could unfold with a different twist: a U.S.-supplied Trojan Horse undoing future Japanese preeminence. In the meantime, executive talent from Asia and Europe flock to Harvard's program, some attracted by the rage for the marketing theories of HBS professor Theodore Levitt, a prophet of "the global corporation" which "does and sells the same things in the same way everywhere," thanks to the computer, print, and television revolutions that are, in his view, "homogenizing markets everywhere."[73]

Today about 15 percent of Harvard's MBAs come from abroad. The Japanese have gained a few places for its executive talent at HBS by endowing prestigious professorships, with Matsushita Electric and Industrial Bank of Japan each donating $1.5 million. Its cultivation of ties with the foreign bourgeoisie notwithstanding, HBS will more likely remain the favored formative institution for members of the U.S. capitalist class.

HBS and U.S. Capitalism

HBS continues to carry out four important functions for U.S. capitalism: 1) class cohesion, 2) consulting, 3) trade union management, and 4) ideology.

Class Cohesion

A favorite ritual of the HBS Club of New York is its annual Business Statesman Award, which almost always goes to the leading representatives of finance capital: Rockefeller, Dillon, McNamara, Rohatyn, and Wriston among its past recipients.[74] HBS alums are herded into this festival of the ruling class and then subsequently targetted for donations to the HBS Fund, a lavish and delightful way of ensuring class reproduction. One non-Harvard manager explains how service to HBS helps the career development of its alumni. Noting that an HBS graduate had been "struggling" in his first three years at his corporation, he:

> finally...became area director for contributions to HBS. And Harvard picks this up right away and has him put his picture in our weekly paper. Well, I have to tell you this, from that day forward his career has just taken off. He jumped twice ...You know it can't be a coincidence...For three years...nobody knew the poor guy existed; he was doing a good job, but all of a sudden, once it became generally known, he just took off.[75]

Michael Useem has spoken of an "inner group" in U.S. capitalism, referring to the few members of the capitalist elite who hold numerous interlocking directorships in the Fortune 500 and the major foundation and university governing boards.[76] Most HBS faculty, while outsiders to the "inner group," nevertheless possess considerable inside knowledge about several corporations, ties to which they make known in HBS's "Company Contact Register." A sample entry: HBS Professor John Quelch lists himself as a "company contact" for General Foods, General Mills, General Motors, Reebok, and United Airlines. His colleague Malcolm Salter is well-connected with competing auto-industry firms including Chrysler, Ford, General Motors, and Volkswagen, as well as to the United Auto Workers.[77]

As far as directorships themselves, in the Fortune 500 the HBS faculty hold close to four times as many as that of its nearest business school competitor. Moreover, the case method of instruction, based on concrete study of individual firms, compels faculty to make contacts with corporations, ensuring that most of the professoriate will have 10, 20, and in a few cases more than 50 corporations with which they are in a position to broker information.[78]

Consulting

Several members of the HBS faculty earn salaries from consulting that rival the earnings of Fortune 500 executives. J. Paul Mark's much maligned study of HBS, *The Empire Builders*, opens with a narrative showing how strategy wunderkind, Professor Michael Porter, exploits his students for his consulting business through the use of the case method. When Porter served as a consultant to the National Football League in its struggle to destroy its USFL competition, he put his "Business Policy I" students to work on the problem. Conceding to the *New York Times* that "my teaching and consulting are very closely entwined," Porter did not mention that the "laundry list" of strategies he handed to the NFL was largely culled from the suggestions of his MBA students. Porter's Monitor Company was labelled "an ethical embarassment" in *Time* magazine's Harvard 350th anniversary issue but an unrepentant Porter told colleagues: "There's nothing at all unethical about what I do for companies, unless you call making money for them unethical." When Porter was subsequently able to gain more favorable coverage of his work from the *New York Times*, HBS Professor Joseph Bower saluted him for his craftiness with its reporter: "You certainly charmed the fangs off the snake."[79]

Porter aside, the HBS faculty engage in practices ranging from the morally questionable to the malodorous and greasy. As Mark observes about the naivete of corporations willing to aid HBS professors in research for their course's case studies:

> Few companies ever turned down requests from professors to do research. To them, it was unimaginable that the sensitive information they gave to HBS for free, in the name of academic research, was being sold to their nearest competitors for large sums of money, although that was sometimes the case. The fact was that some faculty considered brokering information to be part of the job.[80]

It is little wonder then that HBS Dean John McArthur remarks, "MBAs find ethics [to be] Mickey Mouse."[81]

The case method has its critics at other theory-based business schools, such as Chicago, and Bok himself declares the case method deficient in tackling conceptual and ethical issues. Ironically, Mark has suggested that the best corporate case studies at HBS have been written by journalists, exploding the myth of the vaunted expertise of the HBS professoriate. In the end, the lucrative consulting network at HBS makes it highly unlikely that this method of pedagogy will be abandoned in the forseeable future.

Trade Union Management

HBS professors are frequently consulted by managers who are intent on thwarting unions and working-class insurgencies. But Harvard's postwar contribution to management has been less to combat unions directly and more to instill in unions a pro-business, anti-communist outlook. In waging the international class war, Harvard, with the collaboration of the AFL-CIO, set up its longstanding Trade Union Program, which recruits union officials around the globe for seminars. Halberstam's study of Nissan briefly describes how the company's anti-communist union leadership became identified and then invited to participate in courses at Harvard.[82] The program has raised more controversy abroad than in the United States, with allegations surfacing in 1983 in the *New Zealand Times* about its CIA backing. The CIA, particularly in the early decades of the Cold War, poured ample resources into conservative trade unions throughout Europe and Latin America.[83] In the early 1970s, an official University brochure providing the details on the Harvard Trade Union Program openly states, "Overseas candidates are selected by the United States Departments of State and Labor and the Agency for International Development."[84]

The Harvard Trade Union Program is, alas, regarded as an example of the University's spirit of liberalism and tolerance, but critics such as columnist Bob Kuttner have excoriated Bok and the program's faculty advisor, former Secretary of Labor John Dunlop, for giving pro-union lip service to workers and then supporting union busting drives at Harvard itself.[85]

Whatever ambivalence Harvard may project about trade unions, the University has been in the forefront of techniques of labor control through its pioneering programs in scientific management (for more details, see my essay on science).

Ideology

In a political culture with democratic aspirations, managerial ideologies are redolent of elitism ("We rule because we know more"), so the myth of entrepreneurship and the rugged individual retains appeal, even within a caste that so demonstrably subverts this ideal as the MBA. For the most part, HBS secretes an ideology that is scientific in much of its veneer, and bureaucratic/managerial in its core. At certain moments, however, this bland inculcation of managerial values becomes punctuated by ideological gusts celebrating the entrepreneur and the heroic individual. As the HBS brochure, *The Business of the Harvard Business School*, expresses it: "...the general manager is not unlike... an explorer—leading an enterprise through uncharted territory in uncertain and unpredictable conditions with imperfect navigational instruments."[86] HBS professors themselves clamor for more courses on entrepreneurship. Oddly, only 11 percent of Harvard MBAs in a recent survey described themselves as "self-employed," which in J. Paul Mark's view is the barest minimum requirement in the definition of entrepreneurship. At the same time, over 80 percent *wish* that they could become entrepreneurs.[87] The reality is that the MBA route, by nature a safe road to affluence and authority, is ill-suited to operating in the risky, anarchic world of the entrepreneur. It comes as little surprise then that many entrepreneurs, Steve Wozniak of Apple, for instance, are college dropouts. Despite the U.S. economy's domination by highly bureaucratized corporations, with the top 200 holding some 60 percent of all manufacturing assets in 1983,[88] the belief, in Robert Engler's words, that "multinational business goliaths are just like small boys selling lemonade" may ultimately serve as one of the "manipulative masks for rule by irresponsible technocratic bureaucracies over a citizenry whose dominant tone is trained passivity."[89] The Harvard MBA, doubtless sincere in these entrepreneurial aspirations, may not recognize how neatly this ideology serves the maintenance of power. Finally, HBS has a legacy of sexism that continues to pervade its ideology. With only three women among HBS's 90 tenured faculty, this is hardly a revelation. HBS used to engage in such Stone Age practices as shepherding away the wives at their husbands' graduation and lecturing them, in one wife's recollection, on how "their husband's career was the most important thing." HBS authorities advised MBA wives:

> they should not rock the boat and do anything to upset their husbands' careers. If their husband was going to be transferred,

they should go happily. It means more money and it means a better career for him.

Upon being told what her place would be by HBS officialdom, one woman reflected:

I was appalled...But at the time I went along with it...They told me that I should...and Gordon [her husband] was sure that his career was very important.[90]

Today sexism at HBS is still less subtle than in most parts of the University, manifest in such episodes as former Pepsico executive and HBS Professor Andrall Pearson's constant reference to women as "gals" and demeaning questioning of a female student on whether she would buy a proposed product in the supermarket.[91] Nevertheless, even with the best intentions as Pearson himself eventually apologized to offended women students, the case method has built up a backlog of thousands of cases from the 1930s onward celebrating white male entrepreneurship, with scant attention to problems confronting women and minorities. Despite sporadic struggle by the Women's Student Association for greater diversity in the curriculum, the reality that the HBS faculty resembles an exclusive white men's club disables it from carrying out any such reformation.

Education as a Class Act

I believe in what the students are calling our monstrous corporate state because it keeps America alive and the colleges should be turning out students who can staff it.

Chase Peterson,
former Dean of Admissions,
Harvard University[92]

Pervasive corporate influence is evidenced in the governing structure, the sciences, and foremost of all in the business school of Harvard University. Though the governing board continues to devolve power to the University's administrative elite (see the introductory essay by Weissman), there is a recognition, expressed in 1970 by Yale president Kingman Brewster, "that the university and the corporation share a joint trusteeship symbolized by the many people from business and finance who play the stalwart, anonymous role of protecting the integrity" of educational institutions.[93] This is no haphazard outcome, but has rather developed by design. In a moment of rare candor in 1908, Charles W. Eliot, generally regarded as Harvard's greatest president, noted that "dangerous" classes have no significant role in governing Harvard, because universities based on private funding are able to escape "class influences such as that exerted by farmers as a class, or trade unionists as a class." Higher education is, therefore, controlled in Eliot's approving words by "the highly educated, public-spirited, business or professional man."[94] The fascinating aspect of Eliot's discourse is how it illustrates Antonio Gramsci's powerful thesis about the manner in which narrow elites convert their self-interest into the universal interest: for Eliot, farmers and workers, the majority, are selfish; corporate elites are "public-spirited." Today the Bok regime mirrors this in declaring pro-divestment, anti-corporate candidates for Harvard's Board of Overseers as narrow-minded and dangerously single-issue in focus, whereas the nominees of state and corporate elite background receive the University's seal of approval for putative dedication to the general interest. With the help of such sustained mystagogy, the University remains, now more than ever, firmly in the grasp of corporate power and privilege.

Even so, the capitalist class is periodically rife with division, and the universities might have provided a partial antidote to the worst pathologies of the Reagan-Bush era. Instead the festering wounds of this epoch of private opulence and public squalor have been opened further by the major leadership of universities, who have urged on corporate takeover of public culture, often in the name of helping U.S. enterprise remain competitive with that of Japan. For the university itself, pursuit of these policies are producing two odd but predictable developments: 1) a division in the faculty between an entrepreneurial stratum possessing handsome six-figure incomes and circles of friends that may includes heads of corporations and heads of state, and a humanist wing whose commitment to an older ideology of professionalism compels them to shun the temptations of the market, only to find their privileged middle class status threatened by skyrocketing costs such as housing, which in turn are fed by the predatory speculation and expansion of their own universities; 2) the universities, similar to multinational corporations that mouth patriotic slogans and then quickly shift investment abroad, solemnly pledge to Congress their desire to save U.S. jobs by enhancing academic-industrial links and then rush to sell expertise exclusively to the highest bidder, in the case of Harvard its largest contracts going to firms from Japan and West Germany.[95]

As "the commodity relation" seeps into major regions of administrative and intellectual life, the university witnesses a phenomenon manifest "at its most grotesque," observes the philosopher Lukacs, in the "'lack of convictions,' the prostitution of...experiences and beliefs" that may be "comprehensible only as the apogee of capitalist reification."[96]

In the overall balance, the academic leadership may have made one serious miscalculation in their newfound eagerness to replicate capitalist enterprise. While capital is notoriously mobile, able to pick up stakes and flee entire nations, universities are inherently immobile and, still heavily dependent on public funding, less able to ignore a sustained political challenge. High-tech capitalism, at the moment brash in its triumph over unions and community control, may discover that the emerging postmodern university is the weakest link in its chain of production, what David Noble calls "the Achilles heel of the multinational marauders, the point of vulnerability." Challenged to refrain from further robbery and impoverishment of U.S. civic culture, the corporations and their academic allies might just be compelled to beat an abrupt and hasty retreat.[97]

Appendix I: Radiation at Harvard
The Silkwood Syndrome

The Harvard Corporation retains an aloof demeanor in the face of demands that it become responsive to the community at large. But in a series of shocking revelations by the Nuclear Regulatory Commission (NRC) and a congressional subcommittee, the dangers of Harvard's lack of accountability have been brought home to the public. In a surprise inspection in March 1986, the NRC cited numerous violations at Harvard, summarized in part by the *Boston Globe*:

1) "Radioactive material was stored in unlocked labs and dumped in ordinary trash cans at the Biochemistry Building at 7 Divinity Avenue..."

2) "Radioactive materials were poured down a sink drain in Buildings B1 and C2 of the Medical School in Roxbury...Materials were also disposed in sewers at the Medical School without checking whether the levels of radioactivity exceeded federal regulations."

3) "Radioactive materials were transported to the Environmental Health and Safety Office...in plastic garbage pails with unsecured lids..."

4) "Radioactive ash was brought to the Harvard-owned New England Primate Center...without any safety evaluation. Furthermore, it was stored inside a trash bin at a publicly accessible area."

5) "There were also several procedural violations: eating, drinking, and smoking in labs using radioactive materials; levels of radioactivity above contamination limits; lab workers without radiation training; and radiation-monitoring meters that were miscalibrated."[98]

The NRC fined Harvard, $2,500, in what Massachusetts Representative Ed Markey termed "a slap on the wrist."[99] Harvard's Vice-President Robert Scott quickly reassured the community that the University has corrected all of the problems. But its postwar history with radioactive and nuclear materials does not inspire confidence in the University's policies. In October 1986, Markey's congressional subcommittee on conservation and power revealed that from 1953 to 1957 researchers at Harvard-affiliated Massachusetts General Hospital "injected terminally ill brain tumor patients with uranium to determine the dose at which kidney damage begins." The *Boston Globe* continues: "From 1961 to 1965, MIT scientists injected twenty elderly subjects with radioactive radium or thorium." Describing the people in these government sponsored experiments as human "guinea pigs," Markey reports that subjects received dosages in some cases over ninety-eight times the recognized level for safety at the time. "American citizens," he states, "became nuclear calibration devices for experiments run amok." MGH spokesperson Martin Bander showed little remorse for these scientists' actions, saying that Markey "ignores the purpose of the study to make it sound like it was very unethical research." He says his hospital was taking the first steps for "treating brain tumors."[100] (Those impressed by such uplifting "ends justify the means" rationalizations by Harvard may wonder why the researchers injected such material to damage the kidneys of these patients.)

Unlike Harvard, MIT has been forced to answer for its nuclear politics. Vincent Raulinaitis, a machinist employed for 21 years at MIT's Laboratory of Nuclear Science, learned by accident that the metals he had been handling were contaminated with radioactive material. After exposés in the *Boston Globe* and outside arbitration involving his union, Raulinaitis in 1984 secured a confidential agreement with MIT that lowered the maximum permissible level of radiation by 50 times.

At Harvard, there are obstacles to a similar triumph. For one, the Board of Overseers has often provided ample representation to the most unreconstructed apologists for nuclear power. The president of the Harvard Board of Overseers at the time of the 1986 NRC inspection was Joan Bok (Derek's cousin-in-law) who serves on the board of directors of several nuclear utilities. Also on the Overseers was Carter energy czar James Schlesinger, who in an interview with *US News and World Report* remarks that "I personally would very much prefer to live next door to a nuclear power plant." He adds that nuclear power "is clean and attractive. The risk of an accident...is exceedingly remote."[101] Harvard also invests heavily in nuclear power utilities, as well as sinking over $10 million into the company most notorious for nuclear villainy, Kerr-McGee, the employer of Karen Silkwood.

Another telling indicator of Harvard's insensitivity to worker and community safety is its voting record on related measures in the corporations in which they are major shareholders. Voting against a resolution for General Electric to stop further generation of nuclear waste and to conduct a health study of the effects of its older reactors, Harvard explained that it followed its "precedents of voting against or abstaining on resolutions that would halt nuclear related activity." Even more frightening was Harvard's refusal to support a shareholder resolution asking American Cyanamid to provide public disclosure of potential chemical hazards and to report on what preventive measures it had taken to reduce accidents at its pesticide manufacturing facility. The resolution came on the heels of the Union Carbide disaster in Bhopal, India. In characteristic form, Harvard, then owner of $8.5 million in Cynamid securities,[102] claimed that "the meaning of the term 'public disclosure'...was not clear,"[103] and that Cyanamid appears to be complying with some of its provisions anyway.

The historical record does not support Harvard's warm regard for Cyanamid's management. In 1978, American Cyanamid workers went on strike to express their outrage at the suppression of employee illness data and distortion of statistics on carcinogens at the company's Bound Brook, New Jersey plant. American Cyanamid plant manager Eldon Knape was unmoved. "We don't run a health spa," he declared. In 1979, having realized that the dangerous presence of lead compounds could produce birth defects, American Cyanamid gave its women workers at their Willow Island, West Virginia plant three alternatives: quit, take a demotion, or undergo sterilization. Five women chose the last course, four of whom later told the *New York Times* of their deep regret.[104]

When it came time to support a mild proposal designed to inform workers of the chemicals at their workplace, Harvard's vaunted commitment to humanism and the free marketplace of ideas suddenly did not apply.

Appendix II: The Harvard Corporation's Members and Investments

With over $90 million sunk into tobacco industry powerhouse and leveraged buy out specialist Kolberg, Kravis, and Roberts, Harvard is today under fire for a portfolio serving corporate raiders and merchants of death.[105] In its $5 billion portfolio Harvard keeps a higher percentage of its investments in liquid stock market transactions than do many firms that are tied up heavily in bonds and treasury bills. Partly for this reason, the Brady commission in its inquiry into the 500-point stock market crash of October 1987 fingered Harvard as one of the possible culprits. They noted that its managers were the second largest buyers and fourth largest sellers on the day before the crash. On the morning of that fateful day, Harvard apparently unloaded massive numbers of securities, feeding the atmosphere of panic.

Another blemish on Harvard is Corporation member Robert Stone, also on the governing board of Pittston, the mining corporation that has provoked major labor unrest by slashing health benefits for a workforce vulnerable to black lung and other lethal maladies. Stone's affiliation with the University led Pittston workers to carry their protest to Harvard Yard, which has resounded with the chant: "Stone is a stain on Harvard."

Besides Stone, Harvard Corporation membership includes Derek Bok, Henry Rosovsky (Harvard dean, professor, and director for Corning Glass, Paine Webber, and American Medical International), Charles Slichter (University of Illinois physicist and director for Polaroid), Coleman Mockler (CEO of Gillette and director for Bank of Boston, First National Bank/Boston, Fabreeka Products, John Hancock, Raytheon, and Gillette), and Judith Richards Hope (corporate lawyer and director for Woodward and Lothrop, Conrail, and the Budd Co.). A seventh member of the Corporation will be named shortly. For a university that has been the nation's leader in promoting programs in business ethics (according to *Time*), the prominence on its main ruling body of Pittston, Bank of Boston (convicted in a Swiss money laundering scheme and for years accepting bags of money from Boston's top organized crime family, the Angiulos), Gillette (heading the list of animal rights activists for cruel and unusual treatment of lab mammals), Raytheon (a defense contractor that even pro-industry *Aviation Week* identifies as among the most vulnerable to tougher federal fraud statutes), and Paine Webber (whose analysts in 1985 were flush with praise for investing in post-Bhopal pesticide kingpin, Union Carbide) suggests that Harvard's homilies on corporate behavior are not meant to be taken too seriously. The Corporation's investments are handled by the Harvard Management Co. led by Walter Cabot of the famous Boston Brahmin clan whose family fortune was built in part through the opium trade of the nineteenth century, nourished in the twentieth by substantial ownership of the United Fruit Co., who promoted the toppling of the democratically elected government of Jacobo Arbenz in Guatemala in 1954, and in the present, by presiding over a university's portfolio that stands among the most morally sanctioned of the non-profit sector.

Over $163 million of Harvard's portfolio remains invested in firms doing business in South Africa. The following is a list of Harvard's top investments in 1988.

FIRM	Market Value (Millions of Dollars)
Kolberg, Kravis, and Roberts	94
IBM	54
The Henley Group	49
Polk and Taylor Buildings	34
Harken Oil	31
Philip Morris	28
Student Loan Marketing Assoc.	28
Dow Chemical	28
Digital	27
Exxon	25
Warburg, Pincus Capital	25
HACO Corporation	24
Property Capital Trust	23
General Motors	20
Welsh, Carson, Anderson, and Stowe	20
NYNEX	17
Middle South Utilities	17
Bellsouth Corporation	16
General Electric	16
Dimensional Fund Advisors	16
Cilluffo Associates	16
Boeing	15
CMS Energy	15
Bankers Trust	15
Dun and Bradstreet	14
Ford	14
Flserv, Inc.	13
Pacific Telesis	13
Delta Airlines	13
HLM Partners	13
Upjohn	13
Outboard Marine Corporation	12
Wells Fargo	12
Oracle Systems	12
United Technologies	12

Notes

1. In a speech at Mather House on October 8, 1986, liberal dean and current Corporation member Henry Rosovsky warned students that today the biggest danger to Harvard comes from those he called "the Academic Bolsheviks." The *Crimson*, October 9, 1986, p. 8.

2. Ten donors, including Rockefeller himself, each contributed $5 million just before Harvard's 350th anniversary in 1986. Many universities have one or two donors, a Bill Cosby, i.e., who can deliver multimillion dollar sums. A mere handful have a phalanx of centimillionaires and billionaires who can raise $50 million at the drop of a mortar board. *U.S. News and World Report*, August 25, 1986, p. 55.

3. Peter Dobkin Hall, *The Organization of American Culture: Private Institutions, Elites, and the Origins of American Nationality* (New York: NYU Press, 1984), p. 269.

4. *Ibid.*, pp. 269-270.

5. The *Crimson*, June 6, 1984, p. 13.

6. See *How Harvard Rules* (1969 edition).

7. For lists of these directorships on the Corporation, see the Harvard Watch reports compiled by Robert Weissman, especially "The Hidden Rule: A Critical Discussion of Harvard University Governing Structure," issued by Harvard Watch, December 7, 1987, pp. 51-53.

8. Standard and Poor's cited in James Schwartz, "The Crimson Handshake" in the *Crimson: 350 Years of Harvard* (special edition, 1986), pp. 14-15.

9. *Ibid.*

10. "The Many Paths to Riches," *Forbes*, October 23, 1989, p. 148.

11. James K. Glassman, "Being There," *The New Republic*, May 26, 1986, p. 14.

12. Lopez compiled these figures for 1974 and found the HLS dominance to be more pronounced, as these firms ranged from 33 to 60 percent of its members with HLS degrees. But before sociologists declare this proof of the waning of Harvard, they should note that the explosive growth in the size of these firms may well have necessitated the tapping of talent from more sources. In most elite firms, HLS typically has triple the places over the nearest university rival. See E.H. Lopez, *The Harvard Mystique* (New York: Macmillan, 1979), pp. 40-44.

13. *Ibid.*, p. 41.

14. E. Digby Baltzell, *Puritan Boston and Quaker Philadelphia* (Boston: Beacon Press, 1979), pp. 230-235.

15. See Upton Sinclair, *The Goose Step* (self-published, 1923).

16. Hall, pp. 266-267.

17. Schwartz, p. 14.

18. The *Crimson*, November 14, 1986, p. 3.

19. Kate Wenner, "How Harvard Fails America," *Village Voice*, June 12, 1977, an article oft cited by Lopez, p. 225.

20. Schwartz.

21. C. Wright Mills, *The Power Elite* (New York: Oxford University Press, 1978 [1956]), p. 67.

22. Lopez, p. 17.

23. Chris Farley, "Harvard's All-Male Clubs," *Boston Globe*, February 22, 1988, p. 13.

24. Conversation with author.

25. Karl Marx from Vol. III of *Capital*, quoted by Göran Therborn, "What Does the Ruling Class Do When It Rules," in A. Giddens and D. Held, eds. *Classes, Power, and Conflict* (Berkeley: University of California Press, 1982), p. 247.

26. N. Chomsky, *American Power and the New Mandarins* (New York: Vintage, 1969), p. 27.

27. Jürgen Habermas, *Toward a Rational Society: Student Protest, Science, and Politics* (Boston: Beacon Press, 1970), esp. chapter 1.

28. Quotations of Towne, Scott, and Mann from David Montgomery, *Workers Control in America* (Cambridge: Cambridge University Press, 1979), p. 158.

29. Marquand quoted by Baltzell, p. 261.

30. White, p. 62.

31. P. Anderson, "Origins of the Present Crisis," in P. Anderson and R. Blackburn, eds., *Towards Socialism* (Ithaca: Cornell University Press, 1966), pp. 32-33. The opening sentence of my article is adapted from this by now classic essay.

32. Gaisford quoted by M.I. Finley, "Crisis in the Classics," in J.H. Plumb, ed., *Crisis in the Humanities* (Hammondsworth: Penguin, 1964), p. 12.

33. Lewis Lapham, *Money and Class in America* (New York: Weidenfeld and Nicolson, 1988), p. 20. Lapham's unique contribution to social theory is his designation of the U.S. upper classes as an "equestrian class."

34. T. Eagleton, *Literary Criticism* (Minneapolis: University of Minnesota Press, 1983), p. 200.

35. Edward B. Fiske, "Liberal Arts Studies, Long in Decline Are Reviving Around the Country," *New York Times*, November 9, 1986.

36. Vellucci quoted by Joel Gurin and Nancy Pfund, "Bonanza in the Bio Lab," *The Nation*, November 22, 1980, front cover. The latest episode confirming Vellucci's remark is the announcement on September 1988 of Harvard's formation of the Medical Science Partners (MSP), a venture capital fund designed to commercialize faculty biomedical projects. Condemned by even the generally pro-Harvard *New York Times* and *Boston Globe*, MSP, writes Jaron Bourke, is "unlike previous forms of funding relations with the biomedical industry" insofar as Harvard now has a direct "role and interest in

the marketing of its faculty's research." We are coming full circle and Harvard is becoming less beholden to outside corporations. It is becoming *a corporation* itself. A common quip is that Harvard Law School, for instance, will soon open its own law firm. Stay tuned for more details. See Jaron Bourke, "Still a Bad Idea: A Critique of Harvard's MSP," *Harvard Watch Report*, October 24, 1988.

37. Schwartz cited by G. William Domhoff, *Who Rules America Now* (Englewood Cliffs: Prentice-Hall, 1983), p. 99.

38. Ernest L. Boyer, *College: The Undergraduate Experience in America* (New York: Harper and Row, 1987).

39. Martin Kenney, *Biotechnology: The University-Industrial Complex* (New Haven: Yale University Press, 1986), p. 103.

40. Yamamoto quoted by Kenney, p. 90.

41. "Agenda at Harvard," *In These Times*, November 19-25, 1986, p. 4.

42. *Labor Notes*, November 1986, pp. 1, 10.

43. Gurin and Pfund.

44. Gray quoted in Kenney, p. 54. This section also relies heavily on the presentation of Gurin and Pfund.

45. *Ibid.*, p. 65.

46. *Ibid.*, pp. 58-59.

47. *Ibid.*, p. 63.

48. *Ibid.*, pp. 62-63.

49. Steven Weisman, "Harvard Will Do Research for Shiseido," *International Herald Tribune*, August 5-6, 1989, p. 13.

50. *Ibid.*, p. 65.

51. On Boesky's investors, see *New York Times*, November 19, 1988, p. D1. Aside from Ptashne, Martin Peretz's family had over $8 million invested in Boesky's scam. For the leap in Genentech, see Gurin and Pfund, p. 545.

52. Gurin and Pfund, p. 545.

53. *Ibid.*, pp. 545-546.

54. "For profit or science? Questions over an AIDS test," *Boston Globe*, June 28, 1988, pp. 43, 56.

55. *Boston Globe*, October 19, 1988, p. 1.

56. Gurin and Pfund, p. 545.

57. Richard Higgins, "Study Finds Secrecy in University Labs," *Boston Globe*, June 8, 1986.

58. E. Mandel, "In Defense of Socialist Planning," *New Left Review*, 159, September/October 1986, p. 25.

59. *Ibid.*

60. David Noble and Nancy Pfund, "Business Goes Back to College," *The Nation*, September 20, 1980, pp. 251-252.

61. J. Paul Mark, *The Empire Builders: Inside the Harvard Business School* (New York: William Morrow, 1987), see back cover for statistics.

62. Shad's quotation from *Boston Globe* cited in "Making Money the Old Fashioned Way," *Subterranean Review*, Spring 1987.

63. *New York Times*, December 13, 1987, p. 44.

64. John Goldberg, letter, *New York Times*, August 13, 1987.

65. James Petras, "Speculators, Lumpen-Intellectuals, and the End of U.S. Hegemony," *Against the Current*, March-April 1987, pp. 6-7.

66. Walter Kiechel III, "New Debate About HBS," *Fortune*, November 9, 1987, p. 35.

67. David Halberstam, *The Reckoning* (New York: Avon Books, 1987), pp. 253-258.

68. *Ibid.*, p. 737.

69. *Ibid.*, p. 257.

70. *Ibid.*, p. 623.

71. Lapham, p. 231.

72. Halberstam, pp. 695-696.

73. For this citation from Levitt's controversial strategy, see Randall Rothenberg, "Brits Buy Up the Ad Business," *New York Times Magazine*, July 2, 1989, p. 18.

74. Mark, p. 72.

75. Diane Rothbard Margolis, *The Managers* (New York: William Morrow, 1979), pp. 43-44.

76. Mike Useem, *The Inner Group* (New York: Oxford University Press, 1984).

77. Mark, p. 269.

78. *Ibid.*, pp. 258-259.

79. *Ibid.*, pp. 12-13 and 259. Concerning Porter's remark that "There's nothing at all unethical about what I do...unless you call making money...unethical," Porter is, of course, an active self-promoter and rarely mentions the enormous sums of money he loses for his clients. According to Alex Beam of the *Boston Globe* (September 20, 1989, p. 71), "Michael Porter is the architect of a costly and ruinous restructuring of McGraw-Hill...After reading Porter's best-selling management manual, *Competitive Strategy*, [McGraw-Hill president Joseph] Dionne invited the wispy-haired HBS wunderkind to devise a strategy for pumping new life into the moribund billion-dollar publishing giant...Predictably, Porter's 1984 blueprint organization threw McGraw-Hill into turmoil..." Beam concludes: "Those divisions performed best that were reorganized least."

80. *Ibid.*, p. 259.

81. *Ibid.* McArthur quotation from *New York Times,* October 6, 1980, p. D2.

82. Halberstam, chapter 23.

83. See William Blum, *The CIA: A Forgotten History* (London: Zed Press, 1986) and Juliet Schor and Daniel Cantor, *Tunnel Vision* (Boston: South End Press, 1987).

84. Brochure reproduced in *Introducing Harvard* (Cambridge: Self-Published, 1972) p. 36. It also outlines HBS programs designed to train management in Central America, the Philippines, and other Asian countries. See also the 1969 edition of *How Harvard Rules.*

85. Bob Kuttner, "Ironies abound as Harvard resists all-out campaign to unionize," *Boston Globe,* February 2, 1987, p. 15.

86. "The Business of the Harvard Business School," HBS brochure, 1986, p. 1.

87. Mark, pp. 115-116.

88. Statistics from *Statistical Abstract of the United States,* cited by G. Katsifiacis, *The Imagination of the New Left* (Boston: South End Press, 1987), p. 167.

89. Robert Engler, "Social Science and Social Consciousness: the Shame of the Universities," Theodore Roszak, ed., *The Dissenting Academy* (New York: Vintage, 1968), pp. 184-185.

90. Margolis, pp. 159-160 and 166-167.

91. Mark, chapter 8.

92. Quoted by the *Boston Globe,* article reprinted in *Introducing Harvard* (Cambridge, 1972), p. 53.

93. Brewster quoted in Barbara Ann Scott, "Class Interests and Academic Policy Planning," *New Political Science,* 14, Winter 1985-86, p. 132.

94. Eliot quoted in David Smith, *Who Rules the Universities* (New York: Monthly Review Press, 1974), pp. 85-86.

95. David Noble, "The Multinational University," *Zeta,* April 1989, pp. 17-23. John Judis, "U.S.-funded research becomes foreign affair," *In These Times,* September 20-26, 1989, p. 3. For the decline of the professional ethos and the stratification among the faculty, see Barbara Ehrenreich, *Fear of Falling* (New York: Pantheon, 1989), p. 246.

96. Georg Lukacs, *History and Class Consciousness* (London: Merlin Press, 1971), p. 100. Lukacs was discussing the effects of the triumph of "the commodity relation" in journalism.

97. Noble, p. 23.

98. Fred Kaplan, "Harvard fined over radioactive materials," *Boston Globe,* June 11, 1986, pp. 1 and 27.

99. *Ibid.*

100. "Radiation Tests Employed People as Human Guinea Pigs," *Boston Globe,* October 25, 1986.

101. Schlesinger quoted in *Christian Science Monitor*, January 27, 1977, p. 12.

102. American Cyanamid investment figures from *Harvard University—General Investment Holdings* issued by Presidents and Fellows of Harvard University, June 30, 1986 and June 30, 1988. From 1986 to 1988, Harvard's investment in Cyanamid dropped from $8.5 million to $2 million.

103. "Harvard University Committee on Shareholder Responsibility, Annual Report, 1985-86, October 1986, pp. 8-9.

104. "Cyanamid," in M. Moscowitz, et al., *Everybody's Business: An Almanac* (New York: Harper and Row, 1980), pp. 599-601.

105. See the excellent coverage of Felicia Kornbluh, *Subterranean Review*, December 1988.

Neighborhood Bully
Harvard, the Community, and Urban Development

Zachary Robinson and Oscar Hernandez

The name "Harvard" typically evokes architectural images of neatly huddled relics of Early Americana. Indeed, Harvard's first buildings still form the core of its modern-day campus. But from the twenty-five-story William James Hall to the expansive Science Center and the JFK School of Government complex/theme park, Harvard has sprawled well beyond its original colonial horizons. To the soft accompaniment of rustling ivy and the harsher reality of community displacement, Harvard has emerged as a key shaper of Cambridge. It is the city's largest private landholder and a major landlord. Legally classified as a nonprofit charity, it nonetheless aggressively manages a profitable land and housing portfolio. Often Cantabrigians and their elected representatives must contend with this resourceful adversary for the very survival of their communities. Harvard has succeeded, however, in avoiding a socially responsible course with respect to the urban environment.

In 1969, the student authors of the original *How Harvard Rules* wrote of this situation:

> It is in the management of Harvard's business affairs that the governors of the Corporation come into their own, and Harvard's corporate nature is most clearly visible. In its relationship to the people who live and work around it, the Corporation clearly puts Harvard's interests above all others.

Their warning to us is clear. This essay will consider three landmarks in the history of Cambridge which chart the scope of Harvard's corporate attitudes: 1) Harvard's central role in the 1940 reorganization of Cambridge city governance which substantially undermined local neighborhood political clout; 2) the emergence in the late 1960s of resistance to what SDS termed Harvard's "urban imperialism"; and 3) Harvard's continued expansion and ability to subvert gains won in previous decades of struggle.

Historically, Cambridge was a thriving industrial center, the second largest in the state. But beginning in the mid-1950s, the face of Cambridge underwent profound change. This change, today commonly referred to as deindustrialization, was the culmination of a colossal economic restructuring and urban reorganization that began in the wake of the Great Depression and subsequent World War. Old Cambridge was swept up in the tide. The situation of contemporary Cambridge can be traced clearly to the beginning of this epoch, when its municipal governing structure underwent a pronounced shift.

Plan E

In the mid-1930s, Harvard suddenly took an interest in Cambridge municipal governance. The ward-based system then employed was a guarantor of community stability. Local ward politicians derived support from a complex of ancillary institutions: clubs, churches, ethnic organizations. On the one hand, some politicians shrewdly bartered favors for votes from key constituents to establish their foothold in the municipal bureaucracy. On the other hand, the small size of the ward allowed the developing U.S. left to achieve important electoral gains. Harvard and other local corporate interests sought a political system more amenable to their agendas.

They maneuvered for a system called Plan E[1] with Proportional Representation (P.R.). Plan E is a system of government by city councillors elected at large by preferential ballot. These councillors choose from among themselves a largely ceremonial mayor and appoint a centrally powerful "professional" city manager. The city manager then makes all other major appointments.

The words of Edward A. Crane, in 1935 a Harvard senior, later a Harvard Law School graduate, a director of two banks, a lawyer associated with a large developer, a Cambridge city councillor and a mayor of Cambridge, are worth quoting at length. His thesis is titled *The Law and Practice of Proportional Representation in Municipal Government Including Case Study of Cambridge*. In it, he displays cynical insight into the workings of local politics:

> Success in a city-wide (as opposed to ward-based) campaign cannot help severing some of the false local attachments which now obstruct the public good of the entire city. Election at large is bound to give the successful candidate a greater freedom.

Another advantage of election at large is that it improves the quality if not the quantity of the mayoralty market. It provides a short cut to the mayor's chair… (p. 94).

As well as perceiving an outlet for his personal ambitions, Crane saw deeper into the question of the new political structure. In his vision of well-funded professionalized, de-localized, de-partisanized politics "…there is no more reason for supposing that a voter prefers a neighbor for his representative than there is to suppose that all people patronize lawyers and doctors who live in their ward" (p. 53).

He felt that it was possible to prevent:

…the division of cities along racial, religious and class lines. The best method of combatting this evil of the formation of petty cliques is to cut down the number of councillors [as indeed it was, from 15 to 9] with the purpose of raising the quota [of votes needed for election under a P.R. system]…

Crane also noted that "In no P.R. election has labor become class-conscious and put up its own candidate" (p. 63).

Needless to say, public scrutiny of the straightforward discussion in Crane's thesis would have done much to fan the flames of debate. Accordingly, a note from an unnamed Harvard archivist prominently glued to the inside cover of the thesis in 1947 announced that:

Edward A. Crane requests that we restrict the use of this thesis for a period of five years [during which time he was appointed mayor], allowing it to be used only with his consent. He has explained to me his reason, which is that it contains political ammunition that might be used against him. Crane is in politics and lives in Cambridge…

The struggle over Plan E in Cambridge began in 1938. Harvard displayed great interest in the campaign. A Harvard heavyweight, James Landis, Dean of Harvard Law School, a nationally prominent New Deal Democrat, a part of Roosevelt's "Brain Trust," and a member of the Securities and Exchange Commission, was brought in to handle the nitty-gritty of breaking the "false local attachments." He headed the Citizens' Nonpartisan Committee (CNC), the proponents of Plan E. Other officers of the CNC were Henry Wise, prominent in Federal Urban Renewal circles; Jeremiah Downey, founder of the Cambridge Industry Association; Mary Heard, president of the predominantly Brattle Street-based and Republican Cambridge

League of Women Voters; and Archibald Cox, Harvard Law Professor. Cambridge was widely viewed as a political test for Plan E.

An opposition group, The People's Committee for the Preservation of Democracy in Cambridge, was formed and headed by Councillor Toomey. Councillor Al Vellucci was also involved. The two groups maneuvered for support. The CNC targeted city employees, promising that professionally managed city government would improve their lot. The CNC also targeted the black constituency, primarily through Archibald Cox, promising expanded political opportunity through P.R., though at least Ed Crane knew that his promise was a gross misrepresentation of the use to which Plan E would be put.

The struggle heated up. As Landis called the Cambridge City Council a "cheap gang of politicians" in a front-page piece in the *Boston Globe* of October 10, 1938, Councillor Toomey entered a motion to cut Harvard out of Cambridge municipal boundaries. In response, on October 22, 1938, jack booted members of the Harvard *Lampoon* marched storm-trooper style down Massachusetts Avenue and demanded that its own "frontiers" be guaranteed. Eventually they confronted Councillor Michael Sullivan, whom they kicked to the ground in the ensuing scuffle. The Harvard *Lampoon* embarrassed Landis with its mocking prank gone awry.

The People's Committee and the CNC denounced each other in two-inch newspaper headlines. "HITLER—MUSSOLINI—PLAN E": the People's Committee charged that the P.R. scheme aided the spread of Fascism in Germany and Italy. "SHAME": the CNC charged that the names of Hitler and Mussolini were being used to terrorize voters. It is important to note the extent to which the intuition of the People's Committee reflected the research in Crane's thesis. Crane included a technical study of how the Nazi Party manipulated the German P.R. system to effective result. Crane even went to the trouble of including a sample German ballot.

Plan E failed in the 1938 vote but eventually succeeded in 1940, due in part to steadily increasing rates of municipal taxation, a falling real estate market and the perceived burden to the local economy. The success was also due in part to the increased level of sophistication of the CNC's campaign. They had a corps of speakers whose speeches were specially tailored to the various constituencies that included endorsements from well-known ethnic and religious figures. The People's Committee also adopted a more sophisticated stance in its 1940 campaign literature: "Keep the present form of government in the hands of the workingman—fight Plan E."

At the end of his 1935 thesis, Ed Crane exercised his contempt for the working-class communities:

> I have been continually aware throughout of a certain smugness exemplified in those who do not recognize the natural restlessness that comes from the irresoluble hostility between what is (*sein*) and what ought to be (*sollen*)...regardless of all plans, it is impossible to make people better than they want to be.

Was Plan E *per se* "anti-democratic?" Perhaps city-wide at large elections are not inherently anti-democratic, but at the time it had that effect. Working-class politics were not developed in a class-conscious way in Cambridge. Instead, they revolved around a highly localized geographical consciousness and neighborhood ethnic and religious institutions. It had quasi-feudal features, with ward bosses, nepotism, etc. Plan E changed the tone of politics, creating a sort of mysticism of the professional municipal problem-solver. It changed the focus of politics towards highly organized interest groups. The most undemocratic legacy of Plan E is the role of the city manager. This centrally powerful, appointed executive is today further insulated from the democratic process by a half million dollar "golden parachute" clause in the city manager's contract. Though in the minority, development interests, as well as Ed Crane and his protegés, were able to exploit the inside edge they won with Plan E. In that sense, Plan E was undemocratic. But to the extent that it broke machine politics' backwardness, it was progressive. In order for the communities to fight back, they now have to be much more conscious of their class and other common interests, and conscious of who and what they are struggling against.

The Boston ward structure was next to go in 1949 along with the boisterous James Michael Curley, then the city's mayor. Boston had its own CNC to provide business leadership for these changes, the Boston Municipal Research Bureau. Founded in 1932 by 21 area businesspeople, Harvard President Lowell was chair from 1934 to 1941. Jerome Lyle Rappaport, a young Harvard Law School graduate, led the final campaign to oust Curley. In 1950, Rappaport teamed up with Henry Shattuck to form the New Boston Committee, one of the predecessor organizations to the Coordinating Committee, better known as "The Vault." This powerful corporate interest group has maintained its influence over Boston city government throughout the years.

Blitzing Out the "Slums"

The years 1957 to 1960 marked the first large-scale demolitions of working-class housing in the area. Boston's West End, a 48-acre neighborhood of more than 7,000 people and attendant small businesses, was razed in 1958. Without the efforts of organized community groups (efforts that persist to this day), Boston's historic North End would also have been destroyed. The West End was eventually developed by Rappaport into Charles River Park, home to 2,300 luxury-priced apartments and health clubs, boutiques, a hotel, office buildings, medical research facilities, and parking lots. Cambridge's first urban renewal project (1957) led to the demolition of the Lever Brothers plant and the adjacent Rogers Block, five-acre home to as many as 325 working-class tenant families. MIT President James Killian chaired the Citizen's Advisory Committee which chose the site, later to become Kendall (Tech) Square. During a 1962 New England Regional Space Conference at MIT, Crane described the 1957 demolition as the "blitzing out of slums."

Not only were Cambridge low-income housing units disappearing in favor of luxury apartments, but the city was also undergoing a further economic change not necessarily occurring in the urban reorganization of other U.S. cities. Cambridge was to become a major high-tech research and policy development center.

The transformation of the Cambridge economy from industrial manufacture to a research and development center continued throughout the sixties. In 1964 Killian used his government connections (he had been President Eisenhower's science advisor) to bring a tax-exempt NASA electronics research center to the area. Kendall Square was chosen as the site for the thirteen-story accommodations even though it meant the destruction of housing units. The Watertown Arsenal, another potential site, would not have resulted in the loss of housing. But it was three miles away from MIT and the committee that picked the site considered that distance too far away from university facilities. NASA provided 850 technical jobs. Kendall Square renovation cost Cambridge 3,100 industrial jobs. After two weeks of use the research center moved out.

Between 1957 and 1968 the number of high-tech research and development firms in Cambridge increased by 80. At the same time, 118 manufacturing firms left the city. From 1950 to 1970, while hundreds of low-income units were demolished, 1,900 luxury units were built. Rents skyrocketed. By the mid-1970s, institutional expansion left only two of Cambridge's six and a half square miles for residential use. While Harvard and MIT were the main forces in this transformation, the city government, distanced from community control by Plan E, was also an active participant. In 1966 the city's Housing Authority received authorization for 1,500 public housing units from the federal Department of Housing and Urban Development's Housing Assistance Administration. By late 1969 only 300 units had been acquired and Cambridge was "in jeopardy of having the remaining units taken away by the federal government."

The economic and political power wielded by the banks, the universities, and the real estate owners combined with national economic trends to make possible the rapid and dramatic changes in Cambridge. Shut out of power, the community was unable to defend its interests.

A Turning Point for Activism

The year 1969 was a turning point for student activism at Harvard. It is often assumed that the student movement was only concerned with the Vietnam War and on-campus military training. Yet student awareness of the housing issue had been building since the mid-1960s. Columbia University students joined in 1968 with Harlem residents to protest Columbia expansion into Morningside Park. Likewise, Harvard's expansion into the community could not be ignored. In the four decades ending in 1960, Harvard had acquired 159 units in Cambridge. In the next decade, it bought 834 units. Of these, 172 were torn down outright. Another 29 were allowed to deteriorate, then were condemned and demolished. Of the 623 units Harvard constructed in the same period, 529 were graduate student housing and 94 were for the Cambridge community.

A study done by the Harvard University Committee of Concerned Alumni explained what impact the 94 community housing units had on the Cambridge housing situation.

> A study was done by the Department of Planning and Development in the City of Cambridge on the secondary moves resulting from the occupancy of 94 new apartments at Putnam Avenue and Mount Auburn Street, constructed by the Cambridge Corporation with the help of Harvard.
>
> This research revealed that half of the vacated units were filled by students even though a careful selection process insured that most of the tenants came from the Riverside area. Thus the construction of subsidized units seems to increase the supply of

private units available to individuals associated with the University.

On April 8, 1969, when 300 students nailed six demands to Harvard University President Pusey's door, half of the demands dealt with the ROTC. The remaining three dealt with housing issues:

Roll back rents in all Harvard-owned apartments to the level of January 1, 1968.

No evictions from Harvard's University Road apartments to make way for the Kennedy political science library facilities.

No evictions of black and white working people from 182 units of Harvard housing to make way for the Affiliated Hospital complex in Boston.

The last demand represented work that students had done with Roxbury Tenants of Harvard.

On April 9, 1969, Harvard students occupied University Hall, the main administration building. At issue were the six demands. The following dawn, at the behest of President Pusey and his lieutenants, 400 police stormed University Hall. Two hundred students were beaten and arrested. The violent arrests galvanized the student community. Militancy over ROTC and community housing issues continued during the April student strike.

Phillip Whitten, president of the Student Association Cabinet of the Graduate School of Education, gave a speech at a general School of Education meeting in which he stated:

Do you remember—it was only a few days ago—when, in response to SDS's demands on Harvard housing, Pusey and Ford stated the demands were not factually based? "Can anyone take the demands of SDS seriously?" President Pusey asked. Yet two days later we all took them seriously, because, as the *Boston Globe* reported, they were based in fact and it was the University Administration whose facts were wrong.

His speech received sustained applause.

In a prescient warning, SDS also suggested that, whatever concessions Harvard might make, the University had to be watched: in the past and in the future they would expand and tear down existing housing under the pretext of providing housing to relocate displaced households.

For example, in 1964, high income housing was announced at Wellington-Harrington in East Cambridge. When the people there fought back, it was announced that low income housing would go up instead. A "Citizens Advisory Committee" was even set up. The Cambridge Corporation—a Harvard-MIT front—came in. Then we began to hear about increased expenses and financial difficulties. Now that construction is about to begin, it has turned out that the apartments will...be upper-income, just as the original plans specified...Harvard responded to this pressure by hiring a consultant to draft a community housing proposal. In May the Corporation announced plans for 1,100 low- and moderate-income units for the Boston hospital site. The units could be occupied by University tenants but displacees were to be given priority. A similar number of units were proposed for the Cambridge community, but this never materialized.

The summer of 1969 began with a campaign for rent control. In late June, a community-drafted rent control ordinance was defeated 5 to 4 in the City Council. Intense protest followed but late in July the City Council reaffirmed its decision. Rent control was not achieved until after August 30, 1970, when the State Legislature passed enabling legislation for cities to implement laws locally. Saundra Graham, State Legislator, Cambridge City Councillor, School Board member and community activist, emphasized that the tenant resistance movement was crucial in bringing it about.

Community protest with student support continued in May 1970 when the Riverside Planning Team petitioned the Harvard Board of Overseers for help in reserving the 2.25-acre Treeland Bindery site for 100 low income units. The site was the last remaining open space on the Charles riverfront next to Harvard's newly constructed Peabody Terrace.

On June 10, 1970, the day before graduation, 300 community members and students marched to Harvard Yard and had an overnight tent-in. The next morning, the activists realized that Harvard was not concerned with their grievances, so Saundra Graham and 30 other people took over the commencement stage. "Students protesting the war had taken off their gowns and invited us into the procession. I guess the University just thought we were students until we marched up and went onto the stage." Some people in the audience began to shout "go home," to which Graham responded that she and her group *were* home. In order to get her off the stage, administrators allowed Graham to address the audience and to meet with two Harvard Corporation members immediately after the ceremony.

Harvard refused to give up the Treeland Bindery site. According to the *Crimson* of September 21, 1970, University Treasurer and Corporation member George Bennett said that Treeland was "too valuable to support practical low-income housing." Instead, Harvard proposed an alternate site. They acquired a site at River and Howard Streets for the outrageously inflated price of $540,000. After a struggle to maintain community control over the project, the Riverside Community Coalition oversaw the completion of 32 low-income town houses.

Saundra Graham summarized the struggle this way: "I want people of modest means to be able to live in Cambridge. We didn't go out to intimidate Harvard, we were being put out of our homes. It was a matter of survival...We successfully stopped Harvard from buying up the whole community—they only got half of it."[2]

Tenants vs. Corporate Landbankers

Harvard consolidated its real estate holdings by forming the Harvard Real Estate (HRE) organization in 1978. HRE, previously headed by Sally Zeckhauser and more recently by former national finance director for Michael Dukakis, Kristen Demeng, is chartered as a nonprofit organization. It pays a property tax only on some of its holdings. HRE pays no income tax.[3] In fact, many of the high-capital redevelopment projects in the Boston area (including Harvard's MATEP power plant in Boston) have received (Chapter 121-A) tax breaks. Until the formation of HRE, Harvard had traded and managed property through other real estate brokers such as Hunneman and R.M. Bradley. Harvard also worked the real estate market through the Mid-Cambridge Corporation, which it controlled, enabling it to present itself as a smaller landlord than it really was.

As of 1950, Harvard's land holdings were limited to its campus. Thirty years later, a November 1980 institutional land use survey conducted by the city's Community Development Department found about ten million square feet of Cambridge land owned by Harvard. Harvard has formed a so-called land bank. The land bank strategy allows an institution to amass a great enough accumulation of land to provide a substantial amount of long-term control over the real estate market and land-use patterns. A corporate landbanker can skim profits in any of three ways: by milking rent while a structure deteriorates, by leasing underlying land to a developer, or by acting itself as a developer. All the while, control of the land is retained for possible future institutional expansion.

MIT also owns a large concentration of Cambridge property. According to the November 1980 institutional use survey, MIT owned about eight million square feet of Cambridge land. The accumulation of these large land holdings, beginning aggressively in the mid-1960s, brought a heavy cash influx to the Cambridge real estate market. Other speculators could hardly fail to notice this strong trading activity. Harvard and MIT acted as market leaders here; their massive acquisitions laid the foundation for later speculation.

The terms of the speculative drive were most unfavorable to tenants. According to the minutes of the Massachusetts Housing Finance Agency at its March 25, 1969 board meeting,

> the relocation department of the Cambridge Redevelopment Authority estimates that...some 500 persons and families are evicted every year by actions of private landlords in the process of assembling private development sites, raising rents or converting structures into higher-income producing uses[sic].[4]

A brief statistical comparison of Cambridge with its similar-sized neighbor, Somerville, is revealing. Between 1950 and 1980 the drop in family households was 13 percent higher in Cambridge than in Somerville. As families left Cambridge, they were replaced by young professionals and students, who were more likely to live in smaller households and move often. In 1980, 60 percent of Cambridge residents had been living in a different house five years earlier. (The figures for the Boston metropolitan area and for Somerville were 39 percent and 42 percent, respectively.) A high rate of real estate speculation in Cambridge is made possible in part by the transience of its population.

Saundra Graham reported that landlords evicted tenants "for no other reason than to speculate on property. We *had* to have a hotline. People would call and we would surround the house ten feet deep with people to prevent evictions." In order to avoid the controversy around its evictions, Harvard began to subsidize mortgages to professors as a way to continue to acquire property. "Individual professors would receive 100 percent mortgages [no down payment] at 6 percent interest. In the mortgage clause, it would stipulate that the housing had to return to Harvard. It was giving twenty mortgages a year to professors, and it told them that if you want the house, you've got to get the tenants out." The practice of acquiring control of property through subsidized mortgages to professors with a right of first refusal clause for Harvard continues to this day.

Selling homes to faculty provides economic advantage to Harvard. Community activist Mike Turk points out that, "when Harvard sells a three-unit building to a faculty member and therefore decontrols it [removes it from rent control] by owner occupancy, the price of the building is such that it creates an overwhelming economic incentive to charge vastly higher rents or set the stage for condo conversion."[5] The benefit to Harvard comes in two ways: first, by exerting upward pressure on local property values generally; second, the University can recover the more valuable decontrolled buildings through right of first refusal.

Cambridge tenant resistance to evictions, to unaffordable rents, and to buildings that decayed as rents were milked eventually brought about rent control in Cambridge. Direct protest and rent control had an effect on Harvard's land bank strategy. Unwilling to deal with tenant militancy at its commencement ceremonies, Harvard finally negotiated with Riverside residents, though Harvard did persist with acquisitions, albeit at a slower pace and, through its faculty, at one remove. Harvard, the largest rent-control landlord in the city, has also had to deal with the Rent Control Board, a city government agency that was created to give the community a margin of control over housing costs.

Given the role that tenant resistance had in the formation of the Rent Control Board, Harvard's dealings with it have not been what one might imagine. Fred Cohn, landlord, lawyer, Harvard graduate and key figure on the Rent Board, generously offered Harvard counsel on Rent-Board strategy. This fact came out when Harvard slipped a bill for Cohn's services into a statement of its operating expenses at a Board hearing. Besides the conflict of interest, Cohn's services certainly give Harvard an inside edge on Rent-Board hearings. Indeed, Harvard has been able to use its superior resources, legal and otherwise, to turn rent-control regulations to its advantage. According to Sally Ackerman, landlord and Rent Control Board member, "Harvard is a well-organized landlord which by law is entitled to rent adjustment."[6] Of the roughly 100 buildings owned by HRE and open to the general public for rental, 75 buildings (according to Zeckhauser), and by other accounts more, have had adjustments since 1978 in addition to the general city-wide adjustments given by the Rent Board.

In a letter of protest that appeared in the *Crimson* on October 7, 1986, tenants explain the nature of the adjustments that HRE has received:

> We are tenants living in an eighteen-unit rent-controlled property at 472-474 Broadway in Cambridge, owned by Harvard University. Soon, however, many of us will no longer be able to

pay the rent on our apartments. We are all faced with an imminent rent increase of 75 percent, the effect of two separate cases
now being heard at the Cambridge Rent Control Board. This
means that from current rents of about $335 per month we will
all at once have to pay about $585 for apartments with one small
bedroom. Harvard Real Estate, Inc. bases its request for this
increase on the following two factors: 1) they claim to have spent
$83,000 last year on improvements to the exterior of the building;
2) they seek to double the already substantial profit margin on
our building. Harvard claims that the costly external capital
improvements were necessary, yet many seem entirely cosmetic.
The sudden large outlay for improvements was certainly increased by the repairs being long overdue, a result of systematic
long-term neglect, about which tenants challenged Harvard University 10 years ago; timely repairs would have been less costly.
From the figures presented by Harvard Real Estate to the Rent
Control Board it is clear that Harvard Real Estate is well able to
meet all its operating expenses for the building at current rent
rates; even the recent external capital improvements would be
absorbed by the current rates. Why should any landlord, especially Harvard, a non-profit institution, be allowed to seek great
and sudden increases in profit?

Tenants in Harvard-owned buildings at 9-13a Ware Street attempted to resist a similar building renovation scheme. Harvard had
suddenly become conservation-conscious in 1982 when it decided to
install various energy-saving devices in buildings it hadn't properly
tended to in years. Harvard agents broke into apartments to replace
old windows with aluminum-framed, double-glazed thermopane
ones. Charges and counter-charges of assault and battery were filed
in court as tenants tried literally to stand in the way of a Harvard rent
hike.

Current rent-control law entitles Harvard to these dramatic rent
hikes, as Sally Ackerman observed. Regulations 72 and 76 of the city's
rent control ordinances are in fact being artfully exploited by Harvard. These regulations allow landlords to recoup all money—plus a
15 percent annuity—spent on certain capital improvements to buildings through a rent increase to tenants, regardless of whether current
profit margins could absorb the outlay. There are limited grounds
under which a tenant can contest the expenditure. Furthermore, rents
never seem to go down after the landlord realizes his profit. Harvard,
with its vast reserves of capital, can practically insulate apartment
walls with dollar bills. The interest is better than on many other
investments, and the risk is nil when tenants can be evicted for
nonpayment and new tenants are easy to find.

Not all landlords are able to capitalize on rent-control regulations. Most don't have the reserves of a Harvard endowment. In their acquisitive zeal, many comparatively small-time investors have adopted highly leveraged mortgage positions. This means that they have financed down payments on further purchases by adopting second or third mortgages on previous purchases. Often, landlords don't have the cash on hand to exploit regulations 72 and 76, let alone to handle routine maintenance. To increase profit in the face of large debt, some landlords resort to activities such as arson or submitting false evidence to rent adjustment hearings. They often disregard normal maintenance work.

The case of a mid-Cambridge lodging house bought by Barbara DeMarneffe in 1968 represents the small speculator's position. The Rent Control Board approved her biannual rent increases as a matter of course. Ordinary maintenance and repair were neglected until 1981, when steadily deteriorating conditions led tenants to organize and contest her petition for a rent increase. Her response was unusual and desperate, though it does reflect the private landbanker's point of view. She began eviction proceedings against all tenants. She wanted to stop operation of her building, contending that it was too much trouble to make the underlying investment worthwhile. Fortunately for the tenants involved, the courts did not think highly of her argument. To avoid being convicted for the operation of substandard housing, she settled out of court with the tenants' association.

The case of Craigie Arms, a Harvard-owned apartment building at 122 Mount Auburn Street, turned out differently. HRE allowed the physical condition of the Craigie Arms building to deteriorate substantially. Tenants would have been forced out had the building been condemned. This would harmonize well with the rehab plans Harvard had for the building. In 1981, a female tenant was robbed and sexually assaulted in her apartment. She brought suit against Harvard, alleging that building deterioration had progressed to the point where the locks and intercom system didn't function. The Rent Board ruled that the deterioration in Craigie Arms was due to natural causes, not to negligence. And there is now a tentative agreement with the Rent Board that allows Harvard to remove this building from the Rent Control roll for redevelopment as long as a certain percentage of the rehabbed units remain at rent-controlled rates.

Of the renovations and adjustments, Zeckhauser said, "we feel we want to preserve the life of an asset, keeping it viable for at least the next ten years." She described HRE's current function as working to "preserve the physical integrity of our buildings, which serves the community by making Cambridge a nicer place to live, and maintains property values."[7]

Bill Walsh, lawyer and city councillor, is leading a drive to end rent control in Cambridge. Zeckhauser echoes his charge: "It is not at all clear that people in rent-controlled apartments need those rent levels."[8] This view is a version of Ronald Reagan's Welfare Queen myth: that the few social welfare regulations that exist are not a safety net for those with lower income, but a cushion for lazy people. Instead, removing rent-control restrictions in Cambridge would seal the fate of its lower-income tenants.

Already, thousands of Cambridge families have become victims of displacement. Displacement is a cover term for a number of related phenomena. What it boils down to is that when housing prices go up faster than wages, the tenant has three choices: eat less, move to poorer quality housing, or get out of town. Displacement is not a directly visible phenomenon except in its most tragic manifestation, homelessness. Current estimates of the number of homeless people in the country at any one time range from 300,000 to 2,000,000. The nationwide problem has not been as severe since the Great Depression of the 1930s.

It is fitting to close this essay on Harvard and housing with a look at an intriguing episode concerning the University's own behavior towards growing homelessness in Cambridge. During the winter months, heat exhaust vents are the difference between life and death for the homeless. The heating vents at Leverett House, a dormitory for Harvard undergraduates, are no exception. In the coldest week of the winter of 1985-86, Harvard installed a pair of steeply inclined $850 iron grates over two Leverett House heating vents.

Leverett House residents, who had to walk past the heating vents to enter the dorm's cafeteria, were moved by the desperation of a homeless man trying to keep warm by pushing his arms and legs between the bars of the grates. Outraged by Harvard's attempt to sanitize their surroundings, those residents and other students protested to the House Masters. Students also went to the media. They proposed that the house basement be made into a daytime shelter. For the few days surrounding the incident the University felt the pressure.

The House administration responded to student protest by defending the grates in the Harvard *Crimson;* they were naturally "concerned very much for their [the students'] welfare. It's a matter of our having responsibility for the students." They claimed that two incidents prompted the request for the grates. While there is little reason to doubt the House leadership's concern over student safety, Jim V. Miner, trade supervisor for Facilities Maintenance, stated in the *Crimson* that the University's own planning for the grates had been in progress for "several months" and that the department was trying to find a solution to homelessness that was "compatible with the area."

Subsequently, the Dean of Harvard College, L. Fred Jewett, defended the decision to install the grates in a press conference. Public pressure and media attention—including a mention by Dan Rather on network news—forced the University to take down the grates on Tuesday, January 21, only a week after they had been installed.

That same evening, Dean Jewett addressed an all-House meeting and successfully shifted the focus of debate from Harvard's policy to Cambridge's zoning laws. The House administration emphasized how they and the police had offered to take the homeless people to shelters but that they refused. People who worked at the shelters responded that the large shelters were plagued by violence and robbery and the smaller, more hospitable shelters lacked space. Cambridge zoning laws were blamed for limiting the number of emergency shelters and longer-term housing to 1 per 5,000 residents. The administrators—in a rare show of community awareness—urged students to volunteer at one of the local shelters and to lobby to change the zoning laws.

It is an interesting coincidence that Harvard Real Estate has a longstanding battle with the city over zoning laws that stand in the way of its plans for property located at 10 Mount Auburn Street a few blocks from Leverett House. Administrators framed the problem as if it originated from abstract legal code and not from University policy. This approach had its intended effect: debate and interest in the problem of homelessness waned.

There are two conclusions from the Leverett House episode: First, homelessness is a corollary to the rising cost of housing. Second, Harvard acts to minimize the controversy around housing and dispel concern about homelessness; it takes a managerial approach to community discontent. Only under organized pressure has Harvard recognized its social responsibilities.

Meanwhile, Harvard's unrelenting expansion marches on. The recent overhaul of Harvard Square—completed in time for Harvard's

350th—which cost tens of millions of dollars and the life of one worker, provided the Square with a cavernous, modern subway station, an underground bus depot, new brick sidewalks, simulated gas lamps, and a rehabbed brick, glass and marble newsstand. Buoyed by the ensuing surge in real estate prices, Harvard University continues to promote a great transformation of Harvard Square. In order to clear the ground for a posh new hotel, Harvard razed a building it owned just days before it could be declared a historic landmark. Popular restaurants have been pushed out in favor of banks. In one critic's view, Harvard Square is today a giant "shopping mall with streets." When Cambridge citizens in the late 1980s formed the Coalition to Save Harvard Square, a last-ditch effort to halt the newest round of bulldozings and invasions of Gucci-loafered yuppies, Harvard University set out to throttle them. In 1988, the Cambridge resistance campaigned for new zoning laws which would prevent further office expansion. Despite a majority on the Council who were in favor of the anti-growth coalition, Harvard initially prevailed, though the Council has since tightened its zoning rules. In response, Harvard has hinted that it might turn to the courts to reverse stricter community controls.

The problems of Cambridge are a particular instance of a long-festering and multi-dimensional national urban crisis. Community survival is at stake. At the federal level, the Reagan administration took measures to undermine city rent control ordinances. Cambridge's own hard-won system of rent control today is reeling after a long series of local attacks. Housing, a basic human right, has for many become an unattainable luxury. On the other hand, area unions, such as Local 26 of Hotel and Resturant Employees, have successfully initiated a campaign to make businesses put housing within the reach of their employees. A growing sense of urgency over the future of long-time and working-class residents over continuing Cambridge's tradition of diversity has led community activists to form the Cambridge Rainbow. Working communities and their political representatives must fashion families' quiet desperation and impotent rage into political will that subjects Harvard and other corporate developers to a people-oriented program of city government.

Notes

1. Municipal governing structures are regulated by Massachusetts state law under what is known as the optional system. There are currently five plans available, including *Plan A*—Strong mayor, weak council, all elected at large. *Plan B*—Weak mayor, strong council, elected mostly by wards, some at large. *Plan C*—Commission form. *Plan D*—Mayor and city council elected at large with city manager to administer their policies. *Plan E*—City council elected at large by P.R., which appoints from among its members a mayor. An appointed city manager makes all other major staff decisions.

2. Interview with Saundra Graham.

3. On the tax-free properties in its portfolio, Harvard makes a voluntary contribution to the city of Cambridge; in 1988 and 1989, this annual donation exceeded $900,000. But as city council candidate Jonathan Myers has shown, Harvard would have to pay close to $6 million if it were taxed at the normal rate for its real estate holdings. In essence, working-class taxpayers heavily subsidize Harvard for various fire, sanitation, and police services. See *Crimson*, June 26, 1989, p. A5.

4. Cited in John Mollenkopf and Jon Pynoos, "Property, Politics and Local Housing Policy," *Politics and Society*, 1972, p. 410.

5. *The Harvard Independent*, April 25, 1985, p. 6.

6. *Ibid.*, p. 6.

7. *Ibid.*, p. 4.

8. *Ibid.*, p. 6.

Acknowledgements

We would like to thank Bill Cavellini (Simplex Steering Committee), Saundra Graham (State Legislator), and Mike Turk (Cambridge Rent Control Coalition) for their time and insight.

A History of University Labor Struggles

Vladimir Escalante

In an essay written in early 1987, Vladimir Escalante provides a brief look at Harvard's hostile policies towards working people, ranging from the outright contemptuous in the early decades of the twentieth century to, more recently, the self-servingly paternalistic. On May 17, 1988, the HUCTW (the Harvard Union of Clerical and Technical Workers) achieved a 1,530 to 1,486 victory in an NLRB-supervised union election, in what *The Village Voice* (June 28, 1988) called "one of the largest private sector clerical organizing drives in history, mounted against a powerful adversary." AFSCME President Gerald McEntee described Harvard's behavior as among the "most violently anti-union" campaigns he has ever witnessed. Undaunted by its defeat, Harvard University initially stalled certification of the election, accusing the union of unfair electioneering. In the summer and fall of 1988, the NLRB set up hearings for Harvard's appeal, the University's last-gasp attempt to stave off unionization of its clerical and technical workers, 83 percent of whom are women. In October 1988, the NLRB rejected Harvard's appeal, judging it to be "frivolous." Harvard has since agreed to begin contract negotiations with the union.

Commenting on the work of the HUCTW's leader, Kris Rondeau, Domenic Bozzotto, who heads the union that represents Harvard's food service workers, observes:

> Rondeau has brought local organizing to an art form. She came in and reminded people what unions are all about. Reagan said they were dinosaurs. Rondeau said, "let me redefine a union for you... It's not just for when wages are bad. You need it to question authority."

In response to Rondeau, he adds, "Harvard has told people to be as selfish as possible, just like Reagan's been saying." It is thus little accident that Harvard persisted in efforts at crushing this movement.

For additional information on Harvard's central contribution to ideologies of labor control, readers are urged to consult John Trumpbour's essay on Harvard and the corporations concerning the Business School's efforts at molding pro-business trade unions, as well as his essay on the sciences, which takes up scientific management. It also may be worth pointing out that the two most important Deans of the Bok era, Rosovsky and Dunlop—and Bok himself—are specialists in labor management and labor law. As

Escalante's account will indicate, Harvard's vaunted commitment to neutrality has never applied when the class war is at stake.

Harvard in the History of the Labor Movement

Little has been said or recorded about organized labor at Harvard, despite the intense history of the labor movement in the United States. Conflicts, however, have been evident between workers and the University administration. The anti-labor practices by Harvard have not been so violent or open as in other sectors of U.S. industry, but they are pernicious. As in the case of land and community affairs, the Harvard Corporation uses the academic prestige and credibility of their institution to advantage. When dealing with labor conflicts they try to present the University as a benevolent and altruistic institution absorbed in its academic pursuits. But Harvard is a business, run by people who run other businesses. Education is a big business. Its share of the gross national product is greater than that of the agriculture and automobile industries combined. Thus, one should expect policies similar to those that prevail in the current business environment. Hiring expensive union-busting companies is not uncommon. Boston University, for example, hired Modern Management Methods, commonly known as "3M," to try to prevent the unionization of clerical workers during a drive launched by District 65. Harvard University has usually been more subtle in approaching unionization drives, in part because it has been able to rely on its own staff to deal with unions. In this way many of the practices that other corporations use to deal with or get rid of unions can be engineered "in house" at Harvard.

Throughout this century the labor movement has struggled courageously to improve working conditions. Harvard has been involved in this struggle and has responded to the needs of the dominant class in most cases. As Henry Lee Higginson, Harvard benefactor, said in an anti-union fund-raising letter in 1886: "Educate, and save ourselves and our families from mobs."

One of the many instances in which labor-management struggle erupted was the famous "Bread and Roses" Strike in 1912 in Lawrence, Massachusetts, an early center of industrial development. More than half the population of Lawrence consisted of immigrant families who worked under precarious conditions in the mills of the American Woolen Company. More than one third of the men and women died before the age of 25, often within the first years after beginning work. A reduction in salaries precipitated a strike, which quickly attracted moral and material support from numerous trade unions, socialist groups, and sympathetic individuals throughout the nation. The mayor of the town called in the local militia, and the governor ordered out the state police. Harvard cooperated with the mill owners by offering academic credit to students who joined the strike-breaking National Guard under the motto: "Defend your class!" Strikers and their families were attacked by police; martial law was declared and citizens were forbidden to talk on the street. Strikers died at the hands of the police and the militia. Eventually, however, the company gave in to the workers' demands.[1]

Another example of Harvard defending its class was the famous Sacco and Vanzetti case. These Italian immigrants were anarchists and labor organizers in Boston during a McCarthy-like era in U.S. history when the Establishment was running "red raids" under the leadership of U.S. Attorney General Palmer. They were arrested and convicted on very weak evidence for the holdup and murder of two men.

On April 9, 1927, Judge Thayer ordered their execution. As a result of worldwide demonstrations and massive petitions for executive clemency, Governor Fuller of Massachusetts appointed an Advisory Committee to study the case. Its members were A. Lawrence Lowell, President of Harvard University, Samuel W. Stratton, President of MIT, and Robert Grant, a retired probate judge.

According to Louis Joughin's and Edmund Morgan's *The Legacy of Sacco and Vanzetti* and Grant's autobiography, the Advisory Committee was dominated by Lowell, who at once and without vote assumed the chair. It was popularly known as the Lowell Committee. Lowell ran the proceedings and wrote the original draft of the findings four days before the counsel completed their arguments. He also suppressed part of the record of the hearing. As stated in *The Legacy:*

> Sacco's alibi...hinged on an Italian banquet given on April 15. Lowell on his own initiative offered evidence that no banquet was held on that date...Twenty-two pages of the hearings report deal with this problem. Then there appears a notice that certain newspaper files were examined by the Committee. That is all.

The record is shamefully incomplete. Incontrovertible evidence was assembled that proved Lowell's material was wrong; he accepted the new proof and apologized to the witnesses whose word he had doubted. Absolutely none of this is in the printed record, and the only excuse given at a later date was the feeble observation that "colloquies" were not taken down. As Joughin, a social historian, and Morgan, Royall Professor of Law at Harvard, conclude in their book: "Lowell was involved in the issue to such a degree that he held the power of life and death in his hands, but he failed in accuracy, in judgement and fairness...The official representative of New England culture sanctioned the sending of two men to their death in the face of reasonable doubt."

After labor legislation became acceptable in the United States, Harvard, like other corporations and businesses, embarked on the task of circumventing it. For example, in December of 1929, Harvard fired nineteen women workers without advance notice and replaced them with men. The case erupted at the end of that year when a letter by President Lowell on the discharge of one of the workers was "inadvertently" published. In Lowell's own words:

> ...the minimum wage board has been complaining of our em-
> ploying women for less than 37 cents an hour, and hence the
> University has felt constrained to replace them with men. Their
> replacement by men was prompted by the fact that men were
> not protected by the law that prescribed minimum wages for
> "scrubwomen."

In other cases the University circumvented the law by changing the status of "scrubwomen" to that of "chambermaids" who were without legal wage protection and earned only 32 cents an hour. The women had to work from 6 to 11 a.m. in Widener Memorial Library, scrubbing and cleaning; often they could not have breakfast or tea breaks and were even charged 15 cents per week for the tea, whether they had it or not. Some of them had been working at Harvard for 30 years under extremely harsh conditions. After the case was made public, Harvard tried to present a fair front to the public and changed its position as the issue developed in the newspapers. University authorities attempted to justify the sudden firings by saying that the women were well aware that men might be employed to replace them at any moment. The case became an issue in the campaign of a Democratic candidate to the Massachusetts House of Representatives who held the Republican party responsible for the laxity with which the Minimum Wage Board had enforced the law. Some liberal alumni, like the Lamonts, worried by what they saw as "one of those absurdities which critics of the social order love," came to the rescue of the fired employees by implementing a fund to "repair the original injustice and to convince the general public that a more humane and generous temper characterizes Harvard..."[2]

The Role of Students and Faculty

Students have often played an important role in the labor struggles at their university. During the 1960s and 1970s they often sided with labor and the community, but the university has tried to create antagonisms among the three sectors. It is not uncommon to hear university officials argue that demands for higher wages or better working conditions would mean increased tuition, room and board fees, or cuts in financial aid for the students.

A pamphlet circulated by students and employees of the food service at Radcliffe College, circa 1967, denounced a 90 cent per hour differential in wages between "chefs" (men) and "first cooks" (women) doing exactly the same job. According to the pamphlet, Miss Russ, administrator of kitchens at Radcliffe, justified the differential by saying that although many women "cooks" have as much training as male "chefs," "two chefs in North House can do the work of four women cooks." Actually, two "cooks" in South House prepared meals for 400 while three "chefs" cooked for 500. She added that: "Women cooks are less confident so they look for the chefs for support and advice," and that women's wages were "merely supplementary to their husbands.'" The food workers were also demanding improved working conditions, including new dishwashers. The Radcliffe administration answered that those demands would cause an increase in room and board fees for the students at a time when the college was also considering the costly construction of an underground parking lot.

A dramatic conflict united students and workers after President Richard Nixon announced the invasion of Cambodia by U.S. forces on April 30, 1970. Universities and colleges across the country exploded in protest and clashed with security forces. At Kent State University students were killed by National Guard bullets. At Jackson State University they were gunned down by highway police. Within days after the invasion, students at hundreds of colleges demanded immediate withdrawal from Southeast Asia; release of all victims of political repression in the United States, including members of the Black Panther Party; impeachment of President Nixon; and an end to military and counterinsurgency research and ROTC programs at universities. A mass meeting attended by more than 2,700 students, faculty, and workers' representatives in Sanders Theater and Memorial Hall at Harvard decided to strike with the above demands, but those attending also asked the University that striking workers receive full pay, that there be no layoffs as a result of the action, and that students have the option of not taking exams while receiving course credit. The participation of workers in the protest was relatively low until a meeting attended by more than 350 University employees, teaching fellows and the strike steering committee decided to start a five-day strike and to picket their workplaces to convince other workers to join the strike. Their demands were identical to those that the students presented. That their action was motivated by an issue of sociopolitical importance—an imperialist war—brings into question the myth that U.S. labor can only carry out militant actions over "bread-and-butter" issues.

The University administration had learned to moderate its response to student protest after the violent arrests of students occupying University Hall in 1969. Later, in the face of the student strike to protest the Cambodia invasion, the administration decided to accept the reality of the strike and asked the faculty to postpone exams and papers for the striking students. The administration's strategy succeeded in avoiding confrontation with students, as the end of the semester was near, and many students—having no more academic commitments—went home. The strategy took up an opposite position with the workers.

The possibility of worker organization adversely affecting University operations prompted the administration to take bold steps against striking employees while justifying its actions with demagogic statements. In a carefully worded declaration referring to the strike, President Pusey urged officers of the University to make "every effort to accommodate interruptions by acts of conscience" relating to the war in Southeast Asia. His words rang hollow when supervisors at different schools and departments began threatening to fire workers if they joined the strike or attended meetings. When thirty secretaries from the Law School Secretaries Association joined the strike, the administration of the school said that time would be docked from their paid vacation and then hired scabs to replace them.

The administration made desperate efforts to reconcile its actions with its own declarations. At one point it questioned the definition of a strike. According to the administration's new definition, in a 'strike' workers could be excused from work to 'express' their feelings about the War, not to shut down the University. The Harvard University Press even published an Orwellian ad in the *Harvard Crimson* that tried to appeal to the radical mood of the moment by explaining why striking meant working as usual in dictionaries of notable Chinese Communist leaders, blacks in the United States, etc.

The administration's efforts to cover its double standard towards workers and students failed. More than 400 students blockaded University Hall with two moving circles on May 11. The administration retaliated by expelling some student organizers although some of the expelled students had not participated. The blockade succeeded in convincing the University not to fire striking workers, but the strike did not extend. Workers were not only confronting the University, but their own unions. Caretakers, mechanics, groundsmen, and the food service workers had no-strike pledges in their contracts, and so could be easily fired for violating the contract. The administration's veiled threats and waning student participation in the protest discouraged the workers from joining or continuing the strike.

Potential conflicts between the student body and the labor body at the University are encouraged by a legal system that tends to view the relation between student and University as a contract for services. Consequently, in labor relations the University administration often tries to portray the students as the providers of the money and the University as administrator at their behest. The inaccuracy of this view becomes clear when one notices that the student body is essentially a disenfranchised sector. The decision-making process at the University is monopolized by a small number of business managers and high-level officials who handle the University's assets in the ways that any business corporation would, always looking at the bottom line, rather than considering other priorities. The student body's lack of influence has been reflected by the indifference shown by the Governing Boards of the University to demands that have had wide support among students and faculty: racial integration of the University, divestment from companies doing business in South Africa, abolishment of the Committee on Rights and Responsibilities (a disciplinary body for the college), etc. Despite the administration's efforts to pit students and workers against each other, unions have usually shown support for students in their campaigns and have often joined students in their demands and actions. During the divestment movement at Harvard in 1986, labor activists—along with other community leaders—played a prominent role in protesting the University's engagement in South Africa and the violations of the contract with the food service workers. For several hours on May 1, 1986, community activists occupied the Holyoke Center office used to plan the institution's 350th anniversary celebration. On September 4th, activists joined students demanding divestment from companies doing business in South Africa by disrupting a black-tie party to honor the most affluent alumni. Bok cancelled the fete when it became clear that the only way to proceed with the event was to arrest the demonstrators. To minimize press coverage of the event, no arrests were made.

The faculty has also been supportive of University unions at various times. Their support, however, is strongly influenced by concern for their own job security, especially among nontenured teaching staff. Indeed it has often been dangerous for faculty members to advocate causes that the Establishment finds unpalatable. A leaflet put out in 1930 by the Harvard University Socialist Club referred to the firing of the "scrubwomen" mentioned above: "If women are fired to save a few cents, what would happen to a professor in George F. Baker's business school who dared to advocate the social ownership of public utilities?"[3]

Striking against Harvard is a controversial issue, not only because of the difficulties in dealing with the University's public image. A broader perspective on the place of the university in society is necessary, one that shows its role in reinforcing the existing power structure and socioeconomic order. The university provides the technical means and personnel needed to maintain that structure and order. Therefore the dominant classes have a stake in its control. In that sense, any attempt to halt its functioning is damaging to the system. A strike against the university should have the same tactical and strategic value for the labor movement as a strike against any industry of importance to society. The public, however, often sees the university as an institution of higher education rather than a workplace where labor conflicts can arise. The labor movement is currently in poor shape to change that perspective or to exert much leverage on it, especially with respect to Harvard. Unions at Harvard have therefore resorted to other methods of pressure although the possibility of striking has never been ruled out.

In the last few years, Local 26 of the Hotel Employees and Restaurant Employees Union (HERE), which represents the workers in the University food service, has been a particularly creative and combative union not only at Harvard, but in the Boston area generally. For years, union leaders kept a low profile and were more than cooperative with management, negotiated contracts without member participation, and failed to file members' grievances. The membership became so upset that they once threw chairs at their leadership in the meetings. In 1981, they elected a progressive slate that brought the hotels in the area to the brink of a strike before forcing them to accept an unusually good contract. Since then, the union has been highly visible on the campuses of Harvard, MIT and Brandeis University. From 1981 to 1983, the local heard ninety grievances against Harvard. In 1983 the local organized a sit-in in the personnel office in Holyoke Center and maintained a constant strike threat in their efforts to extend the contract. The union claimed that Yale University was paying wages $1.50 to $2.00 an hour higher than Harvard, even though the cost of living in Connecticut was lower than in Massachusetts and the pay increases given by Harvard were being absorbed into higher tax brackets. The Assistant General Counsellor for Labor Relations, Edward Powers, who was negotiating with the union at the time, accepted that the union had a point, but also contended that the University had different priorities. Quoted in the April 7, 1983, *Harvard Independent,* he remarked:

> I'm not saying that they have a good life. I could not raise a family on what they're making. But you have to question priorities...Harvard is a non-profit institution and since we are paying a price that is significantly better than the market wage, you have to wonder what more you can do. After all we have alumni, students, and 12,000 other workers, to worry about too. Yale went through a period in the early 1970s when they reacted to strikes by rewarding them. You got big increases because students were concerned, alumni were concerned, and so Yale made concessions. But recent settlements have not been as good. This year they're getting a raise of a nickel an hour.

Powers later advocated that Harvard not give the workers anything that "other universities would interpret as a victory for confrontational bargaining." These declarations served as catalysts for the union drive to mobilize workers, a drive that ended in a union victory.

In 1986, the union again made headlines on campus when it challenged the firm Harvard had hired to operate the Faculty Club. The firm was hiring outside employees in order to avoid paying overtime for work on Saturdays, Sundays, and holidays. The vice president and general counsel of the University, Daniel Steiner, as well as other officials, claimed that it was not outside employees, but students (who are allowed by the union to work in the food service). They couldn't substantiate their claims, however, and the union launched another strike drive. This time the union employed a tactic similar to one they had successfully used with the hotels in the Boston area. Since the hotels were essentially owned by the insurance companies, the union picketed those institutions to bring pressure directly on the owners. In the case of Harvard, union delegates went to the fancy neighborhoods of Harvard administrators and decision-makers to explain to the residents that their neighbors were mistreating their employees, and that there would be 24-hour pickets in their streets. In the words of Domenic Bozzotto, president of Local 26, "we wanted to give a stomach ache to the decision-makers, not the students." On June 19, 1986, the strike authorization was supported by a vote of 93 percent. Shortly afterwards, the union won their demands and signed a contract with a new firm. It is interesting to note that during the same year students borrowed this tactic to protest the University's investments in South Africa, picketing the house of the University's president, Derek Bok.

Workers' Concerns

The concerns and demands that workers at Harvard have raised could fill many pages. I only mention here some of those which, because of their social content, may have a stronger impact on the community and the University.

According to Domenic Bozzotto, the importance of the Harvard food service workers is not due to their number, but to the fact that the gains they make in their contract negotiations can influence other contracts in the greater Boston area. The union is also important because of the empowerment it has provided minorities in the workplace. Fifty-five percent of its members are people of color, and it conducts its business in five different languages.

Much of the union movement at universities goes beyond bread-and-butter issues, particularly in the case of the clerical and technical workers unions, which consist mainly of women. Unions organizing these workers face not only the difficulties that other unions have in fighting the Harvard "aura," but also the sexism that pervades the institution, the unions and workers themselves, and public opinion in general. The union movement has been dominated by men for so long, it is difficult for many to see women as unionists. Many unions of clerical and technical workers have established strong ties with national feminist organizations. Their unionization thus represents a double problem for the capitalist class in a financial center like Boston. It demands equal wages and working conditions for women as compared to men in addition to the usual demands of overall improvement in labor conditions. Women still make only 64 cents for every dollar that men make in the United States. Although other committed unions have also fought against gender discrimination, the case of the clerical workers has much larger economic implications for the business sector. The clerical and technical sector is one of the fastest growing sectors in the economy and in the union movement, and has become as important as the traditional blue-collar unions in the now declining sector of heavy industry.

The Harvard Union of Clerical and Technical Workers (HUCTW), which has been organizing since 1985, is particularly concerned about making contact with the community and with people who have common interests with the workers at Harvard. Kris Rondeau, chief union activist, points out that in places like Harvard workers are treated as if they are were not responsible, respected, and mature adults.

After combative labor organizations were broken in the 1920s and 1930s by repressive and often violent means, the concept of a union as a 'service' institution became prevalent. According to this concept, unions are only expected to provide or administer benefits that they manage to obtain from the management or from other sources and to cooperate with the management in running the business smoothly. The HUCTW and Local 26 have taken the lead in changing that image and adopting the concept of unions as an organized social collective of workers. The unions are not only fighting for better economic conditions, but also creating an environment in which political, cultural and social issues can be addressed. Their members have the opportunity to become part of an organization devoted to social change. The unions have broadened their perspective in the past years and many of the union activists at Harvard are strongly opposed to the national and international policies dictated by the University and the Reagan administration.

At an academic institution like Harvard that prides itself on being responsible for the development of so many individuals, it seems paradoxical that career development opportunities and promotions are scarcely available for employees. Technical jobs at Harvard are in high demand by skilled individuals who often hold graduate degrees, but job descriptions frequently omit explicit degree requirements and thus offer lower pay. The result is a professional workforce that is underpaid with respect to their qualifications. Furthermore the job descriptions are ambiguous and almost always

add to the explicitly specified duties, "...other duties as required."
This has often allowed for abuses. In one case an employee was asked
to take the place of her supervisor, who had left the job. She received
no raise in pay, but she applied for the job, hoping that her performance would help her in getting a raise. To her dismay, the position
was given to someone else, and then she was asked to train her new
supervisor.

The administration has created a large number of administrative and management positions in order to decrease the number of
potential union members. This large number of pro-management
personnel makes strikes more difficult to sustain at Harvard, and it
restricts the upward mobility of employees in lower levels. In the case
of the food service, those who serve the food in the dining halls have
little opportunity to move to better-paid jobs more often available to
those who work in the kitchen.

Unions at Harvard have the opportunity to solve the problems
mentioned above and to improve the training, quality and efficiency
of the work only if they gain the power to influence the management
of the University.

Anti-union Tactics Today

In 1977 and again in 1981, District 65 tried to unionize the
clerical and technical workers at the Medical Area. Their case gives
many insights into the subtle machinery that Harvard uses when
dealing with labor. On both occasions, Harvard launched a full
campaign to discredit the union and intimidate employees before the
election. Each personnel supervisor was provided with a notebook
prepared by the University titled "Union Representation Election
Briefing Book for Administrators and Supervisors." It contained
information to be transmitted to the employees under his or her
supervision before the 1981 election. Among other points the document states:

> As a practical matter, it is very difficult to get a union out once it
> gets in. Legally, a union can be decertified by a majority vote of
> eligible employees. This involves, however, a lengthy legal pro-
> cess which may take place only under specific circumstances and
> at specific times.

> During the campaign, the union is permitted by law to make
> promises, but the University is not. If the union wins, however,
> no salary increase or benefit improvements would take place
> unless the University agreed to them. As a result of collective

bargaining, pay and benefits can be essentially the same, better than or worse than prior to agreement.

...the across-the-board salary increase in January, 1980, and most benefit improvements would not have automatically been extended to Medical Area staff members had they been represented by a union. Harvard employees represented by unions did not receive the January, 1980 across-the-board increase.

The University would continue all normal activities to the best of its ability during a strike...The law allows an employer to replace economic strikers permanently...District 65 negotiations have often ended in strikes, particularly at the three colleges and universities where it represents staff members.

Over 1,500 Harvard service department employees (Buildings and Grounds, Food Services, Printing Office and Police) are represented by six unions. University supporting staff members not represented by a union have received salary increases and benefits equal to or better than these service department employees.

With these remarks the University administration inadvertently indicts itself for union-busting. The personnel office and General Counsel Steiner demonstrate some of the most common union-busting tactics: buying off the workers by giving non-union employees better conditions (that year Harvard gave an unusually high raise of 9 to 15 per cent to the clerical and technical workers) and threatening the union members with layoffs if they were to use their last resource of pressure, the strike. Interestingly enough, the document contained a description of benefits that the University had already provided in order to refresh the memory of the supervisors about benefits that were, evidently, poorly known or seldom used.

The 1977 election was also preceded by similar documents. They were often sent directly to the employees. In a letter from the personnel office to the Medical Area staff dated June 1, 1977, employees are encouraged to vote "no" on the District 65 representation election with an ominous "fact" list:

Did you know that as a union member you would have to pay union dues, averaging more than $120 each year? Did you know that as a union member you would have to attend union meetings, or pay a fine unless your absence was excused by your shop steward? [The fines were later excluded from the union constitution.] Did you know that the union would introduce a third party into just about every one of your job relationships, so that all sorts of things...would be subject to collective bargaining? Did you know that you might not get any better—in fact might

get less—salary and benefits through collective bargaining? Did
you know that no union can guarantee job security?

Both elections were preceded by a barrage of letters, memo-
randa and fact books, which were amply distributed or mailed to
employees at high cost. Some suggested that the union fees were
arbitrarily imposed on the workers to solve the financial troubles of
the union and were often misused in political campaigns. A 'fact'
book of 36 pages distributed in 1981 hid the book's origins on the
second page (the University administration, of course) in order to
make it look neutral. Its cover was designed to resemble publications
by the government agency on labor relations.

The University often shows false concern for its workers in its
efforts to discredit unions. Although the literature produced by the
University shows a clear bias against union collective bargaining, the
general counsel stated that "Harvard is not anti-union," and that it
was "quite clear" that District 65 would "not bring an improved
quality of life to the University." "District 65 to [his] mind is not a
good union." He added that it was "small, financially unstable and
trying to organize largely for the dues involved."[4]

When Harvard claims that collective bargaining may not provide better conditions for the workers, it puts its motto "Veritas" in
doubt. The improvements in working conditions, pro-labor legislation, and the relatively good standard of living that the working class
has achieved in this and other countries has been preceded by some
kind of collective bargaining, or more generally, collective actions by
workers. If the capitalist class has ever given concessions to the
workers, it has been because they organized themselves collectively
or because the business was trying to avoid their unionization by
buying them off.

The anti-union campaigns at Harvard have been characterized
by the participation of low-level managerial officials encouraged by
the high-level officials. President Derek Bok, a specialist in labor law
and collective bargaining, wrote two letters to workers saying that to
organize under District 65 would not be in the best interests of the
University. Before the 1981 election, a professor told employees that
the school would have difficulty raising funds for the wage increases
the union might bring about. A supervisor also said that if the union
was successful in raising wages, workers might be laid off. The
anti-union campaign was also accompanied by rounds of meetings,
all personally attended by Steiner, in which workers were briefed on
the benefits that the University provided, and what it would mean to

be in a union as compared with the advantages that individual workers could get by dealing directly with management. The campaigns often appealed to sentiments of selfish individualism that conflict with the spirit of solidarity that make up the strength of unions. These campaigns were shortlived in order to produce a peak of tension near the election day that would be quickly dissipated by voting "no" to union representation on the ballot.

In 1982, the organizing fell under the auspices of the United Auto Workers (UAW). After District 65 failed to win an election to represent the Medical Area—losing by only 62 votes—the UAW appealed to the National Labor Relations Board (NLRB). The union charged that Harvard had acted unfairly and denounced the cases of the professor and supervisor mentioned above. The University contended that it cannot control statements of its faculty members, citing the right to free speech. Steiner declared that if the NLRB failed to take proper account of the "academic values" inherent in the case with the free speech issue, it would seek court action. The Board, which has loyally followed the anti-union policies of the Reagan administration, ruled in favor of Harvard.There is another issue in which Harvard has received help from the NLRB. The University claims that a union cannot represent workers in only one part of the institution. It paternalistically argues that collective bargaining is a "meaningless gesture" in those conditions. Previously the board ruled against the University and allowed representation elections only in the Medical Area, but then the University removed the employment office in the Medical Area to better justify its claim. The NLRB overturned previous decisions and forced the unions to seek representation in the University as a whole.

In its anti-union drive, Harvard also has taken advantage of the high clerical turnover rate, which in 1986 it admitted to be 35 percent per year (43 percent according to the unions).[5] Many workers do not invest much in their jobs and are not worried about long-term issues. The University can save in pension and insurance benefits in this way, but the quality and efficiency of the work are negatively affected. The benefits for long-term workers that the unions are demanding would invite more employees to develop skills and experience at the University and end University neglect of senior workers. In one case, a highly skilled technician was being paid $17,000 a year after having worked for 35 years at Harvard. According to Kris Rondeau, senior workers are the backbone of the union and are more interested in winning the union demands.

The University has taken every opportunity to contract out for employees in order to break the unions that represent its workers. For example, it has been giving jobs to low bidders in construction sites for two years. The affected union, the Boston Building Trades General Council, has had a harmonious relationship with University management for years. "Harvard has always come with fair and decent packages," a union official pointed out. The union has accepted reduced rate payments and fringe benefits because of the around-the-year employment provided by the University, and it has preferred not to be involved around other University policies, such as South Africa. The union is therefore distressed by the University's contracting practices. A union official complained: "We are giving them a break and they are turning their backs on us." Other cases are more subtle. Harvard Real Estate is a company that enjoys the non-taxable status[6] that its relationship with the University has given it (see previous chapter on Harvard and the community), but its employees are not unionized even though they share duties and working conditions with the unionized employees of the University's Facilities Maintenance Department.

Union officials do not seem discouraged. Clerical and technical workers have been organized at other facilities, including the Teachers College of Columbia University, Barnard College, Boston University, Yale, the 30,000 workers in the University of California system, and five other public colleges or universities in Michigan (public schools are much easier to organize). Victories at other campuses such as Boston University, where a union-busting firm was hired, have produced a sense of confidence for the union activists. They have helped to build a new relationship with the faculty and administration based on respect that was lacking largely because many of the workers were women. Harvard has based its anti-union campaign on salary and benefit increases—besides attempting to instill fear and uncertainty among workers—but the close vote in the last election for union representation is symptomatic of the fact that the University is missing the point. In the words of Laurie Haapanen, one of the union organizers involved in the Boston University and Harvard drives, the union is "not only about wages and working conditions but about empowerment and feminism. We may not have a Ph.D., but we deserve respect." Jan Schaffer, another Harvard organizer, pointed out that the University authorities do not want to give up their power over the clerical workers partly because they are more aware of the ways in which their work is critical in keeping the University functioning in an orderly way.

The Yale strike of clerical and technical workers organized in 1984-85 by Local 34 of HERE had a considerable impact on the labor movement. It demonstrated the strength that a clerical strike can have. The fall semester was practically lost when strikers decided to "bring the strike home," i.e., go back to work to regain momentum, and set another strike deadline for the next semester. The prospect of losing another semester brought Yale to a reckoning. Harvard has studied this strike and is acting quickly and boldly. The University has amassed enormous resources to fight the union. For example, it has conducted an extensive survey to probe the feelings of their employees by asking questions like, "How do you feel when you hear talk about Harvard?" besides more conventional questions about their job. The survey showed that in general the employees liked and trusted the institution, although they considered that their wages and benefits should be better. Harvard's union-busting campaign is one of the most sophisticated ever mounted in recent labor history, and it is being closely followed by other corporations which depend heavily on clerical and technical labor.

Conclusion

There is no doubt that workers, like students, have a major role in the making of a university and its contribution to society. Their potential interaction with the institution is obviously beneficial not only in the practical aspects, but also in improving the living standards of all members of the university. Clearly this can only happen when labor organizes. For instance, in 1983 Local 26 pointed out the existence of crumbling asbestos in the tunnels where the food for the undergraduate dining halls is transported. The union has also pointed out that students who work at the University lack many of the benefits that organized workers have achieved, like sick days and job security. The clerical and technical workers unions are asserting their right to self-management. They have often demonstrated their capacity to run the university's offices efficiently and smoothly, and the faculty has sometimes expressed guilt at being unable to improve their working conditions in the face of the administration's indifference. Union officials are beginning to talk about "industrial democracy" as the right of employees to participate in the decision-making process and take control of and responsibility for their workplace.

Harvard University has taken liberal stands on many issues as compared with the extreme conservatism of other universities. But it is using those stands to cover practices that are more aligned with the conservative tendencies in the social and political arena today. Harvard is a union-busting organization as far as labor is concerned. The governing boards of the university insist on maintaining the supremacy and elitism that have characterized the institution for centuries and that exclude, for all practical purposes, all other sectors. Their paternalism in "worrying" about the best unions for their employees actually means gross violations of democratic rights. Yet it is those not represented in the government of the institution, those working and living in the most difficult and precarious circumstances, who are certainly entitled to have a greater influence. Considered as a group or collective entity, they are the most productive sector of society. Ultimately this demonstrates the importance of the alliance between workers, students, alumni, faculty, and community, as organized and collective entities, in the struggle to gain control over the educational institutions of society.

Notes

1. Lively discussions of this famous strike can be found in *The Rebel Girl* by Elizabeth Gurley Flynn, 1973, and in *Bill Haywood's Book* by William Haywood, 1929, both books from International Publishers, New York. See also *The Twentieth Century: A People's History* by Howard Zinn.

2. Details of this incident can be found in *The New York Telegram* on January 20, 1930, *The Springfield Sunday Union and Republican* on November 2, 1930 and *The Lean Years: A History of the American Worker, 1933-1941* by Irving Bernstein.

3. See, for example, *No Ivory Tower: McCarthyism in the Universities* by Ellen Schrecker, 1986, Oxford University Press.

4. *New York Times*, May 20, 1982, p. A-22.

5. In 1988, Harvard lowered this estimate to 26 percent per year. The union disputes these figures as inaccurately low.

6. Harvard does make a voluntary contribution of revenues to the City of Cambridge's coffers.

Acknowledgements

This article would not have been possible without the cooperation and help of union activists Domenic Bozzotto, Barbara Rice, Jan Schaffer, Laurie Haapanen, and Kris Rondeau, who gave some of their time to interviews and provided valuable material, and Ed Childs and Jean Alonso, who provided valuable tips and references. The editor wishes to thank Helen Snively for her advice and assistance.

Part IV
Harvard Science
and Pseudo-Science

Blinding Them With Science
Scientific Ideologies in the Ruling of the Modern World

John Trumpbour

A mildly amusing anecdote oft repeated among Harvard faculty concerns one of the University's most generous contributors, the publisher Frank Baird. Baird has funded the chairs of several outspoken representatives of the Harvard Right, most notably that of the arch-conservative Kremlinologist Richard Pipes. During the Vietnam War, Baird, concerned that his generosity might be used to finance the chair of a modish, left professor, told colleagues that from now on he wanted to endow professorships that would be free of dangerous ideological contamination. So these endowments, three in all, would be confined to the hard sciences, noble in their devotion to truth, and not full of kooky speculative ideas that are the staple of practicing sociologists and other murky practitioners in the humanities and social sciences.[1]

Baird's confidence in the ideological innocence of the sciences is a common but declining point of view. In the postwar world, two of the most respected theoreticians of science, the conservative Karl Popper and the anarchist Paul Feyerabend, have declared that one's vision of science determines to a large extent how one views society. Earlier philosophers recognized that there are important connections between philosophy, science, and political theory. Kant's philosophical system owed a significant debt to Newtonian physics, and Lenin thought that his refutation of Mach's positivist version of science was central to the construction of a revolutionary political theory.

Most social orders crave ideas that legitimate existing arrangements and inequalities. In traditional society, the appeal to the Divine, to the sacred, is usually found compelling. Yet the ancient Greeks turned to the values of science, typically biology. Aristotle claimed that slavery is natural and that "the male is by nature superior, and the female inferior." "This principle," he concludes, "of necessity, extends to all mankind." In early modern Europe, rationalism and empiricism again displaced appeals to religion. Hobbes relied on crude anthropological insights to justify absolute submission to authority: "The savage people in America... have no government at all and live at this day in that brutish manner as I said before." Two centuries later, vulgar adherents to Darwin's "survival of the fittest" vision of natural selection felt smug in the conviction that they deserved to be on top of society. As Bertrand Russell commented, they viewed Darwin's theory as depicting "a global free competition in which victory went to the animals that most resembled successful capitalists."[2]

It is in such a context, on the eve of the Social Darwinist moment, that the modern sciences and social sciences came to fruition at Harvard. The initial impetus for the transformation of science at Harvard came in 1846 under the leadership of University President Edward Everett. Acutely aware of the inferiority of U.S. science to that of Europe, Everett recognized that the new industries, the railroads and textiles, needed to harness modern scientific knowledge.

Prior to the rise of large-scale industry, U.S. science was dominated by craftspeople, tinkerers, midwives, and herbalists, those small landholders and autodidacts who saw themselves as fiercely independent and self-sufficient. They saw little value in consulting university scientists for expertise. (The very term "scientist" did not enter the language until the 1840s.) Three out of four North Americans were at that time farmers and agricultural workers, compared to one out of 25 today. Everett foresaw that large-scale enterprise would change all that and, hence, science would be forced to respond more directly to industrial needs. The universities could no longer survive as havens for cranky theologians and windbag parsons.[3]

So in his fateful speech of April 1846, Everett announced to his alumni, faculty, and students that Harvard would inaugurate a new epoch of cooperation between the industrialists and U.S. universities. He proposed that Harvard start a "school of theoretical and practical science" which could provide a "supply of skillful engineers" who would develop the "inexhaustible natural treasures of the country, and...guide its vast industrial energies in their rapid development."[4]

The New England textile magnate Abbott Lawrence said he would give Harvard the financial means to teach the "sagacious heads" needed to direct the "hard hands," America's immigrant working classes. He doled out $50,000, up until then the greatest sum ever donated to a U.S. university, to establish the Lawrence Scientific School at Harvard. Dedicated to applying science to the "invention and manufacture of machinery," as well as to the needs of agriculture, engineering, and mining, the Lawrence School pleased its benefactor so much that he bequeathed an additional $50,000 to Harvard in 1855.[5]

Unfortunately for Lawrence, Harvard probably did not fulfill all his hopes. The man chosen to run its labs, the Swiss emigré Louis Agassiz, saw himself as a pure scientist and did not eagerly pursue research in technical and applied sciences. In many ways, Lawrence himself had a preindustrial sensibility and did not have a sure sense of how science could be harnessed to benefit capitalist enterprise.

Harvard then, for a variety of reasons, failed to become a university renowned for technical virtuosity. The founding of the Massachusetts Institute of Technology (MIT) in the 1860s confirmed this, despite Harvard's continued preeminence in many scientific fields. Instead of following industrial specifications in the narrowest sense, Harvard science and social science became dedicated to scholarly production, but of a sort preoccupied with the propagation of ruling ideologies. Harvard's special commitment to the production of ruling ideology in its sciences is exhibited in three overlapping historical eras: 1) the Social Darwinist (ca. 1855-1900)/Eugenicist (ca. 1910-40), 2) the Imperial (1898-present), and 3) the Scientific Managerial (1910-present).

The Social Darwinist/Eugenicist Periods

The foremost Harvard scientist of the nineteenth century, Louis Agassiz, became the first in a long line of Harvard scientists and social scientists dedicated to producing elaborate classification schemes and genealogies providing scientific confirmation for the superiority of white northern European stocks over the peoples of southern and eastern Europe, Africa, and Asia (see Jonathan Beckwith's essay). A common obsession of this scholarship is the alleged criminal and social pathological tendencies of these "races."

This sort of inquiry did have practical consequences, and not only in the passage of anti-immigration and anti-miscegenation acts throughout the United States. At the Nuremberg trials, Nazi scientists pleading innocence would claim that their experiments on concentration camp victims had important U.S. precedents. They cited the work of the U.S. Army's Colonel Strong, who in the Philippines infected an entire prison population on death row with the plague. Subsequently Strong arranged for other prisoners to receive paralyzing beriberi disease; one died, while many others suffered permanent damage. Strong was rewarded for his research by Harvard University, which later made him Professor of Tropical Diseases.[6]

The Imperial Period

Strong's research harvested and then feasted upon the rotted fruits from the U.S. seizure of the Philippines following the Spanish-American War. But even those Harvard humanitarians opposed to the Spanish-American War, most notably Charles W. Eliot, maintained a confident imperial mindset. They came to recognize that the U.S. could achieve its expansionist aims through cultural influence and economic might, rather than through traditional forms of colonialist occupation. In 1914, Eliot, scientist, Boston Brahmin, and today regarded as Harvard's most illustrious president, called for a cultural and scientific offensive in China: "They [the Chinese] have no knowledge of the practice of scientific medicine...We find the gift of Western medicine and surgery to the Oriental populations to be one of the most precious things that Western Civilization can do for the East." The China Medical Board of the Rockefeller Foundation set out to implement Eliot's vision, working closely with Yale medical officials. Bertrand Russell, who traveled to Peking in 1920, was somewhat bemused by this messianic effort:

> The Chinese have a civilization and a national temperament in many ways superior to those of white men. A few Europeans ultimately discover this, but Americans never do. They remain always missionaries...not of Christianity, though they often think that is what they are preaching, but of Americanism.[7]

The Imperial Period retains a powerful continuity with the Social Darwinist/Eugenicist Period, especially in the latter's eugenic phase (1910-40). Eliot himself served as U.S. vice-president to the First International Congress of Eugenics held in 1912 at the University of London. Harvard, throughout the Social Darwinist/Eugenicist Period, was preoccupied with dangerous classes and the crisis of *domestic* social order, while the Imperial Period focused on the fear of *international* disorder. Both saw population control and mass sterilization as a solution to the impending disarray. Stanford's Lewis Terman, one of the leading proponents of IQ tests in the 1920s, explained the domestic crisis in terms with which the Harvard elites could identify. "It has been figured," he warned,

...that if the present differential birth rate continues, 1,000 Harvard graduates will at the end of 200 years have but 50 descendants, while in the same period 1,000 south Italians will have multiplied to 100,000...[The differential birth rate] is one that threatens the very existence of civilization.[8]

In 1937, Harvard anthropologist Ernest Hooton, president of the American Asssociation of Physical Anthropologists (see Beckwith), told the *New York Times* that:

probably compulsory sterilization alone would serve in the case of the insane and the mentally deficient, but it is very difficult to enforce such a measure in a democracy, unless it has been preceded by an educational campaign which has reached all of the teachable and socially minded individuals of the electorate...I think that a biological purge is the essential prerequisite for a social and spiritual salvation.[9]

A week later, he called on the United States "to encourage a sit-down reproductive strike of the busy breeders among the morons, criminals, and social ineffectuals of our population."[10]

Hooton would not have to look far for such legislation designed to assure genetic hygiene. Former Harvard Medical School faculty member Edwin Katzenellenbogen, later convicted for war crimes at Buchenwald, "among the worst of the Nazi concentration camps," according to *Life* magazine, testified during his trial at Dachau that during his years in the U.S. he had "...drafted for the governor the law for sterilization of epileptics, criminals, and incurably insane for the state of New Jersey [in 1910], following the state of Indiana which first introduced the law in 1910 [sic—1907]."[11]

The guardians of *Pax Americana* during the high water mark of the Imperial Period (ca. 1950-1970) saw a similar international threat from the growing hordes of non-western peoples. Alexander Cockburn reflects on the birth control and sterilization nostrums of the Harvard elite and the super-rich. Noting "the great Rockefeller obsession with the heavy breeders in the Third World," he writes that:

At the height of the Rockefeller birth control programs (which they combined with an obsessive interest in eugenics) their minions used to dream of conducting a vasecto-fallopian blitzkrieg in the Indian subcontinent, succeeding with the scalpel where, in earlier times, Alexander the Great had to admit defeat. Rich people always take a great interest in birth control, dreaming of a world rendered truly delightful by the experience of having to talk only to people as fortunate as themselves.[12]

During the crisis of late Imperial America (1970-present), Harvard science and social science, despite some dissent from within, took the lead in trying to restore domestic tranquility in the aftermath of the unrest of the civil rights and Vietnam era. Three professors at the Harvard Medical School, William Sweet, Vernon Mark, and Frank Ervin, subsequently funded with $500,000 from the National Institute of Mental Health and $108,000 from the Law Enforcement Assistance Administration (LEAA), contributed an intriguing letter to the *Journal of the American Medical Association* (September 11, 1967). They suggested that emotionally disturbed and pathological elements were at the vanguard of political unrest and rioting in the nation's inner cities. Entitled the "Role of Brain Disease in Riots and Urban Violence," their letter notes:

> That poverty, unemployment, slum housing, and inadequate education underlie the nation's urban riots is well known, but the obviousness of these causes may have blinded us to the more subtle role of other factors, including brain dysfunctions in the rioters who engaged in arson, sniping, and physical assault...
>
> Is there something peculiar about the violent slum dweller that differentiates him from his peaceful neighbor?
>
> There is evidence from several sources...that brain dysfunction related to a focal lesion plays a significant role in the violent and assaultive behavior of thoroughly studied patients...[13]

Curiously, back in 1968, the LBJ-appointed Kerner Commission, after extensive interviews with 1,200 people, failed to discover this emotional disease among participants in civil unrest. According to this commission of business and political leaders, the typical black rioter was indeed:

> somewhat better educated than the average inner-city Negro...
>
> He feels strongly he deserves a better job and is barred from achieving it... because of discrimination from the employers...
> He is substantially better informed about politics than Negroes who are not involved in riots.[14]

Undaunted, Doctors Mark and Ervin in 1970 published *Violence and the Brain*, a book recommending stepped-up research into psychosurgery and chromosomal monitoring. With ten million North Americans afflicted with "obvious brain disease" and another five million with brains that "have been subtly damaged," they issued what they called "compelling" data making urgent the establishment of a program for mass screening of citizens. "Our greatest danger no longer comes from famine or communicable diseases," they elaborated. They continued:

> We need to develop an 'early warning' test of limbic brain function to detect those humans who have a low threshold for impulsive violence...Violence is a public health problem, and the major thrust of any program dealing with violence must be toward its prevention.

In 1972, a student of Ervin's at Harvard, Michael Crichton, published the sensationalist novel *The Terminal Man* in which the neurosurgeon declares that "ten million Americans... have obvious damage...Now that shoots down a lot of theories about poverty and discrimination and social injustice and social disorganization... you cannot correct physical damage with social remedies."[15]

Later that year, Dr. Sweet testified before the U.S. Senate on behalf of building diagnostic centers for the prevention of violence. In September 1972, California took the lead, establishing The Center for the Study and Reduction of Violence, directed by UCLA's prestigious Neuropsychiatric Institute. Governor Ronald Reagan hailed the development, pledging support in his January 1973 State of the State address and later investing over $1 million in the Center for fiscal 1973-74, partly from matching LEAA subsidies. Harvard's Dr. Ervin then moved to UCLA, but the Center's activities diminished after students and professors mounted sustained protest, especially in response to its all too typical choice of targets for diagnosis and investigation: junior high schools, "one in a predominantly black ethnic area; the other in a predominantly Chicano area" for a study purporting to locate abnormal sex chromosomes.[16]

The spectre of the lower classes' possessing overactive sex hormones may have received inspiration from Harvard political scientist Edward Banfield, who in his work of major renown, *The Unheavenly City* (1968), brashly pronounced that the "lower class individual lives from moment to moment... His bodily needs (especially for sex) and his taste for 'action' take precedence over everything else..." Banfield searched for solutions to this condition of "present-orientedness," but he had rejected the view that psychotherapy could be relied on to contain the Freudian id run wild. The lower classes are not sufficiently articulate to benefit from its insights, and even if they could "'verbalize'" their anxieties, "there are not nearly enough therapists to treat the insane, let alone the present-oriented." The gravity of the situation was such that some policymakers may ponder whether the "hardest cases" could be:

cared for in what might be called semi-institutions [where]...they might agree to receive most of their income in kind rather than in cash...to have no more than two or three children, and to accept a certain amount of surveillance and supervision from a semi-social worker-semi-policeman.[17]

But most people would probably balk at this, as "'being lower class' is not a crime or committable condition and is not likely to be made one." Instead Banfield offered a more modest proposal: slashing the minimum wage to open jobs for the poor, clamping down with law and order, and, naturally, a stepped up program of population control.[18]

The most recent in Harvard's own saga of such forms of birth and social control concerns the research of the Harvard Medical School's Dr. Stanley Walzer. Throughout the 1970s, Walzer conducted research which claimed that people born with an XYY chromosome pattern should be monitored for possible criminal and anti-social tendencies. Though several distinguished scientists picked apart Walzer's findings, his Harvard prestige made some all too ready to respond to the XYY menace. According to Professor Beckwith, "Bentley Glass, the former president of the American Association for the Advancement of Science, looks forward to the day when 'a combination of amniocentesis and abortion will rid us of...sex deviants such as the XYY type.'" Several women have opted for abortions after learning that their fetus had this chromosomal pattern.[19]

Meanwhile, in a *Harvard Crimson* interview Harvard Professor of Psychology Richard Herrnstein suggests that IQ information should be gathered as a part of the U.S. Census in order to observe "dysgenic or eugenic trends in American society." When queried about the purpose of this, he retorted: "If at some time in the future we decide that our population is getting too large, and we need to limit it, we could use census information on IQ to decide how to limit it." Herrnstein is presently campaigning to increase funding for abortions and birth control for the lower classes, while calling for corporations to allow middle and upper middle class women employees to work on computers at home so that they will be better able to bear children, thus replenishing what he considers to be the U.S.'s dwindling intellectual stock.[20]

One government that already takes Herrnstein's ideas quite seriously is the repressive regime of Lee Kuan Yew in Singapore. Prime Minister Lee has set up a Family Planning Board which, according to the *New York Times* (February 12, 1984), urges "Graduates and professionals...to go forth and multiply," while "the less educated" are pushed "to have no more than two children."

In January 1984, to enforce this decree, women with university degrees were given top preference for sending their children to the primary school of their choice, but the less educated received next preference only if they underwent sterilization after their first or second child.[21] (By the way, President Lee sent his own son and likely successor to Harvard's Kennedy School of Government.)

In 1985, Herrnstein wrote a much lauded book with the criminologist James Q. Wilson that minimized the social causes of crime and declared the centrality of genetic contributions to the criminal tendencies of individuals. (Conveniently, Herrnstein and Wilson focused on the crimes of lower class people, omitting rampant white collar crime in their ambitious survey. As Lewis Lapham quips, "among the city officials appointed by Mayor Koch the crime rate of 50 percent surpassed that of any identifiable grouping anywhere in the world.")[22] Herrnstein is at times critical of racism, so he tries to divorce his scholarship from that of the eugenics movement of the 1920s and 1930s. (Oddly, however, the book is unabashed in relying on studies from Germany in the 1930s to prove its thesis!) Those who bear the brunt of his public policy "reforms" are surely those peoples and races trapped in the lower rungs of the U.S. socioeconomic structure. In a recent issue of *The Black Scholar*, Lynora Williams notes that today "some 20 percent of married black women of childbearing age are sterilized, many without knowing the facts of the procedure, some without even knowing the operation has taken place."[23] Native American women have a sterilization rate exceeding 25 percent, while an older (1968) study of women in Puerto Rico, a territory regarded by foundation social engineers as a model for export, indicates figures exceeding 35 percent. In the United States, female sterilization leaped 350 percent between 1970 and 1975, and almost doubled again from 1976 to 1982.[24] Harvard medical and social science has been in the forefront of legitimating the vasecto-fallopian blitzkrieg at home and abroad.

The Period of Scientific Management

The Period of Scientific Management has important continuities with the Imperial and Eugenicist Periods; it shares the previous concern with restoring order and extends it to the economic workplace. Although Scientific Management in part serves as a prophylactic against strikes and other forms of industrial unrest, as will be seen later, the chief advocates of scientific management share in the fervor for eugenics and population control.

With the publication of *Psychology and Industrial Efficiency* shortly before the advent of World War I, Harvard Professor Hugo Munsterberg proclaimed the birth of a new science:

> Our aim is to sketch the outlines of a new science which is intermediate between the modern laboratory psychology and the problems of economics: the psychological experiment is systematically to be placed at the service of commerce and industry.[25]

Munsterberg's ideas represented a modification of the nostrums of the father of scientific management, Frederick Taylor. Taylor, whose ideas began to percolate in the curriculum of the Harvard Business School during the previous decade and who himself served on the University's Visiting Committees, believed that workers' tasks could be made so routine and efficient on the assembly line that he once quipped that eventually a trained ape could carry them out. Taylorism primarily concerned the organization of production; Munsterberg and his followers instead saw themselves as a "maintenance crew for the human machinery," in the words of Harry Braverman. They spoke of "human relations" and "industrial psychology," a maelstrom of ideas designed to select, train, and pacify the workforce. It was seen by Harvard liberals as a sort of Taylorism with a human face. Munsterberg declared that his industrial psychology would provide the "adjustment of work and psyche by which mental dissatisfaction in work, mental depression, and discouragement may be replaced in our social community by overflowing hope and perfect inner harmony." Some of these ideas gained influence during the labor upheaval and class struggle of the Depression, but postwar economic expansion was required for their wider exploitation.[26]

Psychiatrist Elton Mayo of the Harvard Business School emerged as the most influential thinker in the new school of Scientific Management. An intellectual emigré from conservative Queensland, Australia, he treated class struggle and worker discontent as less rooted in genuine grievance and more as a kind of neurosis, to be exorcised by the techniques of psychology and social anthropology. He thus spoke of "the mental hinterland," in which worker discontent ignited the deep recesses of the mind, leading to "the hidden fires of mental uncontrol." Something would have to be done, for "the world-storm rages with increasing intensity; our will to internal cohesion is constantly disturbed by social disorder and...class ha-tred."[27] Though working closely in the late 1920s and 1930s with members of the Business School such as Roethlisberger, the co-author of *Management and the Worker,* and members of Harvard's Anthropol-ogy Department including Lloyd Warner, Mayo possibly received his most important ideas from the biologist L.J. Henderson, who intro-duced him to the thought of Durkheim and especially Pareto. In order to overcome the "anomie" (a Durkheimian concept) of the workplace, the scientific manager needs to foster the development of a "nonlog-ical social order" (a Pareto concept), which hitherto had been de-stroyed by social and technological change. By developing nonlogical impulses or social sentiments among the workers, the friendly man-ager can restore teamwork and harmony to the enterprise and thus heighten productivity.

The influence of this intellectual mishmash should not be un-derestimated. Scientific Management's influence went beyond mere business enterprise. Raymond Callahan's *Education and the Cult of Efficiency* (1962) is the classic study of how business elites and intel-lectuals from the premier universities, Yale, Stanford, Chicago, and Harvard, particularly its President Emeritus Charles W. Eliot, pro-moted the business yardstick in the running of the nation's public schools. Interestingly, the universities resisted Scientific Manage-ment in the running of their own institutions. The Bok regime, half a century later, has finally sought to implement its principles at Har-vard (see the essay by Robert Weissman.)

Scientific Management in education brought with it a vast array of administrative reforms and techniques of control and monitoring of students, most notably IQ and other standardized tests, replete with machine-like, multiple choice questions. The Harvard Graduate School of Education's George Mirick in his primer, *Progressive Educa-tion* (1923), declared that:

> the power of a machine is determined...by measuring the amount of work it can do, and this amount can be stated in what are called foot-pounds or horse-power.
>
> It is in this direct way that mental abilities are measured. A human being is a machine. This machine is moved by nervous energy... As in the case of an electric or a steam machine, the quantity of the human energy and the quality of the human machine can be perceived by the quantity and quality of the work that it does.[28]

Claiming that "scientific testing" had been "perfected," Mirick neglected to mention that in 1912 these so-called culture-free tests found some 83 percent of Jews, 80 percent of Hungarians, 79 percent of Italians, and 87 percent of Russians to be feebleminded, according to Professor Henry Goddard's famous exams sponsored by the U.S. Immigration Service.[29] These figures later supplied the arsenals of those lobbying for restrictions on immigration in the 1920s. Concerning test results of women, Hugo Munsterberg concluded that females exhibited qualities useful at the workplace: "The average female mind is patient, loyal, reliable, skillful, full of sympathy, and full of imagination." Unfortunately, measurement of these valuable qualities also revealed women to be inclined toward mediocrity, because the female mind remains "capricious, oversuggestive, often inclined to exaggeration, is disinclined to abstract thought, unfit for mathematical reasoning, impulsive, overemotional."[30]

Beyond its contribution to the fetish for standardized testing, the practice of scientific management has ramifications for the sorry state of schools today. By 1958, Neal Gross, in his study of public school administrators in Massachusetts, concluded that the leading educators demonstrated an impressive command of the areas promoted by scientific management (finance, personnel, and school plant management) but that their work in directing educational instruction itself was embarrassingly poor. The training of educational administrators in the graduate schools of education throughout the nation had been predicated on business priorities: scientific management and the cult of efficiency. The confirmation of the philistine quality of this curriculum for training educational management came in 1960 when Miami, Florida school administrators banned George Orwell's *1984* and Aldous Huxley's *Brave New World* in the face of complaints by parents that they were "filthy books." After the administrators admitted to never having read these books, the U.S. Commissioner of Education also confessed: "I've never heard of those books, and I don't think it would be prudent of me to discuss them."[31]

This incident illustrating the impoverished training of educational elites should especially be recalled today, when the E.D. Hirsches and the Allan Blooms confidently blame the protest movements of the 1960s for the "decline" in academic standards and "cultural literacy" during the 1970s and 1980s. Meanwhile, the principles of scientific management continue their reign of barbarism in high schools throughout the land.

But scientific management had a much more noxious influence abroad. Indeed in 1937, when Robert Brady wrote *Spirit and Structure of German Fascism*, he noted how much the Nazi mechanisms of labor control paralleled the ideas of Elton Mayo and his "Human Relations" school of management at Harvard. According to Judith Merkle in *Management and Ideology*, the heritage of the international scientific management movement could be found in the labor control techniques employed by the Nazis in a spectrum ranging from welfarism to slave labor. She elaborates:

> On the positive side, there was a Mayoistic concern for the reimposition of organic unity on that formerly isolated unit, the factory worker, through group determination of physical conditions in the factory (the "Beauty of Work" program), and management-sponsored, cut-rate group vacations and spare-time activities (the "Strength through Joy" movement). Throughout these efforts, the attempt was made to substitute group and official "reinforcement" for money incentives by symbolically reorganizing the sacred and ennobling aspects of labor in ways that ranged from the promotion of the Hans Sachs image to the ironic "Arbeit Macht Frei" ["Work makes one free"] over the entrance of Dachau.[32]

This is not to say that the Harvard exponents of scientific management had a strong predilection towards fascism. Most were outspoken in defending western democracy against Nazism. But their confidence in the values of scientific management and lack of concern for economic democracy in the workplace rendered them unable to see how easily their doctrine could be harnessed on behalf of chillingly authoritarian systems of rule. Scientific management is preeminently a means of rationalizing social control, seeking to restore order through class-neutral, technocratic language designed to mask dominance. But its overt message is that of efficiency. For that reason the advocates of scientific management in the United States shared with their German counterparts a passionate support for programs in eugenics. Indeed, some maintained close contacts with German eugenicists throughout the interwar period. Fearful that their support for welfarism would allow less productive people to multiply more rapidly, the liberal leadership of the U.S. Progressive movement warned that the ensuing decline in efficient WASP stocks would undermine the success of scientific management. (Note again how it is Harvard liberals such as Oliver Wendell Holmes who support sterilization laws with gusto [see the essay by Gould].) Eventually, many liberal followers of scientific management retreated from overt advocacy of eugenics when the Nazis carried it to its horrible logical terminus. In her judicious study, Merkle observes the following about Nazi behavior and its debt to the Harvard advocates of scientific management:

> While the efficiency craze generated by Scientific Management was not the sole cause of this campaign of murder, its elevation of efficiency and rationality as virtues above common morality, its pseudo-scientific language and organizational techniques, and its early entanglement with ideas of racial and social efficiency certainly assisted in legitimating a developing climate of opinion that allowed administrators of the efficiently bureaucratized Aryan reproduction and minority liquidation campaigns to function with a sense of duty well done.[33]

Harvard has not been free of such abuses in the postwar world. The largest of Harvard's institutions, its medical-industrial complex sprawled throughout Boston, operates on many of the principles of scientific management. Its willingness to tolerate the injection of lethal dosages of radioactivity into terminally ill patients during the 1950s may be evidence that this prewar ideology could not be so easily discarded (see Appendix I in the essay on Harvard and the corporations). It may be harder than liberals reckoned for them to drain the foul eugenics bath water while holding on to their baby of scientific management.

Scientific management allows moral evasion to seep into public and private life, with its ability to elude outside mechanisms of accountability. Its celebration of specialization and professionalization is one source of the problem. "When the rockets go up...where they land, that's not my department," is a statement attributed to Werner von Braun.

Nevertheless, the ability of scientific management to mask power relations is probably its greatest contribution to ruthless unaccountability. J. Scott Armstrong in 1977 conducted a study of Upjohn's decision to keep a drug on the market that endangered human life. Ninety-seven percent of individuals surveyed considered Upjohn's action morally reprehensible. But when Armstrong used game theory techniques with 2,000 management students, organized into corporate boards, over 79 percent favored the same action as the Upjohn board.[34] How does scientific management produce such outcomes? Hannah Arendt once discussed what she called "the rule by nobody" that allows groups to carry out moral choices that would be considered terrifyingly evil by individuals under ordinary circumstances. Responsibility becomes diffused and, hence, individuals feel no personal responsibility for the consequences of their actions. The psychologist Albert Bandura elaborates:

social organizations go to great lengths to devise sophisticated mechanisms for obscuring responsibility for decisions that affect others adversely...Through division of labor, division of decision-making, and collective action, people can be contributors to cruel practices and bloodshed without feeling personally responsible or self-contemptuous for their part in it.[35]

Science and its Discontents

In the final analysis, these three historical periods provide ample testimony against the prevalent view of science's neutrality, its innocence of politics and ideology. Agassiz himself proclaimed his objectivity and the freedom of his science from politics, but the recent discovery of his memoirs reveals the duplicity of his enterprise. In them, he expresses revulsion for blacks, his utter horror and stomach sickness when he first laid eyes on an African-American.

In the 1970s and 1980s, Harvard rocked the U.S. scientific community as the site of a few of the most fabulous lab frauds and breaches of ethics of these decades.[36] Harvard's original blind faith in the nobility of science left it unprepared for such revelations. In 1951, Harvard's President James Conant, an elder statesman of science, asserted that violating the principles of scientific impartiality, as well as producing "shoddy science," is virtually impossible:

> Would it be too much to say that in the natural sciences today the given social environment has made it easy for even an emotionally unstable person to be exact and impartial in his laboratory? The traditions he inherits, his instruments, the high degree of specialization, the crowd of witnesses that surrounds him, so to speak (if he publishes his results)...these all exert pressures that make impartiality on matters of his science almost automatic.[37]

Conant's belief that scientists need not be virtuous, that scientific quality control is enough to insure impartiality, sounds increasingly anachronistic, as the crisis of confidence in science spreads.

The history of Harvard science portrayed here suggests that political-ethical and extra-scientific considerations have a powerful impact in determining its thematic innovations and trajectory. Harvard's special commitment to producing scientists versed in the techniques of rule is hardly the result of scholarly dispassion and disinterest. From the nineteenth century onward, Harvard professors have come from the most spoiled and pampered intellectual class in human memory. Convinced, however, that their enterprise is animated out of benevolent service to reason, the professoriate cries poverty, claiming that they have sacrificed wealth for the life of the mind— much to the bemusement of more perceptive social critics. In 1860, one of Agassiz's students noted in his diary:

> This morning Prof gave us a rather strong lecture on behavior etc... Told us, poor as he was, he would not change his position for mere living. I thought of the income he is receiving from his book and school, his 1500 a year as Professor; his wealthy wife; the house in which he lives for nothing; his children already engaged to the wealthiest. O consistency, thou art a jewel![38]

The professoriate always carries a certain *ressentiment* against the wealthier capitalist. (The capitalist's quip, "If you're so smart, how come you're not rich?" is met by the professorial sneer, "If you're so dumb, how come you're rich?") But among Harvard profs from the nineteenth century (appointed after 1830), 75 percent possessed estates ranking in the top 1.3 percent of the population of Massachusetts. An Oxford don favorably compared life in Old Cambridge to "English country society." A professor chose Harvard over the Sorbonne, according to a young Bostonian in Paris, because he "knew which side his bread was buttered on...The professors' houses and apartments [in Paris] are small, old, gloomy, tumble down affairs in comparison with which his present residence is a palace."[39]

In the twentieth century, the elaborate corporate connections of the Harvard professoriate have reinforced the desire of its scientists to serve privilege. (See the essay on Harvard's corporate relations for documentation.) And yet, some might respond, as Raymond Aron has, that "the object of every industrial society is to assert the power of man over nature (of which the power of some men over others is an unavoidable consequence)."[40]

However, the ecological destruction and degradation of late capitalist civilization has heightened support from the wider society for a critical science freed from the imperatives of domination. What shape it will take remains to be seen. But if there are any prospects for a freer society, it will demand an understanding of the institutional and ideological mechanisms that provide the privileged with the methods and means to control the powerless. One agent for change is scientists themselves who, despite their privileged status, have increasingly come to realize, in Nietzsche's haunting words, that should they "elevate" themselves:

> above the herd by means of [their] specialty, [they] still remain one of them in regard to all else—that is to say, in regard to all the most important things in life. Thus, a specialist in science gets to resemble nothing so much as a factory workman who spends

his whole life in turning one particular screw or handle on a certain machine, at which occupation he acquires the most consummate skill.[41]

Already a growing minority of the scientific community is eager to dispense with ideas about science's neutrality and ideological innocence. Confronting these dissidents are formidable obstacles, not the least of which remain the movement's internal divisions between 1) "public interest" scientists who desire for the profession and themselves a bigger slice of decision-making power now held by political and corporate elites, 2) advocates of broader "democratic control," a program to be achieved in part through expanded scientific literacy and education, and 3) some social ecologists and feminists who reject outright the logic of Western science.[42] Most agonizing is the premonition that, even if science were freed from the imperatives of corporate and state power, the logic of domination might well remain inscribed in the scientific project. And yet, such pessimism of the intellect should not inspire quietism and the retreat from politics, as the very issues of human freedom and survival are at stake. The potency of science as a form of social control and legitimation is predicated precisely on surrender to its progress as ineluctable and intractable.

For those in search of avenues out of apathy, understanding the historical deployment of the sciences at Harvard might well be a critical place to start.

Notes

1. Most recently, E.O. Wilson and Nobel Prize-winning chemist Dudley Hershbach discussed Baird at a panel, "Social Issues in the Science Classroom," Harvard University, December 9, 1987. Ironically, Hershbach, a holder of one of the Baird chairs, is generally regarded to be a liberal, no friend of the hard right.

2. Aristotle, Hobbes, and Russell quoted by D. Kolodney, introduction to N. Chomsky, "IQ Tests: Building Blocks for the New Class System," *Ramparts*, July 1972, pp. 24-25. My essay, similar to these cited quotations, focuses largely on biological determinism, though it should be remarked that there are dangers from a crude environmental determinism, as exhibited in the behaviorism of Harvard's B.F. Skinner. For a contrast of these two extremes, see N. Chomsky's critique of Skinner and Herrnstein in *For Reasons of State* (New York: Pantheon, 1973). It should be remarked, however, that the school of scientific management featured in my essay has roots in environmental determinism and can be regarded as a forerunner of later doctrines of behaviorism.

3. Leon Kamin, Richard Lewontin, and S. Rose, *Not in Our Genes* (New York: Pantheon, 1984), p. 29, and Ronald Story, *Harvard and the Boston Upper Class* (Middletown: Wesleyan University Press, 1980), p. 66.

4. E. Richard Brown, *Rockefeller Medicine Men* (Berkeley: University of California Press, 1979), p. 24.

5. *Ibid.*, pp. 24-25.

6. J. Braithwaite, *Corporate Crime in the Pharmaceutical Industry* (London: Routledge and Kegan Paul, 1984), p. 89.

7. Eliot and Russell quoted by Ruth and Victor Sidel, *A Healthy State* (New York: Pantheon, 1982), pp. 216-217. For a book that points to the division in U.S. ruling circles between those who preferred traditional colonialist occupation and those who sought economic and cultural levers of control, see Dennis Phillips, *Ambivalent Allies: Myth and Reality in the Australian-American Relationship* (Hammondsworth: Penguin, 1988), p. 100.

8. Terman quoted by Jeffrey Blum, *Pseudoscience and Mental Ability: The Origins and Fallacies of the IQ Controversy* (New York: Monthly Review Press, 1978).

9. "Biological Purge," *New York Times*, February 21, 1937, II, p. 1. For the references on Hooton and Katzenellenbogen below, see the useful chronology in L. Lapon's anti-psychiatry polemic, *Mass Murderers in White Coats* (Springfield: self-published, 1986).

10. *New York Times*, February 28, 1937, XII, p. 8.

11. "The Guilty: The Butchers of Buchenwald Hear the Stern Judgment of Civilization," *Life*, August 25, 1947. For testimony, see Judge Advocate General of the Army (JAG) Record Group 153. *U.S. v. Josias Prince Zu Waldeck,*

et. al., Case No. 000-50-9. Box No. 233, File 12-390, Vol. 1, Trial Record; for Katzenellenbogen, see p. 4199, cited by Lapon on p. 88.

12. Alexander Cockburn, "Ashes and Diamonds," *In These Times,* June 11, 1986, p. 17.

13. Samuel Chavkin, *The Mind Stealers* (Westport, CT: Lawrence Hill, 1978), p. 93.

14. *Ibid.,* p. 92.

15. *Ibid.,* pp. 90-93.

16. *Ibid.,* pp. 94-96.

17. E.C. Banfield, *The Unheavenly City: The Nature and Future of Our Urban Crisis* (Boston: Little, Brown, 1968), pp. 53, 224 and 236. For a valuable analysis of Banfield's work and similar social science literature, see Barbara Ehrenreich, *Fear of Falling* (New York: Pantheon, 1989).

18. Banfield, p. 236ff.

19. J. Beckwith quoted by E.H. Lopez, *The Harvard Mystique* (New York: Macmillan, 1979), p. 91.

20. *Ibid.* In May 1989, Herrnstein published a new essay in *The Atlantic* calling for government response to what he alleges is a decline in the U.S. population's I.Q. Coverage of the debate provoked by his article has followed in *Newsweek* (May 22, 1989) and other widely read forums.

21. S.J. Gould, *The Flamingo's Smile* (New York: Norton, 1985), p. 330.

22. Lewis Lapham, *Money and Class in America* (New York: Weidenfeld and Nicolson, 1988), p. 89. Confirming Lapham's assertion are journalists Jack Newfield and Wayne Barrett in *City for Sale* (New York: Harper and Row, 1988). They write: "The crime rate among ordinary people in the poorest neighborhoods of New York—the 79th Precinct of Bedford-Stuyvesant, the 48th Precinct in the Bronx—is one per hundred. Among the county leaders of the Democratic organization in this one-party city, that rate has become fifty per hundred." See Braithwaite for works documenting the proposition that white collar crime is more rampant than crimes traditionally associated with the lower class.

23. Lynora Williams, "Violence Against Women," *The Black Scholar,* January-February 1981, p. 19.

24. Sue Davis, ed. *Women Under Attack* (Boston: South End Press, 1989), p. 28.

25. Munsterberg quoted by H. Braverman, *Labor and Monopoly Capital* (New York: Monthly Review Press, 1974), p. 142.

26. *Ibid.,* see p. 87 and Chapter Six. For Munsterberg on "adjustment of work," see his *Psychology and Industrial Efficiency* (Boston: Houghton Mifflin, 1913), p. 309.

27. For these quotations of Mayo and a discussion of his Australian past, see Helen Bourke, "Intellectuals for Export," in S.L. Goldberg and F.B. Smith, eds. *Australian Cultural History* (Cambridge: Cambridge University Press,

1988), pp. 95-108, and H. Bourke, "Industrial Unrest as Social Pathology: The Australian Writings of Elton Mayo," *Historical Studies,* Vol. 20, 1982, pp. 217-233.

28. G. Mirick, *Progressive Education* (Boston: Houghton-Mifflin, 1923), pp. 202, 306.

29. Samuel Bowles and Herbert Gintis, *Schooling in Capitalist America* (New York: Basic Books, 1976), p. 196.

30. Munsterberg quoted by S. Shields, "The Variability Hypothesis," in Sandra Harding and Jean Barr, eds. *Sex and Scientific Inquiry* (Chicago: University of Chicago Press, 1987), pp. 200-201.

31. R. Callahan, *Education and the Cult of Efficiency* (Chicago: University of Chicago Press, 1962), p. 254.

32. Judith Merkle, *Management and Ideology* (Berkeley: University of California Press, 1980), p. 202.

33. *Ibid.*, p. 204.

34. J. Scott Armstrong, "Social Irresponsibility in Management," *Journal of Business Research,* Vol. 5, 1977, pp. 185-213.

35. Bandura quoted by Braithwaite, p. 3.

36. See the case of John Darsee in "Fraud in Harvard Lab," *Time,* February 28, 1983, or that of Scheffer C.G. Tseng in *Boston Globe,* October 19, 1988. The case of John Darsee is featured in Alexander Kohn, *False Prophets: Fraud and Error in Science and Medicine* (New York: Blackwell, 1988), pp. 84-88.

37. Conant quoted in J.R. Ravetz, *Scientific Knowledge and Its Social Problems* (New York: Oxford University Press, 1973), pp. 49-50.

38. Story, p. 81.

39. *Ibid.*, pp. 79-83.

40. R. Aron quoted by M. Urban, *The Ideology of Administration* (Albany: SUNY Press, 1982), p. 22.

41. F. Nietzsche, *The Future of Our Educational Institutions* (New York: Russell and Russell, 1964), p. 39.

42. Among these three contending factions, 1) the public interest scientists, 2) the advocates of democratic control, and 3) the ecologists and feminists, there are sure to be problems of policy implementation that provide no simple resolution. For instance, scientists who demand more self-management and control over scientific enterprise may underestimate how much their scientific colleagues, through their dominance of national peer review panels, have already steered the allocation of resources to a small number of elite universities. So much so that President John Silber of Boston University has decried their priorities: "Those who have the Lion's share of research funds do not want any new boys getting into the old boys club. It's an old boys' club, and new boys need not apply." (Ostensibly making the case for a more democratic and egalitarian allocation of resources, Silber, metaphorically speaking, may be lending strong credence to the prevailing feminist critique of science.)

But broader democratic control entails risks, among them the possibility that political representatives will abandon the national or general interest in favor of local projects and assorted pork barrel. Moreover, funding priorities in science may ultimately hinge on epistemological considerations; i.e., if Feyerabend's anarchistic view that scientific breakthroughs come largely through unconventional approaches, serendipity, and "against method," it might make sense to spread scientific wealth and resources far and wide. But if one holds that discoveries tend to be achieved slowly and incrementally by an intellectual vanguard armed with ample resources, then a democracy is more likely to become preoccupied with establishing tight standards for limiting funding to a narrow group of scientists and institutions. In various scientific fields, the best strategy for funding breakthroughs is hardly obvious, including to the scientific community itself.

For the quotation of Silber and a discussion of current funding controversies, see Stanley Meisler, "Halls of Ivory Research the Pork Barrel," *Los Angeles Times,* April 15, 1989, pp. 1 and 16.

The Science of Racism

Jonathan R. Beckwith

I returned to Harvard as a faculty member in 1965 with fond memories of my undergraduate and graduate years there, and with a view of Harvard as a liberal force in society. The memory of Senator Joseph McCarthy's attack on Harvard as a "Moscow on the Charles" must have been an important factor in creating the image of a progressive institution. However, events at Harvard since then and my discovery of aspects of Harvard's past have drastically changed my view. In particular, my concern over contemporary misuses of genetics (my field), the student strike of 1969, and my involvement in efforts to prevent Harvard from tearing down a working-class residential community have led to my increased political awareness and radicalization.

In reading the history of the misuse of genetic theories and their social implications, Harvard's name has continually cropped up. It turns out that Harvard University has been a major source of theories that have been used to rationalize the inequalities in our society on the basis of race, class, and sex.

In the nineteenth century, Louis Agassiz, Harvard professor of zoology, claimed that the science of skull measurement demonstrated that the Negro brain was comparable to the "imperfect brain" of a seven-month-old fetus. He further stated that the skull suture of the black infant closed earlier than that of the white infant, resulting in a situation where, if the Negro learned too much, the brain would swell and the skull wall would burst.

Academic racial theories gained wider acceptance in the early twentieth century, when the eugenics movement burgeoned in the United States, finding support not only in business circles but in progressive ones as well. This movement, which spoke of genetically-based racial differences, and, in general, of superior and inferior genetic qualities of humans, had enormous impact on our society. Sterilization laws were passed in over 30 states, legalizing sterilization of criminals, alcoholics, the "feebleminded," etc., as a result of the testimony of eugenicists. In 1924, the Immigration Restriction Act was passed by the U.S. Congress, enormously reducing the influx of immigrants from countries other than Nordic-Anglo-Saxon ones. This act was based in part on the testimony by eugenicists that southern and eastern European immigrants were causing a deterioration of the gene pool in the United States. The promoters of the eugenics movement included a number of Harvard faculty members. For instance, Professors Edward East and William Castle of the biology department in the 1910s claimed genetic support for the theories that stated that marriages between blacks and whites would yield inferior children. While Castle later reversed his opinion, these arguments were used to support the passage of miscegenation laws in 34 states, prohibiting marriage between different races.

The psychology department also provided support for the eugenics movement, with William McDougall, department chair, in 1921 calling for the replacement of democracy by a caste system based upon biological capacity, with legal restrictions upon breeding by the lower castes and upon intermarriage between the castes. Professor Nathaniel Hirsch purported to demonstrate the genetic inferiority of immigrant classes, supporting his proposals with statements such as: "I have seen gatherings of the foreign-born in which narrow and sloping foreheads were the rule...In every face there was something wrong—lips thick, mouth coarse...chin poorly formed...sugar loaf heads...goose-bill noses..."

Anthropologist Ernest Hooton, still at Harvard when we were undergraduates, also joined the eugenics movement. In a book published in 1935, Hooton raised the possibility of "a criminal career based on the racial heredity of the individual." Carleton Coon, who was professor of anthropology from 1927 to 1948, concluded that physical-anthropological studies demonstrated that blacks were at an earlier evolutionary stage of development than whites. Coon's "evidence" has been widely promulgated for many years by racist groups and, as recently as 1976, a Ku Klux Klan newspaper, in an article entitled "Science Exposes the Equality Hoax," quoted Coon in support of racial discrimination.

Ideas about the genetic basis of various behavioral problems (e.g., criminality) and of racial inferiority were in decline from the 1930s until the 1960s. They were revitalized in the late 1960s and they have been growing ever since. Their public rebirth came with the appearance of an article by University of California psychologist Arthur Jensen in the prestigious *Harvard Educational Review* in 1969. Jensen claimed that there was new evidence that blacks were intellectually inferior to whites because of their genetic heritage. This was followed a few years later by the publication of an article in the *Atlantic Monthly* by Richard Herrnstein, Harvard professor of psychology, who purported to demonstrate that inequality of wealth and status were genetically determined and, therefore, unchangeable. The foundations for the proposals of both Herrnstein and Jensen have been demolished—their data base has been shown to be fraudulent, and the genetic theories were either misunderstood or misrepresented. Harvard Medical School Professor Bernard Davis has recently written and spoken on "evidence" for biological differences between groups, suggesting that such programs as affirmative action are scientifically untenable. He went on to attack medical school programs that he charged were designed to increase the number of black doctors.

In the 1970s, we have seen three Harvard faculty members, E.O. Wilson, Irven DeVore, and Robert Trivers, publicly launching a supposedly new field of science, "sociobiology." According to these theories, which have been promoted in popular magazines and in curricula and films for high schools, hierarchies in our society and the lower achievement of women are genetically determined. Wilson stated in the *New York Times Magazine:* "My own guess is that the genetic bias is intense enough to cause a substantial division of labor even in the most free and egalitarian of future societies. Thus, even with identical education and equal access to all professions, men are likely to play a disproportionate role in political life, business and science."

More recently, there have been further developments in the relationship of Harvard faculty to biological theories of human social relationships. Professors Richard Herrnstein and James Q. Wilson received a good deal of publicity for their book *Crime and Human Nature*, in which they argue that criminals who are high-rate offenders have inherited their criminal tendencies.

As with previous theories, there is, in my opinion, simply no scientific basis for these claims, and some have already been discredited. Instead they reflect merely the social values of these professors and the milieu and society in which they live. These values are used in concrete ways to support the status quo and power relationships as they exist in our society. The reason I point out these instances is to show how Harvard past and present has served as a major source of scientific and other theories that help rationalize the nature of

American society and that are used to support policies that will maintain the social system as it is currently constructed.

In addition to generating theories with significant social impact, Harvard faculty members have had more direct influences on policy. Kissinger's power politics in southeast Asia (e.g., the bombing of Hanoi) and Samuel Huntington's involvement in the strategic hamlet program in Vietnam are only two examples of such contributions. Daniel Moynihan brought his academic theories to Washington under the Nixon administration, helping to support the policy of "benign neglect" toward blacks.

Does this picture represent only one side of the coin? Have there been just as many progressive faculty members who have opposed such views and presented alternate views of society? The answer is, for the most part, no. There is the rare case of Harlow Shapley, the astronomer, who managed to stay on. But, in fact, Harvard has a history of purging faculty with such views. For instance, in the 1930s, the failure of Harvard to promote the Marxist economist Alan Sweezy was widely attacked as a case of political persecution. During the McCarthy era, psychologist Leon Kamin and Helen Dean of the medical school faculty were let go, also for their political leanings.

After the student strike at Harvard in 1969, a number of non-tenured Harvard faculty members who supported the strike were not given tenure. These included a classmate of mine, Chester Hartman, who proposed that Harvard should be more conscious of the destructive impact of its expansion on the working people of Cambridge. Hartman was told that, despite unanimous student support, his contract would not be renewed because of his lack of "loyalty" to the institution (see Chester Hartman's essay). Subsequently, much publicity surrounded the failure of Harvard to promote three members of the economics department, Arthur MacEwan, Herbert Gintis, and Samuel Bowles. Some members of the department stated openly that Marxist economics was not good economics.

However, despite the ongoing tradition of rationalization of social inequalities by Harvard faculty, the last ten years have seen, perhaps for the first time, active opposition to such theories among this same faculty. The writings and public appearances of Stephen Jay Gould, Richard Lewontin, Ruth Hubbard, and others have provided some balance to this particular debate. The same cannot be said for the public stands of much of the faculty in the humanities and social sciences, which the *Boston Globe* (August 31, 1986) concedes has tilted dramatically to the Right in recent years.

There is a mystique about Harvard that affects those who attend it and that lends authority to the pronouncements of those who teach there. It is important to break down this mystique so that pernicious social policy and social values are not permitted to be stamped with the authority of "Veritas." I hope that by remaining at Harvard and speaking out on these issues, I will be able to contribute to this demystification.

Sexism and Sociobiology
For Our Own Good
and the Good of the Species

Ruth Hubbard

During the last third of the nineteenth century, and into the twentieth, defenders of male prerogatives in the marketplace and the home have felt threatened by women's demands for equality. The agendas of the movement for women's rights have been different and so have the responses. In the 1800s, the movement focussed on access to education and the professions, birth control, and the vote. The present focus has been on equal rights (the ERA), reproductive rights, the right to exercise sexual and affectional preferences, and the economic struggle for equal pay for equal work or, more recently, equal pay for work of comparable value. During both periods, Harvard professors have provided arguments to support the status quo. Both times, the arguments have been neither new nor convincing but, because of Harvard's prestige, they have been announced with greater fanfare and have gained a wider hearing than they merited.

Brains or Ovaries

As girls gained access to education, it became clear that girls' brains were up to the task. Women's colleges opened and attracted successful students and so did adventurous coeducational colleges and universities. By the 1860s and 1870s, scientific arguments about the inferiority of women's brains were no longer acceptable in most quarters. The question of the day was no longer: Can women do it? New reasons were required to restrict women's access to higher education and the professions and so the question became: Is it good for them? And who could answer this question better than physicians, scientifically trained men, who had been caring for the health of women?

The times were problematic for "regular" physicians (that is, the men who had been able to go to Europe for their medical training or to the few U.S. medical schools that were beginning to model themselves on the European schools). Women were prominent among "irregular" healers where husband/wife teams were not unusual. Most midwives were women, and women had always cared for the ill at home. So, when women began to apply to the medical schools where the "regulars" were being trained, male physicians had reason to worry that becoming a physician might look like a natural extension of what women had been doing all along. What is more, the prevailing modesty of upper-class women was likely to make many of them prefer to be seen by a woman physician if they had a choice, and in this they would have their husbands' approval. Physicians therefore viewed the entry of women into the medical profession as an economic threat, particularly at a time when, rightly or wrongly, they believed that the profession was already overpopulated.[1] For all these reasons medical students and practicing physicians did not look with favor on women's attempts to enter their profession. So, physicians came forward to explain that it would be detrimental to women's health to become physicians.

Foremost among them was Dr. Edward H. Clarke, who held the chair of *materia medica* at Harvard Medical School from 1855 until 1872, when he resigned his professorship and became a member of the Harvard Board of Overseers. In 1869, Clarke wrote an article for the *Boston Medical and Surgical Journal* in which he argued that women had a right "to every function and opportunity which our planet offers, that man has," if they are equal to it, but he urged moderation: "Let the experiment...be fairly made...[and] in 50 years we shall get the answer."[2]

However, Clarke soon turned against the notion that women should enjoy these opportunities together with men. Let women be educated to the best of their capabilities, but separately. Of course, even if women wanted to take Clarke up on his "experiment," they could not follow his advice because the only medical schools that existed at the time were operated by and for men. So women kept applying to go to these medical schools, and even to Clarke's own institution, Harvard Medical School. Under this threat, Clarke drew back from his proposed experiment and in an address to the New England Women's Club of Boston, delivered in 1872, he put forward the arguments that were published the next year as *Sex in Education; or, A Fair Chance for the Girls*.[3] This book went through seventeen editions in the next thirteen years and a bookseller in Ann Arbor, who claimed to have sold 200 copies in one day, remarked that "the book bids fair to nip coeducation in the bud."[4]

In the Introduction, Clarke stressed that the point is not that one sex is superior to the other, but that they are different and on this he based his assertion that coeducation is detrimental to women's health. A girl obviously can go to school and do whatever a boy can do. "But it is not true that she can do all this, and retain uninjured health and a future secure from neuralgia, uterine disease, hysteria, and other derangements of the nervous system, if she follows the same method that boys are trained in."[5] And if this is not a sufficiently scientific way to say it, here goes: "The physiological motto is, Educate a man for manhood, a woman for womanhood, both for humanity. In this lies the hope of the race."[6]

The rest of the book was built around this "physiological" rallying cry. In the chapter entitled "Chiefly Physiological," Clarke described in painful detail all the ways women's physiology would be injured if girls were educated the same as boys and therefore developed their brains rather than pay due regard to developing their menstrual functions. "The organization of the male grows steadily, gradually, and equally, from birth to maturity," he stated authoritatively, whereas girls must pass through a critical transition when they must "allow a sufficient opportunity for the establishment of their periodical functions...Moreover, unless the work is accomplished at that period, unless the reproductive mechanism is built and put in good working order at that time, it is never perfectly accomplished afterwards."[7] And it is not enough for girls to exercise care in how they *begin* to menstruate, "'precautions should be...repeated...again and again, until at length the *habit* of regular, healthy menstruation is established'" (cited from "the accomplished London physician, and lecturer on diseases of women," Dr. Charles West.[8]) Clarke went on: "There have been instances, and I have seen such, of females in whom the special mechanism we are speaking of remained germinal—undeveloped... They graduated from school or college excellent scholars, but with undeveloped ovaries. Later they married, and were sterile."[9]

Here Clarke was speaking to another fear of the time, for the cry had gone up that the native-born, upper classes were not reproducing themselves, whereas poor, immigrant families were having too many children. Therefore the possibility that education would render upper-class women sterile was alarming to both women and men of his class.

I have quoted Clarke at such length not just because I like his authoritative style, but because I want readers to see the ways he transformed prejudices of his time and class into scientific truths. Rather than go on and quote from the so-called case histories that Clarke cited in his next chapter, entitled "Chiefly Clinical," some of which quickly were shown to be inventions,[10] I want to point out that, of course, Clarke did not go unchallenged. Thomas Wentworth Higginson (Emily Dickinson's friend, abolitionist, and correspondent) pointed out that Clarke's dire descriptions meant little as long as he offered no comparable information about how education affected the health of boys. Other critics objected that his proposal that girls' education be coordinated with the demands of their menstrual cycles was equivalent to no schooling for girls, since girls do not menstruate in synchrony. And what of the teacher, wondered Eliza B. Duffey, "She too requires her regular furlough, and then what are the scholars to do?"[11] Duffey further asked whether Clarke wished to suggest that wives and mothers require three- or four-day menstrual furloughs each month.

Despite Clarke's best efforts, women gradually gained access to medical schools. But the doors of Harvard Medical School remained sealed until late in World War II, when economic considerations and a decline in the quality of male applicants induced this last medical bastion of sex discrimination to admit twelve women to the class that entered in the fall of 1945. Yet even at that late date, in the debate preceding the vote, some faculty members argued that their colleagues who were planning to admit women were ignoring "the fundamental biological law that the primary function of women is to bear and raise children."[12]

Of Eggs and Human Nature

Let us now move to the 1970s when the present wave of the women's movement was becoming a significant political force. As might be expected, again scientists have risen to the challenge and pointed out that the status quo is in tune with nature. I will concentrate on the contributions of another Harvard professor, the biologist Edward O. Wilson, a member of Harvard's elite Society of Fellows and a popular teacher.

Wilson's research has been concerned with the classification and behavior of ants. Therefore it came as no surprise when in 1971 Harvard University Press published his handsomely illustrated *The Insect Societies*. However, this was followed in 1975 by the publication of another book with the more ambitious title, *Sociobiology: The New*

Synthesis. It is rare for a scientific text of 697 pages, that includes a 22-page glossary and 64 pages of bibliography, to become a media event or to sell over 100,000 copies, despite its $25 price and its awkward 10½×10¼ inch format that makes it too large to fit into most bookshelves. Yet, with careful nurturing by the Harvard University Press, including talk shows, cocktail parties, write-ups in *Time* and *Newsweek,* and a rave review in the widely-read *Atlantic* by Fred Hapgood, at the time a writer for the Harvard University Publicity Office, this book propelled Wilson to instant fame. The subsequent publication of *On Human Nature* in 1978 stirred hardly a ripple among Wilson's scientific colleagues, but garnered a Pulitzer Prize for literature.

What is all this about and how does it relate to the way scientists have used their purportedly objective expertise to support the status quo against women's striving for equality? Before examining Wilson's sociobiological arguments in greater detail, I want to make clear that sexism lies at the center of sociobiology because of the way sociobiologists deal with the concept of "reproductive success." Following Darwin, reproductive success is measured by the number of offspring an individual produces who themselves grow up and reproduce. This brings us up against an asymmetry between females and males that arises from two facts: 1) that in many species males can produce far greater numbers of sperm in a lifetime than females can produce eggs, and 2) that eggs usually are larger than sperm. Sociobiologists take these two innocent-looking differences to mean that a female, by definition, has a larger "investment" in each of her eggs than a male has in each sperm. And since each individual is said to be trying to maximize the number of her or his genetic offspring, this asymmetry in size and number of reproductive cells is taken to imply that females are "by nature" more protective of their offspring than males are, since females cannot produce as many.

Many things are wrong with this argument. For one thing it is a metaphor, and a questionable one at that, to speak of eggs and sperm as investments. Females form eggs as part of their metabolism as do males sperm, and it takes no more effort or energy to produce one than the other. Our muscle cells cannot be said to represent more of an investment or to cost us more, and hence be more precious to us, than our liver cells merely because they are larger or because we have more of them. We need both and these kinds of comparisons between them are meaningless. For another, since it takes only one sperm to fertilize an egg, no more sperm can become adults than can eggs. And since the males of most species do not divide into wimps and superstuds, in any given species or population about as many males as females have offspring and have them in about equal numbers.

Yet Wilson and other sociobiologists use this purported asymmetry in the reproductive investments of women and men to account for *the* division of labor (as though there were only one) as described, for example, by the statement that in "an American industrial city, no less than [in] a band of hunter-gatherers...women and children remain in the residential area while the men forage for game or its symbolic equivalent in the form of barter and money."[13] This statement obscures the fact that there is no unique or universal division of labor. It also ignores that among hunter-gatherers women do the major share of the foraging, that in numerous African and Latin American societies the markets, where bartering and the exchange of money happens, are women's domain, and that most women in our own society do not get the chance to stay home "in the residential area" and care for their children, even if they want to, because they need to earn money. Yet Wilson takes the purported asymmetry in "reproductive investments" to justify the prediction he published in the *New York Times Magazine* that "even with identical education and equal access to all professions, men are likely to play a disproportionate role in political life, business, and science."[14] (Indeed, he was apparently so impressed with this prediction that he repeated it, slightly reworded, in *On Human Nature*.[15]) A further example of how literally Wilson takes the investment metaphor of reproduction is his amazingly inappropriate appraisal of female prostitution: "It is to be expected that prostitutes are the despised members of society; they have abandoned their valuable reproductive investments to strangers."[16] Erased are the social conditions under which the system of prostitution operates in our society—the pimps, corrupt police, drug dealers, junkies, teenage runaways, women trying to support children on more than a minimum wage, men buying sex they cannot get any other way, and so on. Prostitutes are neglectful people who squander their investments and do not clip coupons when they come due!

Wilson defines sociobiology as "the systematic study of the biological basis of all social behavior" and promises that his synthesis will come to include "sociology and the other social sciences, as well as the humanities...[as] the last branches of biology."[17]

He asserts that the basic elements of human nature can be identified by means of an elaboration of Darwin's theory of evolution through natural selection that includes the most recent concept of "genetic fitness." This concept involves the assumption that those traits that are "adaptive" come to be inherited. The argument runs as follows: individuals who carry genes for adaptive traits leave more descendants than other individuals do, so that in future generations, these genes outnumber the genes for less adaptive traits. When it comes to behavior, sociobiologists argue that this means we do the things that are good for our own survival and reproduction so that the genes that have made us behave that way in the first place will be spread into future generations.

The kinds of behaviors that Wilson tries to show as adaptive—hence basic components of human nature—are aggression, territoriality, selfishness, and the tendency to establish dominance hierarchies; the various secondary sexual behaviors, such as fondling and kissing, that make relationships between women and men emotionally satisfying; altruistic behaviors that accrue also to one's benefit; and religious-spiritual traits, such as the need to believe in something beyond oneself. "The predisposition to religious belief," he writes, "is the most complex and powerful force in the human mind and in all probability an ineradicable part of human nature."[18] Yet, "[a]lthough the manifestations of the religious experience are resplendent and multidimensional, and so complicated that the finest of psychoanalysts and philosophers get lost in their labyrinth, I believe that religious practices can be mapped onto the two dimensions of genetic advantage and evolutionary change."[19] And, of course, included among adaptive behavior are men's "predisposition" to dominate women and women's greater contribution to child care. "Because [the egg] represents a considerable energetic investment on the part of the mother the embryo is often sequestered and protected, and sometimes its care is extended into the postnatal period. *This is the reason why parental care is normally provided by the female...*"[20] (my italics).

But these are by no means the only behaviors for which Wilson postulates genetic components ("behavioral genes"). Included, among others are homosexuality, schizophrenia (or rather, "a major part of the tendency to become schizophrenic,"[21] whatever that means), and the incest taboo—that is, the avoidance of incestuous behavior. (Apparently Wilson is not aware of the literature documenting the widespread occurrence of father/daughter, brother/sister, and even grandfather/granddaughter incest at all levels of our society.)

Of course, Wilson recognizes that much of human social behavior is cultural, but like other sociobiologists, he believes that he can identify the genetic components of behavior by identifying its adaptive components. They constitute that "stubborn" kernel of human nature that "cannot be forced without cost."[22] He states that "the great majority of human societies have evolved toward sexual domination as though sliding along a ratchet"[23] and warns that although we are sufficiently flexible to make change possible, "the early predispositions that characterize sex would have to be blunted" and "regulations" would be "required" that "would certainly place some freedoms in jeopardy."[24]

Wilson leaves out, or at least underplays, the fact that a crucial characteristic of humans, one of the things that sets us apart from other life forms, is our enormous adaptability, our capacity to occupy and use effectively just about all environments and to endow them with special significance in the effort to survive and to give meaning to our survival. It is highly questionable whether it means anything to speak of "human nature" apart from the ways people function in societies. Yet the sweep of Wilson's generalizations extends from termites to rhesus monkeys to human societies, and draws analogies between human societies that are widely separated in time and space and in their cultural, economic, and political contents. He excuses this by saying that rather than dwell on "details...it is the parallelism in the major features...that demands our closest attention."[25] But what he takes to be "detail" or "major" is of course easily influenced by what he is trying to prove.

A crucial methodological problem in human sociobiology is that it is impossible to prove that adaptive behaviors are inherited biologically and handed on through cultural learning. We transform our cultural and natural environments even as they transform us. To sort genetic from environmental contributions to traits, one must be able to specify and quantify the trait and completely control the organism's genetic make-up and environment. This can be done only for a few traits of organisms that can be grown under carefully monitored laboratory conditions. It is, of course, impossible to do with people. To overcome this difficulty, Wilson and other sociobiologists argue that if they can show that a trait occurs in different societies and, perhaps, among animals as well, this suggests that it is adaptive and has been established through natural selection, therefore that it has become genetic.

This line of reasoning is misleading for many reasons. The most important one is that organisms that look or act alike need not do so for the same evolutionary or genetic reasons. Therefore, biologists usually are careful to distinguish between what they call "analogies" and "homologies." Analogous traits fulfill a similar function and may look similar, but have different evolutionary origins. Examples are the wings of insects, birds, and bats, or the eyes of lobsters, squids, and humans. Homologous traits are traits that have had a common evolutionary history, that often fulfill similar kinds of functions, but their evolutionary paths may have diverged so that they need not look alike. Examples are the hairs and horns of mammals, reptilian scales and birds' feathers. Paleontologists who track evolutionary lines therefore spend much time and care scanning the fossil record so as to distinguish homologies from analogies, which are useless for establishing evolutionary and genetic relationships.

Clearly, behavioral traits cannot be analyzed in this way. Therefore, it is impossible to prove that similar behaviors, though perhaps adaptive, are not merely analogous solutions to similar, or indeed common, problems—how to fly, how to fend off intruders, how to share tasks that need to be done. Observations of behavioral similarities do not permit one to deduce the existence of "behavioral genes." Nor does it clarify the situation to suggest, as Wilson does, that perhaps genes control not behavior, but "tendencies" or "predispositions" to behave in certain ways. For example, he writes:[26]

> [It is] possible, and in my judgment even probable, that the positions of genes having indirect effects on the most complex forms of behavior will soon be mapped on the human chromosomes. These genes are unlikely to prescribe particular patterns of behavior; there will be no mutations for a particular sexual practice or mode of dress. The behavioral genes more probably influence the ranges of the form and intensity of emotional responses, the thresholds of arousals, the readiness to learn certain stimuli as opposed to others, and the pattern of sensitivity to additional environmental factors that point cultural evolution in one direction as opposed to another.

Such assertions are so inclusive and vague that they are meaningless. They certainly cannot be proved scientifically. (What sensitivities, emotions, arousals, stimuli? What does it mean to "point cultural evolution in [a] direction?") The impossibility of distinguishing behavioral analogies from homologies, the many levels of interaction between different genes, the many still unknown events that intervene between gene activities and observable behavior and the complexity of the mutual transformations among organisms and their environments all force me to conclude that Wilson's aim to develop an accurate picture of the evolutionary, hence genetic, basis of social behavior, probably cannot be realized for animals, and surely not for people. Some of the necessary measurements cannot even be conceptualized, and of those we can specify, most cannot be carried out. How can one hope either to prove or disprove claims of "innate predispositions" for such ill-defined and culturally variable behavioral traits as dominance, aggression, maternalism, or selfishness? The inherent difficulties of precisely specifying and assigning these kinds of characterizations make it easy to compose stories that lead one to conclusions that are in line with one's preconceptions.

What Wilson perceives to be "human nature," and what he therefore explicates biologically, is, in its essential features, a stereotyped description of how things are in western capitalist countries, with their divisions of sex, race, and class that determine great differences in the power one has over one's own and other people's lives. To make the evolutionary argument, he tries to show that this stereotype also characterizes other societies—human and animal—that are organized quite differently. This leads to enormous confusion in the use of concepts such as dominance or aggression, and, indeed, in all efforts to understand how the divisions of labor affect roles and power, particularly with regard to differences in social, economic, and political status between women and men.

Assertions such as that men dominate women in all societies conceal more than they reveal until we know how "dominance" is defined. The argument for the universality of male dominance usually is based on the fact that all societies have divisions of labor. We are told that in many of them, men's tasks are valued more highly than women's. But these valuations can easily be in the eye of the anthropologist-beholder. The point is that for egalitarian societies, such as some of the hunter-gatherer peoples in Africa, it may be quite wrong to try to fit their divisions of roles into the power differentials that are implicit in the concept of dominance hierarchies.

We in the industrialized countries have grown up in hierarchically structured societies, so that, to us, dominance hierarchies appear natural and inevitable. But it is a mistake to apply the same categories to societies that function quite differently and to pretend that differences between our society and theirs can be expressed merely as matters of degree. What I am saying is that one cannot rate apples, oranges, and pears on their "appleness." They are not more or less apples; they are *different*.

To take widely different and complex social manifestations and scale them along one dimension does violence to the sources and significance of human social behavior. Western technological societies have developed in their ways for their own historical reasons. Other societies have their histories that have led to their social forms. To try to classify these cultures into categories derived from the way our society operates ignores our history and their histories. To take people who live on islands, in plains, or on high mountain ranges, between the arctic zones and the tropics, in industrial cities, towns, or agricultural communities, and pretend that one can identify and analyze the basic features of their societies by reading and thinking about them rather than needing to experience their diversities is typical western ethnocentrism.

When it comes to comparing cultures the world over with those of Europe and the United States, another problem arises from the fact that every other place on earth has been affected by what has happened in the industrialized countries. David Livingstone's accounts express his shock at the power women exerted in the "petticoat governments" (his expression) with which he had to deal in Africa. And there are comparable reports from early Europeans arriving on the American continent. Euro-American traders, missionaries, and governments have affected customs, economic arrangements, and politics in all parts of the world. If we find similarities between western practices and those of peoples who appear to be culturally as well as geographically distant from us, we must consider the possibility that westerners put them there.

Whither Veritas?

Let me be clear: we are people and not monkeys or ants. Furthermore, each of us is unique. Genes do have something to do with our humanity and with our individual differences, but we cannot know how much they have to do with them. When something cannot be proved, yet the pretense that it can be, or has been, proved is used to argue for or against social policies and forms of government (Wilson tells us that Marxism is "based on an inaccurate interpretation of human nature"[27]), the effort is not a quest for knowledge. It is a political campaign.

The Brown University biologist Anne Fausto-Sterling has well described the problems inherent in doing scientific research on questions that are central to the ways our society is organized.[28] She points out that to do science as objectively as we can, we must try to be aware of the many facets of our subjectivity that are likely to affect the way we view the area of our inquiry. When it comes to sex differences, it is questionable whether anyone can hold opinions, or do research, that express something other than her or his beliefs about how society operates, or should operate, because everything about our lives, including our language, is gendered. In as loaded and value-laden an area as sex differences, everything becomes political, a way of persuading others to promote what we believe to be correct ways for the society to operate. Under those circumstances, it is wrong to ignore, and even deny, one's biases and pretend that one is doing objective research or dispensing objective information.

When Edward Clarke wraps himself in the mantle of medical authority to mouth the prejudices of the men of his class, that is deception. When Edward Wilson opens the last chapter of *Sociobiology: The New Synthesis* with the words: "Let us now consider man [sic] in the free spirit of natural history, as though we were zoologists from another planet completing a catalog of social species on Earth,"[29] that too is deception. He is not an observer from another planet. He is a Harvard professor, and a scientist, with group and personal interests. To pretend scientific detachment when words are as suffused with social values, as are the language of medicine and sociobiology, is naive or malicious. Even Harvard professors need to face the fact that they cannot live outside the political concerns of their time and that some areas of life are so steeped in politics—and sex is one of them—that objectivity becomes synonymous with unacknowledged partisanship.

Some forty years ago, Margaret Mead pointed out that although different societies have different, and often opposite, divisions of labor by sex, no matter how work is shared out—whether women or men carry the heaviest loads, whether men or women go to market— each society believes its way of doing things is inevitable and natural.[30] In our society, in which experts interpret nature for us, physicians and scientists are the ones to assure us that our division of labor reflects biological imperatives. And when they come wrapped in the mantle of "Veritas," who would dare not to believe them?

Notes

Parts of this article are adapted from my review of E.O. Wilson's *On Human Nature* (Cambridge, MA: Harvard University Press, 1978) that appeared in the October 1978 issue of *Psychology Today*.

1. For a discussion of the interplay of some of these elements, see Mary Roth Walsh, *Doctors Wanted: No Women Need Apply* (New Haven: Yale University Press, 1977), pp. 133-137.

2. Cited in Walsh, *Doctors Wanted*, pp. 120-121.

3. Edward H. Clarke, *Sex in Education; or, a Fair Chance for the Girls* (Boston: James R. Osgood & Co., 1874).

4. Walsh, *Doctors Wanted*, pp. 120-121.

5. Clarke, *Sex in Education*, pp. 17-18.

6. *Ibid.*, p. 16.

7. *Ibid.*, p. 38.

8. *Ibid.*, p. 39.

9. *Ibid.*

10. Walsh, *Doctors Wanted*, p. 129.

11. Eliza Bisbee Duffey, *No Sex in Education; or, an Equal Chance for Both Girls and Boys* (Syracuse, 1874), cited in Walsh, *Doctors Wanted*, p. 128.

12. "Committee Report, Harvard Medical School," 1944, p. 2, Harvard Medical School Dean's Records, cited in Walsh, *Doctors Wanted*, p. 232.

13. Edward O. Wilson, *Sociobiology: The New Synthesis* (Cambridge, MA: Harvard University Press, 1975), p. 553.

14. Edward O. Wilson, "Human Decency Is Animal," *New York Times Magazine*, October 12, 1975.

15. Edward O. Wilson, *On Human Nature* (Cambridge, MA: Harvard University Press, 1978), p. 133.

16. Wilson, *On Human Nature*, p. 126.

17. Wilson, *Sociobiology*, p. 4.

18. Wilson, *On Human Nature*, p. 169.

19. *Ibid.*, p. 172.

20. Wilson, *Sociobiology*, p. 317.

21. Wilson, *On Human Nature*, p. 169.

22. *Ibid.*, p. 147.

23. *Ibid.*, p. 124.

24. *Ibid.*, p. 133.

25. *Ibid.*, p. 89.

26. *Ibid.*, p. 47.

27. *Ibid.*, p. 190.

28. Anne Fausto-Sterling, *Myths of Gender: Biological Theories About Women and Men* (New York: Basic Books, 1986).

29. Wilson, *Sociobiology*, p. 547.

30. Margaret Mead, *Male and Female: A Study of the Sexes in a Changing World* (New York: Dell, 1949).

Ideology in Practice
The Mismeasure of Man

Stephen Jay Gould

To the preceding essays, critics respond that we need not worry, that racist and sexist scientific ideologies are typically the abstract theorizing of professors, safely confined in the Ivory Tower without effects on the wider society. Richard Herrnstein, in particular, once rebuked Noam Chomsky for his warnings about these pernicious doctrines on the grounds that, after all, this is America and *not* Nazi Germany (see N.J. Block and Gerald Dworkin, eds., *The IQ Controversy.* [New York: Pantheon, 1976]). In this brief epilogue to his book *The Mismeasure of Man*, Steven Jay Gould exposes the practical consequences through the story of Carrie and Doris Buck, tragic victims of a Supreme Court ruling by Harvard's favorite liberal son, Oliver Wendell Holmes, whose commitment to such social theories eventually led to the sterilization of thousands of women in Virginia and elsewhere.

In 1927, Oliver Wendell Holmes, Jr. delivered the Supreme Court's decision upholding the Virginia sterilization law in *Buck v. Bell*. Carrie Buck, a young mother with a child of allegedly feeble mind, had scored a mental age of nine on the Stanford-Binet. Carrie Buck's mother, then 52, had tested at mental age seven. Holmes wrote, in one of the most famous and chilling statements of our century:

> We have seen more than once that the public welfare may call upon the best citizens for their lives. It would be strange if it could not call upon those who already sap the strength of the state for these lesser sacrifices...Three generations of imbeciles are enough.

The line is often mis-cited as "three generations of idiots..." But Holmes knew the technical jargon of his time, and the Bucks, though not "normal" by the Stanford-Binet, were one grade above idiots.

Buck v. Bell is a signpost of history, an event linked with the distant past in my mind. The Babe hit his 60 homers in 1927, and legends are all the more wonderful because they seem so distant. I was therefore shocked by an item in the *Washington Post* on February

23, 1980—for few things can be more disconcerting than a juxtaposi-
tion of neatly ordered and separated temporal events. "Over 7,500
Sterilized in Virginia," the headline read. The law that Holmes upheld had been implemented for 48 years, from 1924 to 1972. The
operations had been performed in mental-health facilities, primarily
upon white men and women considered feeble-minded and anti-social—including "unwed mothers, prostitutes, petty criminals and
children with disciplinary problems."

Carrie Buck, now 72, lives near Charlottesville. Neither she nor
her sister Doris would be considered mentally deficient by today's
standards. Doris Buck was sterilized under the same law in 1928. She
later married Matthew Figgins, a plumber. But Doris Buck was never
informed. "They told me," she recalled, "that the operation was for
an appendix and rupture." So she and Matthew Figgins tried to
conceive a child. They consulted physicians at three hospitals
throughout her child-bearing years; no one recognized that her Fal-
lopian tubes had been severed. Last year, Doris Buck Figgins finally
discovered the cause of her lifelong sadness.

One might invoke an unfeeling calculus and say that Doris
Buck's disappointment ranks as nothing compared with millions
dead in wars to support the designs of madmen or the conceits of
rulers. But can one measure the pain of a single dream unfulfilled,
the hope of a defenseless woman snatched by public power in the
name of an ideology advanced to purify a race. May Doris Buck's
simple and eloquent testimony stand for millions of deaths and
disappointments and help us to remember that the Sabbath was
made for man, not man for the Sabbath: "I broke down and cried. My
husband and me wanted children desperately. We were crazy about
them. I never knew what they'd done to me."

Part V
Education, Ideology, and Social Control

"Cleaning House"

Hiring, Tenure, and Dissent

John Trumpbour

"Our educational system is not a public service, but an instrument of special privilege; its purpose is not to further the welfare of mankind, but merely to keep America capitalist," observed novelist Upton Sinclair in the 1920s. Sinclair's interest in business propaganda and repression in U.S. universities was heightened in the aftermath of the celebrated case of Scott Nearing, whose contract as assistant professor of economics at the University of Pennsylvania was terminated allegedly because of the trustees' disapproval of his campaign against child labor. In historian Joel Singer's precise summary, an editor of a newspaper controlled by pro-child labor interests attacked Nearing's speeches "against the greedy exploitation of children as sacrilege, and called on the University trustees to rid themselves of such a dangerous professor."

It has been over seventy years since Nearing's case called attention to the relationship between special interests and power in higher education, but little of substance has changed on the question of who really rules the university. Today few boards of trustees will directly intervene to sack a professor; instead crafty administrators and supine elements among the professoriate make sure that critical thinkers do not get out of hand. In Nearing's day, his work against child labor found intellectuals ready to dismiss him as an "agitator"; in today's university, he would be disparaged for lacking "rigor" and "objectivity." Curiously, two decades after Penn torpedoed Nearing, Harvard itself moved against two of its own economics professors, Alan Sweezy and Raymond Walsh, an action allegedly precipitated by their criticism of the sacred laws of the free market—and, most distressing, their outspoken advocacy of laws protecting child labor.

Beyond these controversial cases of yesteryear, are there sources of job security in today's academic world? Sociological studies of tenure candidates indicate that quantity of publication counts much higher than quality, but the two most decisive elements in academic success are different: 1) possession of a degree from an elite graduate school, and 2) charm and interpersonal skills. Lionel Lewis's study of 3,000 letters of recommendation concerning tenure candidates shows that success depends much less on intelligence and more on convincing fellow faculty that a person is a team player, a charming person with good interpersonal skills: in short, someone resembling C.

Wright Mills's description of "the cheerful robot." Theodore Hamerow's recent study of the history profession adds that faculty (all assumed to be male) whose wives are popular and gracious hostesses have a special edge. He writes:

> Until quite recently it was not unusual for letters of recommendation to dwell on the candidate's wife as well as the candidate himself. The two were frequently described as a "delightful pair" who would add greatly to the social life on campus. While the usual adjectives to describe him were "gifted," "promising," "bright," or the unambiguous euphemism "clean-cut," she was generally portrayed as "delightful," "attractive," "vivacious," and "likable"…The rise of the feminist movement has made people aware that such forms of endorsement are condescending and demeaning to both spouses. But while the tone of academic personal relations has changed, the substance remains to a considerable extent the same.[1]

Tenure battles are still occasions for controversy at Harvard. Harvard takes pride in tenuring only a small percentage of its junior faculty and today uses this as the main justification for its failure to tenure important radical intellectuals. Tenured conservatives and liberals, though, continue to flourish.

Nevertheless, amidst much coverage by the *New York Times* and the *Boston Globe* in 1986, liberals exploded angrily over refusals to tenure such talented bourgeois intellectuals as Robert Watson in English, and Bradford Lee and Alan Brinkley in history. The liberals do have grounds for upset. Among Brinkley's opponents were Oscar Handlin and Donald Fleming, a pair of craven apologists for Harvard in their own historiography and men who, according to colleagues, accuse Brinkley of being "too journalistic."[2]

C. Wright Mills once remarked that a scholar capable of communicating with the broader public finds her/himself dismissed as a popularizer, or worse still, "a mere journalist." Galbraith is often treated with contempt by many colleagues in economics because he refuses to abide by the conventions of communicating ideas in leaden prose and dull abstractions. Perhaps this is one of Brinkley's sins.

Even so, the liberals have substantially weaker grounds upon which to complain about the tenure process than do radicals. Many liberal junior faculty are denied tenure, but after five to ten years elsewhere, they may be invited back with a lifetime post. Over 80 percent of the history department's tenure appointments have Harvard degrees, symptomatic of a university that is without doubt the most incestuous in the country. Some historians concede privately that Brinkley will likely be invited back later. The radicals, Paul Sweezy, Sam Bowles, Erik Olin Wright, et al., do not have this luxury.

Psychologist Leon Kamin and others sent packing in the McCarthy era cannot expect such magnanimity, regardless of the weight of their intellectual accomplishments. Eugene Genovese, today regarded as the premier historian of North American slavery, was recently denied a Harvard post, thanks to the machinations of Harvard's liberal intelligentsia in history. For a counter-example that proves the rule: when attention was recently brought to such examples of ideological persecution, the history department soon thereafter offered a tenured post to radical Eric Foner; but more than a few senior faculty admitted that this offer was disingenuous, telling the *Harvard Crimson* that they agreed upon it because they knew in advance that Foner definitely would not accept. Theda Skocpol, a Left Weberian and the best comparative sociologist of her generation in the United States, had to hire lawyers to get a tenured slot, Harvard finally backing down in the face of a sex discrimination suit. Over at neighboring MIT, David Noble, without peer as a historian of American technology, was let go in 1984, most observers concede, due to his punishing critiques of MIT's sacrifice of independence in favor of corporate and Cold War priorities.

In the first essay in this section, Joseph Menn explains how the tenure process works at Harvard through visiting committees, a deck stacked for the Bok regime by his loyal lieutenant Burton Dreben. Menn's short essay is significant because until now the role of the Drebens and the visiting committees in elite educational reproduction has typically been ignored. He also sheds light on the sacking of social scientist Paul Starr who, despite having strayed from his radical intellectual heritage, paid the price for failing to adhere to the canons of IBM sociology advocated by the pro-quantification triumverate of Dreben, Rosovsky, and Bok.

Menn's presentation is followed by Lawrence Lifschultz's previous history of Harvard's commitment to destroying the careers of radical economists. (An earlier and unabridged version of his essay was published in *Ramparts*, April 1974.) This section is closed by Chester Hartman's illuminating case study showing how faculty reappointment decisions are precisely about ideology and not competence. Readers are urged to turn to the following three essays, Cynthia Silva, et. al., who treat Harvard's abysmal record of minority hiring, Eugene Rivers's discussion of the promotion policies for blacks in Harvard's administrative apparatus, and Jamin Raskin's later essay on the Harvard Law School, which documents the Bok-supported *jihad* against professors in the critical legal studies movement.

Notes

1. T. Hamerow, *Reflections on History and Historians* (Madison: University of Wisconsin Press, 1987), pp. 125-126.

2. See *Harvard Crimson*, October 6, 1986. For a biting critique of Handlin and Fleming's interpretation of Harvard history, see Suzanne Hildenbrand, "Celebrating Fair Harvard," *History of Higher Education Annual*, vol. 6, 1986. Referring to their *Glimpses of the Harvard Past* (Cambridge: Harvard University Press, 1986). She writes: "Flattery and self-congratulation characterize the book; the only discordant note is struck in the epilogue as Handlin lashes out at critics of Harvard." She also remarks that Harvard Professor Stephan Thernstrom's own contribution to this volume "is...a kind of social Darwinian interpretation of the assumed superiority of Harvard students..."

The Tenure Process and Its Invisible Kingmaker

Joseph Menn

There is nothing as central to the way a university functions as its process for choosing professors. The tenure system has been standard procedure at U.S. institutions of higher learning longer than anyone can remember, and it has been nearly as long since Harvard decided to grant lifetime posts primarily to those outside its own non-tenured staff. It is difficult to see more in the practice than an overly cautious, conservative tendency. Despite the claims of the present dean of the faculty and his immediate predecessor to the contrary, little has been done to alter Harvard's predilection toward tested-and-true outsiders.

A much more subtle and insidious problem is the way in which Harvard chooses among outside tenure candidates and the long-standing secrecy that shrouds this process. One explanation lies in the importance of Harvard in the academic universe: even when its faculty mechanism rejects a scholar, no one wants to be identified as the whistle-blower. Another explanation lies in Harvard's success in keeping the hows and whys of its innocuously named ad hoc committees within a very tight circle indeed, to the extent where full professors and even department chairs can't explain their workings, or can do so only on the basis of hearsay. The truth probably falls somewhere between these answers.

The ad hoc committees came into use in the 1930s, as the James Conant administration sought a quiet, politically expedient means of settling Keynesian/Marxian in-fighting in the economics department. The ad hoc system proved to be an extremely effective public relations front put up by the administration to distance itself from the departments without untoward publicity. The committee would be formed, mostly from scholars outside the University, to evaluate every departmental recommendation for tenure. Then the president could make an informed, objective decision. If anyone asked, the committee members were simply to be chosen because of their expertise. Their names would be kept secret, ostensibly to prevent lobbying, but in reality, at least in part, to prevent any of the principals from crying foul until the process was over. The vote of the committee was also to be secret, but it was assumed the president would defer to the localized knowledge of the committee members. In other words, despite the obvious subjectiveness of the system, there would be nowhere to pin blame, or even points of view, with any certainty.

The ad hoc system spread fairly quickly to the graduate school of education, the divinity school, and the design school. As of this writing, it is poised on the brink of taking over the Law School, a dramatic move that will be touched on later in this essay. The system has undergone slight alterations from dean to dean and president to president, but has remained constant in its basic premise, execution, and justification.

Under repeated and informed questioning, administration figures have gone so far as to say the committees are generally composed of at least three outside scholars, one or more academic deans, a Harvard professor from a distinct but related department, the dean of the faculty and the president. Not even in the face of what one key figure in the process termed "a truly exceptional breach of faith"—the leak of the 4-2 vote by the committee against tenuring sociologist Paul Starr—would anyone involved in the process admit to anything more than an informed, informal consensus. Evidently, voting is just too political to be discussed.

The few men who control the committee system continue to stress secrecy, espousing the same reasons put forward a half-century ago. But through interviews conducted late in 1987, a picture begins to emerge from the shadowy inner circle. Philosophy professor Burton Dreben, considered the greatest academic kingmaker in the country although few professors at Harvard can accurately describe his activities, is a cornerstone of the process. Academic deans, particularly government department chair and now Kennedy School of Government Dean Robert Putnam, identify Dreben as the man Henry Rosovsky, former dean of the faculty, was referring to when he wrote in his annual report of 1979-80: "I have added to my staff a professor whose principal responsibility is to select committee members."

The academic deans are all but interchangeable for the purposes of the committees. But all of those who agreed to be interviewed said they join committees only occasionally, when they involve cases of personal interest. The outstanding exception is Dreben, who in addition to forming the committees, says he sits on every single one outside the philosophy department, where it would be a conflict of interest. Dreben estimates he has participated in more than 260, or about 25 committees per year. Still more intriguing, he says he cannot recall a single instance in which President Bok has disagreed with the sentiments of the committees Dreben has created. Also at odds with the official accounts of the tenure process is the description by Putnam and other department chairs of the intense lobbying process they must undertake in order to secure from Dreben the appointment of committee members with favorable dispositions towards the proffered candidates. According to them, how well a department is regarded by the administration is the single greatest determining factor in the selection of the ad hoc committee members. "The government department is thought of as strong, so it would be a real surprise for me to come testify and see a long table of unfamiliar faces," says Putnam. Paul Starr goes one step farther, saying "The membership is very much the result of a tenure decision, not a cause. There's much artfulness in the selection, and the votes are entirely predictable." Regarding his own controversial case, Starr adds, "My supporters were told certain people would be on the committee, and we were, in effect, betrayed."

As Dreben is quick to point out, he serves at the pleasure of the dean and the president as a means of enhancing their information and power over faculty appointments. Philosophy department chair Warren Goldfarb, who guided his protégé Dreben through the faculty and administrative ranks, says Dreben achieved his present position because of his encyclopedic knowledge of the U.S. academic scene and because he shared certain predispositions and academic attitudes with Bok and Rosovsky. Those attitudes, as Bok and Rosovsky occasionally enunciate, constitute a bias in favor of quantitative work as opposed to qualitative studies, and towards hard rather than soft sciences. This general drift is well known, but little has been revealed about the politics of specific cases. Asked if he held any clear academic biases, Dreben responded, "It depends very much on the field." He declined to elaborate.

Why Dreben remains where he is, picking the people who overturn by his estimate 15 percent of tenure recommendations and, quoting Putnam again, "embarrass departments away from dangerous choices," is another matter. Defenders of the current arrangement say simply that Michael Spence kept Dreben on when he succeeded Rosovsky as dean because Dreben is very good at what he does: no one else would know so quickly to whom to turn in any field to evaluate a candidate (or, to extrapolate a bit, would know where the chosen experts would stand on a controversial nominee). In the less charitable words of a tenured Harvard professor, Dreben has made himself the institutional *"eminence grise* of the tenure process... Spence didn't feel he could do without him. Burt [Dreben] is a little like [J. Edgar] Hoover was." In this professor's view, Dreben has endured because he "understands that Derek Bok doesn't like controversy. Burt is very good at keeping his role secret, and he shares Bok's preference for old, famous men."

Dreben's career, philosophy, and teaching style appear inadequate qualifications for the backstage power he now wields. The son of an Everett, Massachusetts entrepreneur, Dreben attended Harvard as an undergraduate from 1945 to 1949. Since then he has been away from the University for only two years, one year on a Fulbright to Oxford and the second teaching in the mid-1950s at the University of Chicago. An appropriate foreshadow of his later style and influence was his stint in Harvard's semi-secret Society of Fellows, a multi-year program that takes eight incipient geniuses annually, gives them complete freedom and a handsome stipend, and trains them in the important matters of wine-tasting and cigar-smoking. Were the fellowships more widely known, they would almost certainly have been as sought after as the Rhodes, which the fellowships already surpass in prestige. Dreben studied philosophy during his term as a fellow, especially the work of his sophomore tutor, W.V. Quine. Dreben never got a doctoral degree, but his expertise on Quine and the impression he made during his post-graduate years at Harvard— particularly on two other fellows, Goldfarb and Rosovsky—were sufficient to secure his career.

Ironically, to those who have been denied tenure by his committees, Dreben's publishing record may be the skimpiest at the entire University. He has co-written a single book, published in 1979 with Goldfarb, on mathematical logic, his specialty. Only a handful of articles round out his written contributions to the field, although he says he's been working on a historical overview for some time. One explanation for Dreben's reluctance to publish put forth by students and co-workers is his alleged belief that philosophy is a dead science and that Wittgenstein was the last true philosopher. Students describe Dreben as brilliant, forceful, and at this point in his life, not as ambitious as traditional academics. Besides his numerous advisory posts, Dreben served as dean of the Graduate School of Arts and Sciences in the 1970s. He now heads the Society of Fellows in addition to constructing the ad hoc committees.

While in his 1980 report on the matter Rosovsky states that the ad hoc committees, "the capstone of our system," enjoy widespread faculty support, he does identify several problems with them. Among these are the common year-long delays between departmental recommendation and firm offer, department complaints about the trial-like atmosphere of the committee meetings in which professors are called to testify for and against candidates, and the timidity of the departments to nominate younger scholars for fear of the system's rigidity and perceived preferences. But Rosovsky writes, "In my opinion the current state of the art in many subjects causes the greatest difficulties for the ad hoc system...the future of many subjects is not at all clear. For example, what are the core areas of sociology? How important is literary theory? Who will pioneer the next great strides in economics?..." Rosovsky concedes in summation, with evident reluctance, that "In these circumstances choice becomes to some extent a matter of taste and is frequently subject to honest and heated dispute. Therefore, ad hoc committees can reach very different conclusions depending on their composition and even mood." Rosovsky does not give an explanation of why, how, and by whom committee members are selected for their closed-door opinions on crucial academic concerns. Here is precisely where the exhaustively eulogized Harvard openness calls for an invocation of debate.

Supporters of the system, including philosophy department chair Goldfarb who says he doesn't know how the committee members are chosen, say its greatest virtue is that it gives more power to the president vis á vis the departments than exists at virtually any other university. The assembled scholars, in Goldfarb's view, provide a maximum of information for the president, who has the ultimate discretion to chart the academic course of departments. In order to protect this power from the faculty, he adds, "Of necessity, it isn't meant to be exposed." Harvard sociologist David Riesman adds that the system "makes Harvard a meritocracy, on the whole...The ad hoc committees above all are what made Harvard Harvard...together with national recruiting, they deprovincialized it." Even this glowing praise does not come from Riesman without its caveats, however: "The presidents and deans can also be deceived, and that's not entirely hypothetical. When the Social Relations Department and psychology were merged it came about from the ad hocs, despite their enormous disparity. They were just misinformed—it was without malice."

There are two glaring failings of the ad hoc system. First, by its *de jure* nature it belies all claims to fairness and openness in the academic process, by giving absolute power to a few opinionated individuals and providing them with built-in distance from their actions—and no need to explain their consequences and motives. Second, it discriminates *de facto* against valid and acclaimed methods and subjects of research, especially in the social sciences. This ongoing fault is compounded by the Harvard administration's refusal to permit informed discussion of these discrepancies, most obvious in fields like sociology and economics, or even to acknowledge their existence.

Ad Hoc Justice at the Law School?

During 1987, it became increasingly clear that President Derek Bok intended to introduce the ad hoc system wholesale to Harvard's Law School. Such a move would be at once the most dramatic extension of the administration's centralized power in memory, an historic step forward for the behind-the-scenes network of the shadowy ad hoc committees, and a tragedy of unequalled proportions for the Law School. It would, however, make perfect sense to Bok, who had been embarrassed by the nationwide attention and alumni grumblings focussed on his troubled *alma mater;* the ad hocs provided the much needed, impenetrable cloak for his actions and biases as he staunched the leftward drift of the faculty.

The Law School is currently divided in three camps: professors associated with the left-leaning Critical Legal Studies (CLS) movement—whose adherents believe that law is derived more from dominant social norms than from abstract notions of justice—conservative scholars, and a moderate, unaffiliated wing. Tenure decisions in the past three years have become highly politicized. In 1986, a CLS professor was the first tenure-track scholar in sixteen years to fail to get the required two-thirds faculty vote supporting his bid for a lifetime position. The following spring, visiting CLS professor David Trubek won faculty approval for tenure. Bok, a former law dean, stepped in for the first time in the school's history. He formed an ad hoc committee and overturned Trubek's recommendation. Later, another ad hoc committee was again convened to thwart the tenure bid of another CLS affiliate, Clare Dalton (see Jamin Raskin's essay). (Dalton had charged Harvard with sex discrimination in a legal brief, the precedent set by Theda Skocpol, who gained tenure in the sociology department after having recently won a similar discrimination suit.) Bok had slated a policy speech for fall 1987 on the issue of institutionalizing the ad hoc process at the Law School, but he postponed it, at least until after the resolution of the hotly contested Dalton case.

Although traditional and CLS professors generally strongly disagree about most subjects, they are uniquely combined in their denunciations of the ad hoc process as it is applies to their school. Martha Field, a moderate, warns "It would be terrible for the law school. It's like putting an institution under receivership." CLS historian Morton Horwitz is equally alarmed: "It's based on a nineteenth century patriarchal system. I don't understand how it wouldn't lead to total abuse." The law professors discovered the same internal biases in the Trubek ad hoc committee as their colleagues in the arts and sciences have wrestled with unsuccessfully for years. "When I heard who was on the committee, I knew it was all over," says Horwitz. "Composition of the ad hocs has to be regularized."

Barring an eleventh-hour compromise, some form of ad hocs at the Law School seems inevitable. Professors are watching and waiting, hoping for some input into how the committees will be formed. "More than anything else, it's a question of who will get appointed to the committees and who appoints them," says Associate Dean Richard Stewart. Professors may not want the ad hocs at all, but they will expend effort to make any version as visible and structured as possible.

Dreben, who has advised the Divinity, Design, and Education Schools on the formation of ad hoc committees, says he will not be involved at the Law School. Speculation is directed instead on how great a personal role Bok will take at the Law School, given his experience there and his handling of the Dalton case. Since the atmosphere is more highly charged than it is in the Arts and Sciences, it is doubtful he will find as knowledgeable, efficient, and politic a surrogate as Dreben. Alternatively, he may appoint someone from outside the University to be a nearly all-powerful troubleshooter. If he takes the step of forming all of the committees himself, he risks something short of open warfare when articulate professors attack the impartiality of the members, should their names leak out. Bok would then have no one to hide behind.

As the situation at the Law School fast approaches a grim and bloody conclusion, hope for reform is appearing on the all-too-distant horizon. The meandering knight-in-armor may be the University's

30-member Board of Overseers. Until 1985, the alumni-selected board was merely a rubber stamp to Harvard's presidential and corporate decisions. Since then, three members have been elected by petition on political platforms. In response, Harvard has nominated some less conservative candidates, including Pulitzer Prize-winning writer Frances FitzGerald. Several of the newcomers have pledged to take up key issues in the University's governance, among them Harvard's South Africa-related investments and its laggard affirmative action performance. Two new overseers, sociologist Gay Seidman and historian Peter Wood are concerned about the ad hoc issue and promise to debate the matter if Bok continues to scorch the earth of the Law School.

Considering the staggered terms for members of the Board of Overseers, it appears that any reforms will come too late for the Law School. If so, the academically progressive toe stuck into that Establishment stronghold will probably get stamped on past the point of recognition. This would be a terrific loss to legal education, and would be one more blot on Harvard's sorry record of intellectual integrity. Even if professors there fend off the ad hoc system or forcibly remold it into a more honest and palatable form, the committees in the Arts and Sciences and at the three smaller graduate schools are becoming more deeply entrenched with each passing year. Dean Spence may move his own pawn in to replace Dreben as his Grand Vizier. Associates of the principals, however, believe Warren Goldfarb a more likely successor for Dreben, who is now nearing retirement. In either instance, Harvard's administration will have no reason to give up its effective, subtle and covert control of academic departments.

Could Karl Marx Teach
Economics in the United States?

Lawrence S. Lifschultz

Since the Second World War, economists in the West, and in the United States in particular, have been a fairly self-satisfied group. With John Maynard Keynes in one hand, and the Federal Budget and Reserve System in the other, they have steered the world's most advanced economy over its traditional hurdles of inflation, unemployment, and uneven economic growth. But in recent years their heady confidence has ebbed. The Vietnam War inflation, the downfall of the Bretton Woods international monetary system, a persisting balance of payments problem, and continuing massive unemployment in the advanced industrial world have all eroded public faith in economists.

Incubating since the early 1970s, the public crisis has come home to roost in academia. Suddenly the economics profession is itself being shaken by an internal war of ideas that threatens not just an old and comfortable unanimity, but the very underpinnings of U.S. capitalist theory. The dispute, centered in economics departments at universities across the country, has pitted orthodox economists against a younger generation of radicals. At Harvard in 1972, the Department of Economics wrestled over what one faculty member termed its "worst division in history," created by a decision not to rehire two radical economists. Meanwhile, at Yale, the Economics Department held its third full departmental meeting of the 1973-74 year to deal with the gnawing problem of Karl Marx. At two previous sessions, students and several younger faculty insisted, as they had for four years, that Marxian economics be made a formal part of the Department's curriculum. Further inland at the Amherst campus of the University of Massachusetts, following nearly three years of in-fighting which included the resignation of two department chairs, the University made a remarkable decision to hire five radical economists, four with tenure.

In the midst of these disputes, the profession gathered in Toronto during Christmas for the 1973 convention of the American

Economic Association (AEA). There they heard what was perhaps the severest self-criticism of the profession ever to be made at one of their meetings. John Kenneth Galbraith, President of the AEA, urged his colleagues to "reassociate with reality," and attacked the current orthodoxy in economic theory because "it offers no useful handle for grasping the economic problems that now beset modern society." Samuel Bowles, the associate professor whose failure to receive tenure generated the battle at Harvard, puts the matter even more sharply:

> The issue [both at Harvard and in economics] is not merely a scholarly dispute. There are political forces in the larger society which are clearly involved. We identified ourselves explicitly with forces attempting to overthrow capitalism. Therefore, we could not agree with those who hold the heights of established orthodoxy on what 'useful knowledge' was. What was 'useful knowledge' to us wasn't useful to them. It was inimical to their interests and vice versa.

For the radical economists, the roots of protest are in the social movements of the 1960s. For them, the academic theories which maintained the essentially egalitarian and just nature of U.S. institutions were exploded in the racial fires that burned brightly through Watts, Detroit, and Newark. Through the late 1960s and into the early 1970s, the conflict between younger leftist economists and their elders remained largely one of argument and debate. But more recently these disagreements of theory have become bitterly antagonistic quarrels over the most concrete of "bread and butter" issues to academic economists—their own jobs. Yet beyond jobs lies a larger, and to consensus-minded economists, darker storm. The battle of generations now being fought is not likely to fade away. On the outcome hinge the intellectual foundations of U.S. capitalism. To lose this battle bodes ill for either side in the wider war.

Harvard: Embattled Giants

Sam Bowles taught at Harvard from 1966 to 1973. He had published work about the economics of education, and how education in the United States has historically reproduced class relationships in society. His promotion from associate to full professor with tenure was supported by three of the best known members of the department: Wassily Leontief of input-output fame, Kenneth J. Arrow (both Nobel Prizewinners), and Galbraith. All three are past

presidents of the AEA. Yet despite such impressive backing, Bowles' promotion was turned down by a vote of the whole senior faculty.
According to Galbraith,

> It is established practice in all economics departments to conceal deeply political differences and to say they are not a factor. I believe Sam's political views were a factor. Anybody who has his general competence, teaching ability, research output, and who had been a good micro-economic model builder would have almost certainly been promoted. The Bowles decision will deeply narrow Harvard's interest in the span of economics. The people whose fame exists in neo-classical model building are embattled and their reaction tends to exclude whoever seems to threaten them.

Other members of the Department staunchly maintain that politics were not a consideration. Otto Eckstein, a former economics adviser to Presidents Kennedy and Johnson, states, "The Harvard Economics Department has not made appointments on political criteria." Department chair James Duesenberry likewise insists the decision was made solely on professional considerations. He argues that one in ten junior faculty at Harvard achieve tenured status and that it is a "surprise when associate professors get tenure rather than when they do not." Concerning Galbraith's strong public comments about the decline of diversity at Harvard, Duesenberry remarks, "Galbraith is not so disturbed. He's just having a good time."

Whether these are good times or not, it is clear that emotions run deep among other Harvard faculty members. Stephen Marglin termed the Bowles decision "inherently political." "It's my judgment," he asserts, "that no radical could be recommended for a tenured appointment in my department. If Karl Marx were available, if Thorstein Veblen were available, the department would not recommend them for tenure."

Marglin insists moreover that most members of Harvard's Economics Department are not "capable of appreciating or judging the quality of work on an alternative model with which they are at best superficially familiar and almost totally unsympathetic." Marglin himself is the only tenured radical in the Department, and received his appointment in 1967 for work he described as "squarely in the orthodox tradition"—done, he says, before his changing political views were well known and before he had altered the orientation of his research. In 1969, there were five radical economists who held posts in the Harvard Department; by 1974, Marglin was the only one left.

The Economics Department followed up the Bowles judgment with a decision not to reappoint Arthur MacEwan, one of the original five radicals. The close timing was perhaps not very judicious, since it prompted an outcry from a significant number of graduate students and from the *Harvard Crimson*. The Department's graduate students' organization called for a meeting with the faculty in order to have the decisions explained.

According to Robert Dorfman, a senior faculty member,

> The students were disturbed. They feel the traditional kind of economics we are oriented toward is evasive concerning the deep seated evils of the capitalist system. Their view is that these personnel actions were not dispassionate actions based on scholarly merit, as they were purported to be...but are ways of evicting certain attitudes from the Department.

Dorfman, who supported Bowles' promotion, further explained, "The students are interested in improving the world, and they want to do it through the only means at their disposal—the university. However, we on the faculty wish to emphasize the fragileness [sic] of the university."

To damp down the discontent that was developing, the Department enacted a surprise reversal in the case of a third radical economist, Herbert Gintis. In 1969-70, Gintis had been in the Economics Department as a lecturer—the lowest level of faculty standing. At the time, the Department voted not to appoint him to an assistant professorship, one rung up the ladder; but in the meantime, Gintis received a position at Harvard's School of Education. Suddenly, three years later, the Economics Department decided to offer him the post of associate professor.

The decision was announced shortly after the Toronto meetings of the AEA, where a resolution condemning political discrimination in hiring practices had been introduced. Disclaiming any influence from public pressure or political considerations, department chair Duesenberry insisted, "We are not bothered by pressure; we look right through it." It was privately made clear to Gintis, however, that he was being offered only a three-year contract at the associate level, and that the possibility of tenure was nil.

The disagreement over the specific appointments came to encompass a number of much larger issues. Galbraith at one stage attributed the Department's "conservative hiring practices" to faculty members' links with corporations. No one was mentioned specifically, but attention was soon focused on Otto Eckstein, professor of Economics and president of Data Resources, Inc., a consulting firm that specializes in economic forecasting. Following publicity and Galbraith's complaints, Eckstein decided with regret to drop to half-time status.

Eckstein appears to have been on the receiving end of much unwarranted innuendo. While he opposed the Bowles appointment specifically, his view on the place that should be given to radical and Marxian economics differs substantially from colleagues such as Duesenberry, who regards the writings of leading Marxists as "corny," and Raymond Powell at Yale, who considers Marxian economics to be "intellectually vacuous" and "contentless" by the "economics of [the] British empiricist scientific tradition."

Eckstein, in fact, regards the Marxist position as a very "valid part of economics as a social science."

> The contribution of Marxian economics, is to integrate economic theory with political theory into a coherent whole. No one has successfully tackled the problem since Marx; and whatever work there is stems from Marx. Neo-classical [conventional] economics simply does not integrate political and economic structure into a coherent whole.

Futhermore, he insists that leading Marxists such as Paul Sweezy have "pushed economics forward."

As for the events at Harvard, Eckstein believes,

> We made a mistake in the way we handled the Bowles appointment. It was such a bloody fight. Emotions ran so deep among my mostly older colleagues. I thought we should have communicated to the students that the vote on Bowles did not mean Harvard rejected radical economics as a legitimate field of study or that we felt we did not have some obligation to offer instruction. There were students who had come here when Harvard was a concentration of radical economics. And we had an obligation to meet these expectations for what they thought they were going to obtain at Harvard. Since there is a major student interest in radical economics, we owe them instruction in it.

However, the issue which Galbraith raised concerning the link between ideology and corporate consulting did not die out. It continued as an important element of the Bowles case, and in a parting statement for the *Harvard Crimson*, Bowles himself pressed the point. The piece was entitled "Hardly a Surprise," referring to his failure to achieve tenure.

> Not satisfied with being once removed from power, many economists—a good portion of the senior faculty of the Harvard

Economics Department among them—have gone into the lucrative and gratifying business of directly advising corporations, government bureaus and presidents. "Relevance" in economics has come to be synonymous with service to governmental policymakers. Not surprisingly, conventional economists have proven of more service in hiding the costs of the Vietnam War than in ending it; they have done better at explaining away poverty than in eradicating it. In their advisory roles, conventional economists have reflected the bias of their theories as well as the political requirements of remaining "in favor" by at best accepting and more often justifying the institution of capitalism as the framework within which decisions are made.

When asked to comment on the characterization Bowles had made of conventional economists vis-a-vis the Vietnam War, Department Chair Duesenberry showed a bitterness of temper which could only have come from months of stress in dealing with contending political factions. He said he had been asked before why, in light of the war's character, he had not resigned from the Council of Economic Advisors under Lyndon Johnson and denied his knowledge to the state.

> I figured they weren't going to stop it, so I thought I might as well stay in the meantime and work for the most stable financial policies. What good would it have done if I had resigned? There would have been an article on page three of the *New York Times* one day and forgotten the next. I am the kind of man who puts one foot before the other. I have no use for these paper humanists. At least I got the tax program and some housing legislation through. As an economist I was not concerned with the big picture...Some of us are bothered by a group of people who claim they have discovered a big set of answers...The Chicago types [Milton Friedman *et al.* at the University of Chicago] think they know all the answers, and they are as much a pain in the ass as the radicals.

Harvard has only once before seen such a difficult time over the issue of appointments in the Economics Department. That was in 1937, when Drs. J. Raymond Walsh and Alan R. Sweezy (Paul Sweezy's older brother) were denied promotion from their posts as instructors. In the words of a *Crimson* editorial of that year, "the discharges may have been based on the outstanding liberal activities of the two men." The University issued a denial, claiming the decision was made "solely on the grounds of teaching capacity and scholarly ability." Students of that generation, who had not been steeled in the rigors of People's Park in Berkeley or Mayday in Washington, circulated an orderly petition objecting to any slur on the "teaching capacity and scholarly ability" of the two men, but to no avail. Both were given concluding appointments and left Harvard in 1939.

There is one other skeleton in the Economics Department's ivy closet. It is not discussed very much and does not involve a question of political discrimination. It concerns the failure to appoint Paul Samuelson to a position on the faculty. Samuelson had been a graduate student at Harvard. His introductory book on economics today stands as the basic text in many first year economics courses. He is also a recipient of the Nobel Prize. "Harvard was reputed to be anti-Semitic at that time," says Otto Eckstein. "There is not much doubt that there was a period when there was some anti-Semitism at Harvard. That had something to do with the Samuelson debacle from which this department has never recovered. The failure to appoint Samuelson created the major rival to us—MIT."

By the spring of 1974, the worst was over at Harvard. The decisions on appointments had been taken, the protests made, and a compromise of sorts struck—even if the contract offer to Gintis appeared a bit inconsistent. Galbraith still grumbled away and was reported to be considering forming a breakaway department called the Department of Social Economics, which would stress the relations between politics and economics. In Cambridge, life eased into summer and faculty members expressed hopes that the disagreeable period would pass and be forgotten.

"The Harvard Economics Department has always operated on a principle of professional courtesy," says Eckstein. "It has lately gone through some decline." In the end, Gintis decided not to take the associate post and instead decided voluntarily to join the exodus. But in Massachusetts, the road of exodus for radical economists led not to oblivion but to a new homeland in Amherst. In the end, five radical economists were hired by the University of Massachusetts- Amherst, joining a faculty of about 30: Sam Bowles, Herbert Gintis, Richard Edwards, Stephen Resnick, and Richard Wolff. The first three are from Harvard, the last two from Yale. All but Edwards, who had recently completed his Ph.D., were given tenure.

The Politics Of Competence

Chair Merton Peck of the Yale Economics Department repeatedly expressed to students his difficulty in finding a "competent" Marxist to teach the courses they asked for. The competency issue stirred a hornets' nest every place it was raised. To some it provoked memories of the chairman of Stanford's Sociology Department in the 1950s who, in response to a suggestion that C. Wright Mills be offered a professorship, said: "But Mills is not a sociologist, he is a Marxist." At Harvard, Galbraith had said: "Competency is always a disguise for something else."

In early 1971, Peck had written to Paul M. Sweezy inviting him to give a graduate seminar in Marxian economics. Sweezy declined the offer and in a letter to Peck stated that he believed there was a larger issue involved. He pointed out that current difficulties could be solved if university departments stopped consistently dropping younger qualified Marxists from their staffs. Sweezy wrote to Peck:

> Every generation of graduate students includes a by-no-means insignificant number of Marxists. But with very few exceptions they are dropped from the academic world before acquiring tenure. And the exceptions for the most part find it prudent to keep their ideology separate from their teaching and research...That this situation creates problems for college and university administrators is obvious, and it seems to me that they have no one but themselves to blame.

Samuel Bowles himself argues that the country is in for more shocks, which should feed the growth of radical economists. "Over our lifetime," he says, "there are going to be enormous strains in the advanced capitalist system to which the current body of economic theory and the current institutions of capitalism will be unable to address themselves. This is the reason why radical economics is going to grow. The system is going to continue to fail to solve the problems..." He adds, with a modest reflection on possible reverses, "even if they wipe us all out, the next day some young social scientist is going to scratch his head and say, ' This sounds wrong.' "

The battle goes on, and Galbraith has suggested that orthodoxy is clearly on the defensive. "Neo-classical economists," he states, "are like the covered wagons or the herds when they are attacked. They have turned their heads together and their rumps out, seeking protection against the enemy."

And in the science that was once known as "dismal," this is how war is fought.

Uppity and Out

A Case Study in the Politics of Faculty Reappointments (and the Limitations of Grievance Procedures)

Chester Hartman

Harvard's decision to deny reappointment to Chester Hartman ranks among the most controversial and contested cases of the past two decades. It is most revealing, if only because his is a rare incident of having a "smoking gun," a letter from his department chair explaining outright that Hartman's progressive political commitment led to his termination. His story also reveals the utter hypocrisy of the Bok regime, forced in Hartman's case to deny appeal on the grounds of "separation of powers," a doctrine conveniently scuttled when it becomes necessary to purge radical faculty (e.g., Clare Dalton at the Law School). That is the real meaning of ethics in Bokspeak.

June 23, 1969

Dear Chester:

I have decided that I cannot support your reappointment at the end of the next academic year and will urge my successor to consider next year as terminal. I am doing this because I am convinced that your method of teaching conveys a sense of political strategy more than the substance of city and regional planning. Furthermore, it seems to me that your loyalties to the [Graduate] School [of Design] and the University have lessened rather than increased during the past three years...

William W. Nash, Jr.
Chairman, Dept. of
City & Regional Planning
Graduate School of Design
Harvard University

I received this letter just before the beginning of the last year of my four-year assistant professorship appointment. Seven years later, a tortuous review process ended inconclusively, triggered initially by protest on my behalf on campus and in the planning profession. What were the reasons behind Harvard's actions in not renewing my contract? What did the unprecedented review process reveal about the nature of the University? What lessons might be drawn from this experience?

To set the matter in some perspective: I was acknowledged as a good teacher; had published well beyond my department's norm both quantitatively and qualitatively; had founded and administered a popular and beneficial field service program; and, finally, Harvard's practice at the time was routinely to give at least seven years (and often an associate professorship without tenure) to productive junior faculty. My dismissal exposed two things: how heavily a challenge to established departmental and University authority can weigh in such decisions; and the limits of procedural due process in the university world.

Professor Nash's surprisingly candid letter referred in shorthand fashion to growing tensions within the field of urban planning and (related) events of the late 1960s as they worked themselves out on the Harvard campus.

I was brought onto the faculty as someone whose work and writing represented the more socially- and politically-oriented directions the planning field was moving into, in contrast to the traditional physically-oriented nature of the profession. Part of that shift was a change of consciousness from the view of planning as a neutral, objective, public-interest function to a stance that highlighted underlying class interests involved in planning decisions and clientele and which embraced the nascent "advocacy planning" philosophy that positioned planners in more openly value-laden roles and activities. At Harvard, I was at the vortex of the conflicts that embodied this schism.

Incoming planning students during the latter part of the 1960s were, not surprisingly, more inclined to the new trends and were highly critical of the department's quality and "relevance." Nearly 90 percent of the Planning Department's students signed a petition to the Overseers Visiting Committee that called for complete overhaul of a department they characterized as "mediocre." Nearly half the students who entered the three-year masters program in 1966 dropped out or transferred, often to MIT, where the planning program was considered far superior. My open sympathy with the students and their demands for greater participation in departmental affairs made me something of a pariah among faculty colleagues. (A tenured colleague asserted, in a later *Village Voice* account of my travails: "You can quote me that all this business about students and faculty having an equal voice is just horseshit. We're not a community of scholars but a school to train professionals.") Perhaps my most blatant violation of club rules was participation in a November 1969 demonstration at the groundbreaking ceremony for the Graduate School of Design's (GSD's) new Gund Hall, protesting the misdirected spending priorities in producing a $10 million edifice when so much that was wrong with planning and architecture education had to do with matters other than Harvard's physical plant. Principal among these was the near total lack of minority students and faculty (the Planning Department had no black faculty members and only four black applicants in 1970, compared with 80 black applicants for MIT's planning department), a problem that likely could have been remedied by spending a tiny percentage of these funds.

A major focus of my troubles was the Urban Field Service (UFS), which I began in 1968 to substitute real-life, community-based experience for more traditional studio-based learning via simulated problems. A program popular among students, UFS mounted some 40 projects involving 200 students (mostly GSD, but also from MIT and other Harvard departments). Small supervised teams aided low-income community group clients in projects that ran the gamut from designing playgrounds and community centers, to starting a tenant management corporation in a public housing project, to helping fight off neighborhood-destroying urban renewal and highway projects—including, in two instances, institutional expansion by MIT and Harvard. In the latter UFS project I clashed head-on with the University's administrative vice-president and President Pusey's assistant for civic and governmental relations, both of whom were openly critical of my role. In one notable instance, a UFS team helped a community group oppose an official city plan prepared by the consulting firm of Nash-Vigier—run by two tenured colleagues. One of the major sources of student dissatisfaction was the lack of attention they were receiving from their teachers, which they attributed to the fact that, as in most design schools, senior faculty had outside consulting firms that often took up most of their time and attention. A lurking, related issue was the extent to which faculty appointments might be made with an eye to the needs of these firms; Francois Vigier's rapid advancement—he became an assistant professor in

1965, received tenure in 1968—was seen by some as not unrelated to the existence of the Nash-Vigier consulting firm.

Running the UFS involved a constant battle with colleagues over credit for student work, budgetary hassles, and other conflicts. Most of the faculty opposed giving students this option, and of course underlying their opposition were feelings about the kinds of people we were helping and what we were helping them with. In a February 17, 1970 *Crimson* article, architectural historian Dolores Hayden, then a GSD student, reported that one of her architecture professors told her, "You are fooling yourself if you think you have learned anything by working on a UFS project this semester. If you want to work for these black people [the client group in this instance was white], you should quit school. This work has no place in the School." The sabotage efforts were extraordinary. When the Ford Foundation was on the verge of giving UFS a sizeable grant, a disparaging phone call to a high Foundation official by a senior member of my department scotched the deal. For two terms in a row, UFS wasn't even listed by my chair in a departmental handout given to students outlining the various ways of meeting the "planning problems" curriculum requirement. UFS was a lightening rod for the conflicting currents in the planning field and focused substantial opposition to my place on the faculty.

The "lessened loyalty" charge went beyond intra-GSD matters, to the April 1969 student strike and my open support of it. Beyond general support was the work I and some planning students carried out around one of the central strike issues, the University's relations with its surrounding community, both as landlord and expansionist institution. I was a principal formulator and spokesperson for the set of demands limiting expansion and developing housing for University personnel and residents of adjoining Cambridge and Boston neighborhoods. On television, I heatedly debated Corporation Fellow Hugh Calkins on Harvard's housing policies and obligations—and was roundly criticized for that performance at a faculty meeting the next morning.

Trying to Get Some Answers

Upon receiving Chairman Nash's letter, I wrote twice, asking him to clarify his sources of information, terms, and judgements regarding teaching methods, "political strategy," "the substance of city and regional planning," the meaning of loyalty in a time of change, and possibly competing loyalties to one's institution, faculty colleagues, students, and clients. I never received a reply, even though we had a quite good personal relationship dating back to my student days in the department and had co-authored a review article.

The issue of my reappointment rapidly became a *cause célèbre* within the GSD, in other parts of the University, and in the planning profession. Two-thirds of the GSD students signed a petition demanding that I be rehired; the official GSD alumni organization passed a resolution criticizing the department, rejecting the official reasons for my non-reappointment, and recommending appointment of a fact-finding committee. The American Society of Planning Officials' board of directors demanded that I be rehired; academics, alumni, and professionals from all over the country formed the Ad Hoc Committee to Reinstate Chester Hartman; the *Crimson* gave exhaustive coverage to the case, and articles appeared in the Boston press as well.

The appointment of a new GSD dean for academic year 1969-70 complicated matters. Maurice Kilbridge, a largely unknown Business School expert in systems analysis, was chosen to replace the internationally known architect José Luís Sert. It was widely assumed that President Pusey had appointed Kilbridge in order to end the School's administrative and financial chaos, since Sert's superb architectural skills (as demonstrated in Holyoke Center and the married students housing on the Charles) were in no way matched by his administrative talents. A central fix-up issue was the Planning Department, which had been chaired for seventeen years by one or another of its three tenured professors—Nash, Vigier, and Reginald Isaacs. Moving "the oligarchy" (as the trio was known) out of its entrenched position was clearly part of Kilbridge's marching orders. His mostly successful efforts subsequently led to a move unprecedented in Harvard's history, when the three brought charges against Kilbridge before the Harvard Corporation in 1971, asking that he be removed for violating several of the University's statutes in his attempts to reorganize the department. The charges were rejected "with prejudice."

But while at first Kilbridge seemed, to me and many others, a breath of fresh air, he soon proved to be a waffler, in well over his head, a man of unreliable words and actions. When I first met Kilbridge during the summer of 1969, he appeared supportive and friendly. Within a short time, however, he revealed himself as the central antagonist in my reappointment controversy. In December, he officially wrote me of his decision not to reappoint me, without giving any reason. When I asked for the reasons, he wrote, offering a totally different rationale from the Nash letter: that I was too specialized for a small faculty. (At different times, and by different GSD officials, other reasons were given: students were dissatisfied with my courses—although enrollment figures and student ratings placed me at the very top of the GSD faculty; my research and publications were inadequate—although I had published three articles and guest-edited a special issue on planning education in the major refereed planning journal, whereas the other thirteen members of my department had together published one article in that journal.) I then requested a personal meeting with Kilbridge to review his reasons. When I sent him a copy of my notes on his replies, asking that he make any corrections he felt were necessary, he wrote me a memo, stating that my version was inaccurate, and objecting to and characterizing as "contemptible" my "practice of recording and reporting, for whatever use, private conversations without the pre-knowledge of the other party." In an answering memo, I said I didn't regard the information I was seeking as private in nature, that I had openly, and without objection, been taking notes on his replies (not tape-recording), and merely wanted to assemble an accurate version of his reasons. We got no place, and he ended his final memo on the subject with, "If you are wired for sound, I hope you have a short circuit."

Within the GSD community, however, Kilbridge took a far more ambiguous position. (One of the more surreal moments was when I saw him in his office wearing a purple "CHESTER" button the students had designed and ordered to demonstrate support for me.) In early 1970, he wrote and distributed a leaflet, "SAVE THE URBAN FIELD SERVICE," which began: "I have learned of a whispering campaign against the Urban Field Service. Since I believe the Urban Field Service is one of the FINEST PROGRAMS IN THIS SCHOOL, I will not allow it to be destroyed by any person or group for self-indulgent purposes." This mystifying document was accompanied by a statement to the *Crimson* that "there has been no opposition at all to this program from students, faculty or administrators" and contained as the first of several listed "facts": "So far as I know, he [Hartman] intends to remain at GSD in that capacity [UFS Director]." This bizarre "offer"—made first to me in this form—included conditions that would obviously be unacceptable to me, since I would no longer have a faculty appointment. It was quickly and widely regarded for what it was: a disingenuous attempt to make it appear that I was rejecting the GSD, rather than the other way around.

The Hartman Review Committee

The GSD decision on my reappointment was not reversed, and I left Harvard at the end of academic year 1969-70 for a joint appointment at the National Housing Law Project (then part of the University of California-Berkeley Law School) and the University of California Department of City & Regional Planning. But the pressures and contradictions were sufficient to force the GSD to establish something apparently unprecedented in Harvard's history: outside investigation and review by a committee of non-GSD Harvard faculty, which would report back to the School. The step was explainable partly in terms of "the times," and partly due to the incredible absence of set University procedures for handling grievances concerning denial of academic due process and failure to employ traditional academic criteria in rehiring decisions. Forming a committee took nearly two years; the committee took over three years to issue its report; and the GSD took over a year to dispose of the matter.

At first, the GSD was unable to form a review committee using the procedures it had established, which called for the GSD faculty to nominate and elect five persons, one of whom had to be acceptable to me (I submitted a list of three persons I regarded as acceptable). Dean Kilbridge, in a memo to his faculty calling for revised procedures, noted that only two of the twelve persons approached were willing to serve under the conditions laid out to them, and that the University's General Counsel had raised problems with the original procedure. (Samuel Bowles, one of the three persons I proposed, indicated he would accept only if the "star chamber" character of the procedures were removed, and wrote Kilbridge: "It seems to me anomalous that one of the parties in this conflict...should be entrusted with the selection of the committee charged with hearing the case. The appointment of grievance committees by management has never seemed a particularly just way of adjudicating labor-management disputes." Bowles also noted, when re-asked to join under the revised procedures described below: "Upon being invited to join the committee, I was told that 3 of the 5 committee members had already been chosen and had agreed to participate. Yet you twice refused to identify who these 3 are...I cannot imagine the motivation behind this bizarre tactic, but it did nothing to allay my reservations concerning your general procedures.")

In May 1971, the GSD established new procedures: in lieu of granting me the right to have one acceptable committee member, I was given a one-time right to challenge one of the five originally selected members. For "balance," Dean Kilbridge was given a similar one-time challenge. The new procedure also took away one of the two grounds for appeal originally set forth (to which I had devoted over half of my original 25-page "brief"): my claim that the faculty had not given "adequate consideration" to its reappointment decision. In his memo urging the GSD faculty to revise the grounds for appeal *ex post facto*, Dean Kilbridge argued that "adequate consideration" was "meaningless"—although the American Association of University Professors (AAUP) defines the phrase quite precisely in terms of answers to these questions:

> Was the decision conscientiously arrived at? Was all available evidence bearing on the relevant performance of the candidate sought out and considered? Was there adequate deliberation by the department over the import of the evidence in the light of relevant standards? Were irrelevant and improper standards excluded from consideration? Was the decision a *bona fide* exercise of professional academic judgment?

To its credit, the review committee, when finally established, chose to include this issue in its investigation and report.

The GSD faculty held a new election in May 1971 under the revised ground rules. But they failed to ask me to submit nominations for the new election, as called for by the new procedures, and when I brought this to their attention they acceded to my demand that they hold a new election, but then carried it out in a way so as to ensure a virtual repeat of the results of the tainted previous election. I proposed that the new election list consist entirely of new nominees, otherwise the faculty, out of expedience or malice, simply would reelect the same persons previously known to have accepted appointment. In any case, I argued, any new names on the list would automatically be identified as those I had nominated and therefore would be at a disadvantage. My proposal was rejected, and the faculty proceeded to reelect four of the five previously elected. Not one of the more well-known and highly regarded faculty I proposed (a different list, of course, from the three names I had earlier submitted when I thought I was guaranteed that at least one would be asked to serve) was chosen—among whom were Kenneth Arrow, Albert Hirschman, Archibald Cox, John Rawls, Doris Kearns, Stephen Gould, Wassily Leontieff, and Alvin Poussaint. I exercised my challenge right in order to remove an Applied Mathematics professor I regarded as fairly reactionary; Dean Kilbridge exercised his challenge right and removed Sam Bowles.

Once replacements were made, the Hartman Review Committee (HRC)—four of whom were still people selected under the earlier procedure—consisted of Donald G.M. Anderson of Applied Mathematics (a professor well identified with the University's "law and order" wing during the late 1960s student uprisings, who chaired the committee, did most of the interviewing, and drafted the report); David Birch of the Business School (a former colleague of Dean Kilbridge); Joseph Harrington of the School of Public Health (who had, for several years prior to my appointment, taught a course in my department during the reign of the "oligarchy"); Christopher Jencks of the Education School; and Charles Conrad Wright of the Divinity School.

The HRC began its work in June 1972 and in August 1975 issued its 319-page report (only 58 pages of which are appendices reproducing documents). It was essentially a monumental collection of facts (many important ones unknown to me previously), but with few real conclusions and fewer recommendations. The Committee's bottom-line finding was: "We are not prepared to say that there was a violation of Dr. Hartman's academic freedom, as traditionally understood." On the other hand, I had "legitimate grievances, both procedural and substantive, against a department which was incapable of living up to the reasonable expectations of its junior faculty members, and to a lesser extent an administration which did not act to correct this situation." My reappointment decision represented "a failure of departmental competence and of administrative oversight." The Committee noted critically the failure to obtain outside evaluation of my work and the lack of any

> systematic attempt…to assess, influence, or even find out precisely, what Dr. Hartman was doing in regard [to teaching performance]…Had the City and Regional Planning Department gathered even the limited evidence regarding Dr. Hartman's qualifications at our disposal, and weighed this on its merits in professional terms, the decision might have come out either way. In the absence of such an effort, though, the possibility that Dr. Hartman's views on planning education were held against him increases.

And there was considerable material of a personally complimentary nature: e.g., "He [Hartman] gave far more to his work, and to his students, than was asked of him…There is no real question of his commitment to the educational task of the University, the School or the Department."

The Pusey Connection

The most important piece of new information I learned during the course of the Committee's investigation was the extensive and extraordinary involvement by President Pusey and the Harvard Corporation in the matter of my reappointment. Professor Vigier—with his own anti-Kilbridge ax to grind—was the source of this information. Four letters from Kilbridge to Pusey came to light. The first, dated June 5, 1969, detailed the arrangement reached regarding the conditions of Kilbridge's appointment (and presumably was the fruit of earlier conversations or meetings between the two). One of the seven conditions in that letter read: "The GSD, especially Dean Sert or Professor Nash, will make a decision on the reappointment of Professor Hartman and he will be notified in writing before June 30, 1969, whether or not his contract will be renewed." Professor Vigier, in his testimony before the HRC, interpreted this clause as follows: that the president did not wish to be embarrassed by receiving a recommendation for reappointment and that Dean Kilbridge was not disposed to embarrass the president.

A second letter, dated September 5, 1969, dealt with separating the issue of how to secure continued foundation funding for the UFS from the question of whether I would be reappointed. Another, dated October 16, 1969, discussed an item on the Corporation's October 20 agenda (placed there at Kilbridge's request) to create a separate Corporation appointment for me as UFS director, in addition to my assistant professorship; it ends, "You may see in this a hint of strategy, which I shall be pleased to discuss with you at your convenience." A final letter, dated December 10, 1969, notifies the president of the dean's letter to me of that same date telling me I was not to be reappointed.

Kilbridge never brought these letters to the Committee's attention. He maintained he simply forgot about them. (The HRC had its own problems getting hold of this correspondence after learning about it. University Counsel Daniel Steiner sent a file copy of the June 5 letter only to [by then ex-] President Pusey, not to the Committee; only after much prodding did Dean Kilbridge produce copies from his files.) That a relatively obscure Business School professor, plucked out to become a Harvard dean, should simply forget about the existence of letters to the president of Harvard, regarding the conditions of his appointment and subsequent strategizing, strains belief.

The HRC also took other testimony suggesting "command influence." Corporation Fellow Hugh Calkins recalled that Pusey "report[ed] to the Corporation...well before the official department [sic] action in early December, that the department [sic] had decided not to reappoint Hartman." Did this relate to an oral guarantee of non-renewal to which the June 5 letter was obliquely referring? (The HRC asserted that President Pusey "initiated" actions to have the matter of my reappointment resolved.) William Doeble, the GSD's Acting Dean during late 1969 when Dean Sert was on sabbatical, told the HRC that I had been mentioned by name by President Pusey in meetings of the Council of Deans as part of his disapproval of faculty involvement in the University Hall takeover, and one student testified before the HRC that Kilbridge told him Pusey had commented to him sardonically, "Hartman should have had the courage to stay in the Hall when the police broke down the door." (I had been inside University Hall, as an observer, in the manner that many faculty, right and left, toured the building during the occupation.) Four GSD students signed an affidavit to the HRC stating that, at a social gathering during the summer of 1969, Kilbridge said that even if the department recommended renewing my appointment, Pusey and the Corporation probably would reject the recommendation.

What is the meaning of all this? Why so extensive involvement of the president and Corporation in the mere reappointment of an assistant professor (neither promotion nor tenure was at issue)? Did Kilbridge, as he claims, merely want a messy matter dealt with before he took office? Or did what they say never happens at Harvard actually happen: politically motivated dictation regarding an academic appointment by the real powers at the University?

Stonewalling and Questions of Veracity

A key factor in the HRC's unwillingness or inability to find for me was the virtual stonewalling by all the major figures in the controversy. Reginald Issacs refused to have anything whatsoever to do with the Committee; the other two tenured members of my department, William Nash and Frank Vigier, refused to participate in the Committee's deliberations and requests for information beyond their original oral or written submissions; Dean Sert declined comment; President Pusey and Corporation Secretary Sargent Kennedy also failed to cooperate fully with the Committee's investigation; Martin Meyerson (then President of the University of Pennsylvania and a former member of my department, who was called in by President Pusey as a special consultant on how to deal with the troubled department) declined comment when approached by the Committee.

The HRC delicately castigated the non-cooperators (e.g., "The fact that Dean Sert and Professor Nash have not chosen to clarify the situation is most unfortunate indeed."), but refused to draw any inferences from the stonewalling ("the burden of proof falls on the accuser, and the benefit of doubt redounds to the accused"); it merely passed on to the GSD faculty itself responsibility for dealing with its colleagues.

A further barrier was the questionable veracity of Dean Kilbridge and others. The HRC expressed considerable doubts on this score: "there remains a lingering doubt in the minds of many members of the committee, as to whether he [Kilbridge] has been as candid and forthcoming as he might have been"; "the members of the review committee find it hard to believe that a matter so obviously important to the investigation [the Kilbridge-Pusey correspondence] could simply be forgotten"; "the credibility of other witnesses involved is often subject to serious question." Nevertheless, the HRC refused to draw any negative inferences from this pattern. Its tone was at best mildly critical. President Pusey's extraordinary involvement in my reappointment was pronounced "an unfortunate incident." The Kilbridge-Pusey contacts are "probably mildly embarrassing but essentially trivial." As for the June 5, 1969 letter from Kilbridge to Pusey and its attempted coverup, the Committee wrote: "The hesitancy with which matters surrounding the…letter have been treated may be entirely innocent, due to nothing more than fallible recollections, but do serve to accentuate interest in the matter." Certainly no one could accuse the Committee of indelicacy. What comes through clearly is a paramount unwillingness to think ill of or embarrass a president of Harvard or other higher-ups. Deans and presidents are at worst quixotic, enigmatic figures, never truly suspect or culpable.

Back in the GSD's Court

The review process did not end with the HRC report. That document then was transmitted to the GSD faculty for final action. The School's Academic Policy Committee (APC) prepared a 32-page "summary" of the report, a sanitized reader's digest version about which the *Crimson* (October 13, 1976) noted: "On issue after issue, the [GSD's] academic policy panel took a markedly less critical view of the handling of Hartman's case." To give one of many examples: whereas the HRC labelled my ex-department's reappointment procedures "certainly execrable" and "shockingly lax," the APC characterized them as merely "informal." Donald Anderson himself was clearly miffed at what the GSD was doing to his work: in a letter to the APC he noted, "Your account puts the department in a better light than it deserves...I am surprised that your committee chose to restate and reargue points of our report." Anderson's letter also describes some of the APC's material as "misleading" and notes several inaccurate quotes from the HRC report.

The APC also ducked completely the question of non-cooperation, the matter most clearly referred to the GSD. The HRC called upon the Design School faculty members to take "due note of this fact and take such action as they deem appropriate." What the colleagues of the faculty members criticized by the HRC deemed appropriate was that censure could not even be considered "in the absence of known standards and accepted procedures in this area." In a June 11, 1976 letter to me, Richard H. Peairs, Associate Secretary of the AAUP, noted about the failure to cooperate: "The often exquisite distinctions which must be appraised in resolving disputes of academic right and privilege require that all participants appreciate the weighty obligation to contribute their best energy and knowledge to such tasks..." The action that had just been taken by the Faculty Senate of City College (CUNY), which I brought to the GSD's attention, was also ignored. That body, in February 1975, censured five tenured members of its history department for failure to cooperate with the legitimate requests of a Committee of Inquiry. The CUNY Senate felt that no prior warnings or stated standards of conduct were necessary for this expectation of cooperation or for the censure they issued. The resolution of censure noted that:

> a refusal to cooperate with this legitimate inquiry is unworthy of academicians and constitutes a direct attack on the principles of faculty self-government and of judgment by one's peers...A resolution of censure is simply the means provided in Robert's Rules of Order for a parliamentary body to criticize or express disapproval and this is, we believe, entirely appropriate in the case at hand.

The GSD held a special meeting (October 13, 1976) to act on the HRC report, as filtered to it by the APC. They refused my request to be present or represented, despite support for this by the AAUP. As the June 1, 1976 *Crimson* noted,

> While Hartman will not be permitted to attend, the faculty members charged with wrongdoing may do so. They will have not only the advantage of stating their case directly to the faculty, but also of voting on GSD's resolution of the affair...Many [in fact, half] of the school's faculty members arrived after Hartman departed and know virtually nothing about the controversy. Ignorant thus about the facts and issues involved...and probably reluctant to study the 300-page review committee report, these professors will be swayed by the dialogue at the meeting.

Predictably, the GSD voted to accept their APC's findings and recommendations: that the decision was made by the department alone on legitimate grounds; that no remedial action was required. The faculty's sole concession to the defects and criticisms catalogued in the HRC report was a request to the APC to examine grievance procedures with a view to recommending improved procedures for the future. (A December 17, 1987 letter from GSD Dean Gerald McCue, in response to my inquiry as to what follow-up there had been to this motion, elicited this response: "This issue has not come up in any form during my deanship [McCue was named GSD dean in 1980]. In fact, it has been my experience in academia in general that such issues arise very seldom. Because the issue has not appeared while I have been at Harvard, I have not had the occasion to look into the subject...")

All in all, not exactly responsive to the HRC's critique of the School and its call for reform: "Fully as much as Dr. Hartman, it is the School of Design which is the loser in this sorry situation. It has been ill served and brought into disrepute. It is up to the Faculty of Design to set its house in order."

I made one last appeal, to President Bok (a formal AAUP investigation or court cases seemed to hold little promise, and I was also reaching my own personal limit of energy expenditure on a matter by then over seven years old). In a November 1977 letter, I asked him to review the actions and inactions of the GSD faculty. Bok's reply stressed "separation of powers," holding that "where there has been extensive consideration by duly constituted faculty bodies of claims of infringement of a faculty member's rights, I do not think that my role as President is to try to reach my own decision on the merits and to substitute my judgment for the Faculty's should it be different." "The pursuit of justice in our society," Bok homilized, "is frequently marred by imperfections, but in most cases people are acting in good faith in attempting to resolve difficult questions and reach fair decisions. In my view many people at the GSD and elsewhere at Harvard spent countless hours in resolving your allegations in this manner."

Some Final Thoughts

What is to be learned from my experience?

One lesson concerns the limits of liberalism. Overt, activist leftists simply are not welcome at Harvard University, regardless of their performance by traditional academic criteria. My actions, particularly those related to the 1969 strike—a truly searing experience for the Harvard powers-that-be—and my UFS work as it impacted on the University's corporate activities, were beyond what the University administration and departmental colleagues would put up with from a faculty member. As the HRC put it (albeit in somewhat too narrow terms), "There is reason to believe that Dr. Hartman became the symbol of the [GSD] faculty's distaste for the events of that spring."

A second lesson concerns the thinness of procedural due process when it comes to internal self-criticism and self-examination. A law professor who read this account in draft was simply astounded at the blatant violation of accepted canons of fairness in the process of selecting the "outside" review committee, the work of the review committee itself, and the manner in which the GSD then disposed of the committee's report. Like most bureaucracies, Harvard is hypocritical and self-protective, preferring to shove problems under the carpet or handle them in an ad hoc way, rather than establish the kinds of procedures that are the backbone of the liberal society the University presumably is defending. Trouble-makers are gotten rid of, principles compromised when the interests of the old boys are threatened. Untruths may be told, stonewalling permitted, with no real effort to discipline or punish.

Third, an incredibly protracted review process—seven-plus years—certainly works against the interests of fair play. While likely no one consciously decided and planned to stretch things out so far, nor was there any voice or interest arguing against such delays and the negative effects they have on those who allege and appeal injustice. Key figures tire of the issue. Those who remain at the institution are far more concerned with current relationships and realities than remedying injustices long past, done to someone long gone.

Finally, it may be important to affirm that, as time- and emotion-consuming as it all was, and as ultimately unsatisfying as the final decision was, I don't regret having made the effort. With the benefit of hindsight, I might have done some things differently, possibly involving lawyers more formally (as opposed to informal advice-seeking), especially in regard to procedural matters. But I think I did about as well as I could. Outside support—from professional colleagues outside the University, the press, students, as well as others at the University—was critical to getting even as far as I did, and it likely is rare to have a case as well documented as mine was (its "bottom line" aside, the massive HRC report is a goldmine of revealing and supportive material). It is comforting to know that the kind of urban planning and education I represented has taken root, not only in the profession, but in the best of the nation's planning schools. It is perhaps not irrelevant to note that, in 1980, the Planning Department was transferred from the Design School to the Kennedy School, in an attempt to reshape it and salvage it—an unsuccessful effort that has left it as a tiny degree option within the Public Policy Program there. Finally, Dean Kilbridge resigned in the late 1970s following highly critical reports by the Overseers Visiting Committee to the GSD and strong student and faculty opposition, which included a unanimous vote by the Architecture faculty asking President Bok to undertake "a full investigation" of the School, citing an "atmosphere of tension and distrust."

Acknowledgements

I am grateful to Richard Appelbaum, Amy Fine, Daniel Klubock, Margaret Levi, Dorothy Miller, Marcus Raskin, Philip Schrag, and Michael Tanzer for helpful comments on earlier drafts of this article, and to Kurt Jordan for his technical assistance. For advice and support during the many years and dozens of back-and-forth documents that constituted my participation in the review process, I am grateful to Ed Barshak, Louis Henkin and Daniel Klubock. Finally, I would like to express my deep appreciation to the very many students and other colleagues in the academic and professional world whose political and personal concerns and activism on my behalf effectively forced the University to deal with something that it otherwise would have ignored.

Minority and Third World Students

Cynthia Silva, Lisa Hinds, and Roberta Young

Harvard University regards itself as standing at the cutting edge of social justice. Its leaders, ever ready to acknowledge and condemn racism in U.S. society, are taken aback by suggestions that racism has been central to the operation of the University itself. It is one thing for deans to deplore what is politely called "insensitivity" on the part of individual students; it is quite another to confront racist practices as a whole way of life. This essay is an attempt at refreshing Harvard's institutional memory, and suggests that students will have to learn how to combat the subtler and often more insidious constellation of ideas and practices that encourage minority and Third World students to acquiesce in their own subordination.

The Presence of Minority Students—and Faculty Response

Harvard University today operates under the Charter of 1650, a fondly commemorated document except on those unhappy occasions when it is thought notorious for perpetuating the rule of the all-white Harvard Corporation. What is less known is that the Charter calls on Harvard to provide for "the education of the English and Indian Youth of this Country." The commitment to "Indian youth" was quickly forgotten, save for the enrollment of a few Native Americans between 1653 and 1715. Caleb Cheeshahteaumuck, class of 1665, was the only Native American to be granted a degree during this period. Harvard thereafter remained an exclusively all-white bastion until the late nineteenth century when several African-Americans enrolled, among them George Ruffin (1869), the first black judge in Massachusetts; Robert Terrell (1884), the first black municipal judge in Washington, D.C.; and W.E.B. DuBois (1890), a central figure in twentieth century American intellectual life. The first black students at Harvard came to the Medical School in 1850, but the University unceremoniously kicked them out, deferring to outrage from a large faction of irate white students.[1]

Those black students who finally did attend were hardly greeted with acceptance. DuBois was not permitted to live in campus dormitories, and was refused entry into student organizations. The Harvard Glee Club rejected DuBois and his better-than-average voice because, as he recalls it, this would pose for them the recurring problem of a "nigger" on the team. He spoke of his Harvard experience in stark terms: "I was at Harvard, but not of it." DuBois had brushes with the likes of Harvard science Dean Nathaniel Shaler (class of 1862), who confidently declared that blacks were "unfit for an independent place in a civilized state." Shaler followed in the footsteps of his predecessor, Harvard science Dean Henry Eustis (class of 1838), who, firmly in accord with Louis Agassiz, proclaimed that blacks were "little above beasts" (see Jon Beckwith's essay). For most Harvard students at this time, their only contact with blacks came through the hiring of "scouts," servants modeled after a lord-serf institution started at Oxford. DuBois recalls that, while attending a commencement social function, "a lady seemed determined to mistake me for a waiter."[2]

At its 350th anniversary, Harvard gave a somewhat different portrayal of its history, proclaiming that the University had at least been a haven for dissent and abolitionists. But in the 1850s, a mere eight out of 35 instructors were anti-slavery, and these few, described in a judicious study by Ronald Story, "were... cautious by temperament and opposed to unnecessary confrontation and 'violent denunciation.' " According to Harvard professor F.D. Huntington, the anti-slavery professors regarded democracy as rule by a "cultivated and educated" few. Even so, anti-slavery activist Charles Sumner found himself twice rebuffed for a law professorship, while others expressed relief when the abolitionist Longfellow left the University upon Sumner's election to the Senate. In Charles Francis Adams' words, Harvard professors in the antebellum period delivered speeches "of the most ridiculous ultra-conservative character."[3]

Increasing Commitment to Diversity?

Today, the Harvard administration is less likely to give speeches of a "ridiculous ultra-conservative quality," but that is little solace for minority students who, after two decades of soothing rhetoric since Harvard began admitting people of color, have witnessed slow progress, and in many measures ongoing regress. Through student pressure, African-Americans gained the first significant concessions from the administration (i.e., the formation of the Afro-American Studies Department in 1968, the hiring of black admissions officers, and the active recruitment of black students beginning in 1969). Soon other minority groups struggled to increase services and opportunities for their constituents. (Puerto Rican students gained inclusion in the minority recruitment program in 1970 and Chicano students in 1973. Harvard denied Asian-Americans minority status until 1976, despite recognition as such by Title VI, Chapter 60 of the Civil Rights Act of 1964.)

The minority population in each class escalated from 158 for the class of 1978 to 344 for the class of 1983 where it stagnated for the next six years. Most insidious in all of this seemed to be the existence of what the Third World Students Association (TWSA) in 1986 charged was "an unstated ceiling" on minorities, leading to a situation where the gains for Asians in the decade was accompanied by a decrease in the number of African-Americans. In 1987 and especially 1988, however, Harvard made a relatively substantial increase to around 450, with 14 percent of the incoming class of 1992 Asian, 9 percent African-American, and 5 percent Hispanic. It remains to be seen whether such gains will be sustained and improved upon; Harvard itself suggests that the leap was due to a larger pool of applicants infused with enthusiasm about Harvard through prominent media coverage of its 350th anniversary. Critics have countered that some of Harvard's improvement has been provoked by the announcement of an investigation into Harvard's under-representation of Asians, who apparently are denied entry even when they vastly outperform white students. [4]

Against historic gains must be registered several key setbacks. A marked decline in black students from working-class and inner-city backgrounds has occurred in the past two decades, a serious blow to diversity. The Third World Students Association report of 1986 indicates that by the end of the 1970s, working-class blacks dropped from 40 to 25 percent of the total black incoming class, the decline apparently continuing into the 1980s. A Harvard admissions officer has outright stated that the University prefers to admit black students who come from middle class backgrounds and primarily white high schools: "It is right for Harvard and better for the students, because there is better adjustment and less desperate alienation." Concerning the situation with law school admissions, Thomas

Fox, a recent graduate of Harvard Law School (HLS), observes that: "There's the same amount of [minority] students here every year. That's not commitment. That's just keeping to a certain number so they're not accused of being overtly discriminatory."[5]

The Faculty Record

Among the faculty, hiring of minorities remains dismal. Black faculty stars such as the Medical School's Alvin Poussaint have not been given tenure, provoking HLS professor Derek Bell to reflect, "Simple brilliance is not enough..." Bell concludes that it has only been through student unrest that the University grants tenure to African-American intellectuals. According to a study of 434 faculty positions in the ten departments of Economics, Government, Psychology, Sociology, English, Visual and Environmental Studies, Fine Arts, Chemistry, and Biology, a mere sixteen people are minorities and, excluding foreign scholars, only eight minority professors came from the United States.[6]

There are only three tenured African-Americans out of 383 senior professors on the faculty of Arts and Sciences in 1988, down from five in 1980. In these eight years, Asian-Americans increased from twelve to fourteen, Hispanics dropped from four to two. Of the 946 tenured members of all Harvard's faculties in 1988, fifteen are black men and a mere two are black women. In 1980, Harvard issued the Dean Whitla Report, admitting that Harvard's minority recruitment could be judged "at best, passive recruitment." (We shudder to imagine what it could be "at worst.") When the Minority Students Alliance (MSA) interviewed deans and department chairpersons about implementing the document's mild reforms, "the overwhelming majority *could not even remember* the report," states Curtis Chang of the MSA. "A major report by the Dean's office and the Faculty Council—produced in response to minority students' initiatives—was effectively buried."[7]

In 1988, Thomas Fox reflected on the then presence of only two black tenured professors out of 59 at Harvard Law School: "There are no mentor relationships to be forged. Whereas white students are able to network and get a lot of jobs here, we're not brought into the fold, the inner circle. We go to their parties, participate in their study groups, but there is a certain line we can't cross. The interaction, to a certain degree, is really superficial."[8]

The Afro-American Studies Department itself became weakened in the mid-1970s by the University's refusal to allow the hiring of Africanists in the program, thus cutting off connections to the African past. Dean Henry Rosovsky defended the narrowing of the black experience to the United States, saying "I always thought it [Afro-Am] was an American subject." Students were also stripped of voting rights in the Department, a ploy that ludicrously blamed them for potentially undercutting faculty quality. In reality, the requirement that Afro-American Studies faculty must be sponsored by another major academic department (i.e., history, sociology, government, etc.) has hindered any progress in the department's faculty recruitment.[9] Yale, with this same dual department regulation, has watched its Afro-Am program decline, whereas Princeton, which has granted its department independence, is undergoing an intellectual renaissance led by Cornel West.

Rising Provocation

While apparently not as prevalent as at some campuses such as UMass and Wisconsin, racial incidents with ugly overtones appear to be on the rise at Harvard. In 1987, two white males heaved a frozen orange and grapefruit through a Currier House window, shattering it close to where a black student sat. The student was phoned minutes later by people declaring themselves the "Negro Hit Squad." Some African-American students deemed the punishment that Harvard delivered these culprits fair, until Harvard allowed one of them to play football, despite his probation. In that same year, Asian students cleaning up after a dining hall dance were harassed by a group sporting Crimson team jackets. "Hey Chinkos! How about it chinks?" they shouted, attempting to start a fight.[10] In 1986, Cambridge police stopped three black Harvard law students and, when they showed their Harvard IDs, asked "Where did you boys steal these?" even after they offered additional photo identification. Three years later, the city police yanked two black Harvard students off a bus under the pretext that they may have robbed a convenience store, despite a subsequent FOIA request indicating that the suspect had repeatedly been identified as a blond-headed white male.

Harvard no longer has Ku Klux Klan chapters as it did in the 1920s, but the campus Conservative Club enthusiastically hosts members of the international wing of the KKK, spokespersons for the apartheid regime of South Africa. Because of disruptions at these presentations, Harvard's administration has defined the issue as freedom of speech, without also looking into the broader question of a growth of racial insensitivity among students and faculty. When black students accused a history professor of making racist utterances in his lectures, Dean Spence appealed to academic freedom and the need for a diversity of opinion. But the virtual absence of black and minority faculty makes that appeal to diversity ring hollow.[11]

Minority students have pushed administrators to be more vigilant in punishing those students involved in racist activities. Nevertheless, care must be taken not to strengthen the administration's hand in also persecuting the progressive political forces. Those fighting racism, such as anti-apartheid activists, have frequently been the target of University disciplinary inquiries and inquisitions; student activists must make clear that acts of racism are qualitatively more heinous and should not be equated, say, with a peaceful sit-in against apartheid that in 1987 brought the suspension of a Harvard graduate student.[12]

Accepting Western Hegemony?

While complaints about the insensitivity of the University to minority student concerns abound, students have not generally identified the institutional reasons for this insensitivity. Rather than engage in an analysis of the institution, its functions, and their relationship to it, they have focused on the prejudices of various administrators and faculty. The students' task is not merely to wrest control of resources from a hostile or indifferent bureaucracy. Rather, the conflict involves control over definitions of reality. The University serves to socialize and train the next generation of guardians of the extant social, political, and economic order; and minority and Third World students, no less than others, must confront the functions of their education directly.[13]

The history of minority student organizing activity at Harvard suggests that there have been only occasional insights into the larger hegemonic functions of the University, such as in the recognition of the University's interest in detaching Afro-American Studies from African history. Validating that connection would run counter to the prevailing interpretation of Afro-American history as distinct from Africa and to its function in engendering political impotence. Students saw that, for Harvard, supporting the study of Africa within the context of Afro-American Studies would be tantamount to endorsing Pan-Africanism.

In the majority of instances, however, minority student organizers seem to have failed to appreciate the nature of the struggle in which they are engaged. In their attempts to organize, they seem to have missed some of the most important questions: what role is the University preparing their constituents to play once they graduate, how do those roles affect their communities, and how can they organize themselves to resist the hegemonic culture? Part of the problem here is that Third World students born in the United States (and sometimes abroad as well) frequently appear not to recognize the necessity of resistance on this level. Their record of organizing gives very little impression that they see the need to develop intellectually and culturally compelling alternatives to the dominant frames of reference. Without this recognition, organizing efforts will inevitably focus on improving the comforts of campus life, preparing the way for minority and Third World students to participate more fully in the intellectual mainstream (and the socio-political system beyond campus) even as they strive to maintain cultural integrity.

Further still, the record of Third World student organizing gives the impression that U.S.-born Third World students are alone in their need for redress and removal of institutional barriers. For example, the Third World Student Alliance's 1986 "Program of Demands for Third World Students" notes that most of Harvard's courses on Africa, Asia, and Latin America are taught from the perspective of the colonizer or the western social scientist and argues for the institution of Ethnic Studies courses which would "seek to study a people's experience as primarily defined and perceived by the people themselves." Their demand is well founded, but when it comes to concrete proposals they only specify that the University offer courses in American Indian, Asian-American, Chicano, and Puerto Rican Studies, seemingly stopping short of including Third World people outside the United States in their concerns.[14]

While this points to a kind of self-centeredness, the failure of U.S.-born Third World students to address issues of concern to Third World nationals points again to their failure either to recognize western hegemony or to see a need to challenge it. While minority students decry the administration's attempts to distance them from their culture, they have not acknowledged the University's role in cultivating an acceptance of the rational/technocratic western world view among Third World nationals.[15] One is left to conclude that minority students are either unaware of the impact this has on the relationship between Third World nationals and their respective peoples and cultures, or that they tacitly endorse the dominance of the West. In either case, they leave Third World nationals alone in their struggle to maintain intellectual and cultural integrity, to say nothing of their struggle against the political and economic domination of their home countries.

Finding the Missing Links—Some Concluding Thoughts

The success of attempts to organize a movement among Third World students at Harvard (or on other campuses) will depend not so much on a change of heart among administrators and faculty as on the ability of organizers to identify their constituents, clarify their goals and relate their activities to the concerns of all Third World students and the communities which they represent. Toward that end, organizers must recognize that Third World student organizations should be working groups comprised both of Third World nationals and U.S.-born minorities. In order to develop such coalitions, organizers will have to confront honestly the political, socioeconomic, racial, and cultural differences and conflicts between and among Third World peoples.[16] A revitalization of Third World organizing will also require an agenda that looks beyond the campus to incorporate issues of concern in the communities and countries which Third World students represent. In addition to questions of divestment and apartheid, Third World students must focus on international development, the role of international monetary agencies in the affairs of developing nations, regional politics, and the conditions of minority communities in the United States as well.

As they begin to confront the challenges faced by Third World nationals, minority students from the United States must begin to understand that their own struggle for recognition and cultural integrity is intimately related to the struggle against Western hegemony in Third World political, economic, and intellectual life. In order to organize a movement of Third World students effectively, the bonds of intellectual dependence on western tradition must be broken. The role of the University as a reproducer of the social system must be recognized, and students must make a choice: they can choose to support the dominant political, economic, and cultural systems, which exploit the natural and human resources of the Third

World, ensnare developing nations in debt, divert funds from social programming to military buildup, elevate Europeans and Euro-Americans to the apex of the social hierarchy, and subordinate all forms of knowledge and critical thinking to narrow technical rationality and expertise. Or, they can choose to resist the hegemonic forces, within the University and beyond, that inhibit critical thinking and discourse, and support authentic motion on behalf of social transformation and human justice.

Notes

1. For the history of blacks at Harvard, see forthcoming study by Calvin Titcomb. Information on these black graduates comes from an unpublished paper delivered by him during Black History Month, 1987, Adams House, Harvard University.

2. For Shaler and Eustis, see Titcomb. For DuBois's reflections, consult his autobiographical *Dusk of Dawn* (1940). DuBois is excerpted in the following: W.E.B DuBois, "That Outer Whiter World of Harvard," in William Bentinck-Smith, ed., *The Harvard Book* (Cambridge: Harvard University Press, 1982).

3. See chapter 5, Ronald Story, *Harvard and the Boston Upper Class* (Middletown, CT: Wesleyan University Press, 1980).

4. For earlier figures, see "Commitment to Diversity: A History and Program of Demands for Third World Students at Harvard University," Third World Student Alliance (TWSA), 1986. For latest figures, Katherine Bliss, "Freshman Class Sets Application Records," *Harvard Crimson*, July 8, 1988, p. 1.

5. For quotation of Harvard admissions officer, see D. Karen, "Who Gets into Harvard?," Ph.D. thesis in Sociology (1985), cited by Andrew Hacker, "Affirmative Action: The New Look," *New York Review of Books*, October 12, 1989, p. 64. For Fox, see Pamela Reynolds, "Bakke opened doors, but some feel not wide enough," *Boston Globe*, June 29, 1988, p. 11. For data, TWSA report, "Commitment to Diversity."

6. For Bell, see Diane Lewis, "Harvard Professor considers NY Move," *Boston Globe*, June 29, 1988, p. 22. For data, see MSA Report (1988), summarized by Curtis Chang, "Harvard Minority Tenure," *East Wind*, vol. 1, #2, 1988, pp. 27-28.

7. See Chang, *loc. cit.* and Lewis, *loc. cit.*

8. Reynolds, *loc. cit.*

9. TWSA report, "Commitment to Diversity." Another factor that must surely sap the vitality of these departments is the reality that a majority of the white faculty often discourage students from becoming "too involved" with these intellectual enterprises. For instance, a panel on minority graduate students at Harvard held in Spring 1989 brought confessions from virtually all the participants that their academic advisors had warned that they would probably lose intellectual credibility if they chose to focus on research primarily concerning minority communities.

10. AWARE newsletter (Spring 1989).

11. For some of these incidents, see Eleanor Clark, "Shades of Difference," *Subterranean Review*, Spring 1987, p. 10. Also Chang, *loc. cit.* Chang has been the most trenchant critic of Harvard's claim to seek a "diversity of opinion."

12. For a discussion of how administrators use anti-racism as a tool to repress progressive students, consult Alan Wald's essay on the University of Michi-

gan, "Racism and the University," *Against the Current*, May-June 1988, pp. 8-14.

13. Cf. Samuel Bowles and Herbert Gintis, *Schooling in Capitalist America* (New York: Basic Books, 1976) and Raymond Williams, *The Sociology of Culture* (New York: Schocken Books, 1981) for a detailed discussion of the role of educational institutions in reproducing social, cultural, political, and economic relations.

14. See TWSA report, "Commitment to Diversity."

15. Edward H. Berman illuminates this point in the context of intellectual work supported by U.S. foundations in the Third World in *The Influence of the Carnegie, Ford, and Rockefeller Foundations on American Foreign Policy: The Ideology of Philanthropy* (Albany: SUNY Press, 1983), see chapter six.

16. It is important to recognize that students from certain Third World countries have serious reasons for avoiding activism, including the reality that many return home to repressive regimes which routinely jail and torture dissidents. Not all of these governments are clients of the U.S. or Western European powers, so these students are frequently unresponsive to progressive critiques of Western institutions. Moreover, many Third World nationals, like their First World counterparts, are well aware that political activity jeopardizes careers, the loss of which can mean in poorer countries a future life of poverty and severe deprivation.

Authors' note
The first part of this article was composed primarily by L. Hinds and R. Young, with editorial and research assistance provided by J. Trumpbour and members of the *How Harvard Rules* collective. The second part was written mainly by C. Silva, with research assistance from Z. Robinson.

Meritocracy and the Manipulation of Ethnic Minorities
The Epps and Evans Affairs

Eugene Franklin Rivers

Harvard University, self-anointed the nation's premiere academic institution, assumes the role of functional apologist for racial and cultural discrimination among many other managerial responsibilities. From the evidence currently available, beneath the mountains of well intentioned official rhetoric lies a very disturbing reality. Regarding blacks in particular, Harvard and the Reverend Jerry Falwell's Liberty Baptist College have much more in common than appears on the surface.

While our friends at Lynchburg, Virginia will inform us in no uncertain terms that the social marginality of blacks is the fruit of their god's infinite good sense, Harvard arrives at essentially the same conclusion—but in hushed tones, over coffee in the Faculty Club, and without the assistance of divine revelation. These beliefs find their formal and verifiable expression in Harvard's policies concerning affirmative action. Discrimination in hiring and promotional practices on the basis of race is a logical by-product of Harvard's larger institutional objectives. There are two forces that shape this political reality. First, Harvard is in many respects a *de facto* white supremacist institution that discourages black involvement at the administrative and senior faculty level. This fact is camouflaged by an utterly deceptive liberalism.

The second political force is the considerable ideological energy that is invested in legitimating racism in Harvard's managerial vision. In the present case, the pivotal buzzword is meritocracy.[1] Meritocracy has had a fascinating history at Harvard, as well as within the broader historical evolution of elite academic institutions in the United States. Its strategic deployment by elites in various crisis periods most frequently has served to obfuscate deeper epistemological, policy, and ideological questions concerning the nature and purpose of educational theory and practice.[2] As Samuel Bowles and Herbert Gintis have convincingly argued, the meritocratic ideology is crucial to the process of legitimating the socio-economic and cultural reproduction of inequality by justifying privilege and attributing poverty (and occupational immobility) to a strictly personal failure.[3]

In a number of respects, the philosophical or sociological arguments against meritocracy do not provide the most dramatic illustrations of either the danger of its pretense or the injustice of its applications. This is especially true concerning racial discrimination at Harvard. Issues of race have been a source of considerable controversy, especially in the case of blacks, who have been the subject of much of the discussion of race and meritocracy in the United States as well. The controversies at Harvard, however, conceal subtle and problematic realities.

In the following discussion, we will briefly consider a few representative cases that are uniquely instructive as to how Harvard rewards the dedication and loyalty of its black administrators and staff. The experience of blacks at Harvard suggests that perseverance and performance do not necessarily result in the expected rewards, or depending on the political climate, even token concessions. While a number of heartwarming exceptions exist, they serve primarily to legitimate the myth that success depends solely on individual effort by fostering an illusion of equal opportunity. The racial discrimination that Harvard's "black help" experiences in no significant way violates Harvard's "sacred" commitment to "Veritas" (its motto, which connotes truth and integrity). The miscarriage of justice which our examples have suffered are, in the present political context, entirely consistent with the University's larger objectives. Put indelicately, the University's mystical meritocracy is a moral and intellectual fraud.

Let us begin by considering a case of discrimination in which race was not directly implicated. The denial of tenure in the Economics Department at Harvard to radical economist and associate professor Samuel Bowles in 1974 came as no surprise to students and faculty acquainted with the intra- and interdepartmental faculty politics at the University. Bowles had distinguished himself as one of the most talented and well-known economists in the country (see Lawrence Lifschultz's essay). But Bowles's failure to exhibit an acceptable degree of ideological conformity disqualified him from a Harvard professorship. Consequently, he paid the political price for his unauthorized scholarly and intellectual perspective.

Of course, had Bowles quietly bowed before the throne of neoclassical orthodoxy, or, as some others did, danced the neoclassical shuffle until being appointed, he might have been promoted for good behavior. There is a valuable lesson here. Even a white male radical economist could repent of his sins, renounce "the god that failed," and "make something of himself" according to the political rules of the game. Bowles refused. In the Bowles affair, meritocratic considerations were of secondary importance for clearly political reasons. However, as we have suggested, he could have played by the unwritten political rules of the game and possibly been rewarded.

Beneath Harvard's cosmopolitan appearance is a "separate and unequal" reality. For whites at Harvard, there are at least some unstated rules which, though in principle unjust, nevertheless operate for those who want in. For blacks there are no such "rules." This reality is complicated by the incoherent and disorganized responses on the part of black staff and students. In other words, blacks have on occasion, inadvertently reinforced their own discrimination by substituting rhetorical postures for real politics. Instead of becoming a political force to reckon with, blacks at Harvard can sometimes be characterized as an interest group which exhibits neither the determination nor collective foresight to mobilize itself around its long- or short-term objective interests. Therefore Harvard's strategic responses to questions of racial discrimination in admissions, hiring, and appointments follow a fairly predictable pattern. Historically, it has consisted of a series of appropriately cosmetic gestures which in most contexts in no way reflect reforms. Moreover, these gestures reflect an understandable and occasionally refined indifference to black concerns.

First, however, we shall comment upon the more controversial case of Martin Kilson, Professor of Government.

On December 13, 1979, the *Harvard Crimson* ran a cover story entitled "Dean Reprimands Government Professor." Susan Faludi reported that the preceding day Dean Henry Rosovsky had "officially reprimanded Martin L. Kilson...for making improper advances to a freshman woman [sic] who filed a complaint of sexual harassment against Kilson." Further, the article notes that Rosovsky informed Kilson that "if [Kilson] repeated the action he would consider placing the matter before the [Harvard] Corporation which has the power to revoke tenure." Kilson admitted that he had committed an act of impropriety, though he claimed he had not intended to offend the student, suggesting further that his "generally affectionate air could be misinterpreted."

A follow-up article appeared on the third page of the same edition of the *Crimson*. In a more general discussion of the subject of sexual harassment, Faludi suggested that the matter of sexual harassment involved more than a few "isolated case(s)." She implied, in fact, that as a general phenomenon it represented a "pervasive pattern" among Harvard's overall faculty. There is little reason to question the general accuracy of this claim. However, the *Crimson* articles curiously omitted another dimension of the Kilson story. Professor Kilson is black and the female student is white.

The consensus among a broad cross-section of the administrative and support staff was striking: they collectively suspected that there was more going on in the Kilson case. Their suspicions were correct—especially since, as one black junior faculty member pointed out, and as the Faludi articles had suggested, there had been a "pervasive pattern" of sexual harassment involving presumably white male faculty and yet none of those cases had been accompanied by the kind of media fanfare to which Kilson's was subjected. This incident raised obvious questions which the *Crimson* neglected to ask. Why was Kilson, a black man, the first to receive a "tar and feathering?" Why, if there had been up to this point a "pervasive pattern" of sexual harassment, did the University administration fail to lavish such attention on the other previous cases which involved white men?

(These questions about the treatment of Kilson's case are not intended to obscure the very real problem of sexual harassment at Harvard. But an examination of Kilson's case also illuminates Harvard's seeming double standards.)

From what is generally known (but of course not publicly acknowledged), it seems that Harvard sought to sanction Kilson more for his political and attitudinal transgressions than for sexual harassment. Kilson, from the moment he was granted tenure at Harvard in 1969, had been at the center of innumerable controversies ranging from administrative conflicts around the organizational form and ideological function of "black studies," to moral and strategic differences with the Bok administration concerning the best response to various black student demands upon the University. That Kilson also on occasion publicly stated that Palestinians were human beings deserving of certain human rights further exacerbated the conflict between himself and powerful elements within the University faculty and administration. Kilson's penchant for disturbing the authoritarian equilibrium of John Harvard's plantation exhausted the limits of Harvard's occasional policy of "repressive tolerance." His indiscretion with a white female student provided certain elements within the University with a convenient pretext for settling some old scores and "neutralizing" a black thorn in their flesh.

Even in the case of Kilson, however, Harvard exhibited a measure of fairness. He paid the price for his imprudent commitment to critical intellectual discourse on matters of vital concern to his community. Kilson's case is important because of the considerable misunderstandings surrounding views which have been mistakenly attributed to him. At one level, Kilson's intellectual life embodies both the hopes and contradictions of the liberal pluralist model of race relations of which he has been arguably the most sophisticated proponent. His commitment to what Cornel West calls Parsonsian elitism in his social theory placed him at odds with representatives of black nationalism and the black Left (See John Trumpbour's essay on the National Security State for a critical appraisal of Parsons' thought). Additionally, Kilson's experiences at Harvard reveal a subtle irony which black students rarely comprehend: first, the unpopular positions adopted by Kilson and others reflect the precarious nature of their positions at Harvard; and second, they are playing for advancement at Harvard by *the stated rules of the game. Therefore, they are likely to fail.* As we shall suggest later, their dilemma is insoluble in the absence of a coherent, militant reform movement among black students and their allies.

Whereas the white majority at Harvard is comfortable with the notion that Kilson "earned" his isolation and marginalization, the cases of Archie C. Epps and David Evans are tragic and unnecessary cases of racial discrimination. To begin with Epps, his career commences after graduation from the Harvard Divinity School and develops with his gradual symbolic (as opposed to substantive) incorporation into the administrative apparatus of the University. Epps's career at Harvard has been characterized by an extraordinary level of commitment and devotion which has involved on occasions considerable personal sacrifice and pain. These sacrifices have been made for an institution which has, as our interpretation suggests, exploited Epps' loyalty by using him to run interference for unpopular administrative policies. He has been saddled with the thankless task of absorbing the flak for the white overseers of Massachusetts

Hall who have never accorded Epps the respect that his determined dedication would receive in a just world. No image more vividly portrays this than the April 18, 1969 *Time* magazine photograph illustrating the Harvard strike in which Dean Epps is escorted out of the University Hall by white SDS students during a building take-over. Epps' image in the photograph functions as a visually powerful political metaphor.

The Bok regime continuously relied on Epps to carry out the most indefensible of its policies. In some measure, Epps had embraced and publicly defended Harvard's racist modus operandi. In doing so, he would lose more and more respect from students and faculty. Playing by the rules, Epps surely alienated the progressive constituency. Yet Epps apparently never understood that his very existence at Harvard depended on the unrest he had denounced. Had there been no student-led protests, Harvard would have felt no political obligation to hire blacks in the first place.

Politically isolated and unable to muster public support from even those students and faculty who were ordinarily regarded as sympathetic to affirmative action, Epps would pay the price of his actions. In the summer of 1985, Harvard rewarded Epps for his two decades of service in a manner which can only give the concept of perfidy an entirely fresh meaning.

During the last week of July 1985, A. Michael Spence, Dean of the Faculty of Arts and Sciences, announced that he would recommend to the Harvard Corporation the appointment of L. Fred Jewett '57 as the Dean of Harvard College. Jewett was then Dean of Admissions and Financial Aid for Harvard and Radcliffe Colleges, and had served in that position for thirteen years.

As Dean of Harvard College, Jewett would be the chief administrative officer for non-academic programs and activities for some 6,500 undergraduates. In his capacity as dean, he would supervise numerous administrative agencies and units providing services for students and he would chair the powerful Administrative Board of Harvard and Radcliffe Colleges, as well as the Committee on College Life and the Committee on Housing. Jewett would succeed John B. Fox, Jr. who was stepping down as Dean of Harvard College after nine years of service to become Administrative Dean of Harvard's Graduate School of Arts and Sciences.

As qualifications for administrative posts go, there is little reason to question Jewett's suitability for the position. What is relevant is that when Harvard had an opportunity to hire a qualified black person—and Epps was an obvious candidate—who could, unlike Jewett, send a powerful national message to blacks and other people of color that a career in higher education was a viable option, they rejected the opportunity. Harvard had at least two reasons. First, Epps is a black man. The example of a black person in a powerful position is still undesirable to Harvard. Harvard currently sees no need to incorporate blacks into the administrative apparatus because, for much of the 1980s, black students have been politically dormant. Harvard, however, was not content to simply discriminate against Epps. On Friday, July 26, 1985, the *Crimson* reported the news of Spence's decision, which required Harvard Corporation approval. The article also suggested that Epps, like Jewett, had been a strong contender for the position. There is little reason to believe that Epps was being considered at all, despite the ironic announcement reported on the same page pointing out Harvard's "university-wide legislation prohibiting discrimination...against other members of the...community except on the basis of individual ability to contribute to institutional objectives." According to sources within the administration (who agreed to comment on the condition that they not be identified), Epps never had a chance to compete for the job and was simply misled by his superiors. The matter was rather simple; had Epps been white (whether male or female) he would have been seriously considered. Instead, Harvard used Epps to veil its racist hiring policy. In a *Crimson* article published a few days later Spence discussed the difficulty of the decision-making process and cited the tight competition for the Dean's position. He insinuated that Epps was a "for real" contender, who, we are to believe, was barely beaten out by the stronger candidate Jewett. Epps's presence as a candidate was symbolic, and useful only for conveying the illusion of an open and fair selection process. As one senior faculty member correctly noted, "The reality was that...(Epps) lacked sufficient political backing, consequently he would not receive the appointment." His "individual ability to...contribute to Harvard's educational objectives and institutional needs" was irrelevant. This is how Harvard in the summer of 1985 rewarded Epps for his twenty-one years of service and devotion to its vision of *Veritas.*[4]

Another equally instructive portrayal of Harvard's vision of meritocracy is the related case of Senior Admissions Officer David L. Evans of Harvard-Radcliffe. David L. Evans is one of Harvard's most impressive and under utilized resources. Although his professional training led to a masters degree in electrical engineering from

Princeton, he has functioned during the past two decades as a sea-
soned and unusually perceptive figure in a variety of different contexts as a member of Harvard's administrative apparatus.

From 1970-72, he was Assistant Director of Admissions; he then
assumed the position, from 1972-75, of an Associate Director of
Admissions; and he has been since 1975 a Senior Admissions Officer
at Harvard-Radcliffe College. During this same period, Evans also
served in a variety of overlapping capacities ranging from Freshman
Proctor (1970-77) to residential house tutor (1972-79). Additionally,
he has been the most visible and empathetic administrative presence
for innumerable minority students for sixteen years and is perhaps
most noted for his routine lunchtime visits to the Freshman Union to
provide informal advice and support for those in need. It therefore
came as a surprise, when a white woman with considerably less
experience and administrative expertise was appointed over Evans
to serve as Director of Admissions when L. Fred Jewett left that post
to serve as Dean of the College.

One point should be stressed to avoid confusion. First, women
are not the reason that blacks are discriminated against. Women are,
after all, locked out from most of the University's major command
posts. And yet, white women continue to make much greater gains
than black people of either gender. In part, white women's relatively
greater success in the academy is a function of their superior political
organization as an interest group and their greater numerical presence in society as a whole.

There are other factors of varying importance and complexity
that should be noted. Social psychologist Richard Zweigenhaft conducted a detailed study examining relative success among 40 black,
female, and Jewish Harvard MBAs. His findings, though not in every
detail transferable to the University, are nevertheless important and
relevant to our discussion. For example, he notes all of those interviewed agreed with the comment that in general blacks were lagging
significantly behind women. A few commented that "white women
not only share economic and educational advantages with the white
men...who control...America's corporations...they also share a common culture." One white woman, a 1980 graduate, observed that
white "women were having an 'easier time' than blacks" and explained it in the following way:

> White males at the top have daughters, so they can see a personal
> relationship with young women. Even if their wives didn't work,
> even if they don't have daughters who want to go into business,

they still know young white women personally, and they can respond to their career goals. But a lot of white males don't know any blacks personally, and so they're less comfortable, and less able to respond personally to them.

Evans was, therefore, a victim of white male power. That Evans clearly possessed the superior qualifications necessary to "contribute to Harvard's educational objectives and institutional needs," as the Harvard Corporation's Anti-Discrimination Legislation stated, was of marginal importance. The message? Since Evans was not white, such legislation did not apply.

Further evidence for this conclusion was provided in October 1986 when the same white woman, Laura Gordon Fischer, who had been elevated over Evans to the position of Director of Admissions for Harvard-Radcliffe, received yet another promotion as Director of Admissions for the Harvard Business School's MBA program. As for Evans, he was again not even formally notified of the position's opening! Although some of the details of this case were known by members of various black student associations, alumni and staff, no one stepped forward to draw attention to these incidents. Not even the dashing ideological waterboy for capitalist autarchy Professor Glenn Loury, the black Reaganite of Kennedy School renown, spoke up. It would have been fascinating to hear how Loury would have squared his ejaculations on the virtues of the meritocratic system with the realities of these two of its victims. Or to account for why he conveniently failed to shower the lords of University Hall with the kind of moralism he so prolifically excretes on the pages of *Commentary* regarding Harvard's transgressions.

In a rather intriguing way, the occasionally disgraceful treatment to which these "invisible men" have been subjected by the very institution to which they have been devoted presents an irresistible conclusion. First, their experiences are powerful political arguments against the very visions which they have publicly represented. Second, in the absence of militant and organized demands for black inclusion, Harvard's "objectives and institutional needs" do not require the services of significant numbers of black elites to legitimate its undemocratic vision of empire. Consequently the policy concerns of these fragile elites will be reassigned to the kitchen where they will huddle and quietly await crumbs from the master's table.

Notes

1. For a fuller discussion of the implications and the politics of "meritocracy," see N.J. Block and Gerald Dworkin, eds. *The IQ Controversy* (New York: Pantheon, 1976), pp. 339-383.

2. See Herbert Gintis, "Education, Technology, and the Characteristics of Worker Productivity," *American Economic Review*, May, 1979, and Ivan Berg, *Education and Jobs: The Great Training Robbery* (Boston: Beacon Press, 1971).

3. See S. Bowles and H. Gintis, *Schooling in Capitalist America* (New York: Basic Books, 1976).

4. For the subsequent debate over the Epps affair, see J. Nordhaus, "Article Says University Denied Posts to Blacks," *Harvard Crimson*, April 7, 1987, p. 1. The debate was provoked by an earlier draft of this article.

Sexual Shakedown

Christina Spaulding

The problem of sexual harassment is not necessarily more prevalent at Harvard than at other large universities. Statistics, however, are not the issue. Regardless of the relative severity of the problem at Harvard, the University's response to sexual harassment teaches us a great deal about its institutional character. Specifically, it teaches us about the University's unwillingness to confront discrimination and its lack of commitment to create an authentically open academic community.

Before exploring that response and its implications in more detail, it is necessary to establish a common vocabulary—to define sexual harassment.

Definitions

Sexual harassment is the form of sex discrimination that expresses hostility toward women through sexual behavior. Sexual harassment generally takes two forms. First, it may be environmental, consisting of comments, innuendo, and jokes that, intentionally or not, create an atmosphere that is intimidating, hostile, or offensive to women. The second form is the more classic "quid pro quo" harassment: the abuse of authority to coerce or attempt to coerce sexual relations.

Whichever form the harassment takes, it serves to put a woman who encroaches on male territory in her place by communicating that she is first and foremost a sexual object, and that neither she nor her work will be taken seriously. Sexual harassment poisons the academic environment; it can exclude women almost as effectively as if their presence were explicitly barred.

Institutional Issues

The University's stubborn refusal to take sexual harassment seriously raises important questions regarding the role of academic institutions in society generally, and more narrowly, Harvard's willingness to allow women to participate as equals in the institution.

Largely as a result of ground-breaking litigation in the 1970s and 1980s, many private employers and public universities were forced to address sexual harassment as a serious obstacle to equality of opportunity. Under Title VII of the 1964 Civil Rights Act (which prohibits sex discrimination in employment)[1] and Title IX of the Education Amendments of 1972 (which prohibits sex discrimination in education)[2], sexual harassment has been recognized as a form of sex discrimination.

Because of its tremendous institutional power and prestige, and because it is a private university, Harvard has been somewhat insulated from these pressures for social change. Harvard has benefited from the prohibitive risks of litigation for a female academic employee or graduate student. For those who depend on the esteem of their colleagues for professional advancement, the danger of being branded as a troublemaker is a strong deterrent to bringing a grievance, let alone a lawsuit. Undergraduates are generally unaware of their legal rights and too transient a population to pose a substantial threat to the University. Moreover, the 1984 Supreme Court decision in *Grove City College v. Bell*[3] undermined the force of Title IX's application to private universities. In *Grove City*, the Court held that Title IX applied only to specific programs that received federal aid and not to the entire institution of which the federally funded program was a part. In so holding, the Court ignored evidence that Congress intended Title IX to apply to entire institutions which receive federal funds for any program.[4]

Under *Grove City*, only those Harvard programs that received federal aid were covered by Title IX. The Civil Rights Restoration Act, passed over President Reagan's veto in March of 1988, effectively reversed the Court's holding in *Grove City* and should restore incentives for private universities to comply with Title IX, though the threat of lawsuits still remains slim.

Harvard is potentially more vulnerable to Title VII employment discrimination suits by its nonacademic employees, but the risks of litigation are substantial for these women as well: first, like female faculty, they will have difficulty securing alternative employment if branded troublemakers; second, the financial burdens of suing an institution with Harvard's vast resources may be overwhelming to women of low or moderate income; finally, sexual harassment suits, like rape cases, often put the victim on trial and are emotionally taxing.

Legal duties aside, the question remains whether a university should approach discrimination in its midst as solely an issue of risk management, or whether an academic institution should aspire to a standard of social responsibility higher than the standards upheld by other large corporations. One might hope and even expect that an institution with Harvard's liberal image would assume a leading role in developing progressive policies to insure equal opportunities for all members of its community. History reveals that Harvard has not done so.

Background

Recent incremental improvements in Harvard's approach to sexual harassment were the product of the courage and tenacity of the individual women who have pursued grievances, of embarrassing publicity surrounding specific incidents of harassment, and of intensive lobbying by student groups.[5]

Harvard, like many universities, first adopted a grievance procedure for students' complaints of sexual harassment following a 1978 case against Yale University in which a federal district court found that sexual harassment could be a form of sex discrimination within the meaning of Title IX.[6]

Harvard, however, failed to publish its procedure or any policy statement condemning sexual harassment. Students and faculty thus remained largely unaware of this legal development. The University's essentially "secret" procedure was clearly a formal nod to the narrow requirements of the law rather than a sincere effort to understand and confront discrimination in the University community.

The policy statement eventually published in the Student Handbook described sexual harassment only as "inappropriate personal attention" and "unprofessional conduct." It failed to identify it as illegal sex discrimination. Moreover, this "definition" was significantly narrower than that provided by the guidelines of the Equal Employment Opportunity Commission (EEOC)[7] which had been widely followed by the courts and adapted to the academic setting by other universities.

The grievance procedure, which remained unpublished, was arbitrary and unaccountable. It gave the dean of the faculty virtually complete discretion in the resolution of formal complaints. The flaws of this procedure became apparent as specific cases of sexual harassment received public scrutiny.

The publicized cases of sexual harassment provide the most information regarding the University's handling of sexual harassment complaints. However, because a grossly disproportionate number of the professors who were identified publicly in sexual harassment cases were men of color, focusing on these cases raises some sensitive issues of gender and race.

I would therefore like to emphasize that a 1983 survey of sexual harassment at Harvard, discussed more fully below, found that sexual harassment was widespread across the University and that given the minuscule number of persons of color on the Harvard faculty, it is clear that the vast majority of sexual harassers are white men. The survey also indicated that very few of the women who experienced sexual harassment filed formal complaints with the University. Thus, a significant number of white faculty members whose conduct has been as or more egregious than the conduct involved in the publicized cases, have escaped any formal charges of sexual harassment or public scrutiny of their behavior.

In the 1979-80 academic year, Harvard was first shaken by publicity of Government Professor Martin Kilson's sexual harassment of a freshwoman. In 1982, another case involving harassment of a freshwoman, this time by visiting poet Derek Wolcott, received national publicity.[8] The Wolcott case in particular focused public attention on the University's response to sexual harassment complaints. In his classes, Wolcott had often discussed sexuality as it related to poetry. He subsequently used these classroom discussions as a cover to make advances to a student. Although it was clear that Wolcott had abused his position to manipulate the student into a highly personal conversation (and to proposition her), Dean of the Faculty Henry Rosovsky wrote a letter to the young woman, later published in the *Crimson,* in which he implied that the woman had brought the harassment on herself by discussing sexual matters with Wolcott.[9]

During the same period, Assistant Dean of the College Marlyn Lewis explained that the University's secrecy about the case was designed to give the harasser "time to recover."

Harvard consistently approached sexual harassment as an individual, personal problem of the victim, rather than as a widespread social practice which systematically discriminates against women.

Moreover, administrators' comments demonstrated a very poor understanding of the issue and an obsessive concern that many women "provoke" sexual harassment or make frivolous charges.

During the 1982-83 academic year, following the Kilson and Wolcott cases, the Faculty Council decided to review the University's sexual harassment policies. The Radcliffe Union of Students had lobbied for changes, provided the administration with detailed critiques of the University's policy and procedure and suggested improvements drawn from those of other universities, including Yale, MIT, and the University of Michigan. After a year's discussion, the Faculty Council decided to make no changes in the University's policy, although Dean Rosovsky did release an open letter to the community discussing sexism and sexual harassment. Rosovsky's April 1983 letter restated the University's policy and outlined, for the first time in published form, the procedure for bringing a sexual harassment complaint.

During that same year, Harvard finally agreed to sponsor the study of sexual harassment in the Faculty of Arts and Sciences. The administration expected the study to prove that the extent of sexual harassment at Harvard had been greatly exaggerated. Instead, the survey revealed that sexual harassment in a variety of forms was widespread, that it often had devastating personal and academic consequences for women, and that most cases were not reported to University officials.

The results of the survey were released in October of 1983.[10] At the same time, yet another case of sexual harassment at Harvard was receiving national attention. It was revealed in late September that Government Professor Jorge Dominguez had sexually harassed a junior faculty member and a graduate student in the department. The combination of this particularly egregious case and the results of the survey confronted Harvard with concrete evidence of widespread and serious harassment that it could no longer ignore.

The Survey

The sexual harassment survey was distributed to 2,000 undergraduates (1,000 men and 1,000 women), 1,000 graduate students (500 men and 500 women), and to the entire Faculty of Arts and Sciences in the spring of 1983. The response rate among all groups, male and female, was over 70%.

Because the definition of sexual harassment turns largely on coerciveness, rather than on an "objective" set of behaviors, the study did not set forth a particular definition of sexual harassment. Instead, it provided respondents with a long list of behaviors covering a spectrum of unwanted sexual attention and asked whether and how often the respondents had experienced each of them.[11] The behaviors listed were both verbal—sexual comments and requests for dates—and physical—unwanted touching, actual or attempted rape, or sexual assault. The survey also asked a series of questions regarding the context in which the incident occurred and what the victim had done about it.

From this information, cases were categorized according to their severity. The most serious cases involved repeated harassment (or sometimes a single, very egregious incident), often repeated over the victim's objections, with implicit or explicit threats of reprisal if the victim resisted the attention, and having significant effects on the victim's personal, professional, or academic life. Within this category "very serious" cases were the most coercive and most damaging to the victim. The serious cases included both *quid pro quo* and pervasive, environmental harassment.

From an undergraduate:

When I had trouble with a TA, I felt uncomfortable for weeks before I labeled it sexual harassment, I didn't go to officials because all he did was call me four times in a weekend, visit me,

TABLE I				
	Tenured Faculty	Nontenured Faculty	Graduate Students	Under-graduates
Women experiencing serious or very serious incidents of harassment:	*	8%	13%	13%
upsetting or slightly upsetting incidents of harassment	*	24%	30%	13%
*Because there are so few tenured women faculty, these figures were statistically insignificant.				

TABLE II

Increasing Likelihood of Sexual Harassment*

	freshwomen	sophomores	juniors	seniors
serious or very serious incidents of harassment	4%	13%	16%	20%

*Data available only for undergraduates

ask me to meet him at 9:30 p.m. to discuss a paper. When I got a D- on the second paper (I got an A on the first), he...explained that if I was willing to work 'hard, long, late hours' with him I could still get an A...

The woman eventually withdrew from the course.

While none of the respondents gave specific examples, a number of women junior faculty reported that their colleagues engaged in teasing, innuendo, and joking that was denigrating to women and sometimes directed at them personally. These women reported feeling uncomfortable around their male colleagues and avoiding contact with them—sometimes changing their own research and avoiding active participation in departmental meetings.

Several striking themes emerged from the survey data. First, sexual harassment was, not surprisingly, experienced far more often by women than by men. Second, men and women perceived the issue very differently. Men tended to view harassment as an issue of sexuality whereas women saw it as an issue of power. For example, in response to a section on attitudes about sexual harassment, 47 percent of women compared to 30 percent of men strongly agreed with the statement that "subordinates often put up with unwanted sexual attention for fear of reprisal." And 60 percent of women compared to 25 percent of men strongly disagreed with the statement that "sexual harassment is often an overreaction to normal expressions of sexual interest." Because they saw it as an issue of sexuality, men were more likely to believe that sexual harassment was an essentially individual, personal problem that had been exaggerated and that the University should assume a limited role in regulating such behavior.

From a tenured male faculty member: "All but acts of attempted assault or persistent and repeated pressure for sexual favors despite clear rejection should not concern the university. Mature people should know how to deal with them, and if they don't, it is not the university's business to try to regulate such situations."

Another tenured male faculty member: "Generally the university should treat people like adults by allowing them to solve their own problems whenever possible. Only in cases of outright sexual blackmail should the university step in. Otherwise the whole thing could be magnified way out of proportion."

The peculiar gender dynamics of sexual harassment were also highlighted by women's descriptions of their experiences. To a significant degree, sexual harassment arises from a teacher's inability to perceive his female students as students. In some cases, the problem was essentially willful and indicated a refusal to accept women in the academy. Other cases were less malicious, but nevertheless reflected a professor's inability to perceive his female students as students rather than as potential sexual partners. The harassment was no less harmful because less intentional. Regardless of motive, the sexualization of the student-teacher relationship is a violation of trust and can be extremely damaging to a woman's academic self-confidence. Many women begin college with a lower level of self-confidence than their male counterparts. A teacher's academic interest may therefore be especially important to a female student's academic development. Expressions of sexual interest undermine that crucial relationship and lead the student to doubt the sincerity of the teacher's academic interest.

A typical response from a female graduate student to a man's sexual advances:

> A senior faculty member on my thesis committee would without exception make subtle remarks of a sexual nature when I met with him. Then one day he made a convoluted joke; the subject was a student having an affair with her professor. He then went into a diatribe on the nature of sexual affairs. I felt it was a very inappropriate conversation for the setting...

The woman reported difficulty in working with the professor and a loss of confidence in her academic abilities and professional worth. She felt that she had to be very reserved in her interactions with the professor and met with him less frequently than she should have.

Third, as is typical in sexual harassment cases, women most commonly responded by avoiding any further contact with the harasser. In an academic community, the consequences of such a "solution" may be serious, sometimes depriving a student of access to entire areas of academic expertise, or forcing her to forego needed assistance with coursework.

From another graduate student:

> The incidents are hard to convey because on paper they seem relatively innocuous; it was mostly commentary on the way I dressed, what I was wearing at different times. But there was a hostility in it and these things were said at inappropriate times in conversation, i.e. as interruptions in an academic remark I was making over something, etc.

Although this woman did not even identify her experience as sexual harassment, she resolved the situation by ceasing to work with the professor.

Finally, it was disturbing to observe the frequency with which individuals in positions of trust, especially proctors, tutors, and teaching fellows, exploited students' vulnerability to exert sexual pressure on women much younger than they. Proctors abused their advisory role to make advances on students who had confided in them about personal problems, and teaching fellows took advantage of students who required extra help with their coursework.

From an undergraduate, harassed by her first year proctor:

> I had grown close to my advisor as I confided in him about my emotions about a death in my family. We became good friends as well, although he appeared interested in more than friendship. I realized this because of questions (sexual nature) he began to ask and affectionate gestures. I began to avoid him, which he noticed, and when he asked me why I was avoiding him, we discussed the situation in somewhat indirect terms. The problem however got worse as I felt more pressure to feel differently about him—not just as an advisor and friend. When I was saying goodbye to leave Cambridge for the summer, he cornered me, kissed me and said 'I think I deserved that' ... [the] pressure for a sexual relationship ... destroyed an important avenue of help, advice and guidance which I relied on.

Another typical response from an undergraduate: "This experience occurred with a TF in a course in which I was really struggling. I needed a lot of extra help and was made so uncomfortable by this TF that I had to impose on other TFs in order to (at least) pass—eventually I just gave up bothering other instructors and skidded through the term."

The survey data, and particularly the experiences of women, recounted in their own words, reveal a dramatic difference in the educational and work experience of men and women at Harvard.

Sexual harassment and the fear of harassment shape women's every-
day lives in a manner that men do not have to confront.

Harvard's Response

When the results of the survey were released, Harvard could
have chosen to acknowledge the significance of the survey's findings
and make a good faith effort to address the problems it revealed,
reexamining its written policy and procedure, and taking affirmative
steps to prevent sexual harassment through educational efforts directed at the entire community. Instead, Harvard chose to downplay
the significance of the survey and attempted to minimize its effect on
University policy. First, Harvard sought to manipulate press coverage of the survey—it issued a press release that trivialized and
distorted the data—and second, it relegated students and concerned
faculty members to a minimal role in subsequent discussions of
policy.

After another year of debate and intensive lobbying, Harvard
finally changed its policy and procedure, but earlier promises that
such changes would be developed by a committee including students
and junior faculty were set aside in favor of a largely closed process
that allowed only limited input by those outside the Faculty Council
or administration. Unfortunately, while the end product did embody
substantial improvements, the University's commitment to addressing the problem remained suspect. At the end of the year, the University had still made no specific promises to improve educational
efforts, though it has done so since with the help of Response, a
student-run peer counseling group focusing on sexual coercion.

In the fall of 1984, Harvard, for the first time, forced a tenured
faculty member (Government Professor Douglas Hibbs) to resign
because of his harassment of a Harvard junior faculty member and a
graduate student from another university.[12] The significance of this
step is diminished because it would have been politically difficult not
to fire Hibbs, both because Harvard's lenient treatment of earlier
offenders had been so widely criticized, and because another institution was involved. Professor Dominguez, whose conduct had probably been equally egregious, remained on the faculty. In both cases,
the junior faculty member who had lodged a complaint was forced
to leave Harvard.

Lessons

The single most important factor in achieving this progress was the courage of women who had been victims of sexual harassment. Only they had the makings of legal claims that posed a threat to the University. These women came forward, despite a hostile environment and at great risk to their careers, in an effort to ensure that other women would not need to endure similar experiences.

Although students were not given a role in policymaking, student activism did have some impact. The Radcliffe Union of Students tried to maximize its credibility by presenting the administration with detailed reports and specific proposals for change. The strategy was moderately successful in that some of those recommendations were considered seriously, and a few were eventually adopted.

There were other positive aspects of the effort to effect change at Harvard. The sexual harassment issue drew disparate elements of the women's community together in numbers and in strength that it had not known for several years. Other progressive political groups on campus were supportive and valuable alliances were forged that extended to other issues. The extensive coverage of sexual harassment by the press also provoked thought and discussion in the community.

Some of the lessons, however, were painful. The University's response to the problem was profoundly disillusioning to those of us who had been naive enough to believe that Harvard would respond reasonably once confronted with clear evidence of the problem—particularly when that evidence consisted of such painful and detailed documentation of abusive behavior. Instead, we learned that a large institution that feels itself under seige will go to great lengths to preserve its power at the expense of the most vulnerable members of the community.

The survey itself revealed that a faculty I had once revered for its intellectual sophistication harbored remarkably crude forms of sexism—forms which were not even disguised by an intellectual veneer. The comments that male faculty volunteered in their survey responses disclosed a nearly complete lack of understanding or concern about sexual harassment and its effect on women's lives. The survey was characterized as a waste of time and money and the entire issue was dismissed as the product of "feminist hysteria."

The survey also disabused me of any classist assumptions that sexual harassment achieves its most inelegant expression in the catcalls of construction workers on the street. Instead, the behavior of many men on the Harvard faculty toward female colleagues or students is indistinguishable from that experienced by women who have attempted to break into other male-dominated fields. Sexual harassment is remarkably similar, whether the unwelcome woman is a welder who finds pornographic photos and slogans on her locker, or a faculty member or student who is subjected to continual, degrading sexual comments by male colleagues or teachers.

Although President Bok regularly urges students to aspire to high ethical standards and to a greater sense of social responsibility in their lives, these exhortations are not directed toward Harvard itself. Whether the issue is divestiture or the University's reluctance to confront its own discrimination, the example that Harvard sets for its students is that business is business. Cost-benefit analysis is substituted for ethics.

Despite the much vaunted diversity of its student body, Harvard has failed to become an institution at which a diverse population, sharing a love of academic pursuits, can work together. Instead, Harvard stands exposed in its hypocrisy. Within the nation's (arguably) most prestigious institution of higher learning, women and minorities continue to be marginalized, not by explicit decree, but by a pervasive and thinly veiled hostility.

The final lesson, of course, is not to give up. Because Harvard is *Harvard*, we can't allow it to effectively close its doors to women and minorities. Its tremendous resources and prestige must be shared, even if each step forward requires a bitter fight.

Recommended Reading:

Dziech, Billie Wright and Weiner, Elizabeth, *The Lecherous Professor: Sexual Harassment on Campus* (Boston: Beacon Press, 1984).

Farley, Lin, Sexual Shakedown: The Sexual Harassment of Women on the Job (New York: Warner Books, 1978).

MacKinnon, Catharine, Sexual Harassment of Working Women (New Haven: Yale University Press, 1979).

Alliance Against Sexual Coercion, "Organizing Against Sexual Harassment," Radical America 15 (July-August 1981), pp. 17-34.

Gordon, Linda, "The Politics of Sexual Harassment," Radical America 15 (July-August 1981), pp. 7-14.

Notes

1. 42 U.S.C. section 2000e-2 (1981).

2. 20 U.S.C. section 1681(a) (1978).

3. 465 U.S. 555 (1984).

4. *Id.* at 585 (Brennan, J., dissenting).

5. On paper, the procedures that apply to Harvard's support staff appear to be better than those that apply to students or academic employees. However, my experience in working with a staff member who attempted to bring a grievance indicates that the procedures provide little or no protection in practice. Harvard's employees stand to gain a great deal more protection with the union. They voted to join in 1988.

6. *Alexander v. Yale University,* 459 F. Supp. 1, 4 (D. Conn. 1977) (only one plaintiff was found to have standing to bring a private action under Title IX).

7. 29 C.F.R. section 1604.11(a) (1987):

> Harassment on the basis of sex is a violation of section 703 of Title VII. Unwelcome sexual advances, requests for sexual favors, and other verbal or physical conduct of a sexual nature constitute sexual harassment when (1) submission to such conduct is made either explicitly or implicitly a term or condition of an individual's employment, (2) submission to or rejection of such conduct by an individual is used as the basis for employment decisions affecting such individual, or (3) such conduct has the purpose or effect of unreasonably interfering with an individual's work performance or creating an intimidating, hostile, or offensive working environment.

The EEOC guidelines do not have the force of law. However, such administrative guidelines do carry significant weight in court. It is undisputed that *quid pro quo* harassment—where compliance with sexual demands is made a term or condition of employment—is a form of sex discrimination under Title VII. A federal court first held this type of sexual harassment to be a form of sex discrimination in *Barnes v. Costle,* 561 F.2d 983, 990 (D.C. Cir. 1977). The Supreme Court has recently agreed with lower court holdings that hostile environment harassment is also a form of sex discrimination under Title VII. *Meritor Savings Bank v. Vinson,* 106 S.Ct. 2399 (1986). (The Court held that employers were not automatically liable for sexual harassment by their supervisors, but added that the absence of notice to an employer does not preclude liability. *Id.* at 2408. Thus the exact parameters of employer liability are unclear.)

At least one federal district court has indicated that both definitions of sexual harassment, though developed in the context of Title VII litigation, are equally applicable to Title IX. *Moire v. Temple University School of Medicine,* 613 F. Supp. 1360, 1366 n.2 (E.D. Pa. 1985).

8. *New York Times,* October 21, 1982, p. 22; "Co-ed Complaint," *Time,* June 14, 1982, p. 81.

9. *Harvard Crimson,* Commencement Issue, June 1983.

10. *Boston Globe,* Oct. 27, 1983, p. 23; *New York Times,* Oct. 28, 1983, p. A7; *Boston Phoenix,* Dec. 13, 1983, p. 6.

11. The survey's format was adapted from a similar survey of federal employees conducted by the Merit Systems Protection Board. The results of the federal survey are available in *Sexual Harassment in the Federal Workplace: Is it a Problem?* Report of the U.S. Merit Systems Protection Board Office of Merit Systems and Studies (Washington, D.C.: Government Printing Office, 1981).

12. *Harvard Crimson,* Feb. 5, 1985, p. 1; *New York Times,* February 5, 1985, p. B24.

A Note on the Professional Schools

John Trumpbour

A detailed look into the entire alphabet soup of Harvard's professional schools, including HBS (Business), KSG (Government), HLS (Law), HDS (Divinity), GSD (Architecture), HSPH (Public Health), etc., is beyond the scope of this book.

Briefly summarized, however, there are features that link some of these schools. Certainly the Law, Business, and Government schools share a fetish for the case method, a pedagogical and analytic approach that typically treats problems ahistorically and without context, often refracted through a truncated empiricism and traditionalism. Traditionalism rivets the present to the past, empiricism reproduces what is and elides the question of what ought to be.

More insidious is the professional schools' inculcation of hierarchical values and ratification of class privilege. This is often accomplished through rituals and routines that inflict psychic damage on students and, particularly at the Medical School, outright harm on the wider public. Drawing upon personal experience, one physician-author, Robin Cook, explains medical education in America in no uncertain terms. Discussing his own internship, he reports:

> I'm being exploited under the guise of learning [and] the psychological burden is too heavy... Eventually you reach a point where you don't give a damn. Sometimes, after getting called on a cardiac arrest in the middle of the night, I wish the guy would die so I could go back to bed...that's how tired...I get.

A few off-the-record interviews with Harvard medical interns confirm his account, although one Harvard student admitted to *How Harvard Rules* that he usually feels this way about patients who "will be dead in a year or two anyway." Dr. Cook elaborates on the values internalized from such traumatic forms of education:

> About half the time since third year medical school has been spent in pursuit of the useless and the arbitrary, which are justified by the diaphanous explanation that they are a necessary part of being a medical student or intern and becoming a doctor. Bullshit. This sort of thing is simply a hazing and harassment, a kind of initiation rite into the American Medical Association. The system works, too; God, how it works! Behold the medical

profession, brainwashed, narrowly programmed, right-wing in
its politics, and fully dedicated to the pursuit of money.

I felt I had done my time...Medical practice was at last within
sight. As I walked down the OR corridor, I wondered whether
to buy a Mercedes or a Porsche.

Harvard medical education in particular contributes to the professional mystique of omniscience and omnipotence. One Harvard medical
graduate told Dr. Martin Shapiro, author of *Getting Doctored: Critical Reflections on Becoming a Physician*, that when he admitted to a professor that he did
not know something, the physician-teacher would snap back: "You don't
know. That is *not* a Harvard medical student answer." The medical student
at first learns to feign understanding and later adopts the posture of omniscience that succeeds in intimidating all but the most rebellious among
non-physicians. The patient suffers dearly from this set of power relations.
For example, the U.S., with a higher per capita supply of surgeons, has over
a third more surgeries performed in many fields than, for instance, Britain,
with little evidence of higher quality of health and reduced mortality. Some
studies show evidence that as many as 40 percent of hysterectomies in the
U.S. may be unnecessary, if true mutilation on a mass scale; but few women
have the wherewithal to challenge such diagnoses, this self-assured techno-
barbarism christened modern medicine.

Nevertheless, the Harvard Medical School since 1985 has taken strides
towards reforming its curriculum, which now relies less on unyielding rote
memorization and more on developing skills in mastering the explosive
growth of medical knowledge in the computer era. In terms of pedagogy, it
tries to foster greater cooperation among students in solving medical crises.
While there are still fundamental limits to this curriculum's ability to challenge the dominant ethos and practice of the medical profession, it probably
represents a step forward. Still there exists a minority of conservative students who, partly because their own academic careers and very admission
into medical school was predicated on their mastery of high grades under
hierarchial regimes of pedagogy, complain that they would prefer a return
to stern, authoritarian lectures and rote memorization. (See *Harvard Crimson*,
28 November, 1988.)

Shapiro argues that it is probably unfair to single out medical students
as victims of hierarchical values and grinding conservatism. (He is no doubt
right.) In the following essay, Jamin Raskin explores the production of
consciousness at the Harvard Law School, an institution heretofore shrouded
in mystiques and intrigues of its own. Raskin, with characteristic wit and
wisdom, provides a model for students seeking to produce a critical analysis
of their own professional schools, providing an inside look at the battle over
critical legal studies and a rare view of Bok's unchecked power.

Laying Down the Law
The Empire Strikes Back

Jamin B. Raskin

In 1986 and 1987, the Harvard Law School faculty, held hostage by its rightwing (which was backed up by President Derek Bok), conducted a purge of junior professors associated with the left-wing Critical Legal Studies (CLS). Brilliant scholars but political innocents, four assistant professors were blindsided and forced out of their jobs in a very public display of intolerance.

The site of the most recent, troubled experiment with political pluralism at Harvard, the Law School had become famous during the early 1980s as the home of CLS, a post-modern radical tendency among law professors that challenged the theory and practice of conservative legalism. With powerful alumni in the big law firms hemorrhaging over this enemy within, it was only a matter of time before the empire struck back. Keeping faith with the most intolerant and reactionary elements in the faculty and alumni community, President Bok participated at pivotal moments in the ideological house-cleaning and then reclaimed the whole neighborhood by appointing Professor Robert Clark, the leader of the Law School's rampaging conservative faction, the new Dean in February of 1988. It was vintage Harvard: a series of scandalous offenses against academic pluralism administered by way of bureaucratic inside moves, topped off with a right-wing coup.

The conservatives on the Law School faculty had spent much of the 1980s seething, plotting their revenge. While official Harvard marched right, defending investments in apartheid as good for black South African workers while pulling out the stops to defeat the union drive at Harvard, the younger generation of law professors was not getting the point. Indeed they were going their own way, reviving Legal Realism, mixing it with some healthy radical democratic theory and some high-minded French deconstructionism. While Professor Charles Fried was in Washington fighting to overturn *Roe v. Wade* as Reagan's Solicitor General, the CLS scholars and their liberal allies were placing feminist concerns at the very forefront of the Law

School's agenda. And while the John M. Olin Foundation was making its first shy overtures to the Law School, donating a respectful $900,000 for a Law-and-Economics Program, the radicals of CLS were debunking the silly claims of Law-and-Economics, which teaches that legal judgments should go to the party who would pay the most for the right to win. (On this theory, of course, the easiest way to find out who has a superior legal right is to allow the parties to bribe the judge and see who pays more.) When everyone else was getting in line, Critical Legal Studies kept interfering with the emerging jurisprudence of Attorney General Ed Meese and the Olin Corporation.

The irrepressible Duncan Kennedy, the outlaw from the law-left, even went so far as to engage in a little praxis, lending his support to the clerical and technical workers' organizing drive and the student-led divestment movement. In 1984, he denounced the invasion of Grenada from the steps of Memorial Church, declaring, "It's illegal, it's immoral, it's stupid," as the Conservative Club jeered him from the steps of Widener Library. Meanwhile, the liberals on the Law School faculty held the line on civil rights and civil liberties, defending the basic principles of justice that 1985 Kennedy School honoree Ed Meese was selling off like so many pieces of Wedtech stock. Many liberals also signed a petition condemning the invasion of Grenada and periodically expressed opposition to Reagan's Central America policy. And both liberal and radical professors supported periodic outbursts of student activism challenging the corporate orientation of the placement office and the extraordinary white male predominance on the faculty. (The activism around these issues apparently produced results in 1989 when the number of minority professors doubled from two to four out of 61 tenured professors, catapulting the Law School into the vanguard of Harvard's lackadaisical affirmative action efforts.)

All of these measured acts of resistance could have been tolerated, but CLS professors also committed the ultimate heresy: they changed the content of their teachings and the dynamics of their classrooms. They began to teach law not dogmatically as a body of scientific knowledge to be drilled into the minds of mushy-headed students, but as a series of socially contingent decisions about the uses of state power. Instead of being coerced through the Socratic method into accepting the right answer as defined by the case decision, students would be invited into a discourse on the meaning of the law and the social vision that informs it.

These changes, generally welcomed by students chafing under the ordinary drudgery of law school, were profoundly threatening to those professors who identified with crotchety Professor Kingsfield, hero of *The Paper Chase*. Many older professors built their academic reputations not on fancy reinterpretations of legal discourse or structural historical analysis, but on a straightforward mastery of the terms and mechanics of particular fields, like civil procedure or taxation. Now they were implicitly being accused of teaching the legal equivalent of auto mechanics. Their world view was being undermined. So the "traditionalists" (conservative reaction being the tradition at Harvard) fought back, enlisting the help of Massachusetts Hall, which was only too eager to put the upstart CLS back in its place. Radical ideas in doses larger than an intellectual vaccine, after all, threaten a university which has been otherwise successful at purging any influences of the civilizing movements of the 1960s and 1970s. As Professor Derrick Bell points out, establishment institutions are willing to accept minorities and dissenting voices only so long as they remain minorities and dissenting voices,[1] and CLS clearly had captured the momentum in legal scholarship and was poised to transform legal pedagogy.

Official Harvard, moreover, reacted because it has an investment to protect in the Law School that is far more important than academic freedom. Since 1817, the Law School has been the major ideological transmission belt for conservative legalism in America. It now services the giant law firms that in turn service America's giant corporations, including Harvard itself; in the space of three years, by way of the Socratic method in the day and the Platonic relationship at night, the carrot of large salaries and the stick of debt, the Law School takes huge numbers of the entering classes of more than 500 students and turns them into corporate lawyers ready to produce hundreds of thousands of billable hours.

Acting to protect this crucial and profitable function, the guardians of the corporate state on the Law School faculty and in the University pounced on CLS like tag-team sumo wrestlers. First, pressure was brought on Dean Vorenberg to quietly persuade CLS professors to end their outspoken challenges to the curriculum, the corporate orientation of the placement office, and the lopsided majority of white male professors. When these efforts failed, a massive anti-CLS publicity campaign began in order to stir up the older, moneyed alumni. In 1985, the conservative Harvard Journal of Law and Public Policy sponsored a talk by Boalt Hall law professor Philip

Johnston called, "Do Critical Legal Scholars Belong On Law Faculties?" Finally, in 1986 and 1987, the conservatives brought down no fewer than four tenure nominations associated (voluntarily or not) with CLS. Because tenure requires a two-thirds vote of the faculty, the determined rightwing of perhaps a dozen professors found that it need only sway a handful of colleagues to torpedo a tenure candidate; where that strategy failed, the conservatives appealed to President Bok to exercise his effective veto power over tenure decisions.

The first professor to fall, by a narrow vote, was Daniel Tarullo, who in 1986 became the first junior professor to be denied tenure at the Law School in 17 years. An excellent teacher and recognized authority on international trade and corporations, Tarullo was attacked for his academic work. The same strategy was then used against Zipporah Wiseman, a professor of commercial law famous for her teaching. The sleazy campaigns waged against Tarullo, a Cambridge native whose childhood suspicions of Harvard's class snobbery were only reinforced by his treatment at the hands of his intellectual inferiors, and Wiseman, a professor at Northeastern Law who had been lured away by a virtual promise of tenure from Dean Vorenberg, were rationalized as necessary to uphold "standards." While these standards were presumably based on academic performance, given the horrendous or non-existent intellectual achievements of most of Tarullo and Wiseman's detractors, it is plain that the real standards upheld were ideological. In any case, the real point for the Right was tactical: to flex its muscle for the coming tenure battles, to keep the tenured electorate from adding any more liberal professors who could tip the balance the wrong way, and to generate so much rancor that President Bok would have a pretext for intervention.

It was a shrewd strategy that paid off handsomely in the spring of 1987 when contracts and legal history professor Clare Dalton was defeated by a handful of votes. The Law School faculty voted in her favor, 29-20, but that margin left her four votes shy of the required two-thirds majority. Her defeat followed an unprecedented line-by-line, footnote-by-footnote dissection of her work and an academic smear campaign that resembled a drive-by gang shoot-out. Dalton's work had been given the highest possible ratings by 12 members of the 13-person outside committee the University had paid to examine it. Professor Morton Horwitz quoted Dean Vorenberg as saying that Dalton had received the "strongest" recommendations he had ever seen from an outside scholarly review committee. "The fact that the evaluation of her work by the most distinguished readers in and outside of Harvard Law School was so positive makes it difficult to say that she has not met the most exacting standards for tenure of Harvard Law School or of any law school in the country," thundered Professor Tribe, who had never before criticized a tenure decision to the press. "If a young, relatively conservative male unconnected with Critical Legal Studies had written the same book, I am morally confident that person would have been given tenure."[2] According to Professor David Kennedy, "Every one of the males promoted last year knows that our scholarship could not possibly have withstood the scrutiny that was applied to [Dalton's]."[3]

Yet, when it came time to vote, the guardians of all that is worst in Western civilization became instant experts in Professor Dalton's field of British legal history and declared her work unfit for Harvard. "A relentless attack was launched on her scholarship, that included claims made about historical texts that were utterly tangential and wildly false, with seeming earnestness and in minute detail," Professor Lewis Sargentich told the *Crimson*.[4] Indeed, these were heady days for the misanthropes and neurotics of the Right. Professor David Rosenberg, forever compensating before the big boys for not having gone to Harvard Law School, flexed his intellectual biceps by penning an 80-page memo savaging Dalton's writings. Professor Arthur Miller, who corrected a student in my first year Civil Procedure class with this intervention, "don't say 'new wife,' say 'second' wife; we don't know how new she was," also weighed in on the side of Dalton's all-male, all-white opposition. And Professor Robert Clark assumed a leading role in the sinking of Dalton, opining later to the *Boston Globe* that Dalton's "scholarship does not meet the standards that we ought to have," and that her 1985 Yale Law Journal article on contracts was a "very bad piece of work, full of jargon. It didn't make any original points."[5] Professor Clark would later attack Professor Derrick Bell's three-day sit-in at his office over these tenure lock-outs, lecturing his senior colleague that Bell "would have served his school better if instead of doing this symbolic protest after the event, he had spent time reviewing the scholarship" of the rejected candidates. He added for good measure that "this is a university—it's not a lunch counter in the deep South," where Professor Clark doubtless spent much of his youth working in the civil rights movement.[6]

The next target felled, in the spring of 1987, was CLS-connected Professor David Trubek, a visiting professor who was voted tenure by the full faculty only to have the decision overruled by President

Bok, egged on by the same conservative sycophants who sabotaged Dalton. Sensing that the tactics of gross distortion were dangerous and perhaps ineffective the second time around, the conservatives barely uttered a peep during the faculty vote, choosing the lower road of appealing to Bok behind closed doors to give Trubek the axe—which he promptly did, in an unprecedented interference with the Law School's tenure process. Led again by Robert Clark, the conservatives thus proved themselves willing to sacrifice the long-cherished institutional independence of the Law School to preserve its unquestioning service to the powerful. As Clark told the Harvard *Crimson*, "Every institution needs to have some controls..."[7]

Evidently disgusted with the gathering witch-hunt at Harvard, Professor Trubek took his punishment with pride and went back to Wisconsin. But Professor Dalton, who is married to Harvard political economist Robert Reich and has roots in Cambridge, decided to stay and fight. Twenty-one law professors and Dean Vorenberg urged President Bok to intervene to tenure Dalton in the same way he had intervened to deny tenure to Trubek. The argument relied on a bad precedent, but the logic of Dalton's supporters was inscrutable: if the unexceptional process leading to Trubek's tenure vote was flawed, surely the hysterical proceedings accompanying Dalton's loss also warranted scrutiny. Bok would probably not have looked twice at these entreaties but Dalton also obtained the counsel of Boston lawyer Nancy Gertner, who represented Theda Skocpol in her successful discrimination case against the University, and the threat of a gender and political discrimination suit hung in the air. Bok's hand was forced. He appointed Professor Vagts (who opposed Dalton) and Professor Weiler (who favored Dalton) to interview 15 scholars from other law schools about the fairness of the tenure-process evaluations of Dalton's work. By bagging Trubek, Bok had been too clever by half; now, he had an almost unmanageable situation to contend with. To the liberals, CLS, and most of the student body, the Dalton tenure decision was a test case of Bok's willingness to defend academic freedom by taming the carnivorous forces of the Law School Right. To the Right, the Dalton case would signal whether Bok was a full-fledged participant in the campaign to purge CLS and restore the lost kingdom of Kingsfield. On March 10, 1988, Bok cast his lot with the Right, announcing by press release that he would not ask Harvard's Governing Boards to extend tenure to Dalton.

Less than a year later, Bok would put the icing on the cake by appointing Robert Clark Dean, rewarding him for his reactionary vigor. It was an extraordinary move. Clark, who was for several months himself a member of the Faculty Dean Search Committee, was the professor most likely to exacerbate divisions on the faculty and continue the vendetta against CLS. In a 1985 speech, Clark stated that, "I think that. . .Critical Legal Studies dogmas are deeply pernicious, and have to be combatted in legal education. It is very bad to indoctrinate students with these attitudes."[8]

Said Professor Frank Michelman of the choice: "Clark has been the most intent, adversarial and unyielding in his attachment to right-wing positions. Where do we fit in?" Professor Richard Parker said that, "I was shocked that Bok would have picked a leader of an extreme faction within the faculty. I fear that an ideological test will be imposed on future tenure candidates." But Professor Frug summed it up best: "This was the worst possible choice Bok could have made."[9]

Clark's appointment and the events leading up to it mean that the Law School has become, in Professor Trubek's parting words, the "Beirut of legal education,"[10] a battleground where the strong-arm forces of the Right have preferred purges to pluralism and Derek Bok, once the champion of the Law School's liberals back when he was Dean from 1968 to 1971, now stands behind the conservatives, ready at all times to restore appropriate corporate order. The Right has, for the time being, come out on top, its power based not on law, principle, justice, precedent, or even unvarnished majority rule, but on outside force and bureaucratic intervention.

To understand the origin of the ferocious assault on CLS, a small nationwide movement in legal scholarship that has, at most, eight or nine real loyalists at the Harvard Law School, one must perceive how this tiny beachhead of dissent completely differentiates the Law School from the rest of the University. No Frankfurt School, to be sure, the Law School's intellectual climate is still very different from what you find walking south into the Yard or down to the river. Fifty feet from Austin Hall, for example, stands the beautiful grey Littauer Building, offices of the Economics Department, which long ago purged anyone it could to the left of John Kenneth Galbraith and struck a blow for the free market in the 1980s by abolishing the "radical" sections in the standard Economics 10 course. Also inside Littauer is the Government Department, which manages to combine the profound intellectual project of, say, the *National Review* (Harvard contributors include Harvey Mansfield, James Q. Wilson, Charles Kesler, etc.) with the workplace ethic of *Penthouse* magazine, though perhaps the comparison is unfair to *Penthouse*. Apart from the two serious scholars associated with it, Stanley Hoffmann and Judith Shklar (neither of whom go anywhere near the place), the Government Department is a chance for men (primarily) to champion war and empire (Samuel Huntington), war and patriarchy (Harvey Mansfield), and war and love of war (Eliot Cohen, alas, temporarily lost to the Naval War College), while some of the less sublimated professors spend their time sexually harassing graduate students and young professors (see Christina Spaulding's essay).

If you continue walking towards the Charles, you will find a sprawling shopping center called the John F. Kennedy School of Government which sells Harvard University titles to Texan oil heirs for the low, low price of $500,000 (see the discussion of Joanne Dickinson in John Trumpbour's conclusion) and whole course programs to the Central Intelligence Agency for probably similar bargain-basement prices. Other duties include the promotion of the moralistic pro-family platitudes of neo-conservative Glenn Loury (arrested in December of 1987 for drug possession, not long after his mistress dropped her assault suit against him for battery with a shod foot), and bestowing honors upon devoted public servants like Ed Meese, who celebrated the 200th birthday of the Constitution by using the power of his office to cover up the Iran-Contra scandal.

Compared to the mashed-potato consciousness thus required of professors in the other University departments accidentally bumping into social thought, the Law School permits an amazing range of intellectual inquiry, which is, of course, why everyone is so upset. If Roberto Unger, Clare Dalton and Duncan Kennedy were simply selling legal advice to multinational corporations the way many professors do (it is hard to know precise numbers because the Law School refuses to make these figures public) or making sexual advances on graduate students, there would be no fuss at all: no blocked tenure appointments, no conferences to calm outraged alumni in New York, no extraordinary interventions by the president of the University to sack professors already approved by the faculty.

Compare the treatment of Professor Tarullo with that of Government Professor Jorge Dominguez. Tarullo, a leading international trade scholar and expert in employee-owned enterprise, became the first assistant law professor in seventeen years to be denied tenure. Why? His politics. Dominguez demanded that a female assistant professor of Government have sex with him in return for his looking favorably upon her tenure nomination. Dominguez's punishment?

A six-month sabbatical abroad. Gentlemen professors at Harvard are protected if they indulge themselves in the class vices of avarice and lechery, but thinking outside of received boundaries is treasonous because it interrupts the deep functional processes of the school.

These processes, presumably imperiled by the presence of critical thought on the faculty, were nicely captured in an October 13, 1987 *Boston Globe* article entitled "Autumn Sighting: The Wing-Tipped Harvard Recruiter/For law school's finest, it's options aplenty." [11] The article reported that every October "representatives of more than 700 law firms and corporations on the lookout descend upon this corner of Cambridge to recruit Harvard Law students."

The Law School readies the student body by distributing "a briefing book, 1,000 pages long, with details about each employer. Each student signs up for as many interviews as he or she likes—the average is about 20. The process is controlled by the Law School placement office and is coordinated and computerized so that interviews do not interfere with classes." While the mega-firms plan follow-up interviews with applicants back at the home office, public interest lawyers "throw up their hands at the increasing difficulty of diverting the attention of students from the phenomenally high salaries, the security, and prestige that the private law firms and investment banks offer."

The *Globe* quoted students who were positively flush about the opening of interview season, which will include for most of them about a dozen free "fly-outs" to cities all over America. (A classmate of mine had his picture on the cover of the Harvard Law Record when he qualified as one of the Top Ten Frequent Fliers of America our second year.) "People are coming here to offer us high-paying jobs at great law firms," said Norman Champ (apparently his real name), a second-year student from St. Louis, adding thoughtfully that, "This is like being a kid in a candy shop." He went on to declare exuberant glee at not being a member of the laboring classes: "A hassle would be if we were working a construction site in Boston today."

Other students reported considerable satisfaction with the cocktail parties thrown to kick off the season, such as the one given by the famous New York firm, Sullivan and Cromwell, on the second floor of the Charles Hotel. "This one had the whole array: shrimp, sushi...They had a pasta bar with tortellini, fettucini Alfredo...You just walk in, they put a little name tag on you," noted Anthony Scaramucci, a second-year student from Port Washington, New York. The law firms defended their extravagant annual recruitment practices, which, according to Douglas Phelps, former public interest career coordinator at the Law School, would pay for the entire class of more than 500 to take public interest jobs for a year after law school. "We're not like other industries that produce goods. We offer the services of people," Paul Allison, hiring partner for the Boston firm of Choate, Hall, & Stewart, told the *Boston Globe*. "In general, Harvard Law School has highly qualified people, highly motivated people. And a substantial percentage of the partnership went to Harvard. There is an affinity, a familiarity there."

According to the Law School, only 2 percent of the class of 1987, or nine people, took public-interest or legal services jobs. Sixty-seven percent of the class of 540 went to work for private law firms, where salaries start at $80,000 a year (plus sign-on bonuses) and, in New York, even higher. The rest of the class went to work in investment banking, management consulting, corporate legal jobs, or judicial clerkships that, in most cases (though not all) will lead back to the large firms offering brie, chablis—and ennui. For its students, bright people who got A's in college and hit home runs on the LSATs, the Law School is experienced as a paradox, at once a door opening up to privilege and riches but also a trap, a place where the ones who come as idealists progressively price themselves out of their own convictions. The temptations to join a corporate firm are overwhelming: the magical salaries for summer clerkships (upwards of $1,000 a week), free autumn travel all over America, fancy hotels and expense account lunches, concert tickets and boatrides, immediate social integration and lifetime financial security. These inducements, combined with college and law school loan debts in the tens of thousands of dollars and strong parental pressure to make good on what must be an enormous investment of family capital and pride, push most students into the outstretched arms of law firm recruiters.

For the law firms, it is a simple economic proposition: more associates means more billable hours, which means more money flowing upwards in the pyramid of the firm. Law firms in America now bill $40 billion a year, and the associates are the well-paid wage-laborers of this system. As Chief Justice Rehnquist has stated: "It seems to me that a law firm that requires an associate to bill in excess of two thousand hours per year, thereby sharply curtailing the productive expenditure of energy outside of work, is substantially more concerned with profit-maximization than were firms when I practiced. Indeed, one might argue that such a firm is treating the associate very much as a manufacturer of one hundred tons of scrap metal: if you use anything less than the one hundred tons that you paid for, you simply are not running an efficient business."[12]

Against this institutional background, much thought-crime is taking place at the Law School, where the entire curriculum has been rocked by the mundane (by the standards of reality) but radical (by the standards of Harvard) teachings of Critical Legal Studies. Its very straightforward postulates suggest that the law can only be understood as an instrument of state power for the governance of social conflict and that legal decisions in any given case are radically indeterminate, rather than dictated by some deep inner logic of the law. This first point was, of course, one of the basic insights of Legal Realism in the 1920s and 1930s. So was the second point, now also standard brain-food served by law professors across the spectrum—that is, for every argument compelling one outcome, there is another argument suggesting its opposite. It is a sign of the times that these basic understandings, dressed up a bit with semiotic theory, are taken as heretical by the legal academy, where law must be shown at every turn to be a neutral, apolitical institution. Traditionalists teach what might be called Uncritical Legal Studies: law as a body of principles that exists outside of history and social meaning, an independent field of knowledge. At any rate, CLS professors arguing the contingency of law and its deep responsiveness to social structure usually end up in a normative way "pushing for a kind of internal democratization and reduction of internal hierarchy," in the words of Duncan Kennedy, who tries to combine sophisticated radical theory with a clinical practice focusing on low-income housing rights. [13] Most professors in CLS call themselves participatory or radical democrats and feminists.

While Harvard Law School seems an odd place for radical renewal during the Reagan period, the schisms that have developed there are intelligible signs of the paradoxical nature of legal education. When viewed sharply, from the right angle, law school can be a pure education into social relationships. The study of law may conceal or unearth its real content, it may apologize or criticize, it may teach students to rule or to challenge, it may proceed blindly and dogmatically or historically and theoretically, but it is in essence, and incontrovertibly, the study of conflict and contact between contrary social forces: employer and employee, landlord and tenant, seller and consumer, state and prisoner, government and taxpayer, one nation-state and another, husband and wife, parent and child. The law strikes the balance and draws the boundaries between these forces; to study law is one way to know power.

But traditional legal education excludes recognition of the dynamics of power encoded within it. That is why CLS finds an easy target for subversion in the Harvard Law School curriculum, which is a mirror of the law's past in America, an unwitting barometer of power relationships. Each year of the three-year curriculum belongs to a different time. The first year commemorates the nineteenth-century glory of Harvard Law School's first dean, Christopher Columbus Langdell, by introducing the great institutions of Western history—Property, Contracts, and Torts—the way Langdell taught them, as a kind of natural science, a mathematics for society. Langdell took office in 1870, closed the doors to the non-rich by making a college degree a prerequisite to admission (Abe Lincoln would have been rejected), and introduced the "case method" of studying legal decisions to reveal the scientific doctrines of the law. A legal formalist who believed in rigid adherence to precedent, Langdell championed the absolutist conceptions of property right, contract doctrine, and tort law that defined social relationships in the mid-nineteenth century. He taught these subjects by way of the Socratic method, the perfect vehicle for the communication of scientific truths possessed by the professor. The traditional first year education today still keeps faith with Langdell's insistence upon the student's memorization of case holdings and submission to the authority of the professor.

The second year of the curriculum shifts abruptly to Legal Realism and the statutory New Deal, the modern world of liberal bureaucratic state capitalism, when students take welfare-state classes like Taxation, Labor Law, and Administrative Law. When Legal Realism broke from the incumbent formalist conception in the 1920s, maintaining that law could only be understood as a response to the particular social conflicts it means to regulate, Legal Realism began to lay down the legal infrastructure for the regulatory welfare state. "Twenty-eight of forty-three Harvard Law Review editors who graduated between 1930 and 1932 were employed by the federal government in the following decade."[14] The journey of the Law School into modernity was complete when James Landis, epitome of the hyperactive Roosevelt New Deal, became dean in 1937. Although Legal Realism began with a radical potential, its progress stopped at the point of the welfare state, that raggedy compromise between class justice and class discipline, and it became the ideology of the modern administrative agency. During the second year of Law School, Legal

Realism is invoked mainly for its conservative conclusion as a model for "policy-oriented" interest balancing. Its early radical analysis of the structure and content of law is omitted.

The third and final year before graduation is generally saved for preparation for the contemporary world of big business and high finance. This is the year for Corporate Tax, the Acquisition and Use of Corporate Control, Corporate Finance, Commercial Transactions, Mergers, Acquisitions and Corporate Restructuring, and Securities Regulation.

If there is a theory guiding third-year education, perhaps it is the traces of Legal Process theory, a jurisprudence worked out in the 1950s by Professors Henry Hart and Albert Sacks, who posited the primacy of procedural fairness and order as a value in the meaning of U.S. justice. Legal Process theory reflected the essential durability of legal conservatism, for it replaced Legal Realism's sharper insights—the plasticity of law (including common and constitutional law), the political contingency of property rights—with the old formalist dogma, this time applied to legal process instead of legal substance. Conservatives like Legal Process theory because it tells them that the outcome is fine if the process is fair.

But the essence of the third year is not theory but the practice of corporate law. The third year reasserts Harvard Law School's original calling as a trade school for the class Tocqueville considered to be "the most powerful, if not the only counterpoise to the democratic element."[15] By the third year, students are supposed to "think like corporate lawyers."

CLS professors teach inside and outside of the traditional curriculum, disorienting the ruling paradigm. They disturb the Langdellian peace of the first year by demonstrating the way in which theoretically encased fields of law, such as Contracts, are historically responsive to social and political change and are themselves intrinsic exercises of state power to advance particular ends. Where Professor Fried argues that a legal contract is like a promise in nature, CLS professors, like Gerald Frug, show that a contract is only a contract because the state enforces it, defines its meaning, and sets its boundary points.

Where traditional professors teach Torts, the law of civil wrongs, as a series of moral essences that may have blurry edges (where does negligence end and strict liability begin?), the CLS, led by legal historian Mort Horwitz, teaches the actual historical development of tort law, showing how changes in social and legal vision reflect and interact with changes in social and economic structure. Thus, negligence and strict liability, according to Horwitz, are not just two competing principles within tort law today but the doctrinal expression of different historical demands placed upon the legal system by the society and political economy.

CLS has in fact made a formal inroad into the first year education with the so-called "experimental sections," two of the four first-year groupings that try to examine the law in a more critical and historical way. CLS professors challenge the conventional second year education by recapturing the vital phase of Legal Realism, pointing out the class nature of social legislation, the political nature of judicial decision-making, the inseparability of law and society, and how legal vernacular constitutes a discourse in power. In his Housing Law course (as in his Property course), Duncan Kennedy tries to show how different modes of legal discourse conceal particular social arrangements and advance particular political results.

In Local Government Law, Professor Frug shows the city's progression in American history from a chartered corporation with extensive economic and political powers to a constrained and depoliticized "public" corporation involved primarily in the administration of the community's physical infrastructure. His work is a panegyric to participatory democracy; it invites us to abandon the modern hollowed-out conception of the city and replace it with a city that has the powers of investment, ownership, and autonomy against private corporations and the national military state. In Race, Racism, and the Law, Professor Randall Kennedy, following through on the pivotal work of Derrick Bell, places the question of racism at the very center of American law, recapturing it from the margins where it has been consigned by centuries of legal education. Kennedy explores the dialectic between social struggle and legal change, showing how the Civil Rights movement has been the major catalyst for the expansion of constitutional rights in America. Probing courses in Legal and Constitutional Theory by Lewis Sargentich, Derrick Bell, and Roberto Unger invite students to rethink the "naturalness" of contemporary patterns of social hierarchy and legal understanding. (More whimsical meditations, like Beyond Critical Legal Studies by Frug and David Kennedy, give rise to the association, in many students' minds, between CLS and heady conversations about Derrida and literary theory over cappucino at the Café Algiers.)

CLS courses question the third year of intensive preparation for corporate legal practice in Donald Trump City on moral and existential grounds. Indeed, the very essence of the CLS and liberal challenge to the dominant curriculum is to urge students to do something more creative with their lives than record time in fifteen-minute blocks and emulate Wall Street law partners whose workplace motto, according to Chief Justice William Rehnquist, is "you only eat what you kill." [16] Alternatives are suggested through clinical practice, the curricular innovation that predates CLS but gives the movement's theoretical challenge concrete meaning. Led by Professor Gary Bellow, who came to Harvard as a poverty lawyer in the early 1970s amid much complaint that he had not served on the Law Review, the clinical program allows students to learn to become lawyers by helping very poor clients negotiate the twists and turns of the welfare state. In clinical courses and the parallel student groups, like the Prison Legal Assistance Program or Students for Public Interest Law, students can represent prisoners, tenants, welfare clients, criminal defendants, and the homeless, all the while regaining the confidence in their own skills that has been carefully stripped away from them by the infantilizing hierarchies of law school and law firms. This nearly invisible development at Harvard Law School has generated a student counter-culture that is hard-working and radical in spirit. [17] CLS scholars recognize the importance of connecting radical legal practice with radical legal theory. Bellow told Joel Seligman in 1978 that law students should become active social critics and catalysts for change. "We need to create a learning environment where all courses are concerned with reconstruction..." [18]

The reason that the CLS counter-education is so threatening is that the intellectual center of gravity at the Law School lies no longer with the conservatives on the faculty, but with the liberals. The conservatives, united only by their hostility to CLS, have nothing to bind them intellectually since the progress of each one's moral consciousness stopped at a different point in history. Some of them oppose affirmative action; others don't even like *Brown v. Board of Education*. But the broad faction of distinguished liberals at Harvard Law School was influenced by the political struggles of the last several decades and has adopted for the most part the analytical techniques and contentions of CLS, conferring legitimacy on the movement's intellectual project. This intellectual affinity is natural since CLS and the more conventional liberals share a common ancestry in Legal Realism. They differ primarily in terms of their political style and ambition, the liberals identifying more with the Democratic Party than with the New Left.

In the ranks of the liberals are some of the most notable legal scholars in the country: constitutional scholar Laurence Tribe; Susan Estrich and Christopher Edley, Governor Dukakis' 1988 presidential campaign manager and issues coordinator respectively; the omnipresent civil libertarian Alan Dershowitz; Charles Nesson, another civil libertarian who defended in 1985 a group of students brought before the Law School's kangaroo-court Administrative Board for South Africa divestment protests (and recently, at the center of a firestorm created by remarks he made that he conceded to be sexist); Abram Chayes, who represented Nicaragua in its successful 1985 suit against the United States in the World Court for mining its harbors; Nick Littlefield, the mob-busting expert in government law enforcement; Roger Fisher, the ponderous negotiations specialist; and Henry Steiner, the architect of the Law School's impressive Human Rights Program (founded in 1982), which every year sends twenty-five to thirty students all over the unfree world to make *habeas corpus* petitions for political prisoners and otherwise defend victims of state terror.[19]

Thus, the tenured core of CLS has survived because there is a strong liberalism at the Law School committed to both academic freedom and intellectual engagement with CLS. Nonetheless, it is clear that CLS has taken a beating recently. Its long-term viability is on the line. Not only is it under siege on the faculty, but all of its classroom subversions have not altered the flow of students to service in the corporate state. Partly this is a problem of pure economics, outside of CLS's control; students are forced into corporate employment because of the heavy debts they carry to get through Harvard Law School, which, with expenses, costs about $18,000 a year. These fees practically force young lawyers to go to the corporate firms. And, yet, even with the Low Income Protection Plan, the Law School's modest new loan forgiveness program for public interest employment, CLS has not been able to redirect many students, even many liberal ones, away from the corporate lure.

The pedagogy of CLS has indeed proven remarkably adaptable to the workings of the corporate-legal nexus. CLS professors emphasizing the "flippability" of legal argumentation (in the jazzy slang of Duncan Kennedy) are often the mod-pedagogue favorites of corporate-bound preppies because they teach directly and cynically the skills in legal and rhetorical manipulation that more traditional professors only teach indirectly and mysteriously, by "hiding the ball," in the cogent formulation of Professor Horwitz. As Professor Richard

Pierce of Southern Methodist Law School, a conservative Law-and-Economics advocate, reassured a distressed alumni audience in Texas, "Nothing about CLS merits anger or concern. [Duncan Kennedy's torts course] has a lot more doctrine than the course had when I took it. If I'm hiring someone in the area of tort law, Kennedy's course provides exactly the kind of background I'd like them to have."[20] The easy absorption of CLS into the corporate system sustains a lot of humor (it is often said that you can identify CLS militants because they tie up the Xerox machine at Cravath, Swain & Moore), but it suggests a deeper problem.

What is missing from CLS is a powerful sense that the rule of law can be a force for good, and therefore that people teaching in and studying at the Law School can participate in a movement for social reconstruction. The problem with CLS's famous deconstructive impulse is not, as it is often said, that it leads to nihilism; the problem is that, in isolation, it leads straight back to the status quo. By itself, it is paralyzing. In any case, revelations in 1987 that the founder of literary deconstruction in America, Paul DeMan, was a Nazi collaborationist should be enough to demonstrate that anyone can trash. The question is what you build through the law and within the society. CLS professors should now move away from the demolition of conventional legal doctrine and work to identify, reinforce, and deepen those streams of development within the law that have strengthened democracy, freedom, and international order.

With the ascendancy of Robert Clark, CLS will have to work out a real alliance with liberal professors to prevent the conservative ideological purification of the faculty and the curriculum. Any lingering and self-justifying liberal-bashing impulses should be set aside, not only for strategic but for principled reasons. The Law School's liberals play a significant role in advancing justice in the real world. The Nicaraguan government, for example, turned to liberal Professor Abram Chayes when it wanted to sue the Reagan administration over the illegal mining of its harbors. Professor Tribe successfully defended the constitutionality of rent control before the Supreme Court and also argued (unsuccessfully) in *Bowers v. Hardwick* that the constitutional right of privacy extends to gay people. CLS professors, who talk a lot about participation and "the people," should thus involve the people who are their liberal colleagues in dialogue and action. Just as the liberals might be jolted out of their Dukakis-style complacency, the radicals might learn something about the actual practice of law. Such an alliance could connect with the current exciting political efforts to transform the University by doing legal work for the clerical and technical workers' union and the Alumni Against Apartheid's Board of Overseers' election campaigns.

Moreover, as the country continues along a course of steady degradation of democratic processes and values—from the making of foreign policy by right-wing militarists to the domination of the electoral process by corporate PACs to the loss of public culture outside of television—liberal professors, CLS, and the clinical movement should take the lead in showing law students how desperately their skills and imagination are needed in so many parts of the country to revitalize public institutions and the democratic project. Lawyers do not have to be part of the problem. The next decade can become a period of political energy and experiment, a time for creative invention for the common good.[21] Those who become licensed in the law, who in effect have been given their own set of keys to state power, have a special responsibility to fight for strong democracy, a reduction in official corruption and lawlessness, and an end to what Simone Weil called "the domination of those who know how to handle words over those who know how to handle things," a kind of domination that Harvard Law School has helped to maintain for much more than a century in the United States of America.

Notes

1. See Derrick Bell, *And We Are Not Saved: The Elusive Quest for Racial Justice,* (New York: Basic Books, 1987).

2. Emily M. Bernstein, "Law Profs Question Dalton Vote," May 13, 1987, *Harvard Crimson.*

3. David Snouffer, "Bok Vetoes Trubek, Reviews Dalton Bid," *Harvard Law Record,* Sept. 18, 1987, p. 14.

4. See Bernstein.

5. Steve Curwood, "A Tenure Battle at Harvard Law," *Boston Globe,* July 19, 1987.

6. Brian Silver, "Law Professor Stages 'Academic Vigil,'" *Harvard Independent,* June 10, 1987.

7. "Bok Erodes Law School's Independence," *Harvard Crimson,* August 14, 1987.

8. *Harvard Law Record,* February 24, 1989.

9. All of the quotations in this paragraph are from the "Faculty Reactions Range From Praise to Scorn," *Harvard Law Record,* February 24, 1989,

10. Jennifer A. Kingson, "Harvard Tenure Battle Puts 'Critical Legal Studies on Trial,'" *New York Times,* Sunday, August 30, 1987.

11. Ellen J. Bartlett, *Boston Globe,* October 13, 1987, p. 21.

12. William J. Rehnquist, "The Legal Profession Today," 62 *Indiana Law Journal* pp. 151, 155.

13. "Three Perspectives on Critical Legal Studies," *Harvard Law Bulletin,* Summer 1987, p. 22.

14. J. Seligman, *The High Citadel: The Influence of Harvard Law School* (Boston: Houghton Mifflin, 1978), p. 26.

15. *Ibid.,* p. 64. "Trade School" is also the title of a must-see underground film about the Harvard Law School experience by Michael Anderson, class of '87, which was made as an answer to the $50,000 video propaganda commercial made by the Law School, "The Grand Experience."

16. Rehnquist.

17. The most militant, and somewhat surreal, expression of this student counter-culture is the Counter-Hegemonic Front, which dedicated a bust of Gramsci outside of Duncan Kennedy and Morton Horwitz' offices and conducts well-aimed, if somewhat childish, pranks against the Law School establishment, like putting up "See America, Fly for Free" posters at recruitment time, wearing "Grades Are Random" t-shirts, and disrupting Law Review dinners with drunken toasts to the Lubell brothers, who were victims of a witch-hunt at the Law Review in the 1950s.

18. Seligman, *op. cit.*

19. In 1987, the Human Rights Program sent five students to South Africa to do legal work in the embattled human rights community there. By way of contrast to official Harvard, Henry Steiner's brother, Dan, vice president of the University and chief Robocop against the divestment movement, was forced in 1985 to withdraw an intern program for Harvard students in South Africa when Damon Silvers of the Southern Africa Solidarity Committee discovered that the program involved such deeply reformist activities as coaching junior varsity men's soccer at predominantly white private schools.

20. *Harvard Law Bulletin.*

21. See Marcus G. Raskin, *The Common Good*, (London: Routledge and Keegan Paul, 1987).

Making Students Safe for Democracy
The Core Curriculum and Intellectual Management

Ben Robinson

Introduction

A core curriculum reveals the heart of a university's ideological project. It entrusts to the curriculum the task of acculturating a broad range of students to the institution's ideal of a "cultivated U.S. citizen." But it is a tricky undertaking, especially given the sophistication and diversity of students in the late twentieth century. The ideal itself differs from university to university, depending on the class of people to whom it applies. At Harvard the Core Curriculum aims to produce not just an "educated individual," but to instill the norms of class leadership into a group of people presumably destined for responsible positions in the established social order. A study of Harvard's Core opens a fascinating window onto the shifting tactics of intellectual management and recruitment among the nation's elite.

The Core Curriculum Program is a general education program required of every Harvard Undergraduate. The student must choose ten out of the 80-100 courses offered. The choices must be distributed among the six divisions of the program, which are conceived as reflecting the major approaches to knowledge: 1) Foreign Cultures; 2) Historical Study; 3) Literature and Arts; 4) Moral Reasoning; 5) Science; 6) Social Analysis.

The idea of Harvard's Core Curriculum incubated for several years starting in the spring of 1975, and was implemented over four years beginning in fall 1979. Full Core requirements first applied to 1982's entering class, which graduated just in time for Harvard's 350th birthday gala.

The Core curriculum was Harvard's early entry into the General Education sweepstakes which is now a major arena in the fight to control ideology in academic circles. While this essay limits itself to historically and descriptively situating Harvard's much heralded program, it represents an implicit critique of the bizarrely ahistorical disquisitions of Allan Bloom, author of the bestselling *Closing of the American Mind*, and former Secretary of Education William Bennett. It attempts to widen the debate around academic institutionalization of culture beyond the conservative strictures. Critical movements which have been developing strength on campuses around the country are the source and hope of progressive change. They have met with some success, for example, by replacing a Western Cultures requirement at Stanford University with a more culturally inclusive and ideologically critical sequence known as Cultures, Ideas and Values. This move responds to students' claims that a canon of "Great Books" is a means of systematically excluding from the university cultural contributions by women and non-European people and forms of culture not sanctioned by elite social groups. There have also been debates over requiring sequences in non-western cultures which have democratized curricular arrangements that in the past have been determined by a small clique of intellectuals and administrators.

Background of Curricular Reform at Harvard

a) The move away from classical texts, 1869-1909

Frederick Rudolph, in his history of undergraduate curriculum in the United States, describes how President Charles W. Eliot presided over a fundamental shift in Harvard's curricular philosophy. Eliot maintained that a rigorous curriculum of classical texts and traditional humanist pedagogy, in the style of not only Oxford and Cambridge, but ascetic colonial American Puritanism, was no longer appropriate for a country beginning to socially master its expanding technological might.

While the curricular changes are significant during this period, they represent only a small part of the complete transformation the university was undergoing. This transformation is best illustrated by the founding of Cornell and Johns Hopkins, which embodied the new conception of the university in society. The creation of Cornell in 1866 by Western Union's largest stock holder, Ezra Cornell, provided for the first North American university devoted explicitly—in resources as well as intention—to producing "useful" men in the sense of a modern industrial society, rather than to cultivating the strict and exalted men who presided over the more stern projects of the colonial and infant United States.

Johns Hopkins, opened in 1867 and endowed by wealthy Baltimore railroad investor Hopkins, is the other paradigm of the period, the first North American institution explicitly modeled on a German research university. There are subtle shades of difference between these two paradigms. Cornell brought "service to material and moral aspirations of the middle class," training its students for a practical, immediate application of their studies in the expanding U.S. economy. Johns Hopkins devoted itself to more abstract knowledge, and to training its students to become scholars per se—more lofty industrial servants. Both paradigms, however, were essentially compatible and in the process of merging. The University of Chicago, founded in 1892, was a complete synthesis of the models represented by Cornell and Johns Hopkins, as was Stanford, founded in 1886 by railroad baron Leland Stanford, and headed by David Starr Jordan, who had been hired away from Cornell. With these newly founded universities, tradition and its home in the curriculum and teaching style of the gentleman faculty decisively gave way to a corporate bureaucratic model of higher learning. Rudolph writes of the University of Chicago that "in William Rainey Harper, its first president, it found a man who could do for the University what its chief benefactor, John D. Rockefeller, had done for oil and what J. P. Morgan would do for steel. Harper created an organization in which everything fell into place."

The debt universities owe to the German model of research and scholarship institution is large. But the American developments at the turn of the century started to reverse the direction of influence, as the bureaucratic organization of American universities made an inexorable impression on the universities in Germany's own rationalizing capitalist economy. Max Weber—who not only was responsible for much pioneering study into the nature of bureaucratic organization, but also has assumed a mythic pivotal role in developing our social science analytical concepts—saw the balance of German influence in another light. In a 1918 speech at Munich University on "Science as a Vocation," he stated that

> of late we can observe distinctly that the German universities in the broad fields of science develop in the direction of the American system. The large institutes of medicine or natural science are 'state capitalist' enterprises, which cannot be managed without very considerable funds.... As with all capitalist and at the same time bureaucratized enterprises, there are indubitable ad-

vantages in all this. But the 'spirit' that rules in these affairs is different from the historical atmosphere of the German University. An extraordinarily wide gulf, externally and internally, exists between the chief of these large, capitalist, university enterprises and the usual full professor of the old style...Inwardly as well as externally, the old university constitution has become fictitious.

This context—the maturation of the American university to serve the United States's manifest destiny in the hands of robber barons wealthy with money from oil, railroads and telegraphs—brought forth Charles Eliot as the spokesman for the new university, the university that was to dominate higher education in the twentieth century. Through electives, Eliot marshalled liberal philosophy and laissez-faire economics on behalf of curricular transformation. The logic of the developing economy brought a swift and comprehensive scientific, technical, research, and specialization oriented curriculum to the university. Eliot allowed students the prerogative of choosing chemistry and physics over Greek and Latin. As electives began to dominate the Harvard campus (all subject requirements were abolished for seniors in 1872, juniors in 1879, and sophomores in 1884), the rationale was for all intents and purposes irresistible. Liberating the curriculum was not playing into weak or uncertain hands; rather, the liberation was like letting go a paper boat on a raging stream. By the turn of the century an armada of paper boats filled the same fat industrial stream: no one seems to have thought of electing a course on women's studies, Afro-american studies or comparative history of the working class; the current was just too strong. Electives at the turn of the century represented the freedom to choose industrial progress.

b) The Redbook

Two benchmarks in 20th century Harvard curricular history are the Harvard Committee report entitled "General Education in a Free Society," known as the "Redbook," and the 1963 Godkin Lectures at Harvard, delivered by the President of the University of California, Clark Kerr, and published as the *Uses of the University*. The release of the Redbook coincided with a consolidation of the professional and technical incorporation of the university into society in conjunction with the massive growth of the student body nationally and the clear rise of the United States to international military and economic preeminence. The end of World War II enlarged the student body with the passage of the Servicemen's Readjustment Act of 1944 (the

GI Bill of Rights) which provided for federally-subsidized GI education. The research facilities and university-based think tanks, as well
as the university-groomed Washington "Brain Trusts," without the
external justification of the war, became permanent parts of the
university. Further, they were expanded by an influx of highly-
trained intelligence and War Department personnel returning from
overseas and Pentagon service.

Still, the Redbook was primarily a liberal humanist statement,
not a jingoistic celebration of U.S. culture in the wake of "our" World
War II victory. Among its authors was Nobel Prize winning biologist
George Wald, who later became famous for his outspoken anti-Viet-
nam War activism. While partly inspired by the horror of the exemplary German academy's embrace of Hitler, the Redbook was also
made possible by optimism, the sense of effortlessness which had
accompanied America's climb to world power following World War
II. What is remarkable about the Redbook is the optimism implicit in
the message of the university's new, socially encompassing role as
preserver of democracy and mediator of progress; i.e., that the condition of academe was one with the health of the nation. Though most
of the Redbook does not deal with Harvard but with high school
education, its tone above all is that of the university confidently
formulating the vision of change.

The humanities, sensing a mysterious surge of self-confidence
and self-importance—but not questioning what that confidence was
riding on—declared social goals appropriate to the dawning age of
mass education and the emergence of a new "military-industrial
complex" inextricably bound with the university. Suddenly, the university, a service station to industrialism, had now nearly become
coequal with the most potent forces of society. Organizationally, the
humanities had found a new 'in,' but with this twist: classical learning
was no longer a patrimony required of leaders for the wisdom it
brought them, as it had been under Harvard's colonial mandate prior
to reorientation towards serving industrial progress under Eliot.
Now, after Eliot, the traditional imperative became bounty for a new
class, which would absorb it as a consumer. It wasn't the wisdom of
the "heritage" that was important, but its commonality, its very
baseness in the literal sense of the word. Terry Eagleton has pointed
to Matthew Arnold as formulating an instrumentalization of Western
culture in the realm that had previously been occupied by religion. It
would, in the twentieth century, be Great Books that provided the

shared norms to give North American society, like the British, a coherent self-identity.

Yet the main point about the Redbook is just the opposite: it didn't represent a clarion call to cultural indoctrination. Religion had been sloughed off for sound, productive reasons. Unlike Robert Hutchins' proposals for the University of Chicago, the Redbook looked forward to adapting new, barbaric mass media to cultural enlightenment. It even contains a suggestion for a wide-screen version of Erasmus' *Colloquies*! It was a quintessential pre-sixties North American document in its taboos and its sustained optimism. It saw itself as bringing the fruits of the classical heritage—once reserved for the rich and mighty—to the deserving and eagerly consuming middle class.

Matthew Arnold thought Western society needed a bulwark to maintain order in the absence of religion. But technology, in exchange for its position as ever more exclusive guarantor of capitalist progress since the Industrial Revolution, could more than hold up its end of the bargain. As Weber clearly saw, it provided, along its own technical-rational lines, more than adequate means of reproducing a social order. To use the river metaphor once more, Eliot's paper boats were being carried along as rapidly as ever, only now the river had become so broad that the boats needed radar equipment to check up with each other now and again.

c) The Uses of the University

There was no change in the broad, upward direction of U.S. development at the end of the Second World War. The economic and social processes which occasioned Eliot's reforms were still unquestioned. What had changed, however, was the role the federal government and its particular managerial styles began to play. The New Deal and national war effort set the tone for postwar development, and had an immediate effect on the university. The change in tone can be seen from the different sorts of nationwide education coordinating bodies that were being founded. In 1906 the Carnegie Foundation was established, with the appropriate robber baron backing. In 1913 came the Rockefeller Foundation, likewise endowed. While these groups have not fully ceded their influence, the postwar coordinating organizations leave them almost ceremonial in comparison: in 1946 the Atomic Energy Commission and the Office of Naval Research were founded; in 1950, the National Science Foundation; the OSS became the CIA in 1947; the National Institutes of Health appeared in 1953; NASA in 1958. These organizations, as well as the exploding funding from the Pentagon, became the source of mammoth federal grants to the universities. From 1940 to 1960 federal support to higher education increased over 100 times to $1.5 billion. By 1970 the figure had increased to $4 billion. Other developments in the spirit of the new imperatives of empire, such as the discreetly named field of Area Studies, followed fast: at Harvard there were the Russian Research Center (1948); Center for Middle Eastern Studies (1954); East Asian Research Center (1957); Center for International Affairs (1958). The year 1958 heralded the National Defense Education Act, supporting foreign language and area study. Before the wars the universities were beloved handmaidens, serving them loyally, but still outside of the production court. After the war they went directly big-time. Rah, rah sentiments of optimism in 1960 seemed as shamefully provincial as did slogans of Veritas in 1860.

With the end of the war President James B. Conant began a concerted nationwide recruitment of students, self-consciously engaging in what one book would call "The Making of a University to a Nation"—appropriately with a double meaning. The student body had also become much more ethnically and economically diverse, with about 56 percent coming from public schools in 1960. In 1963 the Harvard and Radcliffe degrees were merged into one.

Clark Kerr took all these developments in stride, laying them out proudly in *Uses of the University*, and declaring the new creation a "Multiversity." After a few decades the university was at last formulating its new powerful role in the United States in its own words. Kerr wrote,

> David Riesman has spoken of the leading American universities as directionless...as far as major innovations are concerned; they have run out of foreign models to imitate; they have lost their "ferment. The fact is that they are not directionless; they have been moving in clear directions and with considerable speed; there has been no stalemate. But these directions have not been set as much by the university's visions of its destiny as by the external environment, including the federal government, the foundations, the surrounding and sometimes engulfing industry.

It was about time that the universities stretch out their new muscles and take control of things. "The university may now again need to find out whether it has a brain as well as a body," Kerr continued.

Uses of the University, unlike the idealistic Redbook, was a clarion call. All these goings on were neither directionless nor nasty, they called for one thing in particular: Management. Kerr overlooked one thing—just as its external arrangements had become vastly complex, so had the University's internal dynamics. Within a year of the publication of *Uses of the University* , Kerr's Berkeley campus erupted in the Free Speech Movement. The students independently began articulating a multiversity Kerr hadn't noticed, and in concepts wholly hostile to the management ethos. Kerr was overwhelmed at one juncture and called the police. Within another year he was dumped by California's then-Governor, Ronald Reagan.

d) A Response to Student Activism

Daniel Bell, author of the influential book *The Reforming of General Education* about Columbia, and later a professor at Harvard, tied together several strands in the reasoning behind the new Core Curriculum movement. Shortly after Bell published *The Reforming of General Education* in 1966, his worst fears about the academy came true—Columbia University erupted in protest. Unlike Kerr, Bell was not caught off guard. Events reaffirmed his belief in the dangerous nihilism of what he called "post-industrial" society.

The issue of the modern crisis is a feeling of vulnerability that is intellectual, not material, for capitalism still has not exhausted its economic potentials. In *The Cultural Contradictions of Capitalism*, Bell notes, "the problems are less those of the adequacy of institutions than of the kinds of meanings that sustain a society." The crisis was brought to the fore by the activist cultural sensibilities of the sixties. According to Bell in *Cultural Contradictions,*

> By the end of the 1960s, the new sensibility had been given a name (the counter-culture) and an ideology to go with it. The main tendency of that ideology—though it appeared in the guise of an attack on the 'technocratic society'—was an attack on reason itself.

How was his analysis used against the students? The very basis of university authority, the reasoning mind, represented rationalism *par excellence*, but that pillar had proven to be resting on a sea of Aquarian egoism. Without proper rational discipline, the old lines of institutional self-regulation were ineffectual. Nor could the university reach out for police protection and legal restrictions—the spirit of academic freedom would balk. The solution turns out to be one of mind over matter, the consummate move of post-industrialism. According to Bell, "The authority of a university is not a civil authority but a moral one. It can deal with disruptions—or threats—not by invoking civil force but by rallying an entire community to establish common rules of common procedure." Bell proposes this as "the reaffirmation of liberalism"—for the whole of the modern world. "The real problem of modernity is the problem of belief. To use an unfashionable term, it is a spiritual crisis, since the new anchorages have proved illusory and the old ones have become submerged. It is a situation which brings us back to nihilism; lacking a past or a future, there is only a void." Bell had neatly relegated the student movement to matters of psychology, denying it the mantel of legitimacy usually granted to bonified political movements.

The Core Curriculum, as we shall see, is a crucial management tool in the era which, as Bell tells us, is characterized by an "end of ideology."

The new Core Curriculum

a) The impact of history

The historical legacy surveyed above resulted in three broad strategies for creating ideological correctives appropriate to the changing role of the university.

1) Initiation—early liberal arts colleges from colonial times until the vocational shift in mid-nineteenth century engaged in teaching an elite group cultural practices which inwardly gave discipline and self-identity and outwardly helped to keep provincial shopkeepers and farmers in disempowered awe. This element endures in the Ivy League.

2) Indoctrination—Chicago best represents the vision of the college as the "community of intellect" cultivating the proper values to stave off barbarism, primarily based on a negative, reactionary conception of the society in which the academy operates. The academy can "save" those who embrace it, indoctrinating them with the correct line of civilized society, but is otherwise isolated. Robert Hutchins, Chicago's crusading president in the 1930s and 1940s, didn't see true education as capable of social reform. He wasn't opposed to reform, he just denied education's role in the process. This mandated blindness concerning the context of one's intellectual activities is an important

component of Hutchins' (and Allan Bloom's) style of indoctrination—the masses can't be reached and need an elite class of caretakers.

3) Civilization—Columbia and the Redbook aimed to bring the happy fruits of education and progress to all, inviting idealism and—in crisis—enlightened patriotism. Civilizing is primarily an outward, positive, and acculturating task, the flip side of Hutchins' indoctrination. One moves to grace through the academy, and the academy itself moves in worldly circles rallying the less fortunate around the flag of good citizenship.

Each of these three aspects of General Education survives in the Core, modified by a dose of the need to maintain order and productivity in society.

It was President Bok—replacing Harvard's top casualty in the 1960s "fall of the American university," hardliner Nathan Pusey—who ushered in the age of management and inaugurated the institutional articulation of Harvard Multiversity. Moving beyond the initial affirmation of the multiversity, Core Curriculum proposals under his aegis came at a time of post-industrial re-tooling. While there are echoes of the Redbook, and the projects are similar, the motivation of the Core Curriculum at its beginning, and now, is far more sophisticated.

There are several reasons, stemming from the disarray of the sixties, for the Core proposal coming at the time it did. From the administrative point of view, the faculty, more than students, had to be rallied behind a sense of common purpose. Dean Rosovsky was a strong administrative figure who also carried weight as a faculty member and had a reputation as a firm resister of student encroachments on academic integrity. (He was one of the "white Berkeleyites" who fled Berkeley in the wake of the Free Speech Movement and Kerr's downfall.) There was no shortage, then, of immediate politics in the realm of authority retrenchment. But the Core's project aims for more than a simple repair of wounded academic egos.

b) The Core Courses

The Core, as much as it marginalizes rival accounts of U.S. society, nonetheless recognizes that they *exist*, say, a Marxist or feminist account. President Conant could allow the Marxist perspective on campus because, as he put it, "studying a philosophy does not mean endorsing it, much less proclaiming it. We study cancer in order to learn how to defeat it.... If an avowed supporter of the Marx-Lenin-Stalin line can be found, force him into the open and tear his arguments to pieces with counter-arguments." But imagine a similar justification of allowing feminism or Afro-American studies on campus! Alas, after the sixties the old strategy had become too simple, and a strategy of mutual co-existence had to be worked out.

The Core represents a realization that liberalism of the John Stuart Mill variety—which proclaims the inevitable victory of "truth" in unregulated conflict—does not suffice to effectively order the flow of ideas. Instead, the Core, like the managerial philosophy that dominates at Harvard's Kennedy School of Government, has absorbed a great deal of materialism. It devalues ideas as it learns to tolerate them. It will still try to keep out through the tenure process, and other gate-keeping strategies, the wrong truths, but it doesn't count on an overall strategy of exclusion. So a course like Theda Skocpol's "Social Analysis 15: Explaining Revolutions in the Modern World" can make the list. And the faculty is probably downright happy with the successful liberalism represented by Barbara Johnson's "Literature and Arts A-50: Black Women Writers." In the Core Curriculum, Mill's open conflict of ideas is reenacted in miniature, in exchange for the more important procedural consensus on the university's role in society. The Core's designers have shown the same confidence as neo-liberal advocates of industrial planning such as Michael Dukakis; namely, that by properly structuring institutional arrangements, violently competing interests can be harnessed and mediated, and yet the interests can go on expressing themselves as distinct interests, on a common stage, as it were.

Responding to the impact of the Core

a) Theoretical basis

The primary task of the Core is maintaining the continuity of power. The Core is a small factor shaping the U.S. power structure, but its contribution is coherent. In the university, "enlightenment rationality" is one dynamic which, through human practice, can lead to continuity in the exercise of power. In so far as scientific specialization does lead to continuity it is abetted by the curricular arrangement of the university. In so far as it leads to fragmentation and the possibility of an external ("irrational, subjective"—sixties-like) reorganization, the curriculum seeks to counter it. In other words, the Core recruits to the the status quo's self-management.

No matter who the individuals are who administer the Core, the measure of the Core's success will be its ability to aid the orderly transitions of rule, to represent and demobilize disorder, and to spread the Good News. The project is not crudely reactionary: It is rather a response to a destructive dialectic of liberalism which the university recognizes as the devil on its shoulder. The Core reflects the fear that the student, scientist, technician and specialist are too neutral, too uncommitted to anything broader than their specialties; that they might be engulfed in an ideology that could pose a threat to the present order. Bok and Rosovsky use the sophisticated talk of ethics, compassion and responsibility to demobilize any wayward passions which might sweep up the "de-classed" apparatchik. The coherence of their vision of the university, of their management of science and humanity inspires confidence. Someplace down the line, after we exercise appropriate criticism within the liberal framework, their confidence wins us over. It is appealing. Not per se, since the ruling interests are too apparent, but it is appealing precisely because the left shares the fear of irrationality and irresponsibility to humanity, of subjectivity and violence.

The Core Curriculum's chutzpah, its claim to harmony, allays our fears of impending disarray—fears which, in the clutch of the late twentieth century, sometimes motivate us more strongly than our hopes. And the cost is that it succeeds in coopting the technical and cowering the cultural: our own proposals for transformation seem too dauntlessly uncontrolled. We accept technical progress and likewise let culture assume the burden of consolation and redemption of humanity.

On the scientific side, the result of such acceptance is that progress might bring "real" gain, but the educated are subjected by technocratic rationality, and the disenfranchised are subjected by the educated. Core courses portray those who are outside of our educational project as objects of policy: not subjects capable of affirmation, but as failure. Either that, or they are better than we are, like the Japanese. And then we subject ourselves to them, not as a foreign culture, but as disembodied rationality—the only measure to which we will make a status concession. This either/or reflects a unique feature of our drive to policy which distinguishes it from earlier colonial racism and makes it so much harder to fully criticize. In our own insecurity (given the vast productive and destructive power of modern economies) we are almost willing to condone the reduction of political affairs to policy for fear of being overwhelmed.

On the cultural side we reassure ourselves with General Education. In General Education we reopen a procedural distinction between *us* and *them*. The reality of their "failure" emerges as we try to avert our own putative decline. If it is General Education which is saving us, then they are unredeemed. We have to self-consciously paint ourselves with the glaze of affirmation by which we can recognize our own: a rational teleology of progress escorted by the free muses of practical reason and aesthetics.

So, it makes sense that we might enjoy so many of our Core courses. The Core catalogue is cheerful. Its optimism is at one with Henry Adams' turn-of-the-century observation on Harvard freshmen:

> Cast more or less in the same mould, without violent emotions or sentiment, and, except for the veneer of American habits, ignorant of all that man had ever thought or hoped, their minds burst open like flowers at the sunlight of a suggestion. They were quick to respond; plastic to mould; and incapable of fatigue. Their faith in education was so full of pathos that one dared not ask them what they thought they could do with education when they got it.

Looking at the catalogue with innocent eyes, its cheerfulness invites fantasy: it can all be mine, like a Conquistador claiming the Amazon. It is the very stuff of affirmation.

If knowledge is power, and confident, optimistic knowledge is ascendent power, then all this cheerfulness will have a dark side indeed for the disenfranchised. Whether we choose to embrace the objectivity of policy implementation out of fear, or the mediated subjectivity of general education out of a need for affirmation, we all too easily wind up as ambassadors of our education. When we expand our vision beyond the curriculum into the vast "extra-curriculum" of the world, we might well wonder if the one thing that we must do is make sure that the curriculum isn't cheerful at all. The tack for curricular reform might be a return to the dour catalogue; to chase students away, to give up on the university as inextricably entangled in the reproduction of the status quo. Think of those students alienated by the exclusivity and presumption of the courses: they free themselves from exercise of the Harvard mandate; they relinquish their mastery and, hence, their ambassadorship. Given the system which has chosen who Harvard students are, might not the most sound strategy be to make the rest of them pessimistic? The catalogue choices might be redesignated, this time as Division, Disarray and Death. And the crucial link of social reproduction could be marginalized and forced to wither in despair. Then what would Daniel Bell and Allan Bloom say?

b) Tactical Response

But we see how far that inward view leads us from the true situation of the university in society. We have forgotten what Clark Kerr had laid out for us: we aren't simply and ideally learning in old Cardinal Newman's idea of the university, we are engaged in meaningful social production. College is now a sober business; students are now critical links in the economic chain. Clearly the point of critiquing the Core is not to write off education as a worthless or reactionary human endeavor. Rather, it is to recognize the student's and the educator's position in the nexus of transformation—the transformation wrought by the family structure, wrought by political and ethnic groupings, wrought by international trade, wrought by the whole range of social practices with which we must now see the university as integrally linked. The curriculum must constantly be changed and reassessed to reflect these transformations and society's changing self-awareness.

We have to reaffirm the presence of the curriculum's constituents—the diverse social groupings that the curriculum claims to be bringing to students' attention—and at the same time be clear about the particular university institutionalization of intellectual representation. In other words, the issue is not just what people, cultures and expressions are going to be given presence in curricula, but how are these curricula going to be organized into the overall social structure? The struggle isn't over when students learn about repressed or underrepresented groups, but continues in the effort to return academic knowledge to the larger community which sustains the university.

The Harvard curriculum gains its political and economic meaning from its institutionalization in a famous and influential university. The question of the value of a course must be framed both in terms of the information being articulated and where and how the formulated knowledge is going to be deployed. Understood in this way, the projects to create more diverse and inclusive curricula must be supplemented by projects which aim at determining how that knowledge is going to be reintegrated into society. This project is one which should both democratize the university as an institution as well as contribute to creating counter institutions, decentralizing the intellectual production of society. In more concrete terms, U.S. society will have to develop labor and community organizations which are capable of supporting technical and cultural production, not just bureaucratic apparatuses. One can get an impressionistic sense of what this might mean by comparing U.S. cultural production with European and Latin American. One thing clearly missing in the United States are forums within the labor movement for formulating and giving voice to positions independent of the news media and the Republican and Democratic parties.

The decentralization of intellectual production is a project of labor and various communities as well as of students and teachers. In giving it clear priority on the campus political agenda, however, students and faculty do not arrogate to themselves an unrealistic role as evangelists of the oppressed classes. Rather, the project lets them affirm their position in society as agents who can effectively help democratize intellectual production. It doesn't require a simple leveling of the distinction between various social activities. If the division of mental and physical labor is wrong, it doesn't disappear when activists ignore the distinction. If the call for more radical social transformation seems pressing, still the democratization of the academy remains a direct way that students and faculty can contribute. All too often, radicalism on campus transforms itself into despair, as though the very intellectuality of the academic isolated her or him from society. But a broad strategy of academic decentralization doesn't imply that issues of intellectual representation, of values and ethics, of science and society, of literature and arts, must take second place to the battle on the assembly line. Rather, it concretely locates such issues in the schema of society's reproduction, and thus invites practical and direct participation in formulating how to give them democratic institutional moorings. The current struggle over the content and teaching of curriculum concerns the internal democratization of the university. The supplemental step should take the democratic process outward and move the university into the community.

Part VI
Strategies
for Transformation

The Progressive Student Heritage

Zachary Robinson

Student Politics: A Long Tradition

Student politics of the 1960s grew out of and had a powerful impact on the off-campus movements of that decade, affirming the ideal of direct participatory democracy. Students became civil rights workers. African-American students from many universities initiated the anti-segregation lunch counter sit-ins. Students fought against the nuclear arms race and for an end to the Vietnam War. As student political action reached a crescendo in the late 1960s, the official commissions to investigate "the crisis on the campuses" multiplied. In 1969, over 400 police violently raided a Harvard administration building which had been occupied by approximately 200 students protesting ROTC and community displacement by Harvard expansion. During the wave of strikes that swept college campuses in the spring of 1970 after Nixon's announcement of the U.S. invasion of Cambodia, the National Guard at Kent State University in Ohio and the highway police at Jackson State University in Mississippi undertook armed intervention, killing six students and wounding nearly twenty others. In the dramatic events of the 1960s, the student movement achieved an unequalled degree of social influence and recognition.

But the extraordinary presence of the 1960s student movement should not eclipse the historic unity of the movement, a continuous presence on the U.S. university campus since the early 1900s. Recalling roots in such Harvard figures as Ralph Waldo Emerson, Henry David Thoreau, Sam Adams and John Reed, a former Harvard student wrote, "The Harvard tradition, I believe, resides today not in the *Crimson* and not in the select clubs and not in the Board of Overseers and not in its imposing plant and not in its dear ivy-clad walls but in its radical student movement, the radical student movement and its allies among the faculty." This statement is challenging in its invocation of tradition, all the more so for the time it was written. It appeared in the December 1936 edition of the *Harvard Communist*.

In 1906 the Harvard Socialist Club was organized as a chapter of the Intercollegiate Socialist Society, affiliated to the Socialist Party, marking the beginning of the organized student movement at Harvard. Four years after its first meeting, the Harvard Socialist Club grew to nearly 100 members. Students have remained organized and active ever since then. They fought for women's suffrage and peace before World War I and for the freedom of Sacco and Vanzetti in the 1920s. Students organized for peace and the basic social guarantees won in the 1930s. They fought against fascism in the Spanish Civil War and in World War II. In the late 1940s, Harvard students worked for the Progressive Party presidential campaign of Henry Wallace. In the 1950s, they worked for peace in Korea. The student activists of the 1960s, 1970s and 1980s continued this social commitment, making it a permanent feature of the modern university in the United States.

Despite the richness of its historical experience, the student movement has had difficulty in maintaining awareness of its heritage. School texts fragment, distort and often omit the history of progressives in the United States. The student movement itself has at times blanked out parts of its own history in the heat of ideological struggle. But conscious appreciation of tradition is a valuable political asset and a precondition for the establishment of a stable identity.

The Material Roots of the Student Movement

The existence of the student movement through eighty-odd years, 20 student generations, makes it a campus institution. A key task for movement historians is to identify what continually regenerates organized politicization among students. The point is not to find out what leads an individual Harvard student to "get radicalized"; rather, it is to locate the student movement in the broader institutional dynamic of the University, to uncover its institutional roots. Three interrelated facets of the modern university in society condition the existence of the student movement: the university has become a major *formulator* of technology, policy and ideology; it has become a *mass institution* both in number and in social cross-section; and it has come to wield *social impact* in its relations with other institutions.

The pre-twentieth century U.S. university was a cross between a secular monastery and a finishing school for the privileged classes.

But the exigencies of industrial development in the United States led the university to assume an active role both in rigorous study of modern society and in direct involvement with the course of its development.[1] To fulfill this active role, to become a major formulator of policy and technology, a special kind of consciousness of society had to develop in the university. The world had to be seen both in its "hard realities," independent of the individual will, and in its possibilities for organizing change and unfolding development. The new attitude toward the world engendered by the university's role as formulator of policy did not fully supplant the ancient humanism of academe. Although the class structure of the social system creates limiting ideological pressures, foundations formed in the university for critical thought beyond dreamy aspiration: social policy was seen to be *made*; it was not simply a given.

When a rapidly industrializing society demanded the services of a new and modern U.S. university, it made students aware of the political issues of that society. These developments were bound to have a stimulating effect on a university movement: articulating consciousness is the *trade* of student and professor. A portion of the students saw social inequities and acted according to their conscience. The Harvard Socialist Club was organized just after the turn of the century and remained a vital force on campus for some years.

The evolution of the modern university did not occur without a political struggle. Currently at Harvard, the issue is joined in the struggle for affirmative action, financial aid, and the new Clerical and Technical Workers Union. The general issue of expanding the opportunity of higher education to a broader cross-section of the population was also a major interest of the student movement at the end of the 1930s and beginning of the 1940s. In 1938, the *Harvard Communist*, arguing for expanded enrollment and financial aid, quoted Roosevelt's Secretary of the Interior, Harold Ickes: "Education is an indispensable tool of democracy in combatting fascism 'even in America.'" The CIO and the AFL, interested in promoting democracy in the United States as well as in raising the social wage of labor, concurred on this point. Harvard resisted. It refused government-administered student aid in the middle of the Great Depression, one of only four colleges to do so.

In spite of institutional resistance, political pressure at the end of World War II intersected with the need to reabsorb the multitude of returning veterans; the university provided a way station. Growing economic need ensured the trend: increasing numbers of young people of diverse ethnicity and national origin, socioeconomic class, and gender were called into the ranks of the student body to receive training necessary for skilled jobs. U.S. higher education embarked on a program of popularization. In the mid-1930s, there were one million university students. Now there are nearly twenty million.

As a mass institution, the university mirrors aspects of society. Certain general social conflicts are reproduced inside the university, transforming it as they are played out. For example, the Afro-American Studies Department is unique among its sister departments at Harvard in being the direct result of determined student struggle in the late 1960s, a struggle which had behind it the historic force of the civil rights movement. The Women's Studies Department, recently formed at Harvard, similarly demonstrates the will of the University's mass base to see all of itself reflected in its institutional environment. In the contemporary period, universities have developed Trade Union, Industrial Relations, or Labor History programs. The relation of these programs to the labor movement and to students of working class background poses complex questions which remain to be resolved.

The modern mass university is shaped through institutional division of labor in a technologically advanced economy and by the complexity of modern affairs of state. But the university exercises reciprocal effect in these spheres. The development in the mid-1940s of nuclear weaponry in and around university laboratories is a striking case in point. The accumulation of enormous financial reserves by the nation's major universities and their resultant economic power is another case in point. No longer can the university's relations with other institutions be considered vague or passive. It is impossible to overestimate the galvanizing effect of the contest over how the university is to be embedded in the network of social relations. This contest lay at the heart of the resurgence in anti-nuclear politics of the Harvard student movement after McCarthyism, and it continues to be seen in the divestiture movement sit-ins of the 1970s and 1980s. The noble motto *Veritas* no longer suffices to characterize the social workings of Harvard. The knowledge pursued here is now clearly bound to a social responsibility by the connections it maintains with other institutions, particularly the military.

The university exists at an important social conjuncture, manifest in the type of social consciousness engendered in an institution which formulates policy and technology and at the same time has an ethical, humanist current: the internal struggles of the mass-based institution which mirror general social struggle and the inter-institutional relations. Between healthy conflict and integration into academe, the student movement takes the place guaranteed it by the very institutional dynamic of the university. U.S. academe has been assimilated to its role in the economic and state organs of modern society, assuming a particularly concentrated form at Harvard. Almost as if to balance, both the American Student Union (ASU) of the 1930s and the Students for a Democratic Society (SDS) of the 1960s at one point had their largest chapters at Harvard (each peaking at around 300). The student movement cannot be "weeded out" as though it resulted from some sort of subversive artifice. The student movement is an organic element of the University.

The 1930s—Unity in Diversity

The 1930s saw industrial unionism come into its own with a wave of strikes and the formation of the Congress of Industrial Organizations (CIO). The fight against Jim Crow opened up. Americans won for themselves a New Deal in the same decade that many other countries fell to fascism in the wake of worldwide depression. The urgent political demands of this epoch unified the various progressive student organizations and drew them out for the first time into a fully ramified national student movement which entered in a programmatic way into the country's general democratic struggle. For the first time also, students campaigned to directly shape their university. As the student movement prepares to enter now into another period of major social change, it will again face precisely these issues of programmatic unity, organizational development sufficient to reflect the diversity of the student body, coalition with the other popular forces in the country, and its unique opportunity to define the university. Much of current relevance can be gleaned from this first successful experience of the 1930s student movement.

The Harvard Student Union (HSU) was the Harvard affiliate of the American Student Union (ASU), mainstay of the 1930s student movement. The HSU coalesced from the other progressive student organizations which predated it on campus. The Socialist Club, first organized in 1906, later dissolved into the Student League for Industrial Democracy (SLID), to which the SDS of the 1960s can trace its roots through its parent organization, the League for Industrial Democracy.

The Liberal Club, founded in 1919, came from a group of alumni who, after World War I, were interested in liberalizing the Board of Overseers and Harvard social science education. In its early years it was an eclectic discussion group, attracting large audiences to talks by such people as Professor Robert Foerster on the factory occupations in Italy, a Korean student on the Korean independence movement, Samuel Gompers of the AFL, J. T. Doran of the IWW, A. J. Muste on the labor movement, Elizabeth Gurley Flynn of the Communist Party on the Sacco-Vanzetti case, and representatives of the Republican, Democratic, Farmer-Labor, and Socialist Parties.

"A new student movement has begun in American Colleges," the National Student League (NSL), student ally of the Communist Party, announced to the Harvard campus in a letter of April 30, 1932 by Alan Lomax.[2]

> Its program is definitely Marxist. It examines critically the culture of capitalism and finds it wanting. Its definite objective...finds expression in the fight for academic freedom for student and instructor, abolition of the R.O.T.C., full social and political equality for Negroes and other minorities and many other issues vital to students...Our program includes creation of discussion groups, publication of a critical magazine, activity along the whole cultural front...and active participation in the industrial conflicts and workers' struggles around us.

The SLID joined with the NSL in organizing a peace demonstration on the steps of Widener Library in November 1933.

In the spring of 1934, the Boston branch of the NSL, in coalition with the SLID, called for an anti-war conference involving students at Harvard, MIT, and Tufts. The NSL *Anti-War Bulletin* of March 28, 1934 warned,

> We have moved into the same charged atmosphere that prevailed just before 1914...Sooner or later, these mounting antagonisms will burst into war. It will be impossible for any great power to stay out...We students will have our decision to make. It cannot be for war...Students form an integral part of the war machine. We are cast for the role of officers, technicians, and propagandists. We are expected to perform docilely our allotted share in transmuting blood into gold...Our concerted action can throw a monkey wrench into the war machine.

This conference began organizing a national Student Peace Week to begin on April 6, the anniversary of U.S. entry into World War I.

The Student Peace Week culminated in a Peace Strike on April 13, 1934. Among the demands: abolish ROTC. Harvard students were called on to boycott class from 11 a.m. to noon that day. About 200 students responded. By 1936, 350,000 students went out for the third annual national student Peace Strike. Eight annual Peace Strikes formed a central part of the 1930s student movement.

At the time of the first Peace Strike in 1934, the Liberal Club amended its constitution to commit it to activism. The following year, the Liberal Club and the Harvard Peace Society joined with the NSL and the SLID to organize the spring 1935 Harvard Peace Strike. By the fall of 1935, these four groups felt the need for "one single body on the campus devoted to public affairs," and the Harvard Student Union was launched. Its motto, according to the 1938 prospectus, was: "Think as men of action; and act as men of thought."

The newly formed HSU sailed straight into its first debate. In order to affiliate to the ASU, the HSU had to vote to accept the basic platform of the national organization. But the Peace Society was apprehensive over its multi-issue character. This cost the HSU the participation of the Avukah Society, a Jewish student group, which refused to join unless the anti-discrimination plank was endorsed. Within weeks, this plank and the whole ASU platform won endorsement, and the HSU affiliated to the ASU, which grew to an organization of 20,000 members nationally.

While the Peace Strikes brought the various student groups together, the HSU was oriented politically by the yearly adoption of a brief program formulated by the membership at an annual convention. These programs "condemned discrimination against racial, religious, and political minorities," supported current human needs legislation, and generally took the position: "Because we want to keep America out of war, we pledge ourselves to make our government a force for peace; because fascism would destroy our generation, we rededicate ourselves to the struggle for democracy." These yearly programs were elaborated in resolutions which dealt with current political events: The HSU stand against discrimination was taken up by its Civil Liberties Committee in opposing the House Un-American Activities Committee. In spring 1941, the HSU and other campus groups, including the *Crimson*, protested against the benching of the Harvard lacrosse team's black player during its match with the Navy's segregated team. Two weeks later, the embarrassed Corporation issued a statement against racial discrimination; the policy of benching black team members when playing against segregated teams was ended. The peace plank was accompanied by a demand for lifting the U.S. trade embargo against the Spanish Republic and instituting a boycott on Japan, and as the threat of world war drew nearer, a demand for international collective security arrangements against the fascist threat.

The HSU program was carried out in several committees, which operated more or less autonomously under the general direction of the HSU Executive Council. (In fact the HSU Executive Council, in voting to affiliate with the ASU, "reserved complete local autonomy.") A review of the committees active in the late 1930s gives an idea of the broad scope of the HSU's political involvement and its exceptionally high degree of organization.

Some HSU committees functioned primarily to foster left-liberal discussions: the Unemployment, Foreign Affairs, Socialized Medicine and Public Health Committees, and an active Speakers Bureau. The HSU devoted sustained attention to campus cultural life, staging through its Student Union Theater several productions of current progressive drama, including Blitzstein's *The Cradle Will Rock*, Odets's *Waiting for Lefty*, MacLeish's *The Fall of the City*, and, with the help of Leonard Bernstein, an adaptation of Aristophanes's *Peace*.

The Debate Committee played a crucial role in the Student Union. With cooperation from the *Crimson* and the Harvard Debating Council, it created the Harvard Congress, carrying political debate from inside the Student Union to non-members. The Debate Committee also helped to assure internal democratic process. But in an organization as broad as the HSU, encompassing members of the Young Communist League (YCL—established at Harvard in 1934) as well as traditional liberals, sharp political differences (on the 1940 Soviet invasion of Axis Finland, for example) were inevitable. The Debate Committee effectively served to turn what could have been disruptive internal political tension into an affirmative feature of this pluralistic organization.

The other committees of the HSU were primarily devoted to more direct action. These were the Peace Strike, Housing, Practical Politics, Labor, College Problems, and Aid to Spain Committees. For many, the struggle of the Spanish Republic against Franco and his allies Mussolini and Hitler symbolized both the agony and the aspiration of the times. The Aid to Spain Committee collected several thousand dollars toward medical supplies for the Republic. It showed movies (e.g., *Spanish Earth*), held lectures, and prominently displayed a photograph of an ambulance it bought for the Republic, emblazoned with the good wishes of Harvard students. Six Harvard students, members of the YCL, volunteered for combat in the Abraham Lincoln Brigade. One, Eugene Bronstein, a graduate student in philosophy, was killed in an aerial bombardment by Mussolini's air force near Brunete, Spain. (His name does not appear among the names of Harvard's war dead in the many campus memorials.)

The work of the Practical Politics Committee overlapped with the work of the Labor Committee, the College Problems Committee, and the Housing Committee, which undertook a survey of the dilapidated dwellings in Charlestown for the Metropolitan Boston Housing Association. The Practical Politics Committee was active in local city council elections, running candidates in Medford and Cambridge. The Committee lobbied the Massachusetts Legislature for the establishment of a tuition-free state college, reduction in Massachusetts sales tax, a plan to tax Harvard, civil service reform, on behalf of Labor's Non-partisan League, against redbaiting by Cambridge politicians, and for progressive politics in general throughout Massachusetts.

The Labor Committee was one of the most active of the Student Union committees. In the fall of 1936, it surveyed working conditions at the major factories near Cambridge in preparation for union organizing. The HSU also sent out carloads of students every Sunday for two months to canvass at workers' homes for the union drives then underway in New England textile mills. In the winter and spring of 1936-37, 30 HSU members canvassed for the United Rubber Workers of America in their drive to organize the Hood Rubber Co. plant in Watertown. Nine were arrested in March 1937 for illegally distributing union literature and later freed by a sympathetic judge. In fall 1937, HSU members went to work for the AFL organizing drives among the garage workers and department store workers of Boston. The Labor Committee was also active in the AFL unionization drive of dining hall workers on the Harvard campus. In this student climate, Harvard would have found it impossible to offer academic credit to student strike-breakers, as it did during the New England textile strikes in Lawrence two decades earlier.

As the "house system" of dormitories formed at Harvard, the College Problems Committee organized for and obtained associate membership status for those commuting students (primarily from lower- and middle-income families) who desired it. Its major struggle was in the Walsh-Sweezy case. Drs. J. Raymond Walsh and Alan R. Sweezy were economics instructors at Harvard who were Marxists and were very popular among students. They were also leading organizers of the Cambridge Union of University Teachers (CUUT), which was a chapter of the American Federation of Teachers but never made a drive for recognition as a collective bargaining unit. The CUUT maintained an advisory relation with the Student Union, and was active in local labor politics. In a February 1937 open hearing, the CUUT, led by Walsh, challenged former Harvard President Lowell's position on an amendment to the child labor laws. During the spring vacation of 1937, Walsh and Sweezy were informed by the administration that they had been given two-year terminating appointments instead of the usual reappointment without prejudice. The administration had begun a new policy of faculty appointment with a basically fiscal rationale and professing concern for faculty members to whom they felt they could not grant tenure.

Student response was rapid. A student investigatory committee was formed to determine if the political views of the two instructors had prejudiced their tenure. A similar faculty committee exonerated the administration, but a letter to President Conant from a Teachers' Union member [3] detailing internal political discussion leads one to wonder whether the union wasn't being closely monitored by the administration and whether the new appointment policy wasn't being used against the union leaders. The HSU College Problems Committee organized student support for Walsh and Sweezy around a petition to the president and Board of Overseers. Despite student and faculty opinion, the University did not change its stance.

Students became aware of their disenfranchisement on educational policy. What they called the "star system" of faculty appointment, with its political implications, became entrenched. Only those who had already made a stellar reputation would receive a faculty appointment.[4] In 1940, students formed the Committee to Save Harvard Education which, together with the Teachers' Union, lobbied unsuccessfully for this faculty appointment policy to apply at most to new appointees. In 1941, students again took up the struggle on behalf of Professors Houghton and Potter of History and Literature, popular among students for their critical approach, who received terminating appointments. In an article in May 1941 on this struggle in the *Harvard Guardian*, a liberal student publication, Robert Seidman noted that

> Our university now exists in a democratic society now being attacked [by fascism] from within and without. In such a period, surely the role of every liberal institution is to propagate by example the ideal toward which the majority of American citizens are striving. If Harvard is to fulfill its function, it should start by the democratic ordering of its own internal life. It cannot come from the Corporation or the Faculty, considering their

current composition. It must come from the student body as a result of insistent demands and pressure. If Harvard students are to maintain and improve the education for which they are spending four years of their youth they must demand and obtain some form of student participation in the formation of educational policy.

As well as taking up the issue of faculty appointment decisions, the College Problems Committee considered President Conant's 1938 report to the Board of Overseers, which dealt with the question of American higher education. Conant had earlier rejected a FERA-administered student loan program and NYA work-study aid as part of his call for a "strict limitation on the size of the student body in the leading schools." The employment office had cooperated with employers who wished to discriminate against black or Jewish students. Student protests against this elitism and bigotry contributed to Conant's pledge in the above report to "recruit from all economic levels of society" by means of an extended financial aid program. In a victory for the student movement, Harvard finally accepted the NYA funds in 1941.

Jolted by economic collapse and the threat of fascism, millions of men and women, young and old, from every ethnicity and all walks of life, immersed themselves in civic activity in the 1930s and 1940s. Many of the fundamental means and concepts of the democratic struggle in the United States were developed then, especially the politics of popular coalition and progressive programmatic unity. The U. S. student movement, in full blossom for the first time, can be proud to have made a pioneering contribution of lasting value.

The Late 1960s—Student Impact

The spring and summer of 1968 brought events that shook the country. Martin Luther King, Jr., who was tying together the struggles against racism, poverty and the Vietnam war, was assassinated in April. The same month saw an anti-war strike of perhaps a million high school and college students, and the student takeover of Columbia University buildings in protest over University war-related research and expansion into the surrounding African-American community. Robert Kennedy and Eugene McCarthy were running reform campaigns in the Democratic presidential primary. These campaigns involved busloads of Harvard students. Kennedy was assassinated just after winning the California primary. McCarthy, facing death threats, soon abandoned his own campaign. Then came the August Democratic convention in Chicago with the accompanying anti-war protest and Mayor Daley's police riot. The 1960s student movement entered the peak of its campus activism.

Three political campaigns, each involving a substantial majority of the student body, are crucial to an understanding of Harvard activism between 1968 and 1973: the student strike of April 1969 which grew out of the struggle against ROTC, the struggle to establish the Afro-American Studies Department, and the unionization drive among graduate students and teaching fellows.

ROTC and the Strike

In the fall of 1968-69, students began a campus debate on the continued presence of ROTC at Harvard. SDS held demonstrations. The Harvard Undergraduate Council and the Student-Faculty Advisory Committee (SFAC—formed in the wake of the 1967 blockade and sit-in against on-campus recruitment by Dow Chemical) passed resolutions calling on Harvard to demote ROTC to extracurricular status. The Faculty Council was under pressure, its liberal credentials at stake. Students, excluded from its meetings, demonstrated at two of them. In February 1969, the Faculty Council finally passed the SFAC resolution on ROTC. Two weeks later, President Pusey announced, "In the Corporation's view it would be shortsighted in the extreme if academic institutions were now to withdraw their cooperation from the ROTC program..."[5] Shortly after, Dean of the College Glimp began renegotiating an ROTC contract with the Pentagon, contravening the Faculty Council resolution. Students continued their demonstrations.

On Wednesday, April 9, 1969, just after spring break, SDS led an occupation of the University Hall administration building. Deans were escorted out and about 200 students filled the building. The administration moved quickly. A Harvard professor, Archibald Cox, had chaired the commission appointed by Columbia University to investigate its 1968 student "disturbances." The administration felt that it had learned the lessons of Columbia. By five o'clock the next morning, over 400 police marched into Harvard Yard. Some removed their identification badges. Students set off fire alarms in nearby dormitories to gain witnesses. Two minutes after Dean Glimp gave a five-minute ultimatum, the police charged. Though other doors stood open, one door was smashed with a police battering ram, presaging what was to happen inside. The skull-breaking violence of the bust and the arrogance of the administration stunned Harvard. The thousand students who witnessed the raid went to the steps of Widener Library to decide their response: Strike!

Over the next few days, students gathered for intense discussion: what would be the program of their strike? The Association of African and Afro-American Students (AAAAS) during the last year had been pressing for an Afro-American Studies Department at Harvard. Concerned to bring this issue to the strike, they prevailed upon the SDS membership to ratify, over the sectarian objections of certain SDS leaders, a demand for a meaningful Black Studies program. The six SDS demands, passed in its April 8 meeting, became eight: the first three relating to Harvard ROTC, the next three on Harvard expansion into Cambridge and Boston, the seventh demanding amnesty for the students who had occupied University Hall, and the eighth for Black Studies. Self-described "moderate" student leaders, the current and former chairs of SFAC, the president of the Young Democrats and a past president of student council, among others, had been engaged in negotiations with the Administration during the previous week, but found them "nothing more than an ineffectual charade."[6] They drafted a four-point proposal which read in part,

> Although it was SDS which actually sat in, it was the Corporation's attitude on ROTC and on expansion which created the situation which led to that sit-in. The Corporation must represent the University community, and not the business community. It must be restructured to reflect the desires of the community: students, teaching fellows, and the Faculty.[7]

There were tensions among the student groups. On Saturday, April 12, a group of graduate students met and formed the Committee on Radical Structural Reform (CRSR) with this analysis of the situation: "the issues which SDS had raised...were not being explained well enough to gain the support they needed to win."[8] They drew up a five-point program. This program explicated the terse SDS demands, drawing on research by students in the Graduate School of Design for the section on Harvard's expansion into residential neighborhoods. It included detailed sections on disciplinary action and on restructuring University decision-making procedures. It demanded that the University establish an Afro-American Studies program, and, in accordance with the AAAAS, further stipulated that students be included in determining its plan. Over the weekend, their proposal won support among moderates, AAAAS, and to some extent SDS. On Monday, April 14, ten thousand students gathered in

Harvard's Soldiers Field stadium, giving an overwhelming mandate to the strike and to the CRSR demands.

Within the next eight days, the Faculty Council passed a resolution to clarify and strengthen its earlier position on ROTC, and a resolution written by AAAAS to create the Afro-American Studies Department with student participation. In May, ROTC announced its plans to cancel its Harvard program.

The other student demands did not fare as well. The Faculty Council set up the Committee of Fifteen, ostensibly an experiment in restructuring, with token student participation. But its purpose became clear. As one faculty member said at the meeting where it was formed, "There is no doubt in my mind that the action of the student group, particularly of its leaders, who perpetrated that physical attack on the university should be punished...They should be expelled from the university."[9] SDS described the committee as a "firing squad"; student participation was irrelevant. The CRSR repudiated the committee. In May, when nearly all of the SDS leadership was indicted, a student boycott was called. This student boycott against the Committee of Fifteen and its successor disciplinary committee, the Committee on Rights and Responsibilities, has lasted continuously and with nearly complete unanimity since then.[10] The University's attitude toward expansion changed somewhat when the Faculty Council endorsed the Wilson report on the local housing problem. But the CRSR concluded in its four-point critique of the report, "It makes no provision for community control in the decision-making process."[11]

AAAAS and Afro-American Studies

The struggle led by the AAAAS for an Afro-American Studies Department began in the academic year 1967-68. Several months of discussion, negotiation, and an April 1968 AAAAS demonstration outside of Harvard's official memorial service for Martin Luther King, Jr. prompted the appointment of the Rosovsky Committee, which recommended the creation of a Standing Committee for Afro-American Studies. On the evening of April 9, 1969, during the University Hall occupation, the Standing Committee announced its program for the Afro-American Studies undergraduate degree. It would require combination with one allied field; the program would not have normal independent departmental status. AAAAS made copies of the program and issued it as a leaflet on April 10. It announced, "Brothers and Sisters—we are being sold out!" Their concern over that morning's bust and their particular concern over the fate of Afro-American Studies at Harvard drew AAAAS into the student strike. After the April 9 Standing Committee announcement they recognized that binding student participation was essential: "The issue of restructuring is very important to us as Black students. The reason we're in the mess we are now, the reason the Standing Committee on Afro-American Studies was able to hand us that piece of bullshit they did a few nights ago is because they had the sole power to decide what Afro-American Studies was going to be."[12] After a complex series of confrontations and negotiations, AAAAS prevailed. The quest for recognition of African-American Studies as a distinct and legitimate academic enterprise, a struggle brought to prominence during the heated political battles of the 1930s in the Harlem public schools and in New York's City College, finally reached fruition in the elite layers of academe.[13] Harvard University, long a bastion of racist exclusion, was compelled for the first time to deal in a substantive way with the historic demand of African-Americans for inclusion.

A Teaching Fellows' Union

Harvard graduate students conducted unionization drives in the spring of 1967 and the spring of 1972. These drives were part of a unionization movement among university teaching fellows (which at campuses such as the University of Wisconsin resulted in a recognized union)[14] and worked with the forerunners of the current union drives among campus clerical and technical workers.[15] In the spring of 1967, the Federation of Teaching Fellows was created "to represent Harvard's more than 900 teaching fellows in the matter of salaries, and to provide them with a forum of expression on other issues of common interest." Although 500 teaching fellows signed its organizing petition, the Federation apparently fell dormant.

Five years later, in February 1972, Harvard announced a fiscal crisis and instituted financial cutbacks for graduate students. The Graduate Students and Teaching Fellows' Union (GSTFU) was formed within a month. Its membership quickly reached 1,000. The GSTFU pressed its demands in administrative committees and Faculty Council meetings. After two successful job actions (walkouts with 80 percent student boycotts) in spring 1972, and a strike in spring 1973, some cutbacks were eventually rescinded; however, the University never acceded to the full union demands.

The fall 1972 GSTFU draft program rounded out its structural politics: as well as demands related to salary and union recognition, it included a proposal for "an Educational Council with equal numbers of faculty, graduate students and undergraduate students [which] shall have final decision-making power on all matters of educational policy." It called on Harvard not to meet the GSTFU demands at the expense of either the pay rates of other University employees or undergraduate financial aid. The draft program also called for the elimination of discrimination in admissions, the establishment of day care services, and full budget disclosure to facilitate open and fair negotiation. Unfortunately, the GSTFU did not begin an NLRB certification drive until after it had lost its political momentum.

Strategic Considerations

The student movement of the 1960s never achieved the stable organizational form it had thirty years before. Nonetheless, in these three campus struggles, it is possible to discern a common strategic perspective. Between rhetorical pronouncements ranging from bland to hyperrevolutionary, students developed an unprecedentedly keen awareness of the institutional dynamic of the university. They sought to create institutional features important to them and to abolish those dominated by or serving other interests. They sought to democratize the university administrative apparatus by empowering various representative councils of students and faculty. They worked to change the relation of the university to the surrounding community and to the military.

On the other hand, the 1960s student movement's understanding of the issues of broader political coalition, of political party and state was severely limited. The institutional possibilities they envisioned, and in part realized, at the campus level were not properly projected at the level of larger social structures. The spontaneous experience of the student movement with these institutions deeply affected their political thinking. Students' most direct experience with issues of the state came in protest over abhorrent U.S. government policies in Vietnam and in the Third World generally. Their spontaneous experience was shaped at the hands of state troopers called in for the "bust." They saw military occupations of rioting ghettos. They were (and are) outraged at the university's supporting relation to the state war bureaucracies. The democratic (electorally representative) side of the state had not shown much promise to them either. Student experience with the possibilities in U.S. mass political parties came during leadership consensus in relentlessly prosecuted nuclear Cold War. It was marked by the debacle of the August 1968 Democratic Party National Convention in Chicago, where Mississippi Freedom Democratic Party delegates were not seated, and where Mayor Daley's rioting police eventually cracked heads in Eugene McCarthy's fifteenth floor Hilton Hotel campaign headquarters. Left and even centrist leaders had been assassinated. The imposing events of this historical moment assumed the quality of perpetuity for student activists unaware of the lessons of the Roosevelt years. The full dimensions of political party and state, a prime nexus of structural transformation, lay outside the purview of the otherwise powerfully elaborated structural politics of the student struggles of the late 1960s and early 1970s.

This limitation had practical consequences, even for student struggles carried out on the campus level. A radical left tendency in the GSTFU, expressing itself in the journal *Upstart*, inveighed against "those who, whatever the label for their politics, see the primary issue as one of developing and maintaining the organizational apparatus of a legally recognized union." Their complete misapprehension of the most basic issues of the state led them to reject "'legal' relations, being recognized as sole bargaining agent," a posture which was ultimately disastrous for their unionization drive. This retreat to defunct anarchism failed to elaborate any new relation to the state, which in any case persisted, and also appeared in caucuses in other teaching fellows' unions. Lacking an understanding of the state, the striking Harvard students of April 1969 were unable to appreciate the central role that institutions such as the Rent Control Board and the community development organizations would play in determining the relation of Harvard to the surrounding community. Instead of projecting a common terrain of struggle for community and student activists, for example in a representative regulatory body, the CRSR strike program focused on expropriating the Harvard Corporation in the name of the students, faculty, and alumni.

However problematic their ideological activity, the students who mobilized the political campaigns of 1968-72 left a legacy of institutional reforms, valuable in their own right, which enriched the political terrain for the continuing student movement. The new way in which students raised political issues and those issues which students newly politicized helped to rejuvenate the U.S. progressive forces.

From history forward

Today, student activists look to the Jesse Jackson campaign and the Rainbow Coalition, to the potential created for a resurgence of democracy in mass politics. A recent national student organizing conference at Rutgers University drew overflow participation. Student militancy in demanding divestiture of their universities' financial interests from apartheid has exposed as myth the notion that student sensibilities have somehow succumbed to "career concerns." Students have a renewed understanding of their power to transform the university. They have a renewed sense of purpose in the nation's political life.

At this time, the student movement must come to grips with its full tradition. Students must fill in the debilitating blank spots created in the polemics of a period now behind us. The student movement has a *living* heritage which indicates possibilities and bears the lessons of complementary moments. Student movement history bears as well the lessons of historical continuity. Its central issues have striking clarity: for peace and against the military abuses of the university, for a determined solidarity in democratic struggles, for a mass academe that educates from a full social cross-section and in representative number, for cultural reform and university restructuring. These issues, raised in the 1930s, resounded in the 1960s—how deeply they must be embedded in the student body and in the function of the university in the current epoch.

Notes

1. For a discussion of this history, see Ben Robinson's essay on Harvard's Core Curriculum.

2. Alan Lomax, with his father John, directed the WPA-funded American Folk Music Archive at the Library of Congress. Pete Seeger, fellow HSU member and noted political folksinger, had a fruitful collaboration with Lomax.

3. This letter is published in part in Richard Norton Smith, *The Harvard Century*.

4. The "star system," which holds little promise for Harvard's junior faculty, remains in place today despite sporadic and ineffectual attempts at reform by the administration.

5. Lawrence Eichel, et al., *The Harvard Strike*, Houghton Mifflin, Boston, 1970, Appendix.

6. *Ibid.*, p. 140.

7. *Ibid.*, p. 141.

8. *Ibid.*, p. 330.

9. *Ibid.*, p. 290.

10. Harvard's disciplinary system has recently undergone minor reform, prompted by student protest of disciplinary actions taken against anti-apartheid activists. Students demanded, among other things, that the accused have the right to an open hearing, and that the University disciplinary committee also include actions of the administration in its area of jurisdiction. These elementary demands were not met. There have been as yet no political cases tried under the new system.

11. Eichel, *op.cit*, p. 246.

12. Eichel, *op.cit*, p. 273.

13. For a discussion of this history in the context of Depression era politics, see Mark Naison, *Communists in Harlem During the Depression* (New York: Grove Press, 1984.)

14. The Teaching Fellows' Union at the University of Califormia, Berkeley, affiliated to District 65 of the UAW, received NLRB certification in the fall of 1988.

15. In April 1972, the journal *Upstart*, put out by a group of radical graduate students and junior faculty, reprinted two articles from the University of Wisconsin's teaching fellows' union. One raised the issue of unionizing unorganized university employees, including clerical and technical workers. (The other article from Wisconsin was by the radical caucus and expressed a view very similar to the views of the *Upstart* staff.) Clerical worker groups conducted joint rallies with the graduate students. It is also interesting to note that the Harvard Union of Clerical and Technical Workers took up a slogan of the teaching fellows' union, "You can't eat prestige."

Acknowledgements

I want to thank Professor John Parsons of MIT. This essay benefitted from the clarity of his patient comments, criticism and suggestions.

"Waiting for Derek"
The Divestment Struggle

Michael West

The issue of South Africa has been central to the progressive political movements of the 1970s and 1980s. In a work of manifest value to current student activists at Harvard, who today have little knowledge of these earlier struggles, Michael West documents the movement's responses to the strategic shifts of the Bok regime, the latter long on calls for national legislation and cosmetic palliatives but short on ending Harvard's own complicity with blood-soaked Pretoria.

West, a Harvard doctoral candidate recently based in Zimbabwe, completed his account in early 1987, shortly after divestment activism peaked. This is a sharply abridged and slightly updated version of his 45-page narrative, the main body of which has been replaced by a brief chronology. The 1987-88 school year represented a decline in South Africa protest; but some momentum has been revived through a coalition of students, labor, alumni, and community members, who on June 6, 1988 succeeded in occupying the offices of Harvard's hired legal guns, Ropes & Gray. Ropes & Gray attorney Thomas O'Donnell in particular serves as co-chair of Harvard's joint committee on divestment. On this occasion, Boston police ended up arresting 18 of the 45 occupiers. During the previous day at Yale, in contrast to the peaceful tactics of the divestment movement, a "conservative" alumnus stormed in and burned down a shanty constructed in protest against South Africa. Back in 1986 when Harvard students installed similar structures, a group of five alumni, two from the class of 1961, showed up after midnight on a Klansman-like mission from God, declaring that they would destroy the shanties. In the words of the class of 1961 ringleader, "If someone put a hut on my property, they'd wind up with a shotgun up their butt." Prompt intervention by a heroic Harvard policeman averted an ugly altercation.

Harvard continues to resist divestment on the grounds that the University pledges to take more humanitarian stands on shareholder resolutions than would regular corporate investors. The historical record raises doubts about this putative humanitarian vigilance. In a June 8, 1988 speech, Peter Wood, a member of the Harvard Board of Overseers, registered his own dissent, noting that of some 56 recent shareholder resolutions concerning South Africa, Harvard supported corporate management an incredible 53 times. Earlier, Harvard justified its stand by appealing to the Sullivan Principles; but when their author, the Rev. Leon Sullivan, called for corporations to cut all ties with South Africa after a nine-month final deadline, Harvard continued to backpedal. It shunted the issue from a Committee on Institutional Policy back to an Executive Committee and then to a joint committee of the Overseers and the Corporation, the last move provoking the Ropes & Gray occupation.

In December of 1988, perhaps in response to the pressure, Harvard announced that it would not divest, but that it would now vote routinely in favor of shareholder resolutions calling for corporate withdrawal from South Africa, unless given compelling reasons to do otherwise. Half of U.S. corporations in South Africa have already taken this step, but Harvard's leadership suggested that they were showing great courage in taking this stand. Wood himself was not impressed, remarking: "Some say this is a small step forward for John Harvard. I think he's shuffling his feet sideways, and he still hasn't stood up" (*Harvard Crimson*, December 13, 1988, p. 6). Meanwhile, in March 1989, Harvard-Radcliffe Alumni Against Apartheid (HRAAA) announced its nomination of Archbishop Desmond Tutu for election to the Harvard Board of Overseers. Tutu's subsequent triumph, as well as the previous battle to achieve representation on the Overseers, is documented in the essay by Chester Hartman and Robert Paul Wolff that follows West's narrative.

In a century that has witnessed the most diabolical outrages against human dignity, few issues have elicited greater universal disapproval than the South African system of apartheid. Political leaders the world over have condemned it. The United Nations has censured it as an affront to its Charter and established a special committee to work for its eradication. Given the transparency of the evil, it is not surprising that anti-apartheid agitation has emerged as the leading protest movement on U.S. college campuses in the 1980s. To many student activists, apartheid is the Vietnam of this decade. Mass movements require an immediate set of objectives and, for the anti-apartheid student activists, this has meant pressuring colleges and universities to divest their endowments from businesses operating in South Africa.

Yet divestment was not the only option available to the anti-apartheid movement. Student activists wishing to make a contribution toward the establishment of a new social order in South Africa could have chosen to concentrate on providing direct material support to the anti-apartheid liberation movements. However, this possibility was never seriously considered, primarily for three reasons.

First, divestment is a specific, simple, and clearly-defined objective that can be applied to any university with a portfolio that includes South Africa-related investments. For many student activists and potential activists, divestment is a much more tangible and obtainable policy than the overthrow of the apartheid regime, though many of these activists would be quick to endorse that as their ultimate goal. University administrators and governing boards are much closer—and indeed more malleable—targets than apartheid. Second, it is much easier to whip up moral indignation against university administrations for failing to divest than to bring around members of a university community to support a black liberation struggle in South Africa. It is one thing to get people to attend a pro-divestment rally or sign a petition. It is quite another to persuade them to make personal financial sacrifices in support of, for instance, a school run by the African National Congress in Tanzania, to say nothing of providing resources that might be used in carrying out military operations in South Africa. Third, it is probable that a great many campus activists have reservations about the efficacy and legitimacy of armed struggle to bring about an end to apartheid. Campus anti-apartheid movements are generally dominated by individuals and groups of liberal political persuasions who more or less operate within the bourgeois consensus of U.S. politics. Support for liberation movements, especially black liberation movements, that might be labelled as communist-inspired, even "terrorist," would leave the anti-apartheid movements vulnerable to redbaiting by their right-wing opponents.

One might also ask why it is that campus anti-apartheid activists have not attempted in any serious way to link their concerns to other domestic and foreign policy issues that have emerged in the 1970s and 1980s, such as the peace movement, the environmental movement, affirmative action, and Central America. The answer appears to be related to the insistence of the anti-apartheid movement—both on and off campus—on maintaining a minimum program so as to hold together the widest possible coalition around South Africa. Apartheid is one of the few issues in U.S. politics on which progressives have a clear political and moral advantage. Who needs cross-issue alliances, the anti-apartheid activists appear to be arguing, when even the Reagan administration has been forced to verbally denounce apartheid as politically indefensible and morally reprehensible.

Harvard's Stake in Apartheid

The wealthiest university in the United States, Harvard has an endowment of well over $5 billion, $163 million of which is currently invested in companies doing business in South Africa. This chapter represents a brief account of Harvard's policies on investment and a chronicle of past struggles for divestment.

The Foundation of Harvard's Investment Policy

The notion that institutional investment should serve ends other than those of dividend-making is a relatively new one. Consideration of responsible social investment as a viable option for the University's financial managers appears to have first gained currency at Harvard in 1970 with the publication of a pamphlet appropriately titled *Harvard and Money*. This pamphlet was the work of a governance committee established by then President Nathan Pusey to suggest ways of improving the University's administration. The committee concerned itself with the questions of whether Harvard had a responsibility for the social conduct of the companies in which it invested, whether it should invest in socially beneficial activities that do not offer immediate financial rewards, and who should decide these questions. The committee's own answers to these questions were steeped in ambivalence. Without denying that the University has social responsibilities outside of its academic functions, it affirmed strongly that "the preeminent task of Harvard remains the advancement of learning."

The authors of *Harvard and Money* looked askance at student-led attempts to influence the determination of the University's corporate policy. Indeed, the governance committee had been appointed largely because of student protests in support of "Campaign GM," a progressive stockholders campaign which involved Harvard. In its deliberations on social investment, the governance committee came up "against two hard political facts." The first of these was that students, "whose major institutional affiliation and only leverage on money other than their own is in the University," are the strongest supporters of social investment. The second "hard political fact" was that many alumni and faculty members who share the students' concerns about the social impact of Harvard's investments are equally opposed to the use of these investments to make political and moral statements. "And it is the alumni on whom Harvard depends for new money." Yet, the political dichotomy that this suggests between students on the one hand and alumni and faculty members on the other was probably false. A poll conducted by the *Harvard Bulletin* showed majority alumni support for Campaign GM, while the Faculty of Arts and Sciences (FAS) voted solidly, though in the official interpretation "perfunctorily," along the same lines.

In its conclusion, the governance committee in 1970 posed a set of seemingly rhetorical questions, the accumulated effect of which appears to argue against social investment. Many of these arguments are still used to oppose divestment from companies operating in South Africa, and so the relevant passages are worth quoting at length:

> What ethically defensible guidelines would permit one to score the relative "virtuousness" of the social conduct of a corporation in which Harvard owns stock? Can the University learn enough about the net social impact of the hundred odd companies in which it invests to make judgements that will neither be, nor seem to be, capricious? If it explicitly brands some companies ineligible on moral grounds, does not the University implicitly confer virtue on others whose stock it continues to hold?... Where Harvard's action is not likely to have real effect, should it make symbolic gestures for their own sake? Alternatively, can the University try to make a real difference, even when the size of its investment does not give it much leverage, by taking the lead in rallying other stockholders? What would be the consequences for the raising of new money, and, if quasi-political questions are involved, for Harvard's tax exemption?

Though it declined to answer any of these questions—many of which, in any case, appear to require little answering—the governance committee expressed the hope that the still deliberating Austin Committee would be more forthcoming.

Foundations II: The Austin Report (January 1971)

Whereas the governance committee was charged with examining the broad question of improving Harvard's administrative structure, the Austin Committee (named after its chairperson, Business Administration Professor Ralph Austin) had a more specific brief — namely, to look into and clarify the University's relationship with corporations. But the Austin Report posed similar questions and arrived at equally similar conclusions as those of *Harvard and Money*. Taken together, the findings and recommendations of these two documents continue to serve as the basis of Harvard's investment policy, particularly its policy toward corporations with South African holdings. The case that President Derek Bok has been making against divestment throughout his eighteen-year tenure has only summarized, or at best elaborated upon, arguments first proffered at the beginning of the 1970s.

The Austin Report is predicated on certain "basic, if not axiomatic," assumptions. Among these are the propositions that Harvard "must remain, before anything else, a center of free inquiry"; that, as an institution, it should remain neutral on all political and social questions, except those that violate fundamental rights, such as free speech, individual political rights, and racial discrimination; that if it departs "from the essentially neutral pursuit of truth," Harvard (and universities in general) run the risk of outside political intervention in their own internal affairs; that the "University is a charity" and its benefactors might object to academic administrators using their money for purposes for which they did not intend or might not support; and that it is justified in entering the political arena only in defense of matters affecting its "classic interest qua University," like government attempts to limit academic freedom and public financing for higher education.

In deciding which stock to buy, the Report suggested that Harvard "should strive fundamentally for maximum return," only making exceptions "on the basis of the University's duty to the more or less immediately surrounding community"—an allusion to Harvard's responsibility to help find housing for families displaced by its expansion policy in Cambridge and Boston. In deciding which stock not to buy, the Report was again willing to make exceptions to its maximization-of-return policy. Yet even in these instances, "investment purity" was an "elusive ideal," for corporations "that offend on some score [say, business contacts with South Africa] may have a particularly good record in another respect [say, nondiscriminatory hiring practices at home]." Even in the case for sanctioning South Africa, "arguments can be marshalled on the other side..." The Report envisaged instances in which it would be appropriate for Harvard to vote its stock "in favor of change for the symbolic effect of a great university's taking a position on a social problem," but it opposed a more activist investor role where Harvard would place shareholder resolutions or join other tax-exempt organizations "in policing the conduct of business corporations." On the question of who should determine portfolio policy, the Austin Report was unambiguous: "The Corporation should ultimately decide all questions that affect the University's investments and its role as a stockholder." As for student attempts to influence Harvard's investment decisions, the Report was even more scornful than *Harvard and Money*. It declared that "operating expenses must not be subjected to financially unrealistic strictures or carping by the unsophisticated or by special interest groups."

"Carping by the Unsophisticated": A Chronology of the Anti-Apartheid Struggle at Harvard

Spring 1972: Student groups demand the sale of Harvard's $21 million investment in the Gulf Oil Company because of its involvement in the then Portuguese colony of Angola. In mid-April two student groups, the Pan-African Liberation Committee (PALC) and the Harvard-Radcliffe Association of African and Afro-American Students (AFRO) issue an "ultimatum" to the Corporation to divest its Gulf stock. The Corporation refuses and the students respond by occupying the president's Massachusetts Hall offices for a week in defiance of a court injunction, ending their occupation only after the University threatened to press contempt of court charges against them. This incident, accompanied by much campus turmoil, is a major factor in the establishment of the Advisory Committee on Shareholder Responsibility (ACSR) and the Corporation Committee on Shareholder Responsibility (CCSR). Shareholder responsibility committees had been established earlier at other universities, such as Yale, Dartmouth, MIT, Princeton, and Stanford.

1977: Founding of the Southern Africa Solidarity Committee (SASC). SASC emerges as the single most consistent group organizing pro-divestment demonstrations and other activities in the late 1970s and throughout the 1980s.

1978: The 1978 ACSR Report rejects calls—including those from some of the committee members—for complete divestment in South Africa-related companies, mainly on the grounds that this would involve "significant financial costs to the University" and possibly "alienate certain groups or individuals on whom the University must rely for future support, financial or otherwise." The ACSR's calculations of the "costs" of divestment are subsequently challenged by Nobel laureate, economist Kenneth J. Arrow.

Spring 1979: A proposal to name a library at the John F. Kennedy School of Government after a wealthy donor, Charles Engelhard, who made much of his fortune from the gold mines of South Africa, leads to a major protest led by SASC, the Black Students Association (BSA), and other groups. A march on the school by 300 people, following a "teach in" on the University's investment policy toward South Africa, provokes school officials to retreat from naming the library after Engelhard, though they were unwilling to cancel other previous commitments with the Engelhard Foundation. The Kennedy School decides to put up a plaque declaring that the library was built with the foundation's money.

The status of the Afro-American Studies Department also became attached to divestment protests and the South African question in the spring of 1979. The struggle is over whether Afro-Am would retain its status as a department or be downgraded to a program. Rallying under the twin slogans of "Harvard out now" and "Give a damn, Save Afro-Am," protesters called for a boycott of classes on April 23. The boycott is relatively successful, with approximately half of all undergraduates staying away from classes.

Nearly 150 FAS and Medical School faculty members, as well as some 3,000 undergraduates, signed a SASC-circulated petition urging Harvard to divest.

Just back from Washington as a member of the Carter administration, Government Professor Joseph Nye in May 1979 ridicules the divestment movement "as a case of academic hubris," especially for their quixotic notion that "the effects of some intellectuals sitting in one part of the world was going to strongly affect events in another part of the world." Warmly received by official Harvard, Nye's argument is a straw man: no anti-apartheid activist would suggest that divestment by Harvard will bring down the apartheid regime.

Spring 1982: Hardliners within the Corporation, apparently led by University Treasurer George Putnam, who is bitterly angry that Harvard suddenly sold its Citibank securities, seek to overturn the policy of automatic divestment from banks that make new loans to South Africa. Confronted by a crowd of over 300 students, the ACSR votes unanimously to keep the ban, a recommendation eventually accepted by the Corporation.

Spring 1983: Despite the immediate setback, the Corporation's hardliners win a subsequent victory, when in early April 1983 the Corporation suddenly announces that it does not take ethical factors into consideration in deciding how to invest the University's endowment. This announcement, tantamount to a repudiation of the Corporation's own stated policy, galvanizes a broad range of groups and individuals into action.

Students set up E4D, the Endowment for Divestment. It is denounced by Bok as "an effort to use economic power to change a University policy with which the donors disagree."

1984-85: Jesse Jackson urges the University to divest, telling a standing-room only audience of 900 in Memorial Church that "the Harvard-South Africa kinship makes crimson become red. It symbolizes collusion with those who spill the blood of the innocent." He encourages students to follow the example of the late Martin Luther King, in whose commemoration the service was held. Bishop Desmond Tutu, in early 1984, told an audience of over 500 of the plight and aspirations of his people. He endorsed sanctions against apartheid, though not quite as openly as Jesse Jackson did at a later date at the same podium since advocacy of divestment is "an indictable offense back in South Africa."

In February 1985, Harvard announces its first divestment from a non-banking corporation, $1 million worth of Baker International stock.

In the largest student demonstration at Harvard in close to fifteen years, over 5,000 people attend a rally held on April 4, 1985 led by Jesse Jackson, the ANC's UN representative, labor leaders, clergy, students, and faculty.

In late April, 45 students force their way past a security guard to occupy the headquarters of the Board of Overseers.

On May 2, 200 students protest the presence of South Africa's New York Counsel General Abe Hoppenstein, invited by the Harvard Conservative Club. They block his exit from Lowell House and lay down on top and in front of his car. Using a considerable amount of force, the Harvard police eventually escort the Counsel General out of the House, "shaken but not hurt." Vice-President and General Counsel Dan Steiner accuses the protesters of seeking to deny the free speech rights of this representative of the white supremacy regime, and condemns their "coercive techniques." The activists counter that many of the facts have been distorted, also noting that they were led to believe they could attend the talk and were rebuffed at the door. They also accuse the police of "obvious use of excessive force." An official University inquiry absolves the police of all wrongdoing. The *Harvard Salient*, the main organ of campus conservatism, admits that inviting Hoppenstein was "a blatantly provocative act and absolutely the wrong thing to do." The Conservative Club is unmoved, later inviting more representatives of the apartheid regime.

1985-86: In September, perhaps trying to maximize the public relations benefit by waiting for the return of students, Harvard announces that back in July it had divested from two more corporations: Allis-Chalmers and Tokheim Corporation. The CCSR, meanwhile, continues to exhibit a Job-like patience with most U.S. firms, only divesting from Baker International (see above) when a senior official of that multinational declares: "If you are looking for hard data, it won't be coming. It's just not important enough to us."

Beyond token divestment, Bok continues his media offensive, including high-profile lobbying of Congress for government imposed sanctions on South Africa and the proposal of an internship program to send Harvard students to South Africa. SASC issues a report objecting to the internship program, showing its failure to include black South Africans in its inception and implementation, that most of the "multiracial" schools to which the Harvard students would be sent had only small proportions of black students, that the University's Berle Report would get Harvard involved in the discredited Bantustan policy, two of the institutions were in South Africa-occupied Namibia, and that the leading black political movements in South

Africa and Namibia were all opposed to the program. Tutu joins the critics. By March 1986, the program is cancelled.

On April 15, 1986, 200 students enter Harvard Yard and construct shanties.

On May Day, 1986, in the most demonstrable display of worker and community support for the Harvard anti-apartheid movement to date, some 200 people demonstrating against Shell Oil march to Harvard Square, where their attempt to enter the Yard in a show of solidarity with the students is thwarted by University officials who order the gates shut.

Fall 1986-1989: See article's introduction and below.

Divestment and Beyond

Harvard celebrated its 350th Anniversary in September 1986. This was an event of national, indeed international, significance, bringing Prince Charles, Cabinet secretaries, as well as leading personalities in the nation's political, economic, intellectual, social, and cultural life to the University's campus to pay homage to America's oldest institution of higher learning. Anti-apartheid activists also came to demand divestment. On the first day of the party (it lasted four days), the activists held a rally and led over 100 people in a candlelight procession through Harvard Square. Following this demonstration, over 60 protesters chanting, "If you want to digest, you have to divest," forced the cancellation of a dinner for some of the University's wealthiest and most influential patrons, prompting one of these distinguished individuals to physically confront the activists and denounce them as "assholes." Taking their campaign into the sky, the activists hired an airplane bearing the sign, "U.S./Harvard out of South Africa. Sanctions. Divest now," timing it to pass over as Secretary of State George Shultz was giving a speech defending the Reagan administration's notorious policy of "constructive engagement." It is worth pointing out that most of the people involved in these events were Harvard alumni and workers. Few students participated in them, as classes do not begin until the latter part of September.

But even as the activists were protesting Harvard's complicity in the apartheid system, the University had already decided to divest almost one-third of its South Africa-related investments. Citing their sale of "strategic goods" to the repressive arm of the apartheid regime, the Corporation agreed in August 1986 to sell $157 million worth of stock in eight corporations, including six oil giants and the Ford Motor Company. As in 1985, however, the Corporation sought to gain maximum propaganda mileage from this move by waiting until after the fall semester began to announce it.

There can be little doubt that pressure from the anti-apartheid movement was a major factor in the decision to make this partial divestment. We need only cite statements to this effect by the University Treasurer, though he subsequently tried to retract what he had earlier said—apparently deciding that it would be impolitic to admit that the University might be compelled by student pressure. The University had to make some concessions on the divestment issue. The level of anti-apartheid activities on campuses nationwide in 1985-86 created a new political reality for university governing boards. In particular, few of these governing boards could have remained unaffected by the University of California's decision to divest completely and sell its $3.1 billion investment in companies operating in South Africa. Further, the almost permanent state of agitation that the anti-apartheid movement had created at Harvard over the past two years had become subversive of the liberal image that the Bok administration has consciously fostered for fifteen years. The University could ill afford to graduate a class of disgruntled and permanently alienated students, at least not if it expects to continue relying on the generosity and good will of its graduates.

One of the most striking features of campus anti-apartheid movements, at Harvard as well as other universities nationwide, is the relatively few black students who actively participate in them. As was pointed out earlier (see chronology), black students initiated the first significant protest action on southern Africa at Harvard in 1972. Blacks played an active role in anti-apartheid activities in 1979 and again in 1983. But, generally speaking, they have subsequently faded from the protest scene. No doubt, one reason for this is the increasing tendency of the white, liberal SASC-led leadership to keep control of the anti-apartheid movement within its own narrow circles, even as it adopts a cosmopolitan posture toward anti-apartheid activities on a national scale. But, more importantly, the decline of black student activism at white dominated universities is probably due to the waning influence of black nationalist ideology among the black intelligentsia in general and black students in particular. It remains to be seen whether the recent response to the more notorious acts of campus racism will regalvanize black activism on apartheid.

While the anti-apartheid movement at Harvard has succeeded in putting South Africa at the top of the University's political agenda, it continues to face a number of challenges. For instance, scores of

U.S. companies have recently announced that they are pulling out of South Africa, but they are not really ceasing business with the apartheid state. For most U.S. corporations, divestment means selling their operations, generally to local South African investors, and continuing commercial ties with these same operations through distribution, licensing, technology transfers, and other indirect means. The anti-apartheid movement should continue fighting for its definition of divestment—the complete cessation of all economic ties with South Africa.

Moreover, even with its latest divestment moves, Harvard still has over $163 million invested in companies doing business with South Africa. Yet this is, in all likelihood, only a temporary state of affairs. Assuming that the University will be able to hold out indefinitely against campus and national pressure for complete divestment, which is an unlikely assumption, the increasing flight of U.S. capital from South Africa might leave it with a portfolio that does not include investments in companies with direct holdings in South Africa. Perhaps the most important challenge for the anti-apartheid movement is what to tackle after divestment? For if one's objective is the elimination of apartheid and not just the divestment of stocks, then the battle is far from over once the University divests, as it will be compelled to do so, one way or another, in the not-too-distant future. U.S. liberalism has still not advanced to the point where it can provide direct support for black liberation movements that are not completely beholden to Western interests, without apologizing for it. Yet, as the apartheid regime steps up its ruthless but futile campaign to wipe out the black liberation movement, students and other anti-apartheid activists must also redouble their efforts to support the establishment of a new society in South Africa.

Democracy, Harvard-Style
The (S)Election of Overseers

Chester Hartman and Robert Paul Wolff

For years now, Harvard has been running elections for its Board of Overseers ostensibly to give its graduates a say in the governing of the University. Actually the elections serve as a veneer of democracy over a powerful group running the University. When a group of Harvard and Radcliffe alumni/ae entered the election process in 1985 in an effort to persuade the Harvard administration to sell its large investments in companies doing business in South Africa, Harvard reacted first by trying to corrupt the election process; then by launching a series of scurrilous attacks on the men and women who put themselves forward as candidates or worked to get the pro-divestment candidates elected; and finally by rewriting the election rules to tilt the playing field so steeply that it will take mountain-climbing gear to keep future pro-divestment candidates in contention.

A fuller description of the governance structure at Harvard and role of the Board of Overseers may be found in Robert Weissman's essay. Suffice it to say here that the Overseers, while historically and technically able to exert real power at Harvard, in recent decades have ceded this role to the seven-person Corporation (aka The President and Fellows—a literal term until early 1989, as before then no woman ever had served on that body). As Overseer George Leighton, a retired federal judge, summed it up, "The Board of Overseers does not advise on policy. What it does is consent."[1]

Each year a committee of the Harvard Alumni Association (to which all alumni/ae automatically belong) nominates ten persons to fill the five newly vacant positions for six-year terms on the 30-person Board. All degree-holders, save Harvard faculty and administrators, are eligible to vote. Although there are roughly 170,000 eligible voters, less than one-quarter actually bother to mail in their ballots.

Nomination and election to the Board of Overseers has traditionally signified a type of patronage—for loyal service to the Alumni Association or Harvard Clubs, largess, or anticipated largess. Nominees are usually corporate executives, lawyers, and the like, with an

411

occasional judge, university president, or foundation executive thrown in. The Board's decision-making activities have been virtually nil, its principal function resting in the various Visiting Committees to departments and other units of the University.

In 1985-86, three West Coast alumni/ae—John Plotz, a deputy public defender in San Francisco; Gay Seidman, a University of California graduate student in sociology and the first woman President of the *Crimson*; and Kenneth Simmons, a black architecture professor at UC-Berkeley—decided to take advantage of the rarely-used nomination-by-petition route in order to focus attention on Harvard's continuing unwillingness to divest its huge investment portfolio of South Africa-related stocks. Along with a few friends and helpers, and calling themselves Alumni Against Apartheid, they mounted a respectable campaign. By speaking to specific issues of controversy and actually running a campaign—virtually unheard of—they were severely criticized by the powers-that-be for "politicizing" the process. Up to that point, elections were extraordinarily dull affairs, and voters made their choices based on each candidate's brief biographical sketch and statement that accompanied the ballot—typical were such snoozers as, "To maintain Harvard's preeminence in today's rapidly changing world will require the continuing support of one of Harvard's greatest assets, its alumni/ae."

The reaction of Harvard's administration to what it clearly construed as an act of *lèse majesté* was dramatic and panicky. Apparently shaken by the prospect of free spirits on a board of loyal drones, President Derek Bok ghost-wrote a letter over the signature of Board Chair Joan Bok (a fact he later admitted after earlier denying his role), urging Harvard grads to vote for the official HAA candidates; this letter was included as part of the ballot packet, along with a highly misleading and one-sided "fact sheet" on the University's position on divestment. This bit of electioneering—roughly equivalent to the Election Commission's printing a political message on the official ballots—produced a flood of outraged letters to the alumni magazine and strong condemnatory editorials in the *Crimson* and *Boston Globe* ("ham-fisted," as the *Globe* described the tactic)—which called for a second, compensatory mailing and a guarantee of impartiality in vote-counting. In embarrassment, the University agreed to turn the vote-count over to an "independent body"—and then chose its own accounting firm.

Somewhat surprisingly, pro-divestment candidate Seidman won, giving impetus to a far more organized effort in the following year. In 1986-87 an expanded organization, renamed Harvard-Rad-cliffe Alumni/ae Against Apartheid (HRAAA), fielded a full slate of candidates (six in all, since one extra seat had fallen vacant due to a resignation). This time two pro-divestment candidates were elected: Consuela Washington, a black Law School graduate who is counsel to the House Energy and Commerce Committee, and Peter Wood, a Duke history professor who led the successful divestment fight there. Others on the slate included NYC Councilwoman Ruth Messinger; former American Public Health Association and Physicians for Social Responsibility President Victor Sidel; Jerome Grossman, President of the Council for a Livable World; and Haywood Burns, then Vice-Provost of City University of New York.

Seidman, Washington, and Wood have not had an easy time of it. They are not members of The Club and are made to know it ("Board Shuns Dissenters," was the headline of an April 27-28, 1989 two-part *Crimson* series on the University's governing boards). The HRAAA-backed candidates "have been the targets of vitriolic personal attacks by Board members who question their commitment to Harvard",[2] they are excluded from key committees, committee leadership and the Board's powerful Executive Committee; and the HRAAA types tend not to have the business, professional and social contacts with the "in" members at the clubs and boardrooms where a good deal of informal interaction goes on. Gay Seidman remarked, "When I first started, I tried hard to be the perfect overseer and do all the right things, but there's a point when I just got to feel so alienated by constant little things that happened that it didn't matter what I did. I was going to be marginalized." Peter Wood observed, "I've been struck by how many cards they've found to play."[3]

Let's look more closely at those cards. Wood, a masterfully diplomatic, non-confrontational type, had assembled and distributed to his fellow Board members materials supporting the divestment position and received agreement to calendar a discussion and vote on the issue. The University thereupon sent Vice President and General Counsel Daniel Steiner and Overseers/Corporation Secretary Robert Shenton on a flying trip around the country to lobby individual Overseers against bringing the issue to a vote. That successful round of visits produced a "compromise"—a joint Corporation/Overseers committee to look into Harvard's policy of "selective divestment" and report back to both bodies. None of the HRAAA-backed Overseers was appointed to the committee. Not surprisingly, the stacked body recommended no more than cosmetic changes in the existing policy; more surprisingly, one of the committee members, Mathea Falco, appended a dissenting opinion ("I'm not sure if there has ever been a previous dissent written to an [Overseers'] report," she noted).[4]

The HRAAA-backed Overseers clearly have had an impact on the University, beyond producing panic. They have moved some of the other Overseers to a pro-divestment position. And, in classic political fashion, the official slate has begun to include some more liberal types, in a clear effort to take away some of HRAAA's appeal. Thus, Pulitzer Prize-winning author Frances FitzGerald, Senator Albert Gore, Jr., and Iran-Contragate Counsel Arthur Liman have been among the recent official nominees—and FitzGerald announced her support for divestment shortly after being nominated.

Meanwhile, Harvard, clearly shaken by the success of HRAAA, seems to have decided that it was time to tilt the playing field. Its vehicle was a committee headed by Federal Judge William Young that had been established in late 1986 to re-examine the procedures for electing Overseers. In September, 1988 (ironically, after a year in which HRAAA was unable to elect any of its candidates), the Young Committee produced the fruit of its efforts.

A simple listing of its recommendations shows the extent to which Harvard was willing to go to rid itself of this threat to its hegemony:

- Tripling the number of signatures required for petition candidacies.

- All petition candidates to be listed separately at the bottom of the ballot and clearly identified as such.

- Ballots with fewer than four votes cast to be thrown out (in order to discourage "bullet voting").

- Preparation of a statement from the Alumni Association explaining why the official candidates have been nominated and why they fit Harvard's needs—i.e., institutionalizing the Joan/Derek Bok letter.

- Reducing from ten to eight the number of nominees for the five seats, the heart of the entire "reform." By reducing by 20 percent the number of official nominees, the Alumni Association stands to increase by 25% the average vote for its remaining candidates, thereby making it very much more difficult for petition candidates to be elected, while simultaneously reducing the degree of choice offered to the voters. The official explanation in the Young Committee Report was that it is too difficult to locate ten good candidates each year from Harvard's 170,000 graduates.

- Finally, the report proposed that for reasons of cost, the counting of the ballots be returned to the Harvard Alumni Records Office.

The Young Committee Report, after routine approval by the Alumni Association's Executive Board, was presented to the Overseers at their September, 1988 meeting (with barely two days' notice), but its provisions were so raw that it apparently met with extensive criticism from diverse Overseers and a vote on the controversial proposals was postponed. Despite strenuous Alumni Association efforts, the report was tabled a second time at the Overseers meeting in April, 1989.

At around this time, HRAAA announced its 1988-89 slate, headed by one of Harvard's most distinguished honorary degree recipients, Nobel Peace Prize-winner Archbishop Desmond Tutu of South Africa. (Others on the 1988-89 slate included Linda Davidoff, Executive Director of the New York-based Parks Council; Ephraim Isaac, formerly Associate Professor of Afro-American Studies at Harvard and now Director of the Institute of Semitic Studies in Princeton; Clara Lopez, Colombian economist, human rights activist, former President of the Bogotá City Council, and the Alumni Association's former Regional Director for Latin America; and Robert Zevin, an expert on socially responsible investment who manages a $1.2 billion investment fund as Senior Vice President of U. S. Trust Co. in Boston.) In the Spring of 1988, Tutu had stated his intention to return his honorary degree unless Harvard divested entirely within a year.

Clearly threatened by the Tutu nomination, the Harvard administration was somewhat uncertain how to respond. Unwilling to attack Tutu publicly, President Bok and his aides ceded leadership to Charles Egan, incoming President of the Harvard Alumni Association and outgoing chair of its Overseers Nominating Committee, and John Reardon, Associate Vice President for University Relations and HAA's new Executive Director.

Egan and Reardon fashioned a curious attack on HRAAA, the gravamen of which was a pair of contradictory theses: the HRAAA candidates, they charged, were "single-issue candidates" who cared only about divestment, rather than the full range of issues facing Harvard—this an echo of the Joan/Derek Bok letter of three years earlier; and, incompatibility, that HRAAA was not really interested in divestment, but instead had an "agenda" of issues, principal among which was an assault on the governance of Harvard. In a letter to Harvard Permanent Class Secretaries, Egan said that in his judgement, and that of the Harvard administration, the election of Archbishop Tutu and the other petition candidates may "play havoc with the administration of Harvard."

Hampered by the unassailable moral authority of Tutu (a quality which one might have hoped would lead Harvard to welcome him onto the Board), Egan decided to focus his attack on HRAAA's Executive Director, University of Massachusetts Philosophy Professor Robert Paul Wolff. Egan asserted that the real issue in Overseers elections was not divestment, but "an attempt by Wolff to advance his own political views. 'Wolff is doing what Joseph McCarthy did, he is creating a banner under which he can float his own social agenda. He is exploiting Bishop Tutu to achieve his own ends.'"[5]

Egan went on to label HRAAA's unsuccessful 1988 candidates "second-rate." Reardon, less restrained than his colleague, couldn't contain himself at the news of Tutu's nomination. "What's to keep [HRAAA] from nominating Fidel Castro next time?," he asked in response to a question at a February, 1989 HAA meeting.[6] And then Egan, Vice President of Hallmark Cards, plunked down $9500 of his own money to pay for a full-page "Open Letter," printed on the inside back cover of the May-June issue of *Harvard Magazine* arriving in all alumni/ae mailboxes just as they were casting their ballots, and signed by Stanford University President and Harvard alumnus Donald Kennedy, a close friend of President Bok. Kennedy's ad urged fellow alums to support the official slate of nominees and vote against "single-issue candidates" (an obvious canard, as evidenced by a reading of the statements of the HRAAA-backed candidates, which spoke to over a dozen concerns and issues besides divestment, including equal admission of men and women, expanding relations between Harvard and Third World learning institutions, enhancement of academic excellence and freedom, and a stronger commitment to training and hiring women and minority scholars). The *Crimson*, on May 3, 1989 reported that the Bok-Kennedy-Egan deal had been brokered by the University's Vice President for Alumni Affairs, Fred Glimp.

Archbishop Tutu won, bringing the number of HRAAA-backed Overseers to four. It says volumes about Harvard alumni/ae that he placed fourth, 4000 votes behind actor John Lithgow and 2000 votes behind Labor Secretary Elizabeth Dole.

The day before the 1989 election results were announced, the Board of Overseers finally passed a slightly truncated version of the Young Report ("I think it was not a good spring for democracy," observed Peter Wood'). A key Alumni Association figure lobbied Board members by phone. Two minor elements of the plan were put on hold: increasing the number of signatures required and the voiding of "bullet" ballots. Efforts to strike the listing of petition candidates separately and institutionalizing the Joan/Derek Bok-style electioneering statement apparently failed by narrow margins, indicating that a large number of the Overseers still are uncomfortable with Harvard's power play. And for the first time in memory, *Harvard Magazine*, the somewhat independent alumni/ae organ, published an editorial in its May-June, 1989 issue entitled "The Overseers' Election." It criticized the University's move on the election process as follows:

> ...[S]uch measures [the Young Committee Report recommendations]...will be seen by many as tactical moves to give the University a more direct part in managing the Overseers' election and to strengthen official slates at the expense of independent candidates and the groups backing them. This impression will not help Harvard...Does Harvard need the kind of partisan feuding that has vexed Princeton and Dartmouth alumni in recent years?...The HAA directors should...do all they can to see that the Board of Overseers is a broadly representative body, reflecting all shades of opinion on University policy.

The implications of the adopted changes are clear. A quick arithmetic calculation shows that had Harvard nominated only eight candidates in 1988-89 rather than ten, Tutu likely would have been dropped from fourth to seventh, and thus would not have been elected.

Three lessons may be learned from this story. First, when playing ball against someone who owns the ball, the bat, and the playing field, and who also keeps the score and calls the balls and strikes, it's a trifle hard to win the game.

Second, the Harvard administration reacts paranoically to even the slightest challenge to its absolute control over all processes of governance and decision. Derek Bok and company simply cannot tolerate even the simulacrum of genuine disagreement.

Finally, despite Harvard's best efforts, HRAAA continues to grow. The next six or seven years will see classes from the late sixties and early seventies returning for their twenty-fifth reunions. The vital center of the Harvard alumni/ae community is shifting politically to the left. If Harvard persists in adopting an intransigent, red-baiting stance in the face of HRAAA's challenge, it may find itself fatally out of touch with its own graduates.

Notes

1. *Harvard Crimson,* April 27, 1989.
2. *Harvard Crimson,* June 8, 1989.
3. *Harvard Crimson,* April 28, 1989.
4. *Harvard Crimson,* April 28, 1989.
5. *Harvard Crimson,* May 10, 1989.
6. *Harvard Crimson,* May 12, 1989.
7. *Harvard Crimson,* June 8, 1989.

Conclusion
Transforming Harvard

John Trumpbour

In the scientific judgement of sociologist Theda Skocpol, Harvard University is "the most arrogant university in the Western world."[1] Those willing to say so, at least for publication, can expect to find themselves set upon by faculty smut hounds, dons whose pecksniffery extends to barking joyously about the existence of academic freedom while clamping their jaws furiously and often fatally upon any quarry foolish enough to exercise its liberties.

The few faculty critics of Harvard aside, student dissidents are greeted with even greater derision. Crammed throughout the University's ranks is a familiar creature E.P. Thompson has elsewhere dubbed *Academicus Superciliosus*. "The one unmistakable means of identification of *Academicus Superciliosus*," notes Thompson, "is that he over-reacts to any sign of student self-activity. Even a polite deputation or petition throws him into a tizzy." *Superciliosus* scurries

> furiously and self-importantly around in his committees, like a
> white mouse running in a wheel, while his master is carrying
> him, cage and all, to be sold at the local pet-shop.[2]

That they are being bought and sold seems rather apparent to the wealthy who help endow many of the University's programs. In an internal memo to Kennedy School of Government Dean Graham Allison, an aide posed the following questions on behalf of Texas millionaire Joanne Dickinson who eventually gave the University some $500,000: "What is the most prestigious title she can buy for $250,000? How much would it cost to be on the Advisory Committee?"[3]

Judged by the standards of Harvard's own *Superciliosi*, $250K is thought to be altogether skimpy, an easily spent pittance. Lewis Lapham recalls attending a conference on world energy and the disparity between the rich and poor nations, a convocation financed by the Russell Sage Foundation to the tune of $250,000. Amidst discussions of the ravages of Third World poverty and the starvation of children, it soon became clear that the academicians assembled had no ideas or solutions "that everybody hadn't already read in *Newsweek*," he recounts. The Harvard delegate then rose, deriding the very notion that they should expect anything could be accomplished on the piddling sum of $250,000. "Who can do anything with $250,000?" he maintained. "The thing to do is to leverage it. Anybody with the right connections in the charity business ought to be able to run it up to $1.5 million before the end of the year. If we had $1.5 million, I'm sure we could come up with an idea." The motion met with roaring applause, and the conference agreed to reconvene upon the arrival of this leveraged infusion of lucre.[4]

In June 1988, Harvard announced that its Kennedy School of Government had received $15 million from capitalist Alfred Taubman to build a center on government that would focus on solving such problems as homelessness. Rather than house the homeless, Harvard would instead house experts on the homeless. Evidently oblivious to the possibility that some might be appalled by this latest plan for expansion, the University reiterated that the center had a more general aim, to conduct research on problems confronted by state and local government.

Meanwhile, a new study cited by former Congressman Paul Rogers suggests that the proliferation of Harvard experts may well wreak havoc with a community's fiscal and outright physical health. Residents of the Boston area, dominated by the prestigious and prohibitively expensive Harvard hospital complex, spend the equivalent 16 percent of gross national product on medical care compared to 9.6 percent in New Haven, a city which shows no evidence of lower quality of care. (The national average is 11 percent of GNP.)[5] As noted earlier, of the nation's 27 largest cities, Boston has recently found itself ranked first in skyrocketing levels of black infant mortality.[6]

So in the midst of this enormous financial drain, who is served by Harvard's wealth and resources? Currently the DuPont Corporation and others are engaged in finding ways to avoid hiring workers who might be "sensitive" to toxic chemicals. And to whom have they turned to devise these tests? The Harvard School of Public Health. When it comes to hazardous materials, Richard Lewontin observes that "the whole movement now seeks to remove the obligation from the corporation and the government to protect all workers and all persons, and to place the obligation on the individual as the locus of the problem."[7]

Confronted by this formidable panoply of institutional power arrayed against sovereign individual, the citizen does not stand much of a chance. In the end, Harvard is able to trim the hapless victim under the twin banners of traditional authority and superior intellect.

What is to be Done?

George Bernard Shaw's own sage wisdom offered that the best thing that could be done with Harvard is to burn the whole University to the ground. A dream with a certain majestic appeal, Harvard's last smoking embers warming the frozen banks of the Charles, there is nevertheless little doubt that the U.S. ruling class would quickly reconstitute their preferred educational service station. They would depart with it just as much as the British aristocracy could live without Oxbridge; the French bourgeoisie, *sans grandes écoles*.

To reject Harvard means, therefore, to reject much more than just Harvard: a social order based on extreme levels of inequality and a political order predicated on popular passivity. Harvard notwithstanding, the society remains in need of what Pound liked to call "a whole volley of liberations."

Under the circumstances, a student movement should not have delusions of grandeur about the triumph of radical social change in the absence of rebellions by the organized working class and mobilized social movements. But students can play a more than negligible role if they recognize the interests they share with these mightier allies, all of whom, whether at the work place, the state house, or the administration hall, seek to achieve power from below. In Cockburn's useful formulation, "the student movement must first *be itself* before it can be a useful ally to anyone." He adds:

> Fortunately the French confrontation of 1968 at least made it clear that students acting as an independent revolutionary force can ignite a much more general conflagration...[8]

Towards that end, what can the student movement contribute to a radical renewal? The terrain upon which the student movement is best equipped to promote progressive social change includes 1) the struggle for empowerment at the university, for students themselves and their allies among the faculty, labor, and the community; 2) the development of an alternative intellectual culture; and 3) the promotion of internationalism among those forces committed to an emancipatory political project.

The Struggle for Empowerment

Proudly saluting his Harvard audience as "Fellow Elitists," Allan Bloom, following a speech in December of 1988, declared that empowerment is a silly notion. On this point, the administration at Harvard and most U.S. universities could not agree more.

A central task of the student movement is to raise the politics of who is granted power on the governing boards of universities. The seven-member Harvard Corporation remains a self-perpetuating and pseudo-feudal organization designed to empower those of wealth and "good breeding." Deserving of a rapid dispatch to the dustbin of Widener Library, it is a mechanism more suited for governing institutions in seventeenth century Stuart England than for a modern democratic polity. On the eve of the twenty-first century, the University awaits the advent of a democratic charter providing representation of students, staff, and members of the local community. Students and faculty have only barely begun to develop and defend traditions of self-governance and, in the ensuing breach, have watched their rights eagerly usurped by the technocrats of Holyoke Center and Massachusetts Hall.

Until the growth of a political coalition able to sustain democratic transformation of the campus, there are few better ways of delegitimating and demystifying upper-class power in the United States other than student direct action. Again Cockburn reflects:

> During such events the rock solid structures of the institution seem to dissolve. The mysterious operations of bureaucracy are exposed...Pretensions of authority seem arrogant and hollow. Before the laughing audience the conjuror has lost his mirrors, his curtain, his false-bottomed hat and his capacious sleeves, and is reduced to simulated jocosity and fervent hopes that the attendants will throw them all out.[9]

For the forseeable future, the combat against racism and the University's complicity with Pretoria will remain the issues of special urgency to the progressive forces on campus. To be effective in linking these to issues of political empowerment, a campaign must be directed not only against the most blatant acts of Ku Kluxery, but also against the liberal and genteel traditions of racism at Harvard. Among the myriad artifacts of such practices, instead of affirmative action in the residential education system, the Bok regime has delivered two decades of negative action — none of 13 House Masters are black. (No doubt, returning white alums would find it disconcerting to have to address a black woman or man, "Master," the ultimate transposition of the quasi-feudal/slave signifiers of rule at John Harvard's plantation.)

Radical students should not shy away from economistic demands, for instance challenging the exorbitant tuition charged by Harvard and many universities, hikes well beyond the general inflation rate that have led to total fees approaching $20,000 for instruction often led by overburdened and undernourished graduate students. Because of the poltroonish quality of most faculty and the hollow-headed careerism of a majority of college students (nationally 75.6 percent agree that "making a lot of money" is an important life goal, up from 39 percent in 1971),[10] there is a need to select issues that can bring the complacent out of their torpor, rather than leave their concerns to the William Bennetts and others all too glad to thunder against the tuition thievery. In the midst of a direct action protest at Massachusetts Hall, enabling them to witness the self-serving and patronizing rhetoric of their Harvard masters, some students will be obliged to abandon wavering liberal illusions and lemming-like conservatism, readying them for a more sustained dose of radical critique.

Alternative Intellectual Culture

Gramsci's legacy to revolutionary theory was his insight that radicals have to achieve "civil hegemony" before they can hope to grasp state power. A distant and daunting task for any of the advanced industrial nations, a hegemonic progressive culture has to be constructed out of a combination of local traditions and more universal values.

Now universities are not the typical sites of outstanding radical culture. Students are taught to absorb ideas passively, dished out to them in antiseptic containers and the students' regurgitations sent back graded A, B, C, D, or F. Lapham remembers at his Ivy League college seeing "the celebrities of the human soul (Plato, Montaigne, Goethe, et. al.) put in guest appearances on the academic talk show," with the audience "expected to welcome them with rounds of appreciative applause. Like producers holding up cue cards, the faculty identified those truths deserving of the adjective 'great.' The students who received the best marks were those who could think of the most flattering explanations for the greatness of the great figures and the great truths."[11]

Progressive students will have to recover the critical edge in the thought of the traditional western pantheon, Plato, Aristotle, Augustine, Dante, Luther, Montaigne, Pascal, Rousseau, Kant, Goethe, Nietzsche, and Tolstoy, while also engaging with their own radical traditions: Marx, Bakunin, Luxemburg, Du Bois, De Beauvoir, Sartre, Lukacs, Brecht, Cabral, Mills, and Marcuse. They will have to rediscover the voices of those thinkers, especially of women and the Third World, who have been summarily ignored or suppressed. The West (as it likes to call itself) has conveniently forgotten that it owes enormous debts to other cultures, to what Martin Bernal has suggested are "the Afro-Asiatic roots of Greek civilization."[12] Aristotle himself referred to Egypt as "the cradle of mathematics," Plato apparently derived significant elements of his thought from that nation, and Herodotus noted that the very "names of nearly all the gods came to Greece from Egypt." In the modern age, Western culture, from Mallarmé's poetry to Pound's Cantos to cubist and primitivist art, has been based on extensive borrowings from Eastern and African civilizations. From Beethoven's extensive use of Turkish marches to the French impressionists' admiration of Japanese painting to the surrealists' inspiration from Native American art of the Pacific Northwest, the cultural avant garde of the West has shunned the view that the rest of the world is intellectually marginal—save, of course, for such notable exceptions as the followers of Hitler, aptly termed "the archetypal monoculturalist" by Ismael Reed for the "pigheaded" belief "that one way and one blood was so pure that it had to be protected from alien strains at all costs."[13]

It also evidently bears reminding that the texts serving as the foundations of Western culture spring from the oral tradition, most notably the *Iliad* and *Odyssey*. Oddly a fundamental premise of western and world civilization courses is the superiority of written over oral culture, thereby sanctioning ignorance of the artistic vitality and creativity of Africans and the indigenous peoples of Australasia and the Americas. Today, African and Latin American writers have recovered some of these earlier oral traditions, indeed producing a literature with greater energy and excitement than the flaccid offerings of contemporary North American and European writers, including that of Bloom's supercilious sidekick, the vastly overrated Saul Bellow. (The Nobel laureate Bellow suggests that we should not study African thought and literature because there is no "Tolstoy of the Zulus." Tolstoy himself would have regarded Bellow, the author of such novels as *More Die of Heartbreak*, as at best a pedestrian scribbler, unworthy of study except perhaps as a measure of the decline of letters in the civilization of Late Imperial America.)

To sum up, progressive students should seek several transformations in the content of university education: 1) a core curriculum that is self-conscious in debating how the canon is chosen;[14] 2) a wider-ranging representation of world literature, challenging "the defense of the West" subtext pervading much traditional pedagogy; 3) exploration of epistemology, particularly in the history and philosophy of science and the social sciences; and 4) the presentation of texts grounded in a historical context. The last point is addressed to the George Wills and Allan Blooms who believe it is morally corrupting and relativizing to teach students that Thomas Jefferson, for example, owned slaves, thus unnecessarily desacralizing the "greatness" of those texts that proclaim a commitment to freedom. Will calls Bloom's critics "dangerously disrespectful of the idea of a text independent of its context," which represents "an affront to the unifying theme of the West's rich tradition."[15] Such efforts at shrouding these works in mystical awe and reverence are more accurately an affront to critical consciousness and will thus require a radical riposte and resistance.

Internationalism

Internationalism has become one of those bloodless clichés, to be unfurled on appropriate occasions by the President of Coca Cola as well as by the embattled leadership of diminutive socialist sects.

Harvard University itself trundles out the internationalist banner, sponsoring significant contact between Kennedy School students and their counterparts from Moscow, southern Africa, and elsewhere. No doubt some good comes from this, but much of the repartee is of the sort that meets the needs and approval of official channels.

Of the many components of the progressive coalition, students are often in the best place to foster internationalism. Not only do U.S. students attend institutions with a large contingent of foreigners, but they also are usually more able to travel and have access to the resources needed to study languages. When Harvard students on their own have forged links to such forces of resistance in South Africa as the United Democratic Front (UDF), they have helped expose the wily calculations behind the University's officially sanctioned "internationalism." Moreover, there is much to be learned from international examples, including the experience of *cogobierno* in Latin America, which produced what one historian calls "the golden age of Argentinean scholarship" by giving students extensive voting rights over appointments and curricular reforms.[16] Currently in the midst of *glasnost*, the Soviet Union is also sloughing off authoritarian modes of pedagogy by granting students a greater say over appointments and curriculum.

The U.S.S.R., to be sure, has spawned its own New Left, a movement whose 18-to-35 year-old representatives have produced a much more dynamic intellectual culture than their current U.S. student counterparts. Led by the courageous personage of Boris Kagarlitsky, previously jailed by the Brezhnevite authorities, he has expressed muted frustration at the lack of interest in their project by U.S. radicals.[17]

Kagarlitsky's plea should not go unheeded. The student Left will fall into a serious strategic error if, in the euphoria over improved U.S.-Soviet relations, it does not exert the "street heat" necessary to bring "détente from below." Contrary to its peaceful rhetoric, the Bush regime has kept defense expenditures at intolerable levels, continuing to spend, writes Russell Baker, as if the Red Army were at this moment occupying Niagara Falls.[18] If students are to see any prospects of improving the amount of support for expanded educational opportunity, they shall have to return to their traditional fight on issues of war and peace. The university continues to stand as one of the most militarized sectors of society, Harvard on its own having previously distinguished itself as a center of CIA-sponsored social science and as the home of the very scientists who invented napalm and the petroleum product best suited to make the burning gel stick to skin. Successful detonations of napalm were indeed first carried out on a Harvard games field and in back of the football stadium. The substance's remarkable ability to "become embedded in the tissues and continue smouldering and re-igniting long after the initial trauma," earned for it the following academic honors: in Japan more deaths than were produced by the dropping of the A-Bombs on Hiroshima and Nagasaki, and in Korea, from the *Armed Forces Chemical Journal* (July 1953), the title of "best all around weapon." Harvard is to this day a mainstay in the advancement of chemical and biological warfare.[19]

Conservatives and liberals will, of course, howl that students and citizens should not meddle in affairs where they lack expertise. This retort is usually the last refuge of scoundrels. From Zola in the

Dreyfus Affair to the critics of the Vietnam War, oppositions to military and national security policy have all been met with this familiar refrain. It is a theme of Buckley's *National Review*, typically used against the minority of intellectuals opposed to U.S. foreign policy:

> Small cliques speaking for the professoriat...come forward...not as scholars in relevant fields but as professors—professors of biology, assistant professors of English, instructors in Romance Languages—they claim the right to challenge the Government to public debate on whatever issues they please. No one would maintain that plumbers, just by virtue of being plumbers, had any such right, or physicians, lawyers, engineers, merchants, bankers, or labor leaders, except perhaps where the issue touched on their special field of interest and competence.[20]

If anything can be learned from this book, it is a healthy distrust of experts. But for all its self-righteous ire and disdain for the intelligentsia, the conservative critique lapses back into paying homage to experts. For Harvard, faith in its own preeminence and authority is one of the verities to be reaffirmed on the University's most solemn occasions. After the assassination of Martin Luther King, Harvard President Nathan Pusey began his eulogy of the civil rights leader, "Though he did not attend Harvard..." This was all the more tragicomic and jarring if only because King showed that, rather than defer to entrenched elites, every person should be regarded as capable of becoming informed and participating meaningfully in affairs concerning human dignity and public welfare.

This book has previously suggested that Harvard today aids and abets ruling class power by supplementing and in some cases supplanting older patrician traditions with newer meritocratic standards for access to privilege and authority. In the short run, the meritocratic ethos may well be difficult to combat (for reasons elaborated in my chapter on the corporations). But in the long run, meritocracy could find itself more vulnerable to attack than the older aristocratic ethos. Immanuel Wallerstein remarks that "the oppressed may swallow being ruled by and giving reward to those who are to the manner born. But being ruled by and giving reward to those people whose only asserted claim (and that a dubious one) is that they are smarter, that is too much to swallow." In past history, people might long accept that a tsar, an aristocrat, or a paternalistic industrialist loved and cared for them, but no one seriously believes that the new meritocrats rule because of some higher duty and devotion to the people. Their selfishness stands exposed and naked, and a realization of this may be a source of Bok's latter day crusade for the elites to adorn themselves in a protective coat of ethics. A similar premonition of future ruling class vulnerability animated both Bagehot and Schumpeter, the former calling on Queen Victoria to supply the needed mystical glue, the latter, having lived through the collapse of the Habsburgs and the assassination of Dolfuss in his days in Vienna, remaining resigned to the likelihood that the social order would pull asunder. Today it is Harvard and the higher education system that supplies part of the mystical glue cementing in place the current social system, though its new surge of confidence, bolstered by recent lacklustre economic performance and brutal repression in the alternative social orders of the East, may in reality be short-lived.[21]

For the student movement, it would do well to take up the gauntlet laid down by C. Wright Mills, who was fond of an anonymous poem about the Wobblies of Texas:

> When that boatload of Wobblies came
> Up to Everett, the sheriff says
> Who the hell's yer leader anyhow?
> Who's yer leader anyhow?
> And them Wobblies yelled right back—
> We ain't got no leader
> We're all leaders
> And they kept right on coming[22]

On campuses throughout the country, the narcotic effects of Reaganism are wearing off. For the oft complacent denizens of Harvard Yard, they will have to renew critical questions and forceful challenges to the University's servants of power wherever they rear their ugly heads. Only in the outcome, to adapt the heroic words of Tom Mann, students might hope to grow more dangerous as they grow older.

Notes

1. *Harvard Crimson*, October 8, 1986, pp. 1 and 6.

2. E.P. Thompson, et. al. *Warwick University Ltd.* (Hammondsworth: Penguin, 1970), pp. 153-154.

3. J. Anthony Lukas, "Harvard's Kennedy School: Is Competence Enough?" *New York Times Magazine*, March 12, 1989, p. 101.

4. Lewis Lapham, *Money and Class in America* (New York: Weidenfeld and Nicolson, 1988), pp. 24-25.

5. In pointing to Harvard's role in inflating the region's medical costs, Congressman Rogers cited the findings of a major study by John Wennberg of the Dartmouth Medical School on Wes Vernon's nationally syndicated radio show, "Cross Talk," February 5, 1989. While Wennberg is both more general and speculative than Rogers about the sources of the exorbitant medical costs in the Boston region, he shows how New Haven, a city with a comparable socioeconomic and demographic profile, is able to deliver medical care at nearly half the cost of Boston. See J. Wennberg, et. al. "Are Hospital Services Rationed in New Haven or Over-Utilized in Boston?" *Lancet*, May 23, 1987, pp. 1185-1188.

6. In 1985, according to figures from the National Center for Health Statistics calculated by the Children's Defense Fund, Massachusetts witnessed its black infant mortality rate leap from 14.2 to 20.8 deaths per thousand, a 47 percent increase, higher than such bastions of the social welfare state as Arkansas (14.2), Texas (15.5), Alabama (17.0), Louisiana (17.2), Florida (17.8), and Mississippi (18.9). While Massachusetts went from best in 1984 to 27th in 1985 out of 33 states with measurable black infant mortality rates, the city of Boston itself stood last among the nation's 27 largest cities. Massachusetts reports that for babies born in 1986 its figures produced a slight improvement, but the state remains towards the bottom of the bird cage. In a February 1988 report, the state's Division of Public Health notes that "in 1980 the infant mortality rate for black infants was 68 percent higher than for white infants; in 1986 the mortality rate for black infants was 159 percent higher than for white infants."

7. Richard Lewontin quoted by M. Raskin in M. Raskin and H. Bernstein, *New Ways of Knowing* (Totowa: Rowman and Littlefield, 1987), p. 121.

8. Alexander Cockburn, "Introduction," A. Cockburn and R. Blackburn, eds. *Student Power* (Hammondworth: Penguin, 1970), p. 16.

9. Cockburn, p. 12.

10. Larry Gordon, "Students Are All Business These Days, Study Finds," *L.A. Times*, January 14, 1988, p. 3.

11. Lapham, p. 19.

12. See Martin Bernal, *Black Athena: The Afro-Asiatic Roots of Greek Civilization* (New Brunswick: Rutgers University Press, 1987). Bernal's theses, provi-

sional in places and in need of further elaboration which he promises in forthcoming volumes 2 and 3, are vulnerable to certain criticisms; in my own view, he may be hasty in trying to distance Homer from the oral tradition, a move he judges necessary to confirm a previous Egyptian colonization and contribution to Greece's achievement of written literacy. For a review hostile to Bernal that seeks to rescue the classicist consensus that the Greeks were either deluded about their debts to Egypt, or else used such claims in polemics to deny the achievements of opponents, see Jasper Griffin, "Who Are These Coming to the Sacrifice?" *New York Review of Books,* June 15, 1989. Bernal's brief riposte appears in the September 28 edition. But even Griffin, in rebuking Bernal for a lack of discussion of this area, concedes that the Greek mind was profoundly moved by the achievements of Egyptian architecture.

13. I. Reed, "America: The Multinational Society," in R. Simonson and S. Walker, eds. *The Gray Wolf Annual Five: Multi-cultural Literacy* (St. Paul: Graywolf Press, 1988), pp. 157-158.

14. In several essays and books, the literary critic Gerald Graff has been the most articulate spokesperson for this mild reform. For historical background, see G. Graff and M. Warner, eds., *The Origins of Literary Studies in America: A Documentary Anthology* (New York: Routledge, 1989).

15. George Will, nationally syndicated column, May 1988.

16. Alastair Hennesy, "University Students in National Politics," in Claudio Veliz, ed., *The Politics of Conformity in Latin America* (London: Oxford University Press, 1967), p. 130. Also cited by G.S. Jones, "The Meaning of the Student Revolt," in Blackburn and Cockburn, p. 52.

17. See Kagarlitsky's interview in the appendices of B. Kagarlitsky, *The Thinking Reed,* (London: Verso, 1988).

18. As this book goes to press, Bush has reaffirmed NATO's goal set in 1978 of 3 percent real growth in defense spending per year. See G. Wilson, "NATO Agrees to Keep Budget Growth at 3%," *International Herald Tribune,* June 9, 1989, p. 3.

19. V.W. Sidel, "Napalm," in S. Rose, ed. *Chemical and Biological Warfare* (Boston: Beacon Press, 1969), pp. 44-47. Dr. Sidel is quoted on the effects of napalm on skin tissue. See also John Cookson and Judith Nottingham, *A Survey of Chemical and Biological Warfare* (London: Sheed and Ward, 1969) and Seymour Hersh, *Chemical and Biological Warfare* (New York: Bobbs-Merrill, 1968.) According to Hersh (pp. 62-63n), Dr. Louis F. Fieser of Harvard, the director of research on napalm, was involved in more macabre projects, including "a weird Army scheme to equip bats with tiny incendiary bombs...The bombs were to be attached by surgery and a piece of string to the chests of would-be bat bombers...After two years of research, a trial run was made in Carlsbad Caverns, New Mexico. On the first day, some bats escaped and set off fires that completely demolished a general's auto and a $2 million hangar. The Army project was abruptly canceled." The Navy's attempt to revive it later was scrapped by August, 1944.

On Harvard's more recent investment and support for the chemical warfare complex, see Jonathan Feldman's study, *Universities in the Business of Repression: The Academic-Industrial-Military Complex and Central America*. (Boston: South End Press, 1989).

20. Will Herberg from *National Review* (1965) quoted by R. Jacoby, *The Last Intellectuals* (New York: Basic Books, 1987), p. 199. The discussion of "experts" owes much to Jacoby's reflections on this quotation.

21. I. Wallerstein, "The Bourgeois(ie) as Concept and Reality," *New Left Review*, 167, January-February 1988, p. 106. Lurking skepticism about the Harvard meritocrats and technocrats prevails in many circles, voiced most recently by former Boston mayor Kevin White in Lukas's article on the Kennedy School of Government: "They're creating a new political class that knows how to administer but doesn't know the people in the neighborhood. They talk about competence. I'd rather not be called competent. I'd be offended by that word."

The defense of the new meritocrats from democratic accountability is typically couched in terms of professionalism. Harvard's Robert Brustein in "The Case for Professionalism" in I. Wallerstein and P. Starr, eds., *The University Crisis Reader* (New York: Vintage, 1971), and Harvard Dean Franklin Ford in his contribution to the *Daedelas* symposium of Summer 1970, point to the folly of holding a surgeon to the canons of democracy. Brustein wrote, "It is unlikely (though anything is possible these days) that medical students will insist on making a diagnosis through majority vote, or that students entering surgery will refuse anaesthesia because they want to participate in decisions that affect their lives…"

Barbara Ehrenreich responds that this defense is "lamentably weak" on numerous grounds. Surgeons, while not expected to take majority votes, do consult with technicians, nurses, and other members of a medical unit in order to make diagnostic and life-saving decisions, patients are routinely told to get second and third opinions before undergoing major surgery, and, beyond that, professionals too often use expertise in one area to subvert community control in others. For instance, at Harlem Hospital during the end of the 1960s, when local groups asked for medical clinics to be open for later hours, doctors and administrators sneered, "Next they'll want to tell the surgeon where to cut." B. Ehrenreich, *Fear of Falling* (New York: Pantheon, 1989), pp. 82-83n.

22. C. Wright Mills, *The New Men of Power* (New York: Harcourt Brace, 1948), see book's epigram. Also cited by Jacoby, p. 94.

About the Contributors

Jonathan R. Beckwith, a professor of microbiology at Harvard, is a frequent contributor to *Science for the People* and active in a wide range of campaigns for science in the public interest.

Alexander Cockburn is a columnist for *The Nation, In These Times, The Wall Street Journal,* and *Zeta Magazine.* He is a member of the editorial board of *New Left Review,* and his latest book is *Corruptions of Empire.*

Vladimir Escalante earned a Ph.D. in Astronomy from Harvard University in 1988. Involved in a broad range of concerns, he helped author a critique of the justice system at Harvard. He has since returned to his homeland of Mexico.

Stephen Jay Gould, Professor of Zoology at Harvard and author of such works as *The Mismeasure of Man* and *The Flamingo's Smile,* is a frequent contributor to the *New York Review of Books.*

Chester Hartman holds an A.B. (1957) and Ph.D. (1967) from Harvard. He is a Fellow at the Institute for Policy Studies in Washington, D.C. and has taught at Harvard, Yale, the Univ. of North Carolina, Cornell, Columbia, and the Univ. of California (Berkeley). His recent books include *Housing Issues of the 1990s; Winning America: Ideas and Leadership for the 1990s,* co-edited with Marcus Raskin; *Critical Perspectives on Housing,* co-edited with Rachael Bratt and Ann Meyerson; and *The Transformation of San Francisco.* He was Executive Director of Harvard-Radcliffe Alumni/ae Against Apartheid in 1986-87.

Oscar Hernandez, an alumnus of the University of Illinois, graduated from Harvard with a Ph.D. in Physics in 1988. He helped spearhead the student campaign against Star Wars.

Lisa Hinds worked on the clerical staff at Harvard for six years. She holds an A.B. from Boston University and has extensive experience in film and graphic design.

Ruth Hubbard is Professor of Biology at Harvard and an important critic of sexism in the sciences.

Andrew Kopkind is a regular contributor to *The Nation* and *Zeta Magazine.* A forceful commentator on U.S. domestic and foreign policy, he also has a European following in such forums as the *New Statesman* and, more recently, *New Left Review* for which he covered the Jackson campaign. Penguin Books assembled a collection of his earlier essays in *America: The Mixed Curse.*

Lawrence S. Lifschultz, a correspondent for the *Far Eastern Economic Review,* teaches at King's College, Cambridge University. He is an expert on Pakistan.

Joseph Menn, a recent graduate of Harvard, is a journalist previously stationed in Guatemala.

Jamin B. Raskin, formerly an editor of the Harvard Law Review and Assistant Attorney General of the Commonwealth of Massachusetts, is currently the general counsel of the National Rainbow Coalition and a regular contributor to *Zeta Magazine*.

Eugene Franklin Rivers, who attended Harvard in the late 1970s, is a minister and community activist in the greater Boston area. He continues participation in the neighborhood and the intellectual initiatives of Harvard's Seymour Society.

Ben Robinson received an A.B. from Harvard in 1987. He is currently a doctoral student in Comparative Literature at Stanford University. He recently returned from El Salvador where he produced a newsletter on developments in Central America.

Zachary Robinson is a Ph.D. student in Mathematics at Harvard. He has been active in the divestment movement and unionization drives at Harvard.

Cynthia Silva has a Master's of Public Policy from Harvard's Kennedy School of Government. She previously served as president of the campus religious and community organization, the Seymour Society. She has appeared on Boston television as a spokesperson for the concerns of African-Americans.

Christina Spaulding, A.B. 1984 Harvard-Radcliffe, was Vice-President of the Radcliffe Union of Students and co-coordinator of the Harvard Sexual Harassment Survey Project. After graduating, she was a volunteer counselor at the Bay Area Sexual Harassment Clinic in San Francisco and lectured on the subject of sexual harassment in education on college campuses around the country. She is a graduate of the Boalt Hall School of Law at the University of California, Berkeley.

John Trumpbour is a Ph.D. student at the Department of History, Harvard University.

Robert Weissman, a recent graduate of Harvard College, ran Ralph Nader's Harvard Watch project, the most vigilant organization in exposing the corporate connections of the University.

Michael West, a doctoral student at Harvard, is a historian of the politics and societies of southern Africa.

Robert Paul Wolff, Professor of Philosophy at the University of Massachusetts, is Harvard-Radcliffe Alumni/ae Against Apartheid's current Executive Director.

Roberta Young is a pseudonym for an undergraduate currently enrolled at Harvard.

Index

About South End Press

South End Press is a nonprofit, collectively run book publisher with over 150 titles in print. Since our founding in 1977, we have tried to meet the needs of readers who are exploring or are already committed to the politics of radical social change. Our goal is to publish books that encourage critical thinking and constructive action on the key political, cultural, social, economic, and ecological issues shaping life in the United States and in the world. In this way, we hope to give expression to a wide diversity of democratic social movements and to provide an alternative to the products of corporate publishing.

If you would like to receive a free catalog of South End Press books or get information on our membership program—which offers two free books and a 40% discount on all titles—please write us at South End Press, 116 St. Botolph Street, Boston, MA 02115.